D0747015

THE EVOLUTION OF ELECTORAL AND PARTY SYSTEMS IN THE NORDIC COUNTRIES

THE EVOLUTION OF ELECTORAL AND PARTY SYSTEMS IN THE NORDIC COUNTRIES

by

Bernard Grofman
University of California, Irvine
Co-Editor

Arend Lijphart
University of California, San Diego
Co-Editor

Agathon Press
New York

ISBN: 0-87586-138-5 (softcover)
ISBN: 0-87586-139-3 (hardcover)

Library of Congress Card Number: 2002011571

Grofman, Bernard.
Lijphart, Arend.
The Evolution of Electoral and Party Systems in the Nordic Countries / Bernard Grofman, Arend Lijphart, editors.
p. cm.
ISBN 0-87586-138-5 (softcover)
0-87586-139-3 (hardcover)
Election law—Scandinavia—History. Political parties—Scandinavia—History.
Includes bibliographical references.
KJC5272 .R43 2002
342.48/07 21

2002011571

Printed in the United States

We dedicate this volume to the memory of one of the leading students of electoral and party systems, Bo Särlvik (1928-1998). We are honored to have his post-humously published chapter appear here.

Acknowledgements

Earlier versions of most of the papers in this volume were presented at the Conference on "The Evolution of Electoral Rules and Party Systems in the Nordic Countries," held under the auspices of the University of California, Irvine Center for the Study of Democracy in Laguna Beach, California in December 1997. It was the tenth in a series of Irvine conferences on topics in political economy, the first of which was organized by Julius Margolis in 1982. The editors would like to acknowledge the generous financial and intellectual support of the UC Irvine Center for the Study of Democracy for this project and for five of the other conferences in the UCI political economy series. Professor Grofman would also like to note the support of NSF Grant #SBR 97-30578, Program in Methodology, Measurement and Statistics (awarded jointly to Grofman and Anthony Marley) for his work on the project.

We would emphasize that this volume was very much a shared endeavor, with the format for many of the tables devised by Jørgen Elklit, the format of the figures devised by Bernt Aardal, and the general structure of the revised chapter expositions based in good part on putting together the best ideas in the presentations of the four original conference papers (Särlvik, Elklit, Aardal and Hardarson). Last but not least, this volume would not have been possible without the invaluable production assistance of Clover Behrend and Cheryl Larsson.

---

1. Papers from the Second Irvine Conference on Political Economy, *Information Pooling and Group Decision-Making* (B. Grofman and G. Owen, eds.), were published by JAI Press in 1986. Papers from the Third Irvine Conference on Political Economy, *The 'Federalist Papers' and the New Institutionalism* (B. Grofman and D. Wittman, eds.) were published by Agathon Press in 1989. Papers from the Fifth Irvine Conference on Political Economy were published in two volumes, *The Economic Approach to Politics* (K. R. Monroe, ed.), published by Harper-Collins in 1991, and *Information, Participation, and Choice: 'An Economic Theory of Democracy' in Perspective* (B. Grofman, ed.), published by the University of Michigan Press in 1993. Papers from the Sixth Irvine Conference on Political Economy, *Term Limits: Public Choice Perspectives* (B. Grofman, ed.), were published by Kluwer in 1996. Papers from the Seventh Irvine Conference on Political Economy, *Political Science as Puzzle Solving*, (B. Grofman, ed.) were published by the University of Michigan Press in 2000. Papers from the Eighth Irvine Conference on Political Economy, *Elections in Japan, Korea and Taiwan under the Single Non-Transferable Vote* (B. Grofman, S.C. Lee, E. Winckler, and B. Woodall, eds.) were published by the University of Michigan Press in 1999. Papers from the Ninth Irvine Conference on Political Economy, *Elections in Australia, Ireland and Malta under the Single Transferable Vote* (S. Bowler and B. Grofman, eds.), were published by the University of Michigan Press in 2000. Papers from the Eleventh Irvine Conference on Political Economy, *Mixed Member Electoral Systems: The Best of Both Worlds?* (M. Shugart and M. Wattenberg, eds.) were published by Oxford University Press in 2000.

About the Editors

Bernard Grofman has been Professor of Political Science at the University of California, Irvine since 1980. He has been a fellow at the Center for Advanced Study in the Behavioral Sciences, Stanford, visiting professor at the University of Michigan and at the University of Washington, and guest scholar at the Brookings Institution, and at a number of universities outside the U.S. His past research has dealt with mathematical models of group decision making, legislative representation, electoral rules, and redistricting. He has also been involved in modeling individual and group information processing and decision heuristics, and he has written on the intersection of law and social science, especially the role of expert witness testimony and the uses of statistical evidence. Currently he is working on comparative politics and political economy. He is co-author of two books, both published by Cambridge University Press, and co-editor of 15 other books; he has published over 200 research articles and book chapters. Professor Grofman is a past president of the Public Choice Society.

Arend Lijphart is Research Professor Emeritus of Political Science at the University of California, San Diego. His field of specialization is comparative politics, with a special focus on relationships between election rules and party systems, the prospects of democracy in ethnically divided countries, and different forms of democracy — especially the contrast between majoritarian and consensus democracy — and their strengths and weaknesses. His best-known books are *The Politics of Accommodation* (University of California Press, 1968), *Democracy in Plural Societies* (Yale University Press, 1977), *Democracies* (Yale University Press, 1984), *Power-Sharing in South Africa* (Institute of International Studies, Berkeley, 1985), *Electoral Systems and Party Systems* (Oxford University Press, 1994), and *Patterns of Democracy* (Yale University Press, 1999). His edited and co-edited books include *Choosing an Electoral System* (Praeger, 1984), *Electoral Laws and Their Political Consequences* (Agathon Press, 1986), and *Parliamentary Versus Presidential Government* (Oxford University Press, 1992). He has also published numerous articles in leading journals on comparative politics and democratic theory.

About the Contributors

Jørgen Elklit is a Professor of Political Science at the University of Aarhus in Denmark. He has published extensively in book and journal form on elections, electoral behavior, and electoral systems in Denmark, covering the entire period 1849-2001. Since the early 1990s, he has also been active as an advisor on elections and electoral systems in a number of countries in Asia, Africa, and Europe, and he has also published on issues related to these activities.

Jan Sundberg is Professor of Political Science at the University of Helsinki, Finland. His main research interest is political parties and party systems published in books and academic journals. He is the former president of the Nordic Political Science Association (NOPSA) and since 2000 member of the European Consortium for Political Research (ECPR) executive.

Ólafur Th. Hardarson is Professor of Political Science and Dean of the Faculty of Social Science at the University of Iceland, Reykjavík. He obtained his B.A. degree from the University of Iceland, and his M.Sc. and Ph.D. from London School of Economics and Political Science. Since 1983, he has been Director of the Icelandic National Election Studies Program. His publications include *Parties and Voters in Iceland* (1995) and various articles in the *European Journal of Political Research and Electoral Studies.*

Bernt Aardal is Research Director at the Institute for Social Research in Oslo, Norway and Adjunct Professor at the Institute for Political Science at the University of Oslo. He has been principal investigator (with Henry Valen) for all Norwegian election studies since 1985. He has published extensively on voting behavior and public opinion in Norway, and is currently member of the executive board of the International Committee for Research into Elections and Representative Democracy (ICORE).

Bo Särlvik, who died in 1998, was Professor of Political Science at Göteborg University until his retirement. He had a long and distinguished career in the field of electoral research. He was one of the founding fathers of the Swedish Election Studies Program in the 1950s, and he played a corresponding crucial role in Britain during the 1970s. Yet another accomplishment of his was *Electoral Studies*, a journal of which he was a long-time co-editor. Särlvik's definition of electoral research was broad indeed; he had deep knowledge not only about voting behavior but also about party systems and electoral systems. His many publications include the award-winning (co-authored) volume *Decade of Dealignment: The Conservative Victory of 1979*, and *Electoral Trends in the 1970s.*

Table of Contents

Introduction

Sparked in part by such seminal works as Rae (1967, 1971) as well as by more recent work such as Lijphart (1984, 1994), Taagepera (1986), Taagepera and Shugart (1989), and Cox (1997), there has been a remarkable resurgence of interest in recent decades in the effects of electoral laws on representation and other aspects of politics. This work has largely fallen into three categories: multivariate cross-sectional cross-national statistical analyses of the relationship between electoral rules and dependent variables such as the proportionality of votes-seats results, degree of party fractionalization, or cabinet stability; formal modeling of the strategic aspects of voter and party behavior; and case studies of the origins and/or political consequences of some particular electoral change(s). Generalizations suggested by this recent work include the following:[1]

(1) Choice of electoral system/changes in electoral system can have significant and lasting direct consequences for party proliferation (Riker, 1982; Duverger, 1984; Shugart, 1992; Blais and Carty, 1991; cf. Taagepera and Grofman, 1985), proportionality of party representation (Rae, 1967, 1971; Yamakawa, 1984; Taagepera and Shugart, 1989; Shugart, 1992; Lijphart, 1994; Cox, 1996), racial representation (Karnig and Welch, 1982; Grofman, Migalski and Noviello, 1986; Davidson and Grofman, 1994: Grofman and Davidson, 1994), within-party and cross-party competition and collusion (Sawyer and MacRae, 1962; Brams, 1975; Katz, 1980; Cox, 1987a, Cox and Rosenbluth, 1994; Ames, 1995), voter turnout (Blais and Carty, 1990), structure of ideological representation (Downs, 1957; Cox, 1990; Greenberg and Weber, 1985; Myerson and Weber 1993; Robertson,

1. The inventory below is taken from Grofman et al. (1999a).

1976; Sugden, 1984);[2] and incentives to cultivate a personal vote through particularistic appeals (Cain, Ferejohn and Fiorina, 1987; Carey and Shugart, 1995; Myerson, 1993a, b; McCubbins and Rosenbluth, 1995). Moreover, through effects on the numbers of parties and/or on the structure of ideological representation and/or on within-party and cross-party competition, change of election systems can have indirect effects on other important aspects of politics such as cabinet durability (Dodd, 1976; Grofman, 1989; Lijphart, 1984), with PR systems tending to have lower cabinet tenure in office than single member district systems using plurality.[3]

(2) Electoral rules that appear identical may significantly differ in their consequences when we consider variations such as in the average number of representatives elected per district (Sartori, 1968; Taagepera and Shugart, 1989) or in national vote thresholds (Reynolds and Grofman, 1992), or nomination procedures, or in even more fine-grain features such as rules restricting campaigning or rules that affect how easy it is for independent candidates to run.[4]

(3) Election systems cannot be understood as operating in a vacuum. Their effects are mediated by other aspects of political institutions and political culture,[5] as well as past history and the shape of party constellations. Seemingly identical electoral rules may give rise to very different types of outcomes in different political settings. Moreover, electoral institutions have ramifications that extend beyond the immediate electoral arena.

(4) The full effects of changes in electoral systems may not occur immediately, since it may take time for key actors to realize the nature of the behaviors that constitute optimizing strategies in the new system (Reed, 1990).

---

2. See also Coleman (1972); Aranson and Ordeshook (1972); and Owen and Grofman (1995) on the effects of party primaries on the ideological structure of two-party competition.

3. For example, Geddes (1995: 269), in her discussion of the prospects for democracy in Eastern Europe, observes that perceptions of government as "disorderly, inefficient, irritating, opportunistic, squabbling and petty . . . . are likely to be exaggerated in countries in which electoral institutions, such as the open list in Poland and single-member districts in Hungary, undermine party discipline." (However, Geddes also notes that "(l)ow opinions of government, especially the legislature, are common even in long-lived stable democracies.")

4. It is also worth noting that choice of electoral systems appears closely linked to other aspects of constitutional design (see esp. Lijphart's 1984, 1999 discussion of the features of the Westminster model versus the consensus model).

5. It is also worth noting that choice of electoral systems appears closely linked to other aspects of constitutional design (see esp. Lijphart's 1984, 1999 discussion of the features of the Westminster model versus the consensus model).

(5) Changes in election systems may give rise to equilibrating forces that moderate the consequences of the changes as voters, candidates and parties adapt their behavior to the new institutional environment in ways that compensate for the changes, so as to partially restore significant elements of the status quo ante (Shugart, 1992; Christensen and Johnson, 1995; Taagepera and Shugart, 1989).

(6) The geographic distribution of partisan support is a key intermediating factor that shapes the extent to which electoral institutions (or changes in them) affect outcomes, especially electoral fairness in the translation of votes into seats (Gudgin and Taylor, 1979, Taylor, Gudgin and Johnston, 1986).

The focus of this volume is on the uses of and consequences of various forms of list proportional representation in the five Nordic countries: Denmark, Finland, Iceland, Norway and Sweden. One major goal of this volume is a simple one, to bring together in one source a synoptic yet comprehensive description of the historical evolution of electoral and party systems in the Nordic countries from the late 19th century until the end of the 20th century, and to combine that description with other key background data on topics such as suffrage and political participation rates and on changes in socioeconomic structure. To achieve that goal we invited some of the leading scholars of Scandinavian politics to prepare country-specific chapters: Jørgen Elklit (University of Aarhus), Denmark; Jan Sundberg (University of Helsinki),[6] Finland; Olafur Hardarson (University of Iceland, Reykjavik), Iceland; Bernt Aardal (University of Oslo), Norway, and Bo Särlvik (Göteborg University) Sweden.[7]

Yet, while we certainly wish to make basic historical information about topics such as suffrage expansion, malapportionment, and the changes in electoral and party systems in the Nordic countries more readily accessible to scholars interested in issues of representation,[8] our ambition for this volume goes considerably beyond merely putting together a set of first-rate country

---

6. We do not find a stark dichotomy between a rational choice and a culturalist approach to be a useful way to think about explanation in the social sciences (Grofman, 2001; cf. Grofman,1996).

7. Professor Sundberg joined the project later than the other authors and was not present at the conference held at the University of California, Irvine that was the launching pad for the volume.

8. Professor Särlvik died shortly after he presented the first draft of his chapter at a conference at the University of California, Irvine organized under the auspices of the UCI Center for the Study of Democracy. His students, Peter Eisaisasson and Ola Jodal, prepared the additional tables and figures required for the full commonality with the other chapters that was agreed upon at the conference. However, with the exception of two minor editorial notes updating some results to 1998, and some very minor copyediting, the text of the Sweden chapter is written entirely by Professor Särlvik.

studies. We have chosen to study the five Nordic nations, collectively, in the light of a general methodological approach that emphasizes comparative methods of analysis (Lijphart, 1971) and what one of us (Grofman, 1999a) has referred to as the logic of an "embedded systems" research design. In so doing, unlike most analytically oriented literature in comparative politics, we focus on "most similar systems." Thus, we have singled out the five Nordic countries not merely because of their common geography, but because they can be shown to share, to a considerable extent, a common political culture (Inglehart, 1997, p. 93, Figure 3.5),[9] as well as reasonably similar economic conditions. Of equal importance to our selection rule for cases is that each of the five countries we consider has made use of list PR. Also, three of the countries have experienced a change from the d'Hondt formula to the modified Sainte-Laguë formula, and this issue was (at least briefly) debated in the other two countries. Because we are dealing with countries with similar political culture, by combining data from the various chapters scholars can investigate the consequences of particular electoral laws and the origins of changes in electoral law in comparative terms with reasonable confidence that they have controlled for many of the factors that might otherwise confound cross-national comparisons.

Moreover, to facilitate comparative cross-national and cross-temporal analyses, each chapter contains basic tables and figures prepared in *a common format* and using *identical definitions and operationalizations.*

One such table identifies the various electoral system eras and the details of electoral system usage for each country, using a shared definition of "electoral era" adapted from Lijpart (1994). Lijphart (1994) has suggested that the comparative study of electoral systems and their effects will benefit if (1) electoral systems are defined by using four major electoral system dimensions (*electoral formula, district magnitude, legal thresholds*, and *assembly size*) and (2) the analytical units are "electoral systems, defined as sets of essentially unchanged election rules under which one or more successive elections are conducted" (Lijphart, 1994: 7ff). Chapter authors follow Lijphart's approach and define a change in electoral system as occurring either with a change in the electoral

9. While there are edited volumes tracking electoral system history for western European democracies (e.g., Carstairs, 1980) and ones describing the electoral and constitutional forms adopted during the post-communist wave of democratization in Eastern Europe, chapters in such volumes tend to be idiosyncratic in terms of topics and degree of specificity, and there is no previously published work on electoral systems devoted exclusively to the Nordic countries viewed from an integrated and theoretically guided perspective, although there are pieces on individual countries..

formula (e.g., from d'Hondt to Sainte-Laguë) or with an upward or downward change of twenty percent or more in district magnitude, legal thresholds, or assembly size.[10] By using *electoral eras* as the unit of analysis, random variations, in e.g., disproportionality and other indices occurring at individual elections, are ironed out when average values are calculated. We find that there are six distinct electoral eras in Denmark, two in Finland (the latter of which involves the shift to a more personalized form of voting), ten in Iceland,[11] five in Norway, and six in Sweden.

Two figures common to the chapters display the Laakso-Taagepera measure of the "effective" number of parties at both the electoral and the parliamentary level,[12] and Gallagher's Index of Disproportionality (a measure of discrepancy between party vote shares and party seat shares),[13] respectively, with line breaks in the figures allowing the reader to easily distinguish the various electoral system eras. Thus, it is easy for the reader to visualize the changes in party constellations and seats-votes proportionality in the context of the major changes that have taken place in electoral rules.

Another common table provides information on major parties and the structure of governing coalitions over the period studied. It provides important background for the reader interested in the linkage between electoral system and party system change.

Several other tables are common to most of the chapters, but report data in a fashion which, because of data availability issues, is not formatted identically across all chapters. Among the topics covered in these tables are suffrage/political participation, malapportionment, electoral rules in the upper chambers, and changes from indirect to direct forms of election, as well as some useful historical background information about the relative size of rural and urban populations and changes in each country's occupational structure. These tables

10. The Netherlands is also located in this same political culture cluster in Inglehart's factor analytic analysis.

11. In the case of multiple tier systems, only changes in the decisive tier are taken into consideration (Lijphart, 1994: 13).

12. Strictly speaking, there are only eight electoral eras in Iceland, but in two cases the magnitude of change comes so close to the Lijphart threshold that Professor Hardarson chose to treat each as a distinct electoral era (see Hardarson chapter for details).

13. The *Laakso-Taagepera index* of the "effective" number of parties is defined as one divided by the sum of the squares of the party vote proportions (Laakso and Taagepera, 1979). It gives the number of equally sized parties that can be thought of as equivalent to the observed distribution of party vote or seat shares. For example, if there were three parties, with vote shares of .45, .40, and .15, respectively, this would translate into 2.6 parties using the Laakso-Taagepera measure.

help place changes in party strength in their demographic context, by allowing the reader to help track changes in socialist party vote with changes in the size of the (enfranchised) working class. They allow the reader to see clearly whatever time trends may be present.

The embedded systems perspective (Grofman, 1999a) calls for analyses that are longitudinal rather than cross-sectional in form so as to get a better handle on causality, but it also asks analysts to do more than simply run time series regressions. In addition, what is desired is an historical and case-specific understanding of the actual mechanisms of change. Thus, not only have we have asked our authors to structure their chapters so as to facilitate the use of their historical and case study material for comparative analyses, but we have also asked them to directly address many of the central questions in the electoral system literature by viewing their chapters as what Eckstein (1975, 1992) refers to as "theoretically driven case studies."

Perhaps the most important of the questions we have asked chapter authors to address are the following two: (1) Does change in electoral system lead to predictable changes in the nature of party representation vis-à-vis proportionality of seats-votes relationships and in the effective number of parties at both the electoral and the legislative level (for example, did the early 20th-century shift from majoritarian methods to proportional representation in each of the Nordic countries lead to an increase in the effective number of political parties; and do other changes in electoral rules have the consequences that our theories would lead us to expect); (2) How can we account for both stability and change in electoral and party systems (for example, how, if at all, was the shift from majoritarian methods to proportional representation in each of the Nordic countries causally linked to issues of suffrage expansion and the rise of social democratic or socialist parties in those countries; and, more broadly, to what extent can changes in electoral rules be traced to strategic calculations and power balances among the relevant actors as opposed to other less clearly interest-driven factors, such as diffusion of innovation). In addition, we have asked our authors to deal with some topics that are much less studied, e.g., the causes and consequences of malapportionment and the nature of the relationship between malapportionment and seats-votes disproportionality, and comparisons between party outcomes in first and second chambers.

A key element of the approach taken here is its insistence on viewing electoral institutions in a broader political context and looking at interactions between electoral and other institutions, especially party systems. Our chapters integrate material on electoral system change with material on party system change, providing a much better understanding of the links between changes in electoral systems and changes in party systems from a longitudinal and historical perspective. In particular, they shed new light on an ongoing debate about the extent to which changes in electoral rules shape party systems, as opposed to party systems being primarily a construct of underlying social cleavages in the society (see Taagepera and Grofman, 1985 for a general introduction to this debate).

While the data in our chapters reinforces already well-known findings, derived primarily but not entirely from post-World War II data sets, about the greater number of (effective) political parties that might be expected under proportional representation than under plurality, and are generally consistent with our theoretical understandings of the likely partisan consequences of various lesser forms of electoral change, they also suggest the need for greater caution in estimating the effects of electoral laws. There need not be a simple and direct causal link between electoral system change and observed changes in party system. In Iceland, from 1908-1933, when the electoral system was basically a majoritarian one, from Duverger's law we would have expected a basically two-party system. While this expectation is confirmed for the earliest part of this period, by 1933, the "the four parties that were to dominate the Icelandic party system for the rest of the century had emerged, even though only three of them had members elected to the Althingi."[14] Similarly, we learn from Aardal's chapter on Norway that "in the last election under the d'Hondt method of list PR (1949) the effective number of parliamentary parties was actually lower than in the last election with majority elections (1918), while the effective number of electoral parties remained the same."

Also, sometimes changes in party system are the causes for changes in electoral system more than vice versa. For example, we see from the Särlvik chapter that changes in social constellations that occurred before any actual change in electoral rules prefigured the switch to a five-party configuration in Sweden. Relatedly, Elklit observes that changes in party system in Denmark (e.g., changes in the effective number of parties) were "primarily caused by societal factors and consequently cannot be attributed to changes in electoral systems." Similarly, Aardal observes that, in Norway, "changes in the party

---

14. See Gallagher (1992), Lijphart (1994).

system and the emergence of new political issues took place without major changes in the electoral system."

The question of electoral system origins is one that has attracted a considerable amount of interest, but almost all of the recent work has been on changes in the post-WWII period, with much of it related to adoption of electoral rules in former communist countries (see e.g., Bawn, 1993; Shugart, 1992; Ishiyama, 1993, 1996; Grofman, Mikkel and Taagepera, 1999), or in Africa. While there have been important theoretical contributions (see esp. Boix, 1999), there is still much to be understood about the determinants of choice of electoral rules.

We can identify a variety of potential causal factors for electoral system choice:

One such factor involves calculations of (anticipated) party advantage.[15] Here, we would expect that the timing and scope of actual changes will be tied to the bargaining power of the parties or their ability to go outside normal channels to institute change (e.g., through popular initiative). For example, demographic and social shifts may lead to changes (or expected changes) in the party system or in the extent to which particular parties or interests achieve representation that trigger changes in the calculations of relative party advantage associated with different electoral mechanisms. Sometimes, there may be other shifts in power balances that allow previously suppressed preferences to prevail. For example, if a minor party's votes are needed to provide assent to some issue that requires more than simple majority support, this may increase their bargaining power enough to allow them to negotiate concessions about electoral laws. On the other hand, absent such shifts, electoral laws (at least in their basics) may, in effect, be frozen in place.

A second factor affecting choice of electoral laws would be diffusion of ideas. For example, the adoption of first-past-the-post (plurality) single member district elections by most former British colonies after independence is often attributed largely to habit. Today, the attractiveness of mixed member systems may be based at least in part on a widespread perception that they are the "wave of the future."[16]

A third potential source of electoral law choices is the view of key protagonists about principles of good government. For example, Reynolds (2000) argues that, in planning for the 1994 elections in South Africa, ANC leaders

15. The fourth, the Communist party, did not win representation until 1937.

16. In this context, it is useful to remember that not all calculations of self-interest need be accurate ones.

opted for proportional representation even though that was not the electoral system most beneficial to the ANC, in large part due to a belief that proportionality of representation was a desirable outcome for the multi-racial democracy they hoped South Africa would become.

Our chapters shed new light on electoral system origins in the Nordic nations, and the reasons for the rise of PR there, as well as the causes of subsequent important but less substantial changes in electoral rules in each of the five countries. Looking at the data in terms of transitions between electoral eras, our chapter authors provide short but insightful discussions of each of the major electoral changes in their countries over the past 100+ years, including a consideration of why the changes were made, which parties or interests favored them, and whether their major political consequences were accurately anticipated, as well as discussing the extent to which electoral rules became constitutionally embedded and thus harder to change. In the Nordic nations we find clear evidence for attempts to use electoral system changes for partisan advantage,[17] but parties usually lack the power to implement the electoral laws they would most prefer and most electoral changes reflect political compromises among members of a political coalition. We also find that the timing of most transitions to a new electoral era can often be attributed to changes in party balance and bargaining power at least as much or more than to changes in the perceptions of relative party advantage.[18]

In the early part of the 20th century, there was a dramatic change in electoral systems throughout Western Europe and the industrialized world, a shift from majoritarian methods to proportional representation. This shift takes place in each of the five Nordic nations; indeed, only the English-speaking nations (except Ireland) resisted this change. Indeed, once PR systems are in place, in the Nordic nations, as almost everywhere else,[19] changes occurred only at the margins. Our authors shed new light about Stein Rokkan's classic thesis (Rokkan, 1970) linking the introduction of (near) universal male suffrage with change from pluralitarian or majoritarian forms of election to proportional representation. Rokkan's argument, in simplified form, is that the primary force behind the introduction of PR was the desire of conservative parties (then dominant) to avoid complete elimination in light of the expected socialist gains

---

17. Cf. Shugart and Wattenberg (2000).
18. See, for example, Aardal's discussion of the decision to introduce apparentement in Norway.
19. See, for example, Elklit's discussion of the changes in Denmark in 1953.

when the working class was enfranchised, coupled with the view of challengers that PR would guarantee them equitable representation. Several of our chapter authors provide some important caveats to Rokkan's thesis. Elklit, for example, shows that the Danish switch to PR was due more to calculations of party advantage in a bicameral system where party advantage was different in the two chambers than to old established parties seeking to protect their position against a new wave of voters; while in Iceland, Hardarson argues that suffrage expansion came largely without party conflict due to an imitation of Danish practices.

Relatedly, our chapters provide new insight into the history of electoral system innovation. For example, we learn from our authors about the use of a mixed member system in Sweden and Denmark long before its post-WWII adoption in West Germany. And, as noted above, we learn about the invention of the modified Sainte-Laguë formula. Also, in the Elklit chapter we learn that Denmark was the first nation to use STV for a national election in 1856, in the form[20] invented by the Danish mathematician and politician C.C.G. Andræ, whose work was published a few years before that of Thomas Hare.

Another important hypothesis that our authors discuss is also due to Stein Rokkan. Rokkan proposed that the shift in the early 1950s in Sweden, Denmark and Norway from the d'Hondt formula for list PR to a special modified form of the Sainte-Laguë formula (with an initial divisor of 1.4) could be seen as a means of improving the chances of "middle-sized" parties achieving equitable representation at the expense of the largest party and the smaller parties. Our chapters show that this specific incentive was not found in all three of the countries that made the switch. Aardal makes the point that there probably was a "contamination effect," in that, at the time of the shift, the three governments in the three countries "belonged to the same social democratic family and maintained close relations with each other. In particular, the growing support for the Communist party after World War II troubled the social democratic parties." In Iceland, d'Hondt was eventually replaced with greatest remainder as a way of increasing proportionality in small constituencies in what Hardarson classifies as the tenth electoral era in Iceland (beginning in 1987). In Finland, the attempts by the Swedish People's Party to replace d'Hondt with modified Sainte-Laguë were several times rejected on grounds that the change might increase party fractionalization.

20. Exceptions are France an, more recently, Greece.

In addition to issues of electoral origins and electoral system effects, as noted earlier, we have asked chapter authors to review other electoral issues including suffrage, the adoption of the secret ballot, voter turnout, malapportionment, and the nature of party cleavage structure.

For example, each of the chapters describes the history of the suffrage in that country,[21] as well as relating changes in suffrage to other changes in electoral and party systems. Some of the chapters (see esp. the Elklit chapter on Denmark and the Sundberg chapter on Norway) cast doubt on the argument of Rueschemeyer, Stevens and Stevens (1992) that an alliance of the working class and the Social Democrats was particularly instrumental in achieving universal suffrage. Norway also requires some modification of the Rueschemeyer et al. claim. In Aardal's view, it is better to say for Norway that "the working class movement contributed to what may be called 'the final push for suffrage'."

Several of the chapters also cast interesting light on early views about the secret ballot. Elklit, for example, observes that (at least prior to 1900), in Denmark, public balloting was initially thought to be the only way to proceed: "Voting was a public function, so it should not be kept secret."

Malapportionment is one of the areas on which our chapters contain a host of new and fascinating material. We learn of the uses of malapportionment as a tool of electoral manipulation in the Nordic nations and we find rural overrepresentation to be a problem that, in most of the Nordic nations, while diminished, was never fully eliminated, sustained as it was by a belief system that justified regional representation even at the cost of considerable population inequality. For example, we find that in Norway, an apportionment rule that was initially designed to foster urban overrepresentation, at a time when the country was almost entirely rural — requiring exactly twice as many rural as urban representatives — persisted into the middle of the 20th century, by which time it acted to favor rural interests. However, even after this clause was eliminated in 1952, the apportionment scheme that replaced it continued to substantially overrepresent rural areas.

In at least three of our countries, for much of their more recent electoral history we find that substantial rural overrepresentation was nonetheless compatible with very near perfect proportionality of party votes to seats relationships. Such a seeming contradiction could occur because, as Hardarson observes for Iceland, "(t)he defenders of the interests of the periphery have

21.Also see Elklit (1999b).

managed to secure their overrepresentation in the Althingi not by an overweighting of the parties of the periphery, but by an overweighting of MPs from the periphery within [virtually all] the parties."[22] Yet, although partisan bias generated by malapportionment may not be found (cf. Grofman, Koetzle and Brunell, 1997), Hardarson argues that, at least in Iceland, this overweighting of rural areas continues to matter because, even holding party constant, MPs from the periphery and the center "differ in their policy views."[23]

Another area where our chapters summarize a considerable amount of data is on the topic of party cleavage structure. Each of the chapters considers the development of traditional cleavage lines such as left-right, and urban-rural, and the split between the communist and the non-communist left, as well as cleavages based on language differences or, in earlier periods in some countries, independence movements, or, in the case of Finland, attitudes toward a powerful neighbor. Each also describes changes that take place in the latter half of the 20th century, such as the so-called "political earthquake" in Denmark in the 1970s discussed in Elklit's chapter, where a trust-distrust dimension supplements the right-left cleavage line, and where developments subsequent to 1973 suggest a further complexification of Denmark's ideological structure. Thus, these chapters shed considerable light on the current evidence about yet another hypothesis of Stein Rokkan, his claim that post WWI Europe was characterized by "frozen cleavages." Also, Elklit's chapter considers historical evidence from Denmark bearing on the Taagepera hypothesis (Taagepera and Grofman, 1985; Taagepera and Shugart, 1989) that (effective number of) parties equals issues plus one.

In sum, we believe that the chapters in this volume will prove a treasure trove of well-organized, analytical, structured data and historical information of interest not merely for students of these five nations but for anyone who wishes to view politics in a comparative perspective, especially those involved in the study of representation and electoral systems, party systems, and the interactions between the two. Moreover, while standing entirely on its own, this volume, with its focus on list PR in the Nordic countries, is intended to be read in conjunction with closely related studies of the single non-transferable vote (SNTV) in Japan, Korea and Taiwan (Grofman, Lee, Winckler and Woodall,

---

22. In Iceland, the level of malapportionment will be reduced in 2003 due to changes in district composition introduced in 1999 and 2000.

23. For example, we learn that, as early as 1906, Finland was enfranchising men and women to a quite similar degree.

1999a), the single transferable vote (STV) in Australia, Ireland and Malta (Bowler and Grofman, 2000), and mixed member systems in various countries of the world that have borrowed in whole or in part from the German model (Shugart and Wattenberg, 2000). The present volume and its three predecessors, together with a planned fifth volume on single member district plurality (a.k.a. first-past-the-post) systems, are intended to provide a comprehensive set of studies of each of the five most important forms of electoral system type.

Each of these volumes also originates in a conference held under the auspices of the Center for the Study of Democracy at the University of California, Irvine.

The Politics of Electoral System Development and Change: The Danish Case

BY
Jørgen Elklit
Department of Political Science
University of Aarhus, Denmark

1. Introduction

The electoral system for national elections to the lower house in Denmark, the *Folketing* — the only house since 1953 — was an ordinary plurality system from 1849 to 1915. Then a very early variant of what is now often termed the Mixed Member Proportional System was implemented (Elklit, 1992: Massicotte & Blais, 1999, 343), even though it was only used in one election, in 1918. Subsequently, an open list, two-tier PR system with the upper, national, level as the decisive level was put in place. This electoral system has prevailed since 1920.

Thus, after the introduction of a parliamentary electoral system in 1848-49, Danish politicians have only legislated major electoral system changes on two occasions over the last 150-plus years. Denmark is a good case in point when it is claimed that national electoral systems are not easily changed. One reason might be that the basic principles of the electoral system have always been specified in the constitution, which has always been difficult to get amended. However, it should also be noted that the present formulation — which was introduced in 1915 to cater for the transition from the plurality to the proportional representation system — was deliberately made so wide that it could cover later changes or ideas not even thought of in 1915. The 1920 change, therefore, did not require constitutional amendments and the relevant article was seen as sufficient and not requiring any adjustment when the constitution was last amended, in 1953.

However, a thorough account of electoral system development and change in Denmark must also consider some of the less important changes *within* this basic structure. This obviously requires a discussion of what constitutes electoral system change and what kind of yardstick to use for identification and measurement of change in electoral systems. This will be taken up below. The suggestion is to subdivide the post-1920 system into four different systems, primarily because of changes in the legal thresholds.

The simple definition of electoral systems as systems for the transformation of votes to seats is also subscribed to here. It will soon become apparent, however, that it is difficult to study one electoral system without also looking at simultaneous electoral systems in the same polity. The way the lower house was elected before 1953 was related to the rules regulating the election of the upper house (and *vice versa*). This point also follows from our inclination to stress the embeddedness of theories of electoral systems as well as the continuous need for contextualization when studying social and political phenomena (see Grofman, Lee, Winckler, & Woodall (eds.), 1999a).

The main purpose of this chapter[1] is to expound the most important causes of the first establishment and later changes of the electoral systems in Denmark by way of demonstrating why these systems have unfolded the way they have and how they have developed from the early 1830s to the late 1990s. One reason for expanding the study of electoral systems into the sub-field of electoral system development and change is that it so far has received much less scholarly attention than it deserves (Nohlen and Kasapovic, 1996: 37). A basic expectation is that changes in electoral system rules and regulations are caused by continuous fights over political decision-making power in the legislature, with the developing political parties as the main actors. The changes in the electoral system are, therefore, path-dependent on previous party system development.

Another aim is to test the relevance of the theory of embedded institutions by analyzing how electoral systems operate in a particular political context, both affecting and being affected by other features of electoral politics such as party systems and social cleavages — or electoral systems operating at other levels (such as for an upper house or for local government). Thus, the electoral system is seen — sometimes simultaneously — both as the dependent and the independent variable, depending on the circumstances.

---

1. The chapter has benefited from comments from Michael Gallagher, Jinshan Li, Anne Birte Pade, Palle Svensson, Lise Togeby, participants in the 1997 Laguna Beach Conference on "Party and Electoral Systems in Scandinavia: Origins and Evolution", and various anonymous reviewers. Assistance from Annette B. Andersen and Ulrik Larsen is also appreciated.

Arend Lijphart has argued that the comparative study of electoral systems and their effects will improve considerably if (1) electoral systems are defined by using four major electoral system dimensions (electoral formula, district magnitude, legal thresholds, and assembly size) and (2) the analytical units are "electoral systems, defined as sets of essentially unchanged election rules under which one or more successive elections are conducted" (Lijphart, 1994: 7ff). One useful consequence of this approach — instead of using individual elections as one's analytical cases — is that random variations in disproportionality and other indices occurring at individual elections are ironed out when average values are calculated.

If significant changes in one or more of the four major electoral system dimensions occur, a new electoral system — *i.e.*, a new case — emerges. Lijphart argues that any formula change *eo ipso* brings about an electoral system change, because formula and calculation rules are discrete variables. For the three other dimensions, a 20 per cent upward or downward change criterion is applied. In the case of multiple tier systems, only changes in the decisive tier are taken into consideration (Lijphart, 1994: 13). Since 1918, the decisive level in Denmark has been the national level.

Here, the approach to what constitutes an electoral system change will be the same as Lijphart's, even though it is not always as easy as it may sound to agree on what actually constitutes a change in a specific electoral system. It is claimed here, *e.g.*, that the *Folketing* elections in 1947 and 1950 were conducted under different electoral systems and that, consequently, the electoral system which Lijphart (1994: 35) has baptized DEN1 (covering the four elections from 1945 to April 1953) must be split so that the first two elections are categorized together with the previous elections and the last two (1950 and April 1953) are seen as constituting a system of their own (cf. Section 3.4).

Table 1 shows the six Danish parliamentary electoral systems implemented since 1849. In order to avoid confusion, a labeling system, which differs slightly from Lijphart's, using Roman instead of Arabic numerals, is employed.

Table 1: The Six National, Lower House Electoral Systems in Denmark Since 1849

Electoral system	DEN-I	DEN-II	DEN-III	DEN-IV	DEN-V	DEN-VI
Elections included	1849-1915 (31 elections)	1918 (1 election)	1920-47 (12 elections)	1950-53 (A) (2 elections)	1953 (S)-60 (3 elections)	1964+ (15 elections)
Electoral formula at the decisive (higher) level	Plurality (1849-1900: "plurality-plurality")	Hare + largest remainders	ditto	ditto	ditto	ditto
District magnitude	1	139	146.5	149	175	175
Electoral formula at the non-decisive (lower) level	NA	*Regional level:* Hare + largest remainders; *Local level:* FPTP d'Hondt in the metropolitan region	d'Hondt	ditto	Modified Sainte-Laguë	ditto
Tier structure*	113 L	140 N - (20 + 24) R - 93 L	148 N- 117 R**	149 N - 105 R	175 N - 135 R	ditto
Number of compensatory seats	NA	29	30.7	44	40	40
Compen-satory seats in per cent	NA	21	21	30	23	23
Allocation of seats in multi-member constituencies final?	NA	Yes	Yes	No	Yes	Yes
Legal thresholds (and effective threshold)	NA	1 seat in a single-member constituency or 1 seat in the metropolitan region	As many votes in 1 of the 3 regions as the national vote/seat ratio or 1 seat in a multi-member constituency (Eff. threshold: Appr.: 1.1 %)	ditto	60,000 votes or in all 3 regions the regional vote/seat ratio or 1 seat in a multi-member constituency (Eff. threshold: Appr.: 2.6 %)	2% of the valid national vote or in two of the three regions the regional vote/seat ratio or 1 seat in a multi-member constituency (Eff. threshold: 2.0 %)
Average assembly ***	104.2	139	146.5	149	175	175

Shaded cells indicate significant changes in basic electoral system dimensions (either a formula change or a change of at least 20%).

* N, R, and L are used to indicate seats allocated at the national, the regional (*i.e.*, the multi-member constituencies), and the local (*i.e.*, the single-member constituencies) level, respectively.

** The number of seats given for DEN-III is after the constitutional changes in summer of 1920, when North Schleswig was reunited with Denmark. For the first two elections in 1920, the tier structure was: 139 N - 110 R.

*** Seats for the Faeroe Islands (since 1849) and for Greenland (since 1953) are disregarde

Table 2: Major Parties and Governing Coalitions in Denmark 1849-1990s

Electoral System	Period	Major "Leftist" (Socialist and Liberal) Parties	Major Center Parties	Major Right (Conservative) Parties	Governing Coalitions
DEN-I	1870-*	Liberals Social Democrats (from the 1880s)	Moderate Liberals (from the 1890s)	Conservatives	Conservatives
	1901-	Social Democrats Social Liberals	Liberals Moderate Liberals	Conservatives	Liberals
	1913-	Social Democrats Social Liberals	Liberals	Conservatives	Social Liberals, supported by Social Democrats
DEN-II	1918-	Social Democrats Social Liberals	Liberals	Conservatives	Social Liberals, supported by Social Democrats
DEN-III	1920-	Social Democrats Social Liberals Communists only after the end of the Occupation	Liberals	Conservatives Various right-wing splinter groups and tiny parties during the 1930s never gained significance	- Liberals, supported by Conservatives, or - Social Democrats, supported by Social Liberals, or - Social Democrats and Social Liberals
Den-IV	1950-	Communists Social Democrats	Social Liberals Liberals Justice Party	Conservatives	Liberals and Conservatives
DEN-V	1953-	Socialist People's Party (from 1960) Social Democrats	Social Liberals Liberals Justice Party	Conservatives The Independents	Social Democrats and Social Liberals (+ Justice Party 1957-60)
Den VI	1964-	Socialist People's Party	Social Democrats Social Liberals	Liberals Conservatives	- Social Democrats and Social Liberals (1964-68) - Social Liberals, Liberals, and Conservatives (1968-71) - Social Democrats supported by Socialist People's Party 1966-68 and 1971-73
	1973-	Socialist People's Party Left Socialists Communists	Social Democrats Social Liberals Center Democrats Christian People's Party	Liberals Conservatives The Progress Party	- Social Democrats - Liberals - Social Democrats and Liberals (1978-79)
	1982-	Socialist People's Party	Social Democrats Social Liberals Center Democrats Christian People's Party	Liberals Conservatives The Progress Party	Conservatives, Liberals, and one or more of the center parties
DEN-VI	1993-	Socialist People's Party Unity List	Social Democrats Social Liberals Center Democrats Christian People's Party	Liberals Conservatives The Progress Party Danish People's Party (since 1997)	Social Democrats, Social Liberals, sometimes with one or more of the other center parties

Pre-parties and early party formation before the 1870s not included.

The chapter is in seven parts. This first section is followed by a section on suffrage and suffrage extensions since the 1830s, while the third section — the core of the paper — in six subsections presents and analyzes the six consecutive electoral systems — the electoral system eras — which constitute the basic structure of Danish electoral system development. The five shifts from one system to another will attract our particular interest and the explanations offered are the chapter's principal contribution to enhancing the understanding of the politics of electoral system development and change. Section 4 then discusses the electoral laws and their various consequences, while the fifth section looks briefly at the malapportionment issue and the sixth and last section is the conclusion.

2. Suffrage

1830s and 1840s

Suffrage provisions for the "Consultative Assemblies of the Estates" of the 1830s and 1840s were strict: Prospective voters were males above 25 years of age who were also owners of an urban house of a certain value, a farm of a certain value (or copy-holders of such farm), or an estate, in one of the three corresponding groups of voters. Prospective voters had to register themselves, so it can be no surprise that only a modest two-three per cent of the entire population were on the voters' roll. Eligibility provisions were even stricter, prospective candidates having to fulfill property requirements double the size of what was required for voters, be at least 30 years of age, and adhere to the Christian faith.

1848

The 1848 cabinet's deliberations over the electoral law for the election of the 114 popularly elected members of the Constituent Assembly are important since the provisions were repeated identically for the elections to the lower, or second, house, *i.e.*, the house elected on the broadest basis (the *Folketing*, as it was to be called), when the new constitution was eventually adopted in 1849.

The main issue in 1848 was whether or not suffrage requirements should reflect the notion that all eligible voters were part of the same electorate and should consequently only be represented through representatives elected in territorially delimited constituencies or if classes (or other interests) should somehow be catered for by some kind of functional representation (as in the previous tripartite elections of the members of the Provincial Consultative Assemblies of the Estates).

The end result was that "universal suffrage" should be provided for, meaning, in the usage of the period, that suffrage should be unrelated to class or taxation. But women, men under 30, paupers (operationally defined as persons either receiving or having received poor relief which had not been paid back or canceled), newcomers to the constituency, and "dependents" (operationally defined as persons privately employed and not having a household of their own) were not given the vote. Furthermore, prospective voters still had to register themselves to be allowed to vote and at the end of the day it became clear that many had not bothered to register to vote in the Constituent Assembly elections scheduled for October 1848. The combined effect of suffrage and registration requirements was that only 6.2 per cent of the entire population was eligible to vote.

1849-1915 (or: DEN-1)

The dramatic nature of the suffrage extension in Denmark in 1849 for parliamentary elections has often been stressed, not only by Danish political historians, but also by comparative political scientists and sociologists (*e.g.*, Rokkan, 1970: 150). But the permanent suffrage provisions (as compared to those of 1848 which were only intended for use in the elections of the Constituent Assembly) were only accepted by the Constituent Assembly after a long and heated debate where most of the cabinet member's arguments for and against from the previous year were recycled (Neergaard, 1892-1916, I: 403-444).

Using again the entire population as our percentage basis (in order to control for changing age structures etc.), we find that 2-3 per cent of the entire population registered as voters for the provincial assemblies in the 1830s, a little more than 6 per cent registered for the Constituent Assembly in 1848, and 14-15 per cent were automatically registered by the local authorities in 1849 and subsequent years (see Table 3). Thus, at both intersections the electorate more than doubled and that might of course be seen as dramatic changes. But the high Danish level of voter eligibility was soon to be overtaken by other European countries.

After 1849, 73 per cent of all men above 30 had the vote. Obviously, the reverse side of the coin is that not less than 27 per cent of the relevant gender/age group did not qualify, because they either (1) were privately employed, but did not have a household of their own, (2) did not fulfill the one year residence requirement for constituencies outside Copenhagen,[2] or (3) were receiving (or had received) poor relief which had not been either paid back or canceled, *i.e.*, the same suffrage requirements as in 1848. The social bias in these requirements is evident. In the mid-19th century, however, such provisions were considered equivalent to universal suffrage, because there were no references to social classes, or tax or income limits.

1915-20 (or: DEN-II)

In the early 20th century, suffrage requirements for the *Folketing* were still as in the mid-19th century, even though the percentage of men above 30 with voting rights had increased from 73 to 90. This increase cannot be explained by the changes in poor relief legislation in the early 1890s only, as half of the increase took place prior to the changes in legislation (Elklit, 1998a: 50-51). Changing residential patterns was probably an important causal element, but there is no need to hide that the available data do not support any clear-cut explanation of the development over time.

A legislative coalition of Liberals, Social Liberals, and Social Democrats had reformed the electoral system for municipal councils in 1908 by introducing both PR and voting rights for women. Thus, it was considered only a matter of time before the latter provision would be implemented for Parliament also, even though a constitutional amendment was needed, as was also the case for voting age and other suffrage requirement revisions. The expansion of suffrage to women in municipal elections and the incremental increase in the percentage of eligible voters among men above 30 made it a foregone conclusion that parliamentary suffrage was about to be expanded dramatically as soon as the political situation was ripe (Dahlerup, 1978). Therefore, voting age was the only suffrage extension issue that was actually debated, as the Conservatives were against any changes while the Liberals and the Social Liberals favored lowering the voting age to 25, and the Social Democrats had long argued for 21 (cf. Section 3.2).

2. Because of the high level of geographical mobility within Copenhagen, the residence requirement was for the entire city, not for the nine individual constituencies.

Table 3: Suffrage in Denmark Since the 1830s (for the Consultative Assemblies, the Constitutional Convention, and the Folketing). Per Cent of Entire Population

	Year(s)	Males	Females	Total	Comments
	1830s and 1840s	2-3	.	3	Only males who were (1) 25 years of ages or more and (2) were owners (or copy-holders) of a town house of a certain value, a farm of a certain value, or an estate were entitled to vote. Prospective voters had to register themselves.
	1848	6.2	.	6.2	Only males, who were 30 years old or more and were *not* paupers, newcomers to the constituency, or privately employed without having a household of their own, were entitled to vote. Prospective voters had to register themselves.
DEN-I	1849	14.5	.	14.5	Same suffrage conditions, but automatic registration was introduced.
	1850s - 1870s	14-15	.	15	Gradual change over time because of the interplay of a number of factors, including migration, residential patterns, political consciousness etc.
	1880s	15-16	.	16	
	1890s	16-17	.	17	
	1900s	17	.	17	
	1910-15	17-18	.	18	
DEN-II	1918			41	Female suffrage + voting age reduction to 29; further, "dependency" and recent arrival were rejected as reasons for not letting people have the vote
DEN-III	1920, July			42	Increased quality in registration
	1920, Sept.			49	Reduction of voting age to 25 (the inclusion of North Schleswig was insignificant in this respect)
	1921-29			50	
	1930s			54	
	1940s			57	
DEN-IV	1950-1953-04			59	
DEN-V	1953-09-1960			62	Reduction of voting age to 23; last provisions about poor relief taken out of suffrage legislation
DEN-VI	1964-71			66	Reduction of voting age to 21
	1973-77			69	Reduction of voting age to 20
	1979-84			74	Reduction of voting age to 18
	1987-98			77	The increase is due to the overall changes in age structure

Note: The extent of the suffrage can be measured in three different ways: (1) relative to the entire population (as here), (2) relative to the age and gender specific group entitled to vote, and (3) relative to the group of adults (which must be defined, depending on the social and cultural views of different time periods: 18, 20, 25, etc.)

However, the notion that the working class and the Social Democrats (though in alliance with other social classes and parties) were particularly instrumental in getting universal suffrage implemented — and parliamentarism introduced in 1901 — is not supported by the available evidence (for a different view, see Rueschemeyer, Stephens, & Stephens, 1992: 91)

Provisions in the 1915 constitutional amendments broadened suffrage considerably (again, it more than doubled, from 18 to 41 per cent of the entire population), since women as well as "dependents" and new-comers (as defined previously) got the vote, and since it was decided that voting age should gradually be reduced to 25, the first step being an immediate reduction to 29. However, recipients of poor relief were still denied the vote, even though the importance of this provision was declining.

1920-1990s (or: DEN-III to DEN-VI)

Since 1920 suffrage extensions have primarily taken the form of lowering the voting age, as indicated in Table 3 above. Voting age was specified in the Constitution until 1953, so changes could only take place in connection with constitutional amendments.

In 1920, it was part of the constitutional amendment compromise that voting age should immediately be decreased to 25, and in 1953 a referendum was used to decide if it should be lowered to 21 or only to 23. In 1953, it was also decided to lift the issue out of the Constitution, even though voting age was still to be decided in a popular referendum. After 1953, three such referendums have approved parliamentary legislative initiatives aiming at step-by-step lowering voting age to present-day 18, while in 1969 a proposal to lower voting age to 18 was rejected by the electorate (Svensson, 1996a: 39), primarily because it was felt to be a too drastic step at the time, and especially so for voters in the rural periphery (Elklit & Tonsgaard, 1978: 39).

3. Electoral System Development and Politics in Denmark from the Early 1830s to the late 1990s

Electoral system development in Denmark started in the early 1830s with the introduction of four provincial "Consultative Assemblies of the Estates", two in the kingdom itself, two in the Duchies of Holstein and Schleswig, respectively, the Danish king also being the Duke of both duchies. There is no need to go into the background for the establishment of these assemblies; suffice it to mention that it was connected both to the aftermath of the 1830 June Revolution in France and to the complicated and intricate relationship between Denmark and the German Confederation of which Holstein — but not Schleswig — was a member.

Elections were conducted in constituencies of varying magnitude (from one to 12 seats), each constituency consisting of one social category of voters (urban dwellers, farmers, or landed proprietors) living in geographically delimited regions (or a couple of towns joined together in one urban constituency).

Elections were direct and open, and they were conducted as ordinary plurality elections, if the constituency had only one seat to fill, and as block vote elections when more seats were to be filled. The electoral term was six years.

As was the case after the 1830 June Revolution, the 1848 February Revolution also had repercussions in the Danish monarchy. The insurrection in Holstein against the absolutist Danish monarch (Frederich VII) in March and the political mobilization of the National Liberals in Copenhagen entailed a swift royal acceptance of a change in cabinet (including new National Liberal ministers). The main purpose was to have a cabinet enjoying popular support, which would allow it to fight the insurrection in the duchies vigorously and prepare for what in the language of the period was termed "a free Constitution" — as well as the change from an absolutist to a constitutional monarchy (Bjørn, 1998).

War-time deliberations about the new constitutional order — including the procedures for designing and deciding on a new constitution — can be followed through the published minutes of the cabinet's meetings. It was decided to have popular elections for 114 of the kingdom's 152 seats of a Constituent Assembly, while the king should appoint the remaining 38 members. 31 additional members should come from the Duchy of Schleswig, but this provision was not implemented because of the war. Five members were appointed by royal decree to represent Iceland, one the Faeroe Islands.

The electoral system for the popular elections was not in dispute. The best organized quasi-political party ("The Society of Friends of the Peasants") suggested that the British plurality system in single-member constituencies be used,[3] as did one of the few newspaper articles on the subject, and it was argued in the cabinet by one of the most vocal and interested ministers. The British system with public nominations followed by a poll (if nominations were not unopposed) was what Danish politicians believed they were copying when they implemented the Danish system with two electoral rounds. The first of these rounds was conducted with a show of hands, but no formal count of the vote — which was decisive, if not challenged — while the second round was with identification of voters and vocal voting in public; but this second round took place only in case of a lawful challenge of the result of the first round. To gain a seat in either round, only a plurality of the votes was required, so the system should be classified as "plurality-plurality" (cf. Lijphart, 1994: 17-18). The issue of open or secret voting was not a matter of dispute: Voting was a public function, so it should not be kept secret.

The main political issue in relation to the electoral system was the 25 per cent of the seats in the Constituent Assembly to be filled by the king. This was fiercely opposed by democratic and progressive elements in the Provincial Assemblies when they were consulted on the proposal, even though the end result of their protests was negative. This particular issue appears to have overshadowed all other matters related to the electoral system.

3.1. *From 1849 to 1915, or: DEN-I*

3.1.1. The *Folketing* Electoral System

The ordinary plurality system introduced in 1849 for elections to the *Folketing* was, as already mentioned, a replication of the system used for the 1848 elections to the Constituent Assembly, and that system was (apart from the members appointed by the king) a Danish adaptation to what was believed to be the British House of Commons electoral system.

Danish politicians did not, however, understand the exact function of the nomination phase in England. That is the reason why the initial show of hands became mandatory, and if the constituency level election committee's decision as to who was the winner after the show of hands was not challenged, this candidate was declared the new MP. Thus, the first round was not only a nomination round. The first round was actually the decisive round in as many as 36 per cent of all individual constituency elections from 1849 to 1900 (when the first round was abolished because secret voting was implemented) and the percentage was as high as 53 in the period 1849-1871, *i.e.* before the development

3. Strangely enough, no reference was made to the fact that most British constituencies in the 1840s returned two members, not just one!

of a stable and permanent party system reflecting the basic social cleavage (Elklit, 1988a: 58-64).

A lawful challenge, however, meant that a second round had to take place among those candidates from the first round who did not withdraw. In the second round, voters were checked against the manuscript electoral register, and only then were they entitled to state "in a clear and loud voice" which candidate they voted for. The actual vote was entered in the electoral register next to the voter's name to render multiple voting impossible and to facilitate vote counting. Some of these electoral registers have survived, mainly in the provincial archives. They are of course available for various forms of electoral behavior analysis, in some cases even in the form of regular panel studies based on the methodology of semi-computerized nominal record linkage (Elklit, 1983; 1988a).

The choice of system in 1848-49 for the election of the new parliament is not surprising. For popular elections, the plurality system was one of very few systems available at the time, and the influence from Britain on the constitutional process was considerable.[4] The main reason for opting for this system appears, however, to have been the simple fact that it was used the year before, and that apparently no other system was suggested.

During the mid-19th century agriculture was the dominant industry in Denmark; industrialization and urbanization only came later, during the last third of the century. The dominance of agriculture was also evident in the residence structure, in the dominant rural/urban social and cultural divide, in the constituency structure, in the development of the party system, etc.

It was only during the 1870s and 1880s that the basic urban-rural cleavage line became equally visible in the party system, where a Liberal party developed (on old roots) as the defender of rural, agricultural, and liberal values and interests, while a Conservative party was formed in response to the Liberal challenge. The party formation processes were certainly more complicated and lengthy than indicated here, since the two parties both reflected earlier pre-parties, but space does not allow us to go deeper into the issue, even though it is interesting to note how clearly the basic rural-urban, partly also left-right, dimension was reflected in a simple two party system.[5] This testifies to the relevance of Taagepera & Shugart's simple rule regarding the relationship

4. As was the influence from Belgium and Norway in other constitutional fields.
5. The party labels reflected this directly as they were "Venstre" (left) and "Højre" (right).

between issue dimensions and number of parties: Parties - Issues = 1 (Taagepera & Shugart, 1989: 94).

When industrialization and urbanization (and subsequent social change) gradually resulted in the development of a working class, a Social Democratic party also developed. The development of a new cleavage (*i.e.*, employees versus employers) explains why there was now basis for the development of a new party (Elklit, 1984: 25). The growth of the Social Democratic party in parliament only came slowly, partly because of the constituency structure (dominance of rural constituencies), partly because of the open voting system which made it difficult for voters to disregard their social networks in the voting situation (Rokkan, 1970: 35). A minor increase in the number of constituencies and a boundary reshuffle in 1894 primarily benefited the cities. Similarly, the introduction of the secret vote in 1901 had a positive effect on the Social Democratic vote in constituencies with a sizable working class electorate (Elklit, 1988a: 296-330).

Thus, the social cleavage system of the turn of the century was clearly reflected in the party system already in the first decade of this century, and even more so when the Social Liberals broke away from the Liberals in 1905. Elsewhere, it has been argued that the development of the "frozen cleavages" which Lipset and Rokkan by and large place in the early 1920s, in Denmark can be traced back to the turn of the century (Elklit, 1988a: 24-45). The Moderate Liberals was another break-away (since 1890/92) so Denmark did for a short period have a five party system, even under plurality, which testifies to the problem of generalizing Duverger's findings, at least at the national level (Rasmussen, 1972: 63; Wildavsky, 1959).

This observation raises some interesting questions about the relationship between the cleavage system, the party system, the suffrage, and the electoral system, which are not answered easily.

3.1.2. Other Houses of Parliament, 1849-1915

The 1849 Constitution also provided for an Upper House, the *Landsting*. It was elected indirectly in large constituencies, in each of which an electoral college was first elected by those voters qualified to vote in *Folketing* elections. Eligibility rules differed, however, as the age requirement for was 40 years, and prospective candidates should also either have a certain yearly income or pay a certain amount of tax.

In 1866, the Constitution was amended, primarily the articles related to the election of the *Landsting*. The changes were so radical and had such important consequences for Danish politics for the following 50 years that they, too, must be considered here, especially since they became a very important part of the institutional set-up in which the *Folketing* was embedded.

Firstly, 12 of the 66 members of the Upper House were to be appointed by the king (*i.e.*, the government of the day, which happened to be Conservative until 1901). *Secondly*, the composition of the electoral colleges was changed, so that only half of the members were elected by all voters eligible to vote in the *Folketing* elections (the ordinary electorate). The other half of the electoral colleges was found in different ways in the cities and in the countryside: In the cities they were elected by those ordinary voters who had taxable incomes above a rather high limit. In the countryside, however, a number matching the number of those elected by the ordinary electorate were appointed *directly* among those who paid the highest taxes (in declining order of tax payments) to function as electors. The consequence was that the taxpaying, land-owning classes in the countryside — together with the conservative bourgeoisie, the industrialists etc. in the cities — got the upper hand in the composition of the Upper House. *Thirdly*, and finally, the electoral colleges were to use the Andræ PR electoral system (see below) when they elected the members of the *Landsting* itself in the multi-member constituencies.

Parliamentarism was not yet the order of the day, and with a strong Liberal majority in the *Folketing* and a Conservative and equally strong majority in the *Landsting* — and the Constitution only saying that the king chooses his ministers "freely" — the road was open for the so-called "Constitutional Fight" over the control of the executive. Space does not allow us to go into this complicated parliamentary battle, which was intertwined with the political parties developing into modern organizations, the gradual development of parliamentary procedures, and the government's use of provisional laws when the parliamentary situation was dead-locked. Only in 1901 did the king accept that he had to take the majority situation in the *Folketing*, the house elected on the basis of the broadest suffrage, into consideration when appointing "his" Cabinet.

One reason for the 1866 Constitutional amendment was Denmark's traumatic defeat in the 1864 war against Prussia and Austria. The development in the complicated Schleswig issue — in particular whether or not the Duchy of Schleswig should be covered by the 1849 Constitution — had in 1855 been the cause of an amendment which limited the Constitution's coverage to the particular matters of the monarchy *strictu sensu*, while a Joint Constitution for the common affairs of the monarchy and the duchies was issued separately. This situation did not last long, but that is not the issue here. More important in this context is that the unicameral parliament of the 1855 Joint Constitution (the Council of the Realm, *Rigsraadet*) had provisions for election by popular vote of 30 of its 80 members, while the king should appoint 20, and the representative bodies of the monarchy and the duchies separately should appoint the remaining 30 members.

The accompanying electoral law provided for the first ever use of an STV electoral system. It was developed by a Danish politician and mathematician, C.C.G. Andræ, a couple of years before Thomas Hare developed his almost identical system (Hart, 1992: 30-31; Holm, 1969; Carstairs, 1980: 77; Rokkan, 1970: 162-163; Andræ, 1905). Due to domestic as well as international problems, the Joint Constitution did not last long, and only one election (in early 1856) was conducted for the *Rigsraad*. But Andræ's STV system continued to attract the interest of Danish constitution and election law drafters and was used in various forms until 1953, primarily in connection with the electoral colleges' election of members of the *Landsting*. The use of the Andræ system in 1856 was facilitated — in a practical sense — through the quite high tax (or income) requirements for potential voters who also had to themselves register as voters, because the combined effect of these two factors was a rather limited number of registered voters.

Stein Rokkan once claimed that the introduction of Andræ's STV/PR electoral system was due to Denmark being — at the time of the system's invention — an ethnically heterogeneous country (Rokkan, 1970: 157). This is a misunderstanding, since the Andræ system was not devised as a mechanism to cater for the conflict between the monarchy and the duchies (or, for that matter, between voters with Danish or German national identification), but for rather traditional conflicts of interest and opinion between voters in multi-member constituencies.

3.2 *The First Major Change, 1915-20, or: DEN-II*

The development which eventually led to the abolition of the plurality system in 1915 and to the first and only use in 1918 of one of the world's first MMP systems[6] (on the basis of one ballot only, not two as is now usually the case) started as a Social Democratic initiative in 1905, following the publication of the results of a new census. It was evident, however, from the very beginning of the course of events which eventually led to this remarkable piece of electoral system legislation that a successful outcome would require the establishment of stable legislative coalitions, probably comprising different party groups in the two houses. The reason was that the 1866 Constitution could only be amended if bills to that effect were passed in identical form in both houses at two occasions separated by a general election (cf. Elklit 1988b; 1992).

Because of industrialization and urbanization, population increase had been particularly dramatic in areas where Social Democratic candidates had huge majorities in constituencies with many more voters than the national average. Thus, Social Democratic seats in the *Folketing* were expensive, counted in votes. Party strategists therefore suggested a constituency reapportionment (maybe coupled with an increase in the number of seats) in order to redress the most blatant violations of the principle of fair districting.

The Social Democratic 1905 proposal was probably inspired by the development in recent elections, since the party again — after some improvement following the 1894 redistricting reform — experienced an increase in its votes/seats ratio. This ratio was even worse for the Conservatives, the other mainly urban party, but there is no reason to believe that the proposal was primarily intended to protect urban interests in general. It was founded in the pursuit of the Social Democratic party's immediate interest in maximizing its share of the seats, but also — and even more so — its access to state power (Dunleavy & Margetts, 1992: 12).

Redistricting had for many years been an item on Social Democratic political agenda, and the constitutional provision in Section 32 seemed clear enough: "The number of members in the *Folketing* must be approximately as the relationship of 1:16,000 inhabitants" — even though it was unclear if that was to be the (approximate) size of each constituency, or only the national average? What deviation from the average was acceptable? How much malapportionment could be tolerated? How often did one have to revisit the issue? It was evident, however, that it would be easy to increase considerably the number of seats without violating the Constitution, because of the general population growth.

---

6. A similar system had been suggested in the German state of Baden as early as 1895 (Betænkning, 1922: 361), while the kingdom of Württberg in 1906 introduced a mixed system for *Landtag* elections (Massicotte & Blais, 1999: 343).

The Social Democratic initiative was not only inspired by experiences from the 1894 redistricting exercise. It also reflected a positive development since the 1890s in the number of votes won, in particular following the introduction of the secret vote, effective from the 1901 general election (Elklit, 1988a: 303ff), and particularly in seats considered winnable by both the voters and the party.

One can argue that the Social Democrats concentrated on changes to the *Folketing* electoral system because that would not by necessity include constitutional amendments (Section 32 in the Constitution also stated that redistricting as well as the *Folketing* electoral system was subject to ordinary legislation through the Elections Act). It would be almost impossible for the Social Democrats to win the support of a majority in the Upper House, which was needed if the reform were to include constitutional amendments. But maybe a smaller reform would be possible, since the electoral system in the *Folketing* might be considered less important by the Conservatives in the *Landsting*. Maybe they would care about the Conservatives being in a permanent minority in the *Folketing* — and if such an amendment through ordinary legislation would not be possible either, then the political gains of being denied equal representation would still be worthwhile for the Social Democrats, in particular among urban working class voters.

The constituency structure had a clearly recognizable element of malapportionment (also after the implementation of the 1894 reform), which partly was to be explained by the constituencies being created in 1848-49 in a different, much more rural, kind of society. This historical legacy is the reason why any increase in the number of seats and any delimitation reform which even to the smallest degree attempted to redress actual imbalances in the voter/representative ratio would benefit the urban parties, and in particular the Social Democrats.

It is, however, also worth approaching this kind of political process analysis from the perspective of the potentially losing actor (Lewin, 1984/88). That would most certainly be the Liberals, the majority party in the *Folketing*, and in government since 1901, when the king had finally accepted parliamentarism. The Liberals had since the early 1870s had a strong majority in the lower house, but a break-away in 1905 of what became the Social Liberal Party had decreased the Government's majority so that it now was very slim indeed. Maybe the ensuing unclear parliamentary situation was another good reason for launching the Social Democratic initiative at this particular point in time.

The balance of power between the two Houses, however, was still as it used to be, *i.e.*, the Conservatives (divided in factions, but that need not bother us here) commanded a majority in the Upper House and the governing Liberals commanded another majority in the Lower House. Both majorities were declining and the long-time perspective was that urbanization and industrialization would lead to such growth in electoral support for the Social Democratic Party that the political landscape would eventually change dramatically. The fracture in the Liberal party added to the uncertainty, in particular because it had not yet been seen how the voters would react (and opinion polls were, obviously, not available).

The Liberal PM, Mr. J.C. Christensen, was a sly parliamentarian who did not — and in 1905 less than ever — want to engage in serious political negotiations with uncertain outcomes. His behavior is only understandable if he is seen as trying to avoid any decisions that would eventually inflict losses on him and his party, especially regarding decision-making power. So he suggested that the number of seats in the *Folketing* should be settled once and for all in the form of a constitutional amendment. The procedures for that were — as mentioned above — complicated and would delay the decision-making process, since many political actors would feel inclined to suggest other constitutional changes, including a long overdue change in the way the *Landsting* was elected/ appointed. This would imply that the career of many members of the Upper House would come to an end, as would the Conservative majority in the House. Obviously, Mr. Christensen was aware of the fact that his proposal meant that he could now rely on the full support of the Conservatives: His own party's main political enemy for decades! So Mr. Christensen's strategy was to postpone and obstruct any kind of positive decision-making until it was absolutely unavoidable.

The political parties had agreed to confine the parliamentary debate in November 1905 to Section 32 of the Constitution in order to avoid complicating elements. But both the Social Democrats and the Social Liberals used the opportunity to mention what other constitutional amendments they would like to see enacted, in particular regarding the suffrage which both parties wished to see truly universalized (even though the Social Democrats would like voting age for both men and women to be 21, while the Social Liberals opted for 25).

The Conservatives (with 11 per cent of the seats for 21 per cent of the votes in the 1903 general elections) suggested the introduction of some kind of proportional representation instead of increasing the number of constituencies and decreasing the level of malapportionment. The other parties reminded the

Conservatives of the discrepancy between, on the one hand, the party's strong attitudes towards equality and fairness in connection with elections and representation in the *Folketing* and the absolute acceptance of the *Landsting* election and appointment system on the other. The parties' positions on these electoral issues remained virtually unchanged for the next many years:

- The Social Democrats' main objective was to have a better (for them) *Folketing* constituency structure, while the number of seats was less important, even though they argued for an increase. They would like to keep the plurality system since they knew that it would benefit them, as it had benefited the Liberals (and still did). They also wanted to abolish the Upper House.
- The Social Liberals, the new party, was also primarily interested in the fairness of the *Folketing* constituency system which they wanted to see complemented with a two-round majority system. For the *Landsting* they suggested equal suffrage.
- The Liberals did not say much — but for reasons of manifesto continuity they had to say that they would like a return to the principles of the 1849 Constitution, *i.e.*, the same suffrage provisions for the two houses and membership size relationships close to 1:2.
- The Conservatives were very keen to have PR in the *Folketing* (but not necessarily an increase in the number of seats). They were also strongly against changes in the *Landsting*, a position which was difficult to defend outside their own circles.

All changes would require acceptance in both houses, which gave the Liberals and the Conservatives,[7] with their respective majorities, the key position, but since both parties did not want to see changes in the electoral system for the house where they themselves held the majority, it can be no surprise that a six-year stalemate developed (Elklit, 1988b). The Social Democrats and the Social Liberals tried continuously, but unsuccessfully, to find support for their ideas, while the Liberals (still headed by Mr. Christensen) came up with a number of different ideas primarily aiming at deferring the decision. One such idea was to resort to a two-step solution, where the *Folketing* suffrage provisions were reformed, in order to allow a more representative *Folketing* to decide eventually on the new constitution. Since the parties were

7. The Conservatives in the *Landsting* was not a unified party at this point in time, but that does not matter in this connection.

known to disagree on the new suffrage requirements, this suggestion was probably also part of Mr. Christensen's delaying tactic.

A decrease in the size of Conservative group in the *Landsting* after the 1910 elections and a couple of deaths among appointed members (who were replaced by members appointed by the government of the day) made it obvious that time was running out for the Conservative strategy, and especially so since Mr. Christensen was no longer Liberal PM, even though he was still influential. The other major factor behind the drive for a solution was a change in the Liberal leadership, where the new party leaders were more positive towards some kind of constitutional amendment settlement. In October 1912, the Liberal government tabled a proposal for an amendment which pointed towards the eventual solution, comprising openings concerning the electoral system to the *Folketing* combined with profound changes for the *Landsting* and suffrage expansions. The Conservatives, however, were still strong enough to block the proposal (even though only 34:31 in the final vote in the *Landsting*).

It was then decided to postpone further parliamentary action until after the *Folketing* elections in May 1913. The Social Democrats and the Social Liberals did well in these elections, and the Social Liberals formed a new government with Social Democratic support. The Conservatives, for their part, did miserably (6 per cent of the seats for 23 per cent of the votes), so their readiness to negotiate grew almost overnight. J.C. Christensen continued to present new ideas and suggest alternatives, which might either attract or deter other actors, so negotiations in Parliament were difficult. Mr. Christensen's main objective appears to have been to delay, as far as possible, any major change, in particular in the *Folketing* electoral system. However, when the Conservatives realized that the *Landsting* would be changed in any case, they decided to enter negotiations in order to have a solution for the *Folketing* that would provide for more proportionality than what would follow from implementing the ideas of the other parties. The negotiations were only completed in 1915 when the Social Liberal government compromised on some of the Conservative suggestions. The stubborn wing of the Liberals then became more willing to compromise, which ensured them some last minute concessions (Elklit, 1988b). The end result was:

- Suffrage expansions, which eventually made suffrage universal (cf. Table 3).
- Comprehensive changes in the *Folketing* electoral system, which included an overall PR system (but with too few compensatory seats, both on regional and the national level) combined with FPTP outside the

metropolitan region and PR in a huge multi-member metropolitan constituency (with d'Hondt and closed lists) (cf. Table 1).

- A complete overhaul of the *Landsting*, which ended up being partly elected indirectly by voters above the age of 35, partly PR elected by the outgoing house.
- Stricter provisions for amending the Constitution, a conservative (without a capital C) measure suggested by Christensen (in case progressive forces should gain even more momentum). The main difference was that a referendum should also be conducted wherein not less than 45 per cent of the entire electorate should vote in favor of the amendment.

The main conclusion is that at least three of the parties (the Liberals, the Conservatives, and the Social Democrats) were mainly driven by self-interest in the electoral system issue. Their main objective was to ensure for themselves as much parliamentary (and of course bicameral) bargaining power as possible, since that would allow them to pursue policy objectives more efficiently. Furthermore, one should not forget that individual office-seeking goals most probably was also a motivating factor behind the parties' behavior. The Social Democrats were most willing to compromise, since they were looking forward to eventually winning a majority in the lower house, especially with the very substantial suffrage expansions which they expected would be to their advantage.

The Social Liberals had a strong bargaining position, especially since 1913. The party's negotiators were instrumental in securing the eventual compromise, but at the price of giving up the party's first choice, *i.e.*, majority elections with run-offs, so it appears that the party valued the reaching of a compromise solution higher than the pursuit of its own policy proposals.

This analysis does not give much support to the conventional interpretation of the introduction of PR as being driven by the old, established parties demanding "PR to protect their position against the new waves of mobilized voters created by universal suffrage" (Rokkan, 1970: 157). On the contrary, one can argue (1) that the Danish party system primarily reflected the cleavage system — in its regional manifestation — and that the party system was "frozen" well before 1915, (2) that the change of electoral system from FPTP to MMP in 1915/18 primarily reflected the parties' striving for parliamentary influence in a complicated parliamentary structure (realizing, obviously, that the Social Democratic vote share was continuously increasing), and (3) that this endeavor had little — if anything — to do with the chronologically parallel discussion about suffrage expansion (and certainly not in the form of a causal relationship running from suffrage expansion to the introduction of PR).

Table 1 also shows how the tier structure was changed as the electoral system DEN-I became DEN-II. The electoral system was changed again in 1920 — to a simpler, two-tier structure — so one has to ask: Why was the 1915 system — only the world's second MMP system — used only once, in April 1918, before being scrapped? This question will be answered in the following subsection.

3.3. *The Subsequent Change in 1920, or: DEN-III*

It was realized well in advance of the 1918 elections that perfect proportionality would not be achieved. The mixture of regional imbalances in electoral support for the parties and the Liberals' access to cheap constituency seats in Jutland (in combination with the possibility of the party getting compensatory seats on the islands and list seats in the metropolitan region) made it a foregone conclusion that the Liberals would still have a seat share higher than their vote share (the system is described in Elklit, 1992).[8] That is why the Social Liberal government had agreed with their Social Democratic parliamentary supporters to propose a new electoral law which should aim at a higher degree of proportionality among parties than was expected under the 1915 law.

However, the new draft law was not put on the table until November 1919 — together with a constitutional amendment proposal — when it was clear that a plebiscite had to be conducted in Northern Schleswig as part of the decision-making procedure on the new border-line between Denmark and Germany after World War I.

The official reason given for the government's constitution and electoral law amendment proposals was the legal necessity created by the expected reunification with parts of Schleswig after the plebiscites decided in Versailles. However, the proposals contained much more than what was related to the reunification, such as various Social Liberal (and Social Democratic) ideas left out in 1915 and also attempts to improve the 1915 Electoral Act without changing its basic principles.

8. Against this background, it was almost acceptable that the Liberals won only 31 per cent of the seats for 29 per cent of the votes.

The opposition parties (Liberals and Conservatives[9]) objected strongly to those changes which were not obligatory because of the reunification. The Liberals were willing to assess the functioning of the electoral law after a couple of general elections, and it appears that they were once again trying to postpone and delay any decision that would eventually cost the party some of its surplus seats in Parliament. Various new proposals were put on the table during the negotiations — including one from Mr. Christensen which was to allocate all seats in unconnected multi-member constituencies.[10]

The party system in the electorate had as its major elements two parties with slightly less than 30 per cent of the national vote (Liberals and Social Democrats), two parties close to the 20 per cent mark (Social Liberals and Conservatives) and a small Business Party in the metropolitan region. The effective number of parties (Laakso & Taagepera, 1979; Taagepera & Shugart, 1989: 79) was just above four in the electorate and just below four in Parliament (cf. Figure 1 or the annex). The effective number of parties had not been below three since 1890 — and was higher in 1906 and 1909 than in 1918 (Figure 1; Elklit, 1992: 197) — so it is difficult to argue that the implementation of MMP/PR in 1918 had any immediate consequences for the party system. Indirectly, it probably contributed to perpetuating the party system of the pre-1915 era.

The electoral system of 1920 is also interesting because of its attempt to strike a compromise between parties being in favor of closed party lists (the Social Democrats), parties primarily wanting to retain the old single-member constituency system (the Liberals), and parties advocating a system where voters in the new multi-member constituencies were allowed to cast a personal (preference) vote for any of the nominated candidates of their favored party (Fink, 2000: 72ff). The solution was (1) to keep the single-member constituencies as so-called "nomination districts" for the candidates in the new multi-member constituencies which allowed the continuation of some sort of relationship between the voters of a constituency (now in the form of a nomination district) and the elected representative, (2) to allow parties to choose between various ways of fielding their slate of candidates (with various consequences for the eventual selection of who was actually elected), (3)

9. The name in Danish of this party was *Højre* ("the Right") until 1915, when the party after the adoption of the new Constitution decided to write a new manifesto and to adopt a new name (The Conservative People's Party) in order to appeal to new segments of the electorate. To avoid confusion, the Conservative party label has here been used throughout.

10. This proposal is identical to the Finnish parliamentary (*Eduskunta*) electoral system of 1906, which Mr. Christensen probably was well informed about.

allowing voters to cast their vote for any of the candidates running in the entire multi-member constituency, and (4) allowing voters who did not want to cast a preferential vote for a particular candidate to vote for the party as such.[11] This liberal system (liberal both towards parties and voters) has — with some modifications — been used since 1920. For a description of the system in its current form, see Elklit and Pade (1996: 26-30).

On various occasions during the 1920s, the Liberals tested the ground to see if support could be found in Parliament for a return either to some kind of plurality or majority system or at least to some variant of the 1915/1918 system, *i.e.*, a substantial number of single member constituencies in combination with some compensatory seats. The subject was also discussed in a Parliamentary Commission (Betænkning, 1922) and the Liberals presented an electoral bill in Parliament; however, the other parties were not interested and no agreement was reached. But it was obvious that the Social Democrats were less hostile to such ideas than the other (and smaller) parties.

The 1930s — especially from 1934 onwards — witnessed a long debate about the possible abolition of the Upper House, where the opposition parties held a majority until 1936, which meant that they could block legislation proposed by the government and its majority in the *Folketing*. The Social Democratic/Social Liberal majority coalition government (since 1929) suggested the abolition of the *Landsting*, a lowering of the voting age to 21 and a kind of unicameralism where the House could sometimes be together and sometimes split in two (like in Norway).

A Social Democratic *Folketing* election victory in 1935 and the Social Democratic/Social Liberal coalition government's winning in 1936 of a slim majority in the *Landsting* made the Conservative leadership accept constitutional changes along the lines indicated above. However, the amendment proposal failed at the referendum in 1939, when only 44.5 per cent of all voters voted in favor, while 45.0 per cent was required. The accompanying electoral law was therefore never enacted, but it is still interesting since it reflects the thinking of the then government as well as some of the Conservatives. The main ideas were (1) to increase the number of seats, (2) to keep the basic allocation principles, but to take the demographic changes since 1920 into consideration when reallocating seats to multi-member constituencies and regions, (3) to double the number of signatures required by new parties, and (4) to require splinter parties

11. These "party votes" were subsequently added to the votes of the party's candidate in the nomination district in question.

with MPs to collect signatures, not only notify the Speaker of the House, if they left their previous parliamentary party group. This demonstrates that many of the ideas implemented in 1948 and 1953 were already on the political agenda in the late 1930s. This is not surprising, since these suggestions mainly reflected the experiences of a politically turbulent decade.

3.4. The 1947-48 Punitive Action Against the Liberals, or: DEN-IV

Most general elections since 1920 had seen the Liberals take more than their fair share of the seats, primarily because of the finality in the allocation at the lower tier, *i.e.*, in the 23 multi-member constituencies (cf. Table 1). This had become increasingly important because of the combined effects of (1) traditional malapportionment in Jutland (no matter how modest) to compensate for the effects of the scattered population in the countryside (the Liberals' traditional stronghold), (2) internal migration from the countryside to the cities since the 1920s, and (3) lack of provisions for recalculation of the seat allocation to multi-member constituencies and regions at regular intervals.

This phenomenon had for quite some time annoyed the other parties, who seized the opportunity to act when the Liberals' metropolitan branch decided to register as a party of its own before the 1947 general elections. The branch fulfilled the registration requirements and participated — legally to the last letter — in the elections in October 1947 as "The Liberals of the Capital", only fielding candidates in this region, where the (ordinary) Liberals consequently did not field candidates.

The result of the election was that the "ordinary" Liberal party won a surplus of not less than 8 seats, as the party had gained 46 final seats at the lower level, while the calculation at the national level showed that it was only entitled to 38 seats. But the crux of the matter was that, on top of this, "The Liberals of the Capital" won three of the 31 compensatory seats because of the number of votes they had won in the metropolitan region, even though their vote shares had been too small to entitle them to a direct lower level seat.

Figure 2 (see Subsection 4.2), showing the fluctuation of the basic index of disproportionality used here, *i.e.*, Gallagher's index of disproportionality, demonstrates how the level of disproportionality in Danish *Folketing* elections was never — since the introduction of PR effective from 1918 — higher than in 1947.

Apart from temporarily solving one of the internal party problems behind the provocation,[12] the Liberals managed to unite the other parties who had all suffered from the party's behavior by being allocated fewer seats than they felt entitled to. The election was certified, since no legal provision had been violated, but a new electoral law was presented, negotiated, and enacted during the first session of the new *Folketing*, so that it could be implemented at the next general election. The main provisions of the 1948 Electoral Act were (cf. Table 1):

- The balance between direct (lower level) seats and compensatory seats was changed by increasing the share of compensatory seats from 21 to 30 per cent. The intention was to make it more probable that seat allocation imbalances from the lower level could be redressed in the overall national allocation of compensatory seats. Table 4 illustrates that this objective was achieved, since both the Social Democrats and the Liberals in 1950 had seat shares identical to the vote shares (40 and 21 per cent, respectively). The same pattern was found for the other parties as well.
- In order to avoid having a party receive more seats than it was entitled to, seat allocations in the multi-member constituencies was made conditional, *i.e.*, on the party not being eventually allocated more than it was entitled to overall.
- The earlier Electoral Act did not provide for recurrent recalculations of the seat allocations to multi-member constituencies and regions in order to compensate for over-time demographic development, internal migration etc. It was now decided to provide for such revisions every five years, and the first revision should take place before the next general election. Seat allocation in Denmark to multi-member constituencies (and regions) is proportional to a composite measure consisting of the sum of (1) the population figure, (2) the size of the electorate, and (3) the geographical area of the constituency (region) multiplied by a factor which had been 10 in 1920, but was now raised to 25. The result of the seat reallocation was such that the decline in direct seats (from 117 to 105) was accounted for by a loss of direct seats in those — primarily rural — multi-member constituencies where the Liberals had traditionally had their strongholds. The average district magnitude (compensatory seats not included) dropped to 4.6 (down from 5.1), and 13 of the 23 multi-member constituencies ended

12. It was virtually impossible for Liberal candidates from the metropolitan region to make it into the *Folketing* because of the surplus of Liberals elected in the two other regions, in particular in Jutland.

with only two, three, or four seats to allocate. Seats at the lower level were allocated by the d'Hondt method (cf. Table 1), and it was probably not fully understood at the time that the combination of this allocation system and only two, three, or four seats to allocate would make the achievement of a reasonable degree of proportionality between vote and seat shares at that level, *i.e.*, the multi-member constituency level, difficult. Of course, the problem of achieving representation for all the major parties — primarily the four old parties — at the lower level disappeared on the national and decisive level, as can be seen in Table 4: The two big parties in 1950 (with a combined vote of 61 per cent) were actually able to take the lion's share (80 per cent) of the 105 direct seat multi-member constituency seats. The allocation of an increased number of compensatory seats, however, was now enough to ensure that both these parties at the end of the day only got their fair share of the seats, *i.e.*, 40 per cent and 21 per cent, respectively (cf. also Table A1A). The low level of disproportionality — even in Denmark — under this electoral system is amply documented in Figure 2.

Table 4 illustrates that both the traditional problems (as illustrated by the 1945 figures) and the specific problem caused by the Liberals in 1947 were redressed completely in 1948 (as demonstrated when the new rules were first used in the 1950 general elections). The Liberals were strongly against the changes, but they could do nothing since all other parties were adamant that they should be taught a lesson.

However, more sweeping electoral system reforms were not on the political agenda, since a Constitutional Amendment Commission was at the same time working on various complicated issues, such as abolition of the Upper House, lowering of the voting age (still 25), and possibly introduction of referendums. Both the institutional and political consequences of changes on these issues were such that nobody dared to complicate the negotiations by also raising the issue of what a new electoral act should look like. That is probably why the 1948 changes were focused strictly on issues related to what the other parties saw as the Liberals breaking the unwritten laws of decent party behavior (Eigaard, 1993: 172).

Table 4: Vote and Seat Shares for the Two Largest Parties (the Social Democrats and the Liberals) in the General Elections 1945-50. Percentages of National Totals

		Social Democrats	Liberals	Liberals of the Capital
		Per cent	Per cent	Per cent
1945 General Election	Vote total	33	23	NA
	Direct seats in multi-member constituencies	41	32	NA
	All seats	32	26	NA
1947 General Election	Vote total	41	26	2
	Direct seats in multi-member constituencies	48	39	-
	All seats	39	31	2
1950 General Election	Vote total	40	21	NA
	Direct seats in multi-member constituencies	52	28	NA
	All seats	40	21	NA

3.5. *The 1953 Constitutional and Elections Act Amendments, or DEN-V*

The 1953 Constitutional amendment process has probably been dealt with most thoroughly by Eigaard (1993), even though his account of the accompanying electoral law changes is somewhat superficial. However, here we shall not discuss other issues from the amendment debate (such as the rules of succession to the throne, introduction of an *Ombudsman*, and Greenland's position in the realm), but only mention that the Upper House was actually abolished. The political-psychological background for the entire amendment included the recent experiences of World War II and the German occupation of Denmark, the psychological need for "a fresh start", and the ruins of the 1939 amendment proposal.

The abolition of the *Landsting* required the consent of a majority of the House itself, and this was more easily achieved when Honorable Members knew that the size of the *Folketing* was going to be increased (to 175, which was a number retained from the final proposal in 1939, plus two from Greenland and two from the Faeroe Islands, giving a total of 179). Other suggestions were to raise party registration requirements for participation in general elections as well as the electoral threshold (cf. Table 1), the major parties thereby trying to narrow the entry into Parliament both for new political groupings and for splinter groups from existing parties. This obviously reflected experiences from the 1930s. However, the general idea was to retain the electoral system basically as it had been since 1920, which also meant redressing the punitive measures taken against the Liberals in 1948. It helped improve the atmosphere among the negotiating parties that the finality of the allocation of direct seats was reinstalled and that the balance between direct and compensatory seats was changed again in the direction of what it was before 1948 (cf. Table 1). The outcome of the 1939 referendum had convinced the politicians that all parties had to support a Constitutional amendment if it should have any chance of passing the 45 per cent hurdle; that of course strengthened the Liberals' bargaining position.

An interesting element in the new electoral law was that the d'Hondt allocation formula at the lower and less important level was replaced by the Sainte-Laguë method in its modified form, *i.e.*, the first divisor being 1.4 and the following divisors 3, 5, 7, etc. With a sufficient number of compensatory seats and the very fair (Hare + largest remainders) allocation formula at the higher (decisive) level, it is difficult to understand the rationale behind this shift, as it would not *per se* change the level of proportionality.

At first sight, the increase of the first divisor from 1 to 1.4 might give the impression that the idea was to make it more difficult for minor and middle-sized parties to win direct seats in the multi-member districts (average size after 1953: 5.9), since such parties would almost by definition only be able to win one direct seat, if any (see, e.g. Rae, 197: 34). However, the change in subsequent divisors more than offset this initial effect, because what really matters is the ratio between successive divisors (Rosensweig, 1981). This can also be seen by comparing the formulas for the *threshold of representation* for the d'Hondt and the modified Sainte-Laguë allocation systems (or by comparing actual threshold-values). Thus, the final result was a modest *increase* in the chances of small and middle-sized parties of winning one or more direct seats in the 23 multi-member constituencies (Laakso, 1979; Elklit, 1999b; Elklit: 1981: 16-20; Elklit, 1993: 55, note 4; Lijphart, 1986: 174-175; Lijphart and Gibberd, 1977). Obviously, the national results would not be different because of the change at the lower level of seat allocation.

The invention of the modification factor 1.4 can be traced to Sweden earlier in the 1950s where the ruling Social Democrats were looking for a mechanism to solve some *apparentement* problems for their junior government coalition partner, the Agrarian Union. Different variants (such as 1.3 and 1.5) were considered, but eventually 1.4 was chosen (Särlvik, 1983: 126-129; von Sydow, 1989: 51-73; see also the chapter on Sweden in this volume). The invention was well suited to solve specific problems of stabilizing the party system by strengthening middle-sized bourgeois parties (which were potentially interesting coalition partners for the Social Democrats) and reducing the over-representation of the Social Democrats, problems considered particularly important in Sweden and Norway (Rokkan, 1970: 160-161).

This particular element in the Danish 1953 electoral system (DEN-V) — legislated in February-March 1953, but decided on as early as May/June 1952 — is obviously modeled directly on the Swedish invention (Elklit, 1999b; Rasmussen, 1972: 55). The interesting point is that electoral systems in Norway and Sweden did not then have compensatory seats, which explains why it was difficult to achieve an acceptable level of proportionality among the political parties. Denmark, however, already had a two-tier electoral system, which was already producing a low level of disproportionality (cf. Figure 2),[13] and it was never intended to change that part of the system. So what was the rationale behind the 1952-53 introduction in Denmark of the modified Sainte-Laguë formula?

The only major change in 1953 in the *Folketing* electoral system was the increase of the electoral threshold, which clearly was a defensive measure by the established parties. It appears, however, that other changes were a very subtle way of winning the support of the Liberals for the general electoral law changes — almost a rehabilitation for the party's sufferings in 1948 — which would ensure their full support for the Constitutional amendment process (Elklit, 1999b). But the threshold changes meant that the effective threshold more than doubled, and the smaller parties protested vehemently, even though nobody listened. The significant change in this dimension of the electoral system is the main cause of the post-1953 increase in disproportionality (cf. Figure 2 and Table 5). The effective number of parties in the electorate remained relatively stable after

13. Apart from the experiences of 1947.

the turbulence of the first post-occupation elections, but the gap between N(v) and N(s) widened, which is another indication of the effectiveness of the new electoral threshold(s).

The main victim of these rules was a new party (The Independents), partly a splinter from the Liberals, partly a right-wing protest party, which channeled both oppositional attitudes towards the new Constitution and remnant pro-expansionist attitudes from the Danish-German border discussion in the late 1940s. The Independents came relatively close to the 60,000 electoral threshold both in September 1953 and in 1957, but did not make it into the *Folketing* until 1960.

The 1960 election was remarkable for an extraordinary turnover of parties in the *Folketing*: The Communists dropped out, losing all six remaining seats, while their post-Hungary 1956 successor, the Socialist People's Party, made a remarkable entry with 11 seats. The Justice Party lost all nine seats, and The Independents made it with more than 81,000 votes (3.3 per cent), which gave them six seats (3.4 per cent).

These considerable changes called for serious consideration of what the electoral threshold should be. In 1961 a decrease was legislated, primarily by lowering the absolute threshold (60,000 votes) to a percentage threshold (2.0), which would fluctuate with changes in electorate size (voting age was lowered to 21 in 1961) and in turnout. The change was driven by the small parties in parliament against the Social Democrats, the Liberals, and the Conservatives, who amongst the three of them commanded more than 80 per cent of the seats. The reason that a legislative coalition could be established in this situation was that the Social Liberal Party (the smallest of the four old parties, getting less than 6 per cent of the vote in 1960) was also a member of a slim government coalition with the Social Democrats. The Social Liberals were, therefore, able to obtain the support of the Social Democrats who obviously cherished government coalition continuation higher than insisting on 60,000 votes as the electoral threshold.

The effective threshold consequently dropped by more than 20 per cent, which consequently meant the establishment of the post-1961 electoral system (DEN-VI) (cf. Lijphart, 1994: 37). The analytical question then becomes whether this 23 per cent decrease in the effective threshold had any noticeable effect on the performance of other variables: Was the average effective number of parties smaller or the average level of disproportionality higher under the DEN-V electoral system than under its successor, DEN-VI?

3.6. Softer Legal Thresholds Since 1964 and Possible Effects Thereof, or: DEN-VI

The 1961 electoral system change was less profound than earlier changes; it nevertheless fulfills the 20 per cent criterion and it therefore counts as a genuine change of system. During the same period, *i.e.*, from 1961 to the present day, voting age was gradually reduced from 21 (accepted in a referendum in 1961), to 20 (1971), and eventually 18 (1978). The average size of the multi-member constituencies (higher level compensatory seats not included) also changed, from 5.9 to 7.9, because of the 1970 Municipal Reform, which also restructured the counties and consequently changed the multi-member constituency structure.

The *Folketing* electoral system still looks and functions very much as it did when it was constructed and implemented in 1920 (Elklit, 1993; Table 1). One can further argue that the system is directly comparable — in any case regarding the effects of the overall national allocation formula on the levels of disproportionality, effective number of parties, etc. — to a number of other two-tier PR systems such as Germany, South Africa, Sweden, and Norway (Elklit & Roberts, 1996).

It was hypothesized above that the threshold changes from DEN-V to DEN-VI would cause a decline in disproportionality as well as an increase in effective numbers of parties. A first test might be to look at average index values and numbers for elections under each of the two systems.

One major objective of Danish electoral systems since 1915 has been to ensure a reasonable level of proportionality between vote and seat shares for all political parties (above the electoral thresholds). The analysis of the degree to which this objective has been achieved requires the use of indices of proportionality (or disproportionality, the other side of the coin). Michael Gallagher's least square index of disproportionality (Gallagher, 1992) has been recognized as an important contribution to the field of electoral system analysis (*e.g.*. Lijphart, 1994: 58ff), since it elegantly weights the discrepancies in vote/seat shares with themselves, thereby allowing larger deviations to influence the index value more than smaller deviations. Average values for Gallagher's index for the six electoral systems considered here are given in Table 5, while individual values are used in Figure 2. By using average values, random variations in individual elections are not allowed to influence the conclusion that the disproportionality index decreased (but only slightly) as expected from DEN-V to DEN-VI. The change in level of disproportionality was also in the expected direction in all four previous cases of electoral system change.

Table 5 includes both the effective number of parties — in the electorate and in parliament — and the relative reduction, *r*, from the effective number of parties in the electorate to the effective number of parties in parliament (Taagepera & Shugart, 1989: 79-80, 106) has also been included. It should be remembered, however, that *r* cannot be compared directly with the Gallagher index, as *r* is the relative reduction in the fractionalization measures N_V and N_S, while Gallagher's index is a disproportionality index reflecting vote/seat share discrepancies among *actual* electoral contestants. It is not surprising, however, that *r* mostly changes in the same direction as the disproportionality index.

At the same time, however, one must admit that the changes in average index values after the shift from DEN-V to DEN-VI in 1961/64 are the most difficult to explain. Gallagher's index declines only from 0.020 to 0.018, while *r* increases from 0.047 to 0.060. Even though the change in the disproportionality index does not falsify the expectation formulated above, the picture is less convincing than in the four other cases of change.

Table 5: Average Measures of Disproportionality and Fractionalization for Six Danish Electoral Systems

	DEN-I: 1849-1915, 31 elections	DEN-II: 1918, 1 election	DEN-III: 1920(A)-47, 12 elections	DEN-IV: 1950-53(A), 2 elections	DEN-V: 1953(S)-60, 3 elections	DEN-VI: 1964+, 14 elections
Gallagher's index	0.243*	0.030	0.015	0.006	0.020	0.018
ENEP	3.36*	4.07	3.74	3.97	3.84	5.16
ENPP	2.69*	3.89	3.65	3.91	3.66	4.85
r	0.199*	0.044	0.021	0.014	0.047	0.060

* *Estimates based on the 11 general elections 1887-1913. Inclusion of previous elections (as well as the 1915 wartime election) is not feasible because of the many uncontested seats, unreliable party labels for a substantial number of candidates, etc. (Elklit, 1984: 28-35).*

ENEP: effective number of electoral parties; ENPP: effective number of parliamentary parties; r: relative reduction from ENEP to ENPP

Sources: Partly Kristensen (1996: 75) and Elklit (1992; 1993), partly new calculations for this paper.

Turning then to the effective number of parties, something has evidently happened, since both effective numbers have increased by about one third from one electoral system period to the next, *i.e.*, a much more impressive change than at any previous shift from one electoral system to another. This shift is also evident in Figure 1, which shows that one has to look at the development over four sub-periods, *i.e.*, the elections in 1964, 1966-1971, 1973, and, finally, 1975-98.

The stability of the party system was still evident in 1964, but from 1966 early forewarnings of the upheavals of the 1970s are detectable. The effective number of parties increased (cf. Figure 1 below) as did electoral volatility. It is remarkable that the disproportionality level did not change much at these elections (cf. Figure 2, also below), but the explanation appears to be that the small parties of this period were not even able to meet the new and softer requirements — a point also made, but in a more general vein, by Rae (1971: 78-79). The lowering of the electoral threshold had as a consequence that more new parties were formed, but since they were unable to pass even the lower threshold, the end result was an increase in the level of overall disproportionality. The changing behavioral pattern of small parties hides the independent effect of the softening of the electoral threshold (Elklit, 1993: 50). In 1971, however, the disproportionality indices have a very telling peak reflecting that several parties were just below the threshold and that the parties who made it into the *Folketing* were correspondingly over-represented. Therefore, it is no surprise that the *r*-value of 1971 (12.8 per cent) is the highest encountered in Denmark since the introduction of PR.

The next election, in December 1973, is often described as the political earthquake in modern Danish political history. The evidence presented above illustrates that political seismologists were not sufficiently aware of early tremors (Damgaard, 1974, is a telling example). These early tremors were the reflections of a development in the electorate indicating that traditional cleavages and issue dimensions in Denmark were becoming more unstable. A trust-distrust dimension was now supplementing the traditional left-right dimension along which it had been fairly easy to order the parties before 1973 — and the voters of the new anti-tax Progress Party scored in the distrust direction (Borre and Andersen, 1997: 18; Rusk and Borre, 1974; Glans, 1984). Since 10 out of 11 political parties were able to make it into the *Folketing* in 1973 (as against only five out of 10 in 1971), the remarkable increase in the effective number of parties (Figure 1) was accompanied by a corresponding decrease in disproportionality (cf. Figure 2). Palle Svensson (1996b) has convincingly argued that neither the democracy nor the political system was in a state of crisis during the 1970s — quite the contrary, as political institutions were able to work to their purpose.

Developments since the early 1970s reflect an increasingly complicated cleavage structure as has been documented in surveys of voting behavior and attitudinal structure (such as, *e.g.*, Borre and Andersen, 1997; Svensson and Togeby, 1992; Nannestad, 1989; Andersen and Bjørklund, 1990; Rusk and Borre, 1974). During recent decades Denmark has become a post-industrial society, which means that the class structure is changing as are the value sets of many voters. The interpretation of this development has often been inspired by Inglehart's studies of postmaterialism and — most recently — modernization and postmodernization (Inglehart, 1997). Borre and Andersen, however, have demonstrated convincingly that the European version of the "new politics" thesis is more conducive to a satisfactory understanding of recent developments in Danish electoral behavior, since their ideological analytical typology[14] enable them to present a coherent interpretation of the "new politics" dimension, where the two-dimensional character of the issue preferences and the party preferences of the electorate becomes easily discernible (Borre and Andersen, 1997: 40-64).

The post-1961 electoral system came into existence because of the lowering of the electoral thresholds, but one cannot claim that the increase in the effective number of parties, the frequent calling of elections (especially in the 1970s and 1980s), or the level of electoral disproportionality — at its second lowest ever in March 1998 (Figure 2) — is primarily caused by this change in one of the electoral system dimensions. The main reason for these changes is attitudinal and behavioral changes in the electorate in combination with changing interrelationships among parties in parliament (Elklit, 1999a; Andersen et al., 1999).

A return to a higher effective threshold was, nevertheless, an issue on the post-1973 political agenda, as it was argued — primarily by politicians from the same three parties who in 1961 had been against the lowering to the current level — that the low threshold *per se* was a cause of problems in Parliament, *e.g.* in relation to coalition building (because of the high actual — as compared to effective — number of parties). Various opinion polls during the 1970s demonstrated that many voters accepted the argument (Svensson, 1996b: 281-285), but the three large parties did not dare to present a bill to this effect

14. 1. Left wing, combining old left with new left; 2. Old socialists, combining old left with new right; 3. Green bourgeois, combining new left with old right; and 4. Right wing, combining new right with old right.

because of their dependence on the small center parties who are usually very co-operative when it comes to government or legislative coalition building. This situation still prevails, so there is no reason to expect changes in the Danish electoral system within the foreseeable future.

4. Electoral Laws and Their Consequences

4.1 The Link between Electoral System and Party System

It was demonstrated above that the Danish case does not support the view that party systems are shaped directly by whatever electoral system is put in place. The 1849-1915 FPTP system eventually developed into a four or five party system (cf. Table 2; Table A-1-A-1; Elklit, 1988a: 35), which then through complicated parliamentary maneuverings created the MMP system of 1915 and the purer PR system of 1920.

Figure 1 demonstrates how that the later — and less important — changes of electoral system similarly did not cause changes in the party systems in question. It has also become evident through the descriptions in sub-sections 3.2 and 3.6 that the changes in the party system — as measured by the effective number of parties — were primarily caused by societal factors and consequently cannot be attributed to changes in electoral systems.

Figure 1.

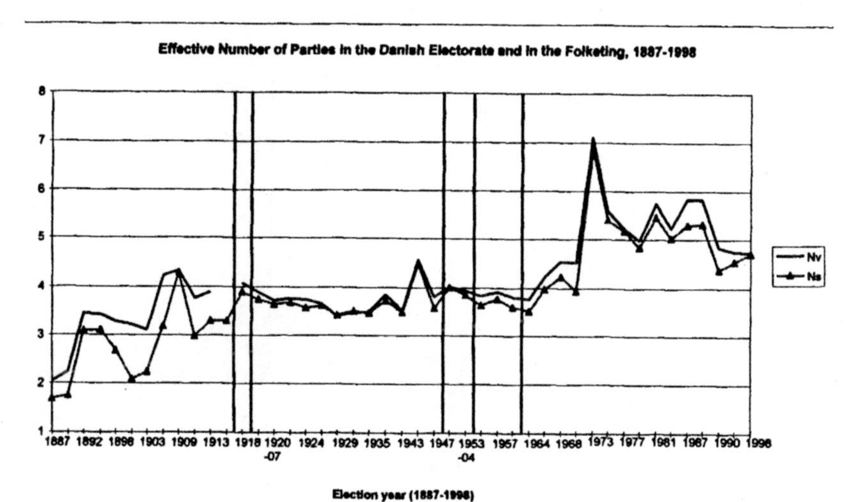

This is of course not to question that the electoral systems do have consequences for the actual format of the party systems: The PR provisions ensure that the vote distribution is mirrored in the seat distribution (for parties above the thresholds) and that obviously is one way of allowing a clear linkage.

4.2. Disproportionality

In much the same way as was the case for the measurement of effective parties, Figure 2 demonstrates — using Gallagher's Index (GI) — that the major change regarding the level of disproportionality occurred in 1918 when some sort of PR was introduced, which immediately brought N(v) and N(s) close to one another (cf. Figure 1).

Later changes in electoral systems — especially from DEN-II to DEN-III and from DEN-III to DEN-IV — have aimed at decreasing disproportionality, while the change in 1953 from DEN-IV to DEN-V also aimed at increasing disproportionality. At all three occasions this aim was achieved, while the fourth change — from DEN-V to DEN-VI, which aimed at decreasing disproportionality, did not achieve this aim because of other developments, in party behavior and in voter attitudes, as discussed in sub-section 3.6.

Figure 2.

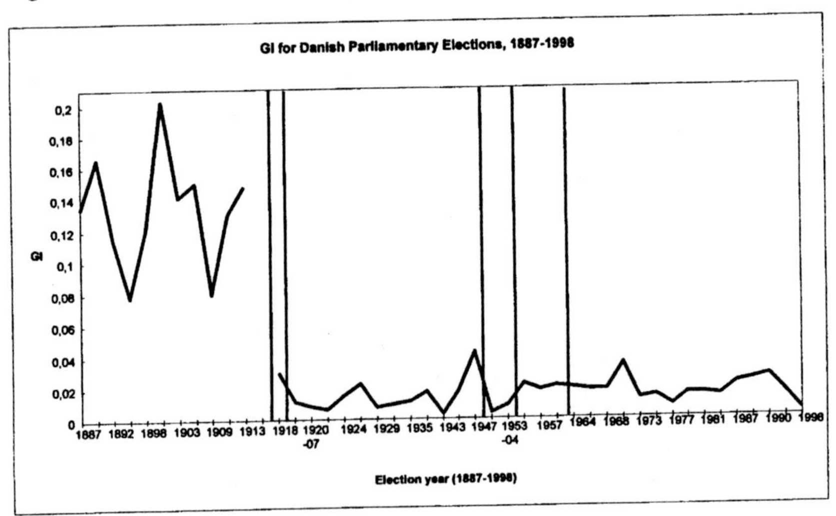

5. MALAPPORTIONMENT

The constituency structure of the 1880s was for all practical purposes identical to that decided on in 1848-49 (apart from insignificant changes because of regulations caused by the Vienna Peace Treaty), *i.e.*, the constituency structure should — if at all possible — be contained within the county structure, the distances to the sole polling place in the constituencies should be as minimal as possible for all voters, municipalities should not be divided among constituencies (apart from Copenhagen), constituencies should be geographically coherent, and provincial towns should be part of surrounding constituencies, not joined together in separate ìtown constituenciesî as known in the pre-1848 the Consultative Assemblies of the Estates. These provisions make a lot of sense when the administrative system and the general infrastructure are considered and the last requirement reflects the idea that voters should form one electorate, not several.

The consequences were that more than two thirds of all constituencies were dominated by voters living in rural districts and the Liberal majority in the *Folketing* was very reluctant to discuss any kind of increase in the number or in the distribution of the constituencies, which could be legislated ordinarily. The result was the more sophisticated kind of gerrymandering, which is caused by unwillingness to change constituency delimitation reflecting an earlier phase in the social and industrial development of society. However, an important political compromise was reached in 1894, which was one important step towards settling the problems which had caused the decade-long parliamentary war between Conservatives in the Upper House and the Liberals in the Lower House; this parliamentary compromise also included a much needed increase in the number of seats in the *Folketing* as well as some border adjustment.

It was unavoidable that the Social Democrats would eventually win some of the new constituencies in the next election, 1895 (cf. Table A-1-A-1), but some elements of traditional gerrymandering is easily detectable in the new constituency structure, which also left almost three quarters of all constituencies untouched — including a substantial number of the small, Liberal-dominated constituencies in rural Jutland.

A major concern for Social Democrats — and urban Conservatives as well — had been the relationship between the number of voters in small and large constituencies. Table 6 illustrates the situation before and after the so-called "constituency compromise of 1894."

Table 6: Smallest and Biggest Constituency in Selected Years 1849-1915 (and the Numerical Relationship Between the Two)

Election Year	Number of Voters in the Smallest Constituency	Number of Voters in the Biggest Constituency	Biggest Constituency/ Smallest Constituency
1849	1,062	2,664	2.5
1881-05	1,500	11,482	7.7
1892	1,522	21,544	14.2
1895	2,182	5,547	2.5
1915	2,450	12,780	5.2

Source: Elklit (1988a: 101)

The differential rate of growth in different parts of the country and in different types of constituencies was one among many incentives for the introduction of PR in 1918/20, even though it probably was less important than those incentives reflecting the need for developing mechanisms which could cater better for the interests of one's party than the FPTP-system.

PR as introduced in 1920 did not change the balance between regions, since the previous (*i.e.*, 1915-20) 93 constituencies outside the capital region were kept as nomination districts, while the capital region was subdivided into 18 nomination districts placed in one of three new capital multi-member districts (*storkredse*). The number of compensatory seats was the same as in 1915, but they were allocated directly to each of the three major administrative electoral divisions, the Capital Region, the Islands Region, and Jutland Region. Provisions for automatically changing the allocation of direct seats and compensatory seats because of demographic development over time were not included, probably because the new allocation system was seen as strong enough to cater for such development.

However, it gradually became evident that this system also had a built-in advantage (*i.e.*, malapportionment) for the Liberals, since that party's distribution of support in Jutland secured that the party during the era of the electoral system DEN-III almost continuously was over-represented in the *Folketing*.

It was only in the late 1940s that this problem of demographic gerrymandering favoring one particular party was eliminated through the implementation of a system for regular automatic allocation of the number of both direct and compensatory seats to regions and multi-member districts on the basis of demographic development in the previous period (cf. sub-section 3.4).

In this way, malapportionment has now been effectively eliminated from the Danish electoral system, and the inter-party strength balance is never affected by this factor. There is, however, still a tiny element of intra-party malapportionment, as parties with a disproportionately strong standing in Jutland might have a systematic tendency to win a slightly bigger share of its seats here than one would expect on the basis of strict proportional distribution, especially in comparison with the Islands region.

6. Is a Conclusion Possible?

The aim of this chapter was — apart from the general description of the development of the electoral systems in Denmark since the 1830s — to provide an explanation of the five cases of electoral system change. On the basis of the main reasons for change, it is reasonable to place the five cases of electoral systems in three groups: (1) 1918 and 1948, (2) 1953, and (3) 1920 and 1961.

The changes in 1918 (and to some degree also in 1948) are best understood as the system's responses to structural societal changes, even though the 1948 case was triggered by the provocation of the Liberals in the capital. Prior to both cases, Danish society had changed dramatically — but of course gradually — and those parties (or regional party groupings) which saw themselves as losing most due to the current electoral system's inability to accommodate the changes in society first politicized the issue (in the first case, the Social Democrats, followed by the Conservatives; in the second case, the Liberals in the capital, followed — during the punitive action — by the other parties). The suggested changes would most certainly inflict a loss on the previous beneficiaries — in both situations the Liberals — who consequently tried to avoid, postpone, or minimize the changes. The attempts to redress the losses caused by structural changes in society were countered fiercely by those political actors who would be paying the price. The behavior of both groups of parties (*i.e.* potential losers and winners) was both rational and easy to explain on the basis of basic party objectives — maximization of one's parliamentary strength, and parliamentary influence potential — very much in line with the argument presented by Bawn (1993). A more systematic test of the factors explaining early 20th century electoral system choice, partly building on Rokkan (1970), which also includes the Danish case, is provided by Boix (1999).

The electoral system change in 1953 was concomitant with a comprehensive constitutional amendment, so the electoral system change was primarily a correlate to external institutional changes. In order to get the necessary 45 per cent of the entire electorate voting in favor of the amendment in the obligatory constitutional referendum, support was needed from across the political spectrum. This gave all the parties — but the Liberals in particular — some bargaining power. The increase in the number of *Folketing* seats was instrumental in creating an environment where most individual future interest could be catered for. Similarly, because of the higher status (and at least to some degree political career security) connected with direct seats than compensatory seats, it was relatively easy for the four old parties to agree on an increase in the share of direct seats compared to the share of compensatory seats, from which they all would benefit — and it could also be seen as a post-1947/48 concession to the Liberals. The introduction of the recently invented 1.4 as the first divisor in the new modified Sainte-Laguë seat allocation formula was most probably only one element in a more subtle arrangement which aimed at making the entire construction digestible for the Liberals in order to ensure that they would not obstruct the constitution amendment process. The three major parties could also agree on the need for a higher formal threshold — even 4 per cent was suggested — which reflected both their immediate interests and their experiences with splinter groups and factions during the inter-war period. The Liberals also had the pleasure of having some of the 1948 changes recalled, which made it even easier for them to accept the final outcome. Again it is evident that the behavior of the political actors was rational and very much as one would have expected.

The two remaining cases — 1920 and 1961 (effective from the 1964 election) — are best understood as revisions of elements in recently implemented systems which for various reasons (mainly political) could now be revised (1953 had elements of that also): The three-tier seat allocation system and the low number of compensatory seats of 1918 proved too favorable for the Liberals (as expected), so the other parties decided to redress that immediately — and the thresholds of 1953 were, not surprisingly, considered too high by the minor parties and were changed in 1961 because of clever political maneuvering by the Social Liberals, the junior partner in a government coalition with the Social Democrats. These two cases of electoral system change are, indeed, best understood as early revisions of the changes of 1918 and 1953, respectively.

It is easy enough to interpret the parties' policy positions in electoral law matters as determined by vote and/or seat share maximization interests, even when this motive coincides with what some political actors claim in relation to the need for strong government and parliamentary stability or — as claimed by other actors, primarily in the political center — the constant need for parliamentary putty.

The above analysis demonstrates that one must also take the general situation into consideration, *i.e.* contextualize the analysis: Is the case of electoral system change caused by (1) attempts to redress structurally caused imbalances, (2) institutional changes in other areas which rub off on the electoral system, or (3) perceived needs for revision of recent changes which did not work out as expected?

What connects the five cases of electoral system change is that — for various reasons — a window of opportunity was open which was seen and exploited by political actors prepared to do so — in 1918, 1920, and 1948 the Social Democrats, the Social Liberals, and the Conservatives who agreed that the Liberals were too hesitant to give up previous advantages. In 1953, the Liberals were able to use their strong bargaining position created by the perceived need for a "yes" in the constitution amendment referendum to have some of the 1948 measures redressed. In 1961, the Social Liberals could capitalize on being a member of a slim government coalition.

Parties still appear to be motivated in their electoral law behavior by their perception of self-interest as being a high seat share in parliament — or at least a high enough share to maintain a key position in relation to legislative as well as government coalition formation. It is equally true that parties have a clear picture of what they would like the eventual electoral system to look like — and especially what they would like to avoid.

This chapter, however, has also demonstrated that basic conflicts among the major parties may also contribute, by making it quite difficult for them to compromise over the electoral system. This leaves more room for the minor or middle-sized parties to maneuver, especially in a fragmented legislature — as the Danish *Folketing* has been, throughout, because a classical two-party system never developed, in spite of the first Danish electoral system (1848-1915) being a plurality system.

Appendix

Table A-1-A-1. Folketing Election Results 1887-July 1920

	Social Democras	Social Liberals	Liberals	Moderate Liberals	Conser-vatives	Others	Total
1887							
Votes %	3	-	58	-	39	-	100
Seats %	1.0	-	72.3	-	26.7	-	100.0
Seats	1	-	73	-	27	-	101
1890							
Votes %	7	-	53	-	40	-	100
Seats %	3.0	-	71.3	-	25.7	-	100.0
Seats	3		72		26	-	101
1892							
Votes %	9	-	32	24	35	-	100
Seats %	2.0	-	29.7	37.6	30.7	-	100.0
Seats	2	-	30	38	31		101
1895							
Votes %	11	-	40	19	29	1	100
Seats %	7.1	-	46.0	23.9	22.1	0.9	100.0
Seats	8	-	52	27	25	1	113
1898							
Votes %	14	-	44	16	26	-	100
Seats %	10.6	-	54.9	20.3	14.2	-	100.0
Seats	12	-	62	23	16	-	113
1901							
Votes %	18	-	45	12	25	-	100
Seats %	12.4	-	66.4	14.1	7.1	-	100.0
Seats	14	-	75	16	8		113
1903							
Votes %	20	-	48	8	21	3	100
Seats %	14.2	-	63.7	10.6	10.6	0.9	100.0
Seats	16	-	72	12	12	1	113
1906							
Votes %	26	14	31	7	22	-	100
Seats %	21.2	9.7	48.7	8.0	12.4	-	100.0
Seats	24	11	55	9	14	-	113
1909							
Votes %	29	19	26	6	20	-	100
Seats %	21.3	15.9	34.5	9.7	18.6	-	100.0
Seats	24	18	39	11	21		113

Table A-1-A-1. (continuation) Folketing Election Results 1887-July 1920

1910							
Votes %	28	19	34	-	19	-	100
Seats %	21.2	17.7	49.6	-	11.5	-	100.0
Seats	24	20	56	-	13	-	113
1913							
Votes %	29	19	29	-	23	-	100
Seats %	28.3	27.4	38.1	-	6.2	-	100.0
Seats	32	31	43	-	7	-	113
1915							
Votes %	-	-	-	-	-	-	-
Seats %	28.3	27.4	38.1	-	6.2	-	100.0
Seats	32	31	43	-	7	-	113

1915: Almost all members were returned unopposed because of the war. Therefore, vote percentages are meaningless.

Table A-1-A-2. Folketing Election Results 1918- September 1920

	Left Socialists	*Social Demo-crats*	*Social Liberals*	*Liberals*	*Business Party*	*Conservatives*	*German Minority Party*	*Others*	*Total*
1918									
Votes %	0.2	28.7	20.7	29.4	1.3	18.3	-	1.4	100.0
Seats %	-	28.1	23.0	31.7	0.7	15.8	-	0.7	100.0
Seats	-	39	32	44	1	22	-	1	139
1920-04									
Votes %	0.4	29.3	11.9	34.2	2.9	19.7	-	1.6	100.0
Seats %	-	30.2	12.2	34.5	2.9	20.2	-	-	100.0
Seats	-	42	17	48	4	28	-	-	139
1920-07									
Votes %	0.3	29.9	11.5	36.1	2.7	18.9	-	0.6	100.0
Seats %	-	30.2	11.5	36.7	2.9	18.7	-	-	100.0
Seats	-	42	16	51	4	26	-	-	139
1920-09									
Votes %	0.4	32.2	12.1	34.0	2.3	17.9	0.6	1.5	100.0
Seats %	-	32.4	12.2	34.5	2.0	18.2	0.7	-	100.0
Seats	-	48	18	51	3	27	1	-	148

Table A-1-A-3. Folketing Election Results 1924 - 1957

	Communists	Social Demo-crats	Social Liberals	Liberals	Justice Party	Conservatives	German Minority Party	Others	Total
1924									
Votes %	0.5	36.6	13.0	28.3	1.0	18.9	0.6	1.1	100.0
Seats %	-	37.2	13.5	29.7	-	18.9	0.7	-	100.0
Seats	-	55	20	44	-	28	1	-	148
1926									
Votes %	0.4	37,2	11.3	28.3	1.3	20.6	0.8	0.1	100.0
Seats %	-	35.8	10.8	31.1	1.3	20.3	0.7	-	100.0
Seats	-	53	16	46	2	30	1	-	148
1929									
Votes %	0.2	41.8	10.7	28.3	1.8	16.5	0.7	-	100.0
Seats %	-	41.2	10.8	29.1	2.0	16.2	0.7	-	100.0
Seats	-	61	16	43	3	24	1	-	148
1932									
Votes %	1.1	42.7	9,4	24.7	2.7	18.7	0.6	0.1	100.0
Seats %	1.3	41.9	9.5	25.7	2.7	18.2	0.7	-	100.0
Seats	2	62	14	38	4	27	1	-	148
1935									
Votes %	1.6	46.1	9.2	17.8	2.5	17.8	0.8	5.0	100.0
Seats %	1.3	45.9	9.5	18.9	2.7	17.6	0.7	3.4	100.0
Seats	2	68	14	28	4	26	1	5	148
1939									
Votes %	2.4	42.9	9.5	18.2	2.0	17.8	0.9	5.3	100.0
Seats %	2.0	43.2	9.5	20.3	2.0	17.6	0.7	4.7	100.0
Seats	3	64	14	30	3	26	1	7	148
1943									
Votes %	-	44.5	8.7	18.7	1.6	21.0	-	5.5	100
Seats %	-	44.6	8.8	18.9	1.4	20.9	-	5.4	100.0
Seats	-	66	13	28	2	31	-	8	148
1945									
Votes %	12.5	32.8	8.1	23.4	1.9	18.2	-	3.1	100.0
Seats %	12.2	32.4	7.4	25.7	2.0	17.6	-	2.7	100.0
Seats	18	48	11	38	3	26	-	4	148
1947									
Votes %	6.8	40.0	6.9	27.6	4.5	12.4	0.4	1.4	100.0
Seats %	6.1	38.5	6.8	33.1	4.0	11.5	-	-	100.0
Seats	9	57	10	49	6	17	-	-	148
1950									

Table A-1-A-3. (continuation) Folketing Election Results 1924 - 1957

Votes %	4.6	39.6	8.2	21.3	8.2	17.8	0.3	-	100.0
Seats %	4.7	39.6	8.1	21.4	8.1	18.1	-	-	100.0
Seats	7	59	12	32	12	27	-	-	149
1953-04									
Votes %	4.8	40.4	8.6	22.1	5.6	17.3	0.4	0.8	100.0
Seats %	4.7	40.9	8.7	22.2	6.0	17.5	-	-	100.0
Seats	7	61	13	33	9	26	-	-	149
1953-09									
Votes %	4.3	41.3	7.8	23.1	3.5	16.8	0.5	2.7	100.0
Seats %	4.6	42.3	8.0	24.0	3.4	17.1	0.6	-	100.0
Seats	8	74	14	42	6	30	1	-	175
1957									
Votes %	3.1	39.4	7.8	25.1	5.3	16.6	0.4	2.3	100.0
Seats %	3.5	40.0	8.0	25.7	5.1	17.1	0.6	-	100.0
Seats	6	70	14	45	9	30	1	-	175

1935: Others: Farmers' Party: 3.2 per cent and 5 seats.
1939: Others: Farmers' Party: 3.0 per cent and 4 seats; National Socialists: 2.4 per cent and 3 seats.
1943: Others: Farmers' Party: 1.2 per cent and 2 seats; National Socialists: 2.1 per cent and 3 seats; Danish Union: 2.2 per cent and 3 seats. The Danish Communist Party had been declared illegal and did, therefore, not participate in the election. The German Minority Party did not participate either, but for very different reasons.
1945: Others: Only Danish Union.
1947: Others: Danish Union: 1.2 per cent, no seats. "Liberals of the Capital" (see text) placed together with (ordinary) Liberals.
1953-09: Others: Only "The Independents".
1957: Others: Only "The Independents".

Table A-1-A-4. Folketing Election Results 1960 - 1971

	Socialist People's Party	Social Democrats	Social Liberals	Liberals	Conser-vatives	The Inde-pendents	German Minority Party	Others	Total
1960									
Votes %	6.1	42.1	5.8	21.1	17.9	3.3	0.4	3.3	100.0
Seats %	6.3	43.4	6.3	21.7	18.3	3.4	0.6	-	100.0
Seats	11	76	11	38	32	6	1	-	175
1964									
Votes %	5.8	41.9	5.3	20.8	20.1	2.5	0.4	3.2	100.0
Seats %	5.7	43.4	5.7	21.7	20.6	2.9	-	-	100.0
Seats	10	76	10	38	36	5	-	-	175
1966									
Votes %	10.9	38.2	7.3	19.3	18.7	1.6	-	4.0	100.0
Seats %	11.4	39.4	7.5	20.0	19.4	-	-	2.3	100.0
Seats	20	69	13	35	34	-		4	175
1968									
Votes %	6.1	34.2	15.0	18.6	20.4	0.5	0.2	5.0	100.0
Seats %	6.3	35.4	15.4	19.4	21.2	-	-	2.3	100.0
Seats	11	62	27	34	37	-	-	4	175
1971									
Votes %	9.1	37.3	14.4	15.6	16.7	-	0.2	6.7	100.0
Seats %	9.7	40.9	15.4	17.2	17.7	-	-	3.4	100.0
Seats	17	70	27	30	31	-	-	-	175

1966: Others: Liberal Center: 2.5 per cent and 4 seats.
1968: Others: Left Socialists: 2.0 per cent and 4 seats; Liberal Center 1.3 per cent and no seat; Justice Party : 0.7 per cent and no seats; Communists: 1.3 per cent and no seats.
1971: Others: Left Socialists: 1.6 per cent; Christian People's Party: 1.999 per cent; Justice Party: 1.7 per cent; Communists: 1.4 per cent. All no seats.

Table 7: Table A-1-A-5. Folketing Election Results 1973 - 1988

	Left Socialists	Socialist People's Party	Social Democrats	Social Liberals	Center Democrats	Christian People's Party	Liberals	Conser-vatives	Progress Party	Others	Total
1973											
Votes %	1.5	6.0	25.6	11.2	7.8	4.0	12.3	9.2	15.9	6.5	100.0
Seats %	-	6.3	26.3	11.4	8.0	4.0	12.6	9.1	16.0	6.3	100.0
Seats	-	11	46	20	14	7	22	16	28	11	175
1975											
Votes %	2.1	5.0	29.9	7.1	2.2	5.3	23.3	5.5	13.6	6.0	100.0
Seats %	2.3	5.1	30.3	7.5	2.3	5.1	24.0	5.7	13.7	4.0	100.0
Seats	4	9	753	13	4	9	42	10	24	7	175
1977											
Votes %	2.7	3.9	37.0	3.6	6.4	3.4	12.0	8.5	14.6	7.9	100.0
Seats %	2.9	4.0	37.1	3.4	6.3	3.4	12.0	8.6	14.9	7.4	100.0
Seats	5	7	65	6	11	6	21	15	26	13	175
1979											
Votes %	3.7	5.9	38.3	5.4	3.2	2.6	12.5	12.5	11.0	4.9	100.0
Seats %	3.4	6.3	38.8	5.7	3.4	2.9	12.6	12.6	11.4	2.9	100.0
Seats	6	11	68	10	6	5	22	22	20	5	175
1981											
Votes %	2.7	11.3	32.9	5.1	8.3	2.3	11.3	14.5	8.9	1.3	100.0
Seats %	2.9	12.0	33.7	5.1	8.6	2.3	11.4	14.9	9.1	-	100.0
Seats	5	21	59	9	15	4	20	26	16	-	175
1984											
Votes %	2.7	11.5	31.6	5.5	4.6	2,7	12.1	23.4	3.6	2.3	100.0
Seats %	2.9	12.0	32.0	5.7	4.6	2.9	12.5	24.0	3.4	-	100.0
Seats	5	21	56	10	8	5	22	42	6	-	175
1987											
Votes %	1.4	14.6	29.3	6.2	4.8	2.4	10.5	20.8	4.8	5.2	100.0
Seats %	-	15.4	30.9	6.3	5.1	2.3	10.9	21.7	5.1	2.3	100.0
Seats	-	27	54	11	9	4	19	38	9	4	175
1988											
Votes %	0.6	13.0	29.8	5.6	4.7	2.0	11.8	19.3	9.0	4.2	100.0
Seats %	-	13.7	31.5	5.7	5.1	2.3	12.6	20.0	9.1	-	100.0
Seats	-	24	55	10	9	4	22	35	16	-	175

1973: Others: Justice Party: 2.9 per cent and 5 seats. Communists: 3.6 per cent and 6 seats. The German Minority Party did not run separately, but together with the Center Democrats in North Schleswig. Therefore, a representative of the German Minority Party was elected as a MP. The same happened in 1975 and 1977.

1975: Others: Communists: 4.2 per cent and 7 seats

1977: Others: Justice Party 3.7 per cent and 7 seats; Communists: 4.0 per cent and 7 seats.

1979: Others: Justice Party: 2.6 per cent and 5 seats; Communists: 1.9 per cent and no seats.

1987: Others: Common Course: 2.2 per cent and 4 seats; Greens: 1.3 per cent and no seats.

1988: Others: Communists: 0.8 per cent; Greens: 1.4 per cent; Common Course: 1.9 per cent.

Table A-1-A-6 Folketing Election Results 1990-1998

	Unity List	Socialist People's Party	Social Democrats	Social Liberals	Center Democrats	Christian People's Party	Liberals	Conser-vatives	Progress Party	Others	Total
1990											
Votes %	1.7	8.3	37.4	3.5	5.1	2.3	15.8	16.0	6.4	3.5	100.0
Seats %	-	8.6	39.4	5.1	5.1	2.3	16.6	17.4	6.9	-	100.0
Seats	-	15	69	7	9	4	29	30	12	-	175
1994											
Votes %	3.1	7.3	34.6	4.6	2.8	1.9	23.3	15.0	6.4	1.0	100.0
Seats %	3,4	7.4	35.4	4.6	2.9	-	24.0	15.4	6.3	0.6	100.0
Seats	6	13	62	8	5	-	42	27	11	1	175
1998											
Votes %	2.7	7.6	35.9	3.9	4.3	2.5	24.0	8.9	2.4	7.8	100.0
Seats %	2.9	7.4	36.0	4.0	4.6	2.3	24.0	9.1	2.3	7.4	100.0
Seats	5	13	63	7	8	4	42	16	4	13	175

1990: Others: Common Course: 1.8 per cent and no seats.

1994: Others: Jacob Haugaard, a comedian who ran as an independent, got elected by winning a direct seat in a multi-member constituency. An independent candidate has never before been able to win a seat, since the only precedent (September 1953) was the case of the German Minority Party formally fielding its candidate as an independent, even though it was public knowledge that the candidate concerned was a prominent member of the German minority as well as its party.

1998: Others: Danish People's Party (a break-away from The Progress Party): 7.4 per cent of the votes and 13 seats

Table A-2-1. Population by Industry 1840-1901

	1840	1870	1880	1890	1901
Agriculture	46	44	45	41	40
Fishing, sailing	3	3	3	3	3
Manufacturing, construction	20	21	23	25	28
Trade and commerce, etc.	4	5	7	9	11
Immaterial industry, services	6	6	7	7	8
Day-laborers, unskilled labor	13	16	9	8	2
Other industries	8	5	6	7	8
Total	100	100	100	100	100

Source: Johansen, 1985: 34. Se Johansen (1985) for definitions and clarifications.

Table A-2-2. Population by Industry 1911-1970

	1911	1921	1930	1940	1950	1960	1970
Agriculture	37	33	30	28	24	19	10
Manufacturing, construction	28	29	29	33	35	35	34
Trade and commerce, etc.	10	10	11	13	13	16	16
Transportation	6	7	7	6	7	7	6
Immaterial industries,	5	5	6	7	8	10	15
Other industries, etc.*	14	16	17	13	13	13	19
Total	100	100	100	100	100	100	100

Source: Johansen, 1985: 35. See Johansen (1985) for definitions and clarifications.
** Including servants and persons not professionally employed.*

Table A-3. Urban and Rural Population 1834-1994

	1840	1850	1860	1870	1880	1890	1901	1911	1921	1930	1940	1950	1960	1970	198	1994
Capital/ Capital Region	11	9	10	11	13	16	18	20	21	22	23	23	20	28	27	26
Provincial towns/ Urban areas	9	12	13	14	15	17	20	20	22	22	24	26	27	52	57	59
Rural districts	80	79	77	75	72	67	62	60	57	56	53	51	53	20	16	15
Total	100	100	100	100	100	100	100	100	100	100	100	100	100	100	100	100

Notes: "The Capital" before 1970 comprises the Municipality of Copenhagen from the beginning, while Frederiksberg is included from 1860 and Gentofte from 1921. From 1970 the figures also include metropolitan suburbs. The definition of "provincial towns" is straightforward until 1960. From 1970 it covers urban areas with more than 200 inhabitants. "Rural districts" are rural municipalities before 1970 and form 1970 districts without urban areas with more than 200 inhabitants.
1921: Figures include changes after the reunification with North Schleswig.
Sources: Census returns and other official statistics.

Indices of Disproportionality and Effective Number of Parties in Danish Folketing Elections 1918-98

Year/Month	I	D	LSq	PWI	Nv	Ns	r
1918	0.015	0.046	0.030	0.018	4.069	3.888	4.447
1920-04	0.005	0.020	0.012	0.005	3.895	3.747	3.800
1920-07	0.004	0.011	0.008	0.004	3.711	3.637	2.003
1920-09	0.003	0.012	0.007	0.003	3.751	3.670	2.162
1924	0.006	0.026	0.015	0.007	3.747	3.564	4.874
1926	0.007	0.028	0.023	0.014	3.651	3.599	1.411
1929	0.003	0.011	0.007	0.005	3.403	3.416	-0.387
1932	0.003	0.014	0.010	0.007	3.472	3.514	-1.203
1935	0.004	0.018	0.011	0.004	3.491	3.463	0.083
1939	0.005	0.027	0.017	0.006	3.842	3.705	3.566
1943	0.001	0.006	0.003	0.001	3.497	3.479	0.504
1945	0.007	0.024	0.018	0.009	4.567	4.476	1.995
1947	0.012	0.055	0.042	0.023	3.801	3.558	6.376
1950	0.002	0.006	0.004	0.001	4.009	3.985	0.595
1953-04	0.003	0.013	0.008	0.003	3.923	3.838	2.177
1953-09	0.007	0.028	0.022	0.009	3.816	3.630	4.874
1957	0.006	0.025	0.018	0.006	3.903	3.763	3.601
1960	0.007	0.033	0.021	0.009	3.808	3.593	5.643
1964	0.006	0.037	0.019	0.010	3.754	3.504	6.672
1966	0.007	0.033	0.018	0.009	4.231	3.963	6.327
1968	0.006	0.037	0.018	0.009	4.543	4.233	6.815
1971	0.013	0.069	0.034	0.018	4.514	3.937	12.792
1973	0.003	0.018	0.012	0.004	7.112	6.856	3.607
1975	0.004	0.022	0.014	0.006	5.600	5.410	3.395
1977	0.002	0.012	0.007	0.002	5.231	5.174	1.084
1979	0.004	0.026	0.016	0.005	4.986	4.834	3.045
1981	0.004	0.027	0.015	0.006	5.754	5.468	4.975
1984	0.004	0.026	0.014	0.004	5.245	5.038	3.950
1987	0.007	0.046	0.022	0.009	5.833	5.308	8.790
1988	0.008	0.048	0.024	0.009	5.835	5.322	8.790
1990	0.008	0.052	0.026	0.012	4.842	4.368	9.790
1994	0.005	0.024	0.016	0.006	4.757	4.541	4.540
1998	0.001	0.009	0.005	0.000	4.740	4.716	0.005

I: Rae's index
D: Loosemore-Hanby index
LSq: Gallagher's least square index
PWI: Li's party weight index (Li, 1995)
r: Difference (in per cent) between effective number of parties in the electorate and in parliament

THE ELECTORAL SYSTEM OF FINLAND: OLD, AND WORKING WELL

BY
JAN SUNDBERG
DEPARTMENT OF POLITICAL SCIENCE
UNIVERSITY OF HELSINKI, FINLAND

INTRODUCTION

The purpose of this paper is to present the most relevant features of the Finnish electoral system and to discuss the major changes in it. According to Giovanni Sartori, proportional representation is a non-effect electoral system, and it affects the party system to the extent that it is non-proportional (Sartori 1997, 47). We will be especially interested in how well the electoral system mirrors the political opinions in elections, and if there have been any subsequent changes during the 20th century, when the system has been in use. The paper is organized as follows. First, we start with a general discussion on the historical and political background and origins of the electoral and party systems. Then we examine shifts in the electoral system eras, the electoral laws and their consequences, the effects of the d'Hondt system, and constituency malapportionment, ending with a concluding discussion.

The electoral system of Finland has been quite stable. In fact, it has been used without major amendments for almost a century. In contrast to the evolutionary change of electoral systems in Scandinavia, the turn to a democratic electoral system in Finland came suddenly. From 1863 to 1906 the Finnish national "Parliament", the Diet of Four Estates, was given certain autonomy to run the country under Russian rule. This old elitist form of the electoral system was replaced in 1906 by a unicameral Parliament, universal suffrage, and proportional representation. This reform gave birth to the modern party system of today. Although the electoral system was one of the most advanced at that time, Finland still lacked independence and democracy. The Senate (government) was controlled by the Russian emperor and the work in Parliament was often done in vain, as laws were not put in force. Frustration grew strongest among the Social Democrats, who saw their social, political, and economic amendments spoiled by the conservative MPs who preferred to cooperate with the Russian-dominated Senate to prevent the reforms from going through.

Finland won independence in December 1917, and the Parliament was put aside as an instrument to solve political conflicts. A civil war started in January 1918, which resulted in a disastrous loss for the socialists and for democracy. After the war, in May 1918, the conservatives prepared to transform Finland into a monarchy. The socialists were denied access to Parliament and a king from Germany was elected. The German monarch was seen as a guarantee of military aid from Germany against the emerging Soviet threat. Germany lost World War I before the monarch moved to Finland and the idea of monarchism was given up (Lindman 1969).

A new constitution was prepared by the non-socialist parties. In the new constitution, which came in force in 1919, the king was replaced with a strong presidency and the Senate was replaced by a Cabinet. The electoral system from 1906 remained unchanged. In fact, no fundamental changes have been made since then. Nevertheless, changes have been made which are important for the electoral system. The district magnitude has been changed by shifting the number of constituencies, the voting age has been lowered several times, and the fixed list system has been replaced by an individual system.

The party system of Finland is characterized by polarized pluralism, with a high degree of fragmentation. One distinguishing feature of the Finnish party configuration has been the permanence of the six main parties. The six parties that existed in the early years of independence are still included in the present Finnish political tapestry.

The earliest political parties in Finland were formed towards the end of the last century, under the impact of the language strife that was taking more and more prominence in the political life of the country. As a heritage from the long union with Sweden, during most of the 19th century Finland maintained the Swedish language as the only language of higher administration and of secondary school and university teaching, although only some 12-15 per cent of the total population spoke Swedish as its native tongue, mostly in concentrated areas along the coast in the south and northwest. This situation meant that ambitious youngsters from Finnish-speaking homes who wanted to acquire a higher education and make a career in the administration had to learn Swedish and, often, practically abandon their native Finnish tongue. The upper class spoke mostly Swedish through out the country.

The language movements crystallized in the 1860s and 1870s into the Finnish Party and the Swedish Party. The Finnish Party demanded increased educational and other rights for the Finnish-speaking majority, and the Swedish Party emerged as a counterforce. In the diet of four estates, Swedes dominated the houses of nobility and of the burgesses, while Finns dominated the clergy and the farmers. The parties were rather loose organizations without a network of local units. A new party that was built from the ground up as a mass organization was the Social Democratic Party, founded in 1899. It did not participate in the language strife and recruited support from both language groups. It began to organize mainly among the industrial workers, tenant farmers, and farm laborers who were not eligible to vote before 1906.

The Russian oppression at the turn of the century led to some political realignments. The Finnish party split into two factions over the question of what tactics to use in dealing with the Russian threat. The so-called Old Finns (retaining the name the Finnish Party) favored compliance and compromise, hoping to save the rest by giving way on some questions. In fact, the conservatives had much to win by dealing with the Russians, as they supported the struggle against the Swedish language and dominance. The wave of Finnization in the public administration would not have been possible without active Russian support. The Young Finns took a legalistic attitude, opposed all violations of the constitutional rights of Finland, and favored passive resistance against the Russians and refusal to comply with illegal orders. The Young Finns broke from the Finnish Party and formed a unit of its own in 1904. On this question, the Swedish party aligned itself with the Young Finns in the constitutionalist front. The old Swedish party was reconstituted in 1906 as the Swedish People's Party, when the parliamentary reform called for an organizational framework capable of eliciting grass roots support for the party.

The farmers organized themselves in a mass party in 1908, when the Agrarian Union was formed by the fusion of two groups formed in 1906 who already had a joint group in Parliament. With the formation of the Agrarian Union (in 1965, the Center Party), the basis was laid for a three front model of interests typical for the Scandinavian democracies. The model was originally made by Stein Rokkan to illustrate the Norwegian poles of conflicts (Rokkan 1987, 63-110), but fits well in the Finnish case, from the beginning of the 20th century up to present day. In contrast to the situation in many other democracies, there is not solely a class struggle between labor and capital, but also one between urban and rural interests, which has also been emphasized as a struggle between the Center and the periphery. The Social Democrats, backed by the labor unions defended the interests of the workers. Later on, the labor movement splintered between Communists and Social Democrats. As the language conflict lost in importance during World War II, the conservatives (National Coalition) stepwise got the role as a defender of capital. In turn, the Center Party, backed by the farmers' interest organization after WW II, have grown into the dominant political force in the rural areas in the north and east.

During the inter-World War period the politics was dominated by a strong turn to the right. The Communist Party, founded in 1918 by Social Democratic refugees in Moscow, was banned in 1919. Also the Socialist Labor Party, which was dominated by communists, was banned and their MPs were imprisoned in 1923 (Saarela 1996). These moves only fueled the nationalists and the pro-fascist movement. Both the Social Democrats and the Swedish minority were in danger. When the pro-fascist movement materialized, with their aims to overhaul the democratic system, the conservative president reacted. The big rebellion meeting and planned march to the capital, Helsinki, was dissolved under army threat. Democracy was saved, the pro-fascist movement founded a political party (IKL), and in 1937 a coalition was formed between Social Democrats and Agrarians. This historical handshake between workers and farmers was given in all four Scandinavian democracies during a period of four years in the 1930s. It prevented the Scandinavian democracies from turning to fascism when the rest of the European continent faced a storm of totalitarianism. In Finland, the agreement was called "the red soil". When the Soviets attacked Finland in the autumn of 1939, the people stood united, thanks greatly to the red soil, and the country managed to preserve its freedom

After World War II, a new period began in Finnish political history. The communist-influenced party, the People's Democratic League, formed at the end of 1944, grew directly after the World War (1945 election) into the second largest in Parliament. In the election of 1958, the communists temporarily became the largest parliamentary party, with one fourth of all seats. During the period from 1945 to 1966, the Social Democrats and Communists continuously competed over who would have power in the labor movement. However, the

Social Democrats exchanged their old wartime leaders for a new leadership, approving of the official foreign policy doctrine. This change of leadership made the Social Democrats a cabinet party, similar to the Center Party, around which practically all coalitions up to the 1980s were centered.

The Center Party has been the most powerful party since World War II, because it has succeeded better than any other party in maximizing its governmental influence. Today, farmers are no more than 7 per cent of the economically-active population, and while the Center Party has successfully enlarged its electoral appeal to all rural residents, it has hardly penetrated the urban areas in the south. In addition, the Conservatives managed to enlarge their support from 1972 to 1987. Their success stemmed from the rapid growth of the urban middle class, who strongly identified themselves with the conservative image of successful careerism. The Conservatives were systematically excluded from cabinet coalitions during a 21-year period, from 1966 to 1987, due to the fear of Russian disapproval. Their attempt to be accepted finally succeeded in 1987 when the Social Democrats and the Conservatives became the main coalition partners in the new government. At that point, the Conservatives had grown from the fourth to the second largest party in Parliament.

As the main parties one by one adapted to the official foreign policy doctrine, the Communists paradoxically lost their advantage. One of President Urho Kekkonen's main concerns was to integrate the Communists into the parliamentary system by offering them offices in cabinet coalitions, as a means of deradicalizing them. The party utilized the position that soon led to a deep ideological conflict between pragmatism (Euro communism) and orthodox Stalinism. From the late 1960s, there was open party conflict between the fractions, which paralyzed its activity. The conflict resulted in internal party splits during the 1980s and a final collapse in 1990, when a new socialist party (Left-Wing Alliance) was formed from the ruins of the old Communist movement. When the Soviet Union collapsed and Finland joined the European Union in 1995, a new era began and replaced the post-World War II period.

2. The Turn to Universal Suffrage

Before the Czar gave his order (in 1905) to the estates to prepare a proposal for the parliamentary reform, the so-called Russianization period took place. This explains why the estates could reach unanimity in great reforms: they were faced with a common enemy. A constitutional committee (the Hermanson Committee) did the preparatory work, and then political negotiations between the estates began. The general aim was to form, nationally, as strong a parliament as possible, in order to be able to resist the Russians. The result was the most modern Parliamentary Act in the whole of Europe in 1906. In fact, the reform was a great victory for the young Social Democratic Party, which was not represented in the Diet. The victory, however, was not primarily the result of a strong Social Democratic mobilization. It was rather a result of the weakness of the Russian government after the revolutionary actions around the large empire. In addition, the four estates were more moderate in their plans; but, faced by a strong Democratic resistance, they had no other choice but to join them. For the first time the Social Democrats managed to have an influence in national politics, through the force of their rapidly growing mass organization. At this stage, the conservatives in the Diet had no chance to make compromises with the Social Democrats.

The most important sections in the Parliamentary Act of 1906 — including the main provisions of the electorate, the constituencies and the voting system — were as follows:

Section 1. The people of Finland, convened in the sessions of the Grand Duchy of Finland, are represented by Parliament.

Section 2. Parliament shall be unicameral and shall comprise two hundred representatives.

Section 3. Parliamentary elections shall be held every third year at the same time throughout the country. The mandate of a representative shall begin when he is declared elected and shall continue until the next elections have been held.

The Czar, however, shall have the right to order new elections before the expiry of the three year period mentioned in paragraph 1. In that case, credentials of representatives, if Parliament is not dissolved again, are in force three years.

Section 4. The representatives shall be elected by a direct and proportional ballot, for which purpose the country will be divided into no fewer than twelve and no more than eighteen electoral districts.

However, if local conditions require an exception from electoral proportionality, one electoral district or several districts may be formed, in addition to those mentioned before, for the election of one representative only.

The suffrage of those enfranchised shall be equal in the elections.

The right to vote may not be exercised by proxy.

More detailed provisions on electoral districts and on the timing and manner of the elections shall be enacted in a special Act of Parliamentary Elections.

Section 5. Every citizen of Finland, both man and woman, who has reached the age of twenty-four years before the year of the election, shall be entitled to vote."

To make universal suffrage workable, the Parliamentary Act was supplemented with decrees which guaranteed the freedom to establish organizations and freedom of speech. The Parliamentary Act of 1906 is the very basis of the current Finnish electoral system. Its basic principles are still in force. At the moment of the electoral reform, Finland turned from having one of the most old-fashioned systems to having one of the most radical. As the electoral reform provided, 1) universal and equal suffrage — women were enfranchised. Finland was one of the first countries in the world to give women the equal right to vote and to be nominated. 2) A proportional election system, with large constituencies, was introduced to give the different political interests an equal right to be represented. 3) For a proper transformation of votes to seats, the d'Hondt counting method was applied. These three fundamental principles are still in force today, though some important modifications have been made.

The prerogatives from the electoral reform of 1906 are often highlighted without mentioning several restrictions. The right to vote was denied to any citizen who:

1) is in permanent service with the armed forces;

2) is under guardianship;

3) for the last three years has not been registered in the local population register;

4) has left her/his taxes unpaid for the two preceding years, for reasons other than lack of means, shown by a certificate from the municipal board;

5) receives poor relief other than temporarily;

6) has relinquished her/his property in order to satisfy her/his creditors, until s/he or she has confirmed the condition of the estate under oath;

7) has been sentenced to a penitentiary for vagrancy, until the end of third year from the date he was released from penitentiary;

8) in final legal judgment has been deemed to be lacking good reputation or is unfit for State service or to attend to somebody else's matters;

9) has been convicted of buying or selling votes in parliamentary elections, or of attempting to do so; of voting in more than one place, or of disturbing the electoral freedom by violence or threat — such shall be disqualified from voting until the end of the sixth calendar year from the date of the final sentencing (Törnudd 1968, 41-42).

Although the restrictions, at first glance, affected the industrial proletariat and landless dwellers, the results of the first universal elections in 1907 was a victory for the Social Democrats. After the first revolutionary attempt in 1905, new confidence arose among the rural and urban workers. As class consciousness emerged and deepened, the Social Democrats dramatically grew in organizational strength. Branches were established in practically all parts of the country. Members poured in and the party became a mass party in good time for the election. The party program was not radical, as it was a plea for extended national and local democracy including social reforms and economic reforms. The demands of socialism, or the like, were unheard of.

Uncertainty before the election was great, as the electorate was tenfold compared to the elections for the Diet. New parties emerged on the electoral arena (Social Democrats and Agrarians), and the old ones reorganized to meet the rising threat from the left. The reorganized Swedish People's Party attracted new categories of Swedish-speaking people in the coastal areas with no former access to politics. The Swedish People's Party became the leading political movement for the Swedish Finns who felt threatened by the moves of Finnization and Russification (Sundberg 1985).

Although issues of language and the relation to Russia were emphasized by the Finnish Party and the Swedish People's Party, the campaign was dominated by domestic social issues. The Finnish Party, also called the Old Finnish Party in contrast to the liberal Young Finnish Party, adopted a far-reaching social reform manifesto. In addition, the newly-founded Agrarian party emphasized primarily social and economic issues related to farming and rural life. The Social Democrats stood for the most aggressive campaigning by demanding land reforms for the rapidly growing number of rural proletariat. This was a well-funded strategy, as the industrial workers at that time were still a small but growing core group for the party.

The 1907 election, the first in Finland, was most important — it formed the party system basically still functioning today. As a result of campaigning and the lack of democratic experience, many of those newly enfranchised had unrealistic expectations concerning the first elections. The electoral turnout was high, as 70.7 per cent of the electorate cast their votes. This result was not surpassed until 1945. The winner of the election was the Social Democratic Party, with 80 seats in Parliament and 37 per cent of the votes. Through this election, the Social Democrats became the biggest political party in Parliament. With that and the strong mass organization, the Social Democrats took the political initiative. All other parties stood against the offensive from the left. The Old Finnish Party (later the National Coalition) was the strongest counter force with 59 seats and 27.3 per cent of the votes. The Liberals (Young Finns) won 26 seats followed by the Swedish People's Party with 24 seats. The Agrarian Union was a small party in this election (9 seats), and it lasted until 1919 when the party took the position as one of the big ones.

As the expectations were high among the socialist workers, the disappointment was perhaps even deeper when the Social Democratic reform initiatives were turned down by the non-socialists, the Russian dominated Senate, or by the Russian Government. The election lost much of its legitimacy and the undemocratic form of government laid the ground for a process which ended in a brutal civil war in 1918.

3. Electoral System Eras

As already mentioned, the electoral system has remained remarkably stable since its introduction in 1906. It is even more remarkable, considering that Finland became independent from one of the most totalitarian and obsolete regimes in Europe, suffered from a civil war, turned for a short period towards monarchism, banned the communists during the inter-World War period, and banned the fascist and pro-fascist parties after World War II. On the other hand, Finland was never occupied during the war.

The interaction between social groups, social issues and electoral systems, in terms of the structuring of party competition, have remained quite the same throughout the period of independence. All electoral reforms have been designed and implemented as non-political technical modifications. The committees producing the detailed plans for these reforms, consisting mainly of legal experts, have not bothered to try to see the electoral system as a strategic environment. Those party functionaries who participated in the workings of these committees have not tried to fully utilize the strategic gains from the small-scale electoral reforms. Moreover, the parties have known from the start that in order to be implementable, the reforms must have broad support. The strategic aspects of law production in Finland have given the parties effective incentives to compromise before government bills are presented to the Parliament

The once radical electoral law from the early 20th century is now one of the oldest in the world. Adjustments of importance have been made in the Act of Organizations with relevance to the electoral results. Some of them have generated political conflicts. As already mentioned, the Communists were banned at different times during the early years of independence, as the Communists reorganized. In 1930, the ban was written into law, prohibiting Communist (or the like) organizations to nominate candidates in elections. The radical right in Finland succeeded to win over the moderate non-socialists to this position, but failed to extend the law to cover the Social Democrats. The communist ban was realized in 1944, after the defeat in the war led to the radical right becoming the target of the same measure. This law of "protection" from 1930 can be seen as an undemocratic parenthesis in Finnish electoral history.

In contrast, the discussion in Parliament around the electoral law has focused on two main themes: improvement of proportionality and candidate selection. From the very beginning, when the d'Hondt method was adopted, small parties have complained about the disadvantageous transformation of votes into seats. Proposals were made to either decrease or increase the number of constituencies, shift from the d'Hondt method to the Saint-Laguë, and to permit the allocation of seats within electoral rings. Except for some shifts in the number and magnitude of the constituencies, neither of the two other sets of proposals was ever accepted by the Parliament. One proposal from the early 1920s was inspired by the Danish system, stating that some of the members of Parliament should be elected in small constituencies and the remaining in a nationwide constituency. Closely connected to this proposal from the same period were attempts made to introduce electoral rings. These rings would enable small parties to pool their votes while still maintaining their identities for the allocation of seats. The risk is greater in electoral alliances, as there is always some uncertainty about which candidate will win and which will lose. In 1923, a proposal was made to combine the principles of electoral rings and nationwide proportionality. Through these movable seats, candidates of the same party from different constituencies could be linked, and then these candidates could be linked with different parties. Proposals of electoral rings have been made by different small parties and resisted by the larger ones several times during the Finnish electoral history. Inspired by the electoral reforms in Scandinavia, during the 1950s and 1960s the Swedish People's Party proposed three times that the d'Hondt system should be replaced with the more fair Saint-Laguë system. These proposals were also defeated due to the risk of increasing fragmentation of the party system (Törnudd 1968, 41-61).

The system of candidate selection has gone through one fundamental change since it was introduced, complemented with a couple of minor changes. Originally, the voter could give her/his vote to no more than three candidates. The voter could choose to support the three candidates listed by marking the ballot with a pencil. S/he was also given the right to alter the ranking order, or to write in the names and addresses of a maximum of three eligible people. The first alternative dominated, and the other two alternatives had no practical significance when votes were transformed into seats. In addition, the law made it possible for a single candidate to appear simultaneously on different lists, as well within the party as in different electoral alliances. More important was the option for one candidate to appear on party lists in different constituencies. With this move, candidates could utilize their support in more than one constituency. This possibility often proved to be a strategic choice, as it can sometimes be problematic for a candidate to estimate in which constituency s/he will get the most votes.

This system remained unchanged until 1935, when the electoral act was reformed. Some changes in candidate selection are worth mentioning. The number of candidates on the list was reduced to two and the chance to alter the ranking sequence was repealed. As the latter option had a minor significance, the reform had only a moderate effect. In 1953 the list system was replaced by single member lists in local elections and, in the 1954 Parliament elections, this system was tested; it was legislated in a new electoral law in 1955. Although lists were still mentioned in the law, that was misleading, as the system became a single candidate choice. The voters could now choose among single candidates without predetermination. By this reform, elections in Finland turned to an individualistic system where the vote is given to a single candidate. Through the candidate, votes are counted for the party or electoral alliance that s/he is representing.

In 1966 the socialist parties managed, for the second time since World War II, to win a majority in elections and Parliament. Their earlier success (1958) did not result in a cabinet coalition, due to the deep antagonism between the Communists and the Social Democrats. However, in 1966 the majority of the Communists had dropped the orthodox mantle for reformism, which resulted in a deep and disastrous conflict within the party. When the Social Democrats at the same time agreed to approve the official Finnish foreign policy, the way opened for a folk front government led by the Social Democrats. The Communists where included, together with the agrarian Center Party. During a four year period, the cabinet was led by Rafael Paasio for the first two years, and then by Mauno Koivisto who succeeded Urho Kekkonen as president in 1982. More important, during this period the electoral law was reformed and a party law was introduced.

Until the late 1960s, the party was not recognized in legislation. When public subsidies were introduced in 1967, the problem became apparent. Public subsidies were seen by the Social Democrats as a matter of justice, as they had no chance to gain funding from affluent donors as the non-socialist parties did. Therefore, in 1969 a party law came into force with detailed rules of party registration and control. Among other things, exclusively democratic party organizations were given the right to register. Also, details of control on how the parties spend their subsidies were enacted in the law (Sundberg 1997, 97-117). The electoral law from 1955 was also reformed in 1969, when the party was given a central role in the electoral process.

As earlier, electoral laws did not make any mention of parties; the nomination of candidates was given to voters' associations. These associations had to collect 30 signatures among citizens who were entitled to vote (until 1955, the number was 50). The candidates nominated by the voters' associations were given the right to join electoral alliances, which represented the party or parties behind the candidates. Thus, the party label could only indirectly appear on the lists through the electoral alliance. In the new electoral law from 1969, registered parties were automatically given the right to nominate candidates without the process of collecting signatures and forming electoral alliances. Originally, only parties were given the right to nominate candidates, but in 1975 this restriction was changed. As a result, voters' associations were given the right to nominate candidates, if every nomination was supported by 100 signatures. The right to give groups of voters a chance to nominate candidates has been successfully utilized in two cases. The first occurred when a popular

MP was denied access to the party list, in an internal party conflict (Communists) in 1983, and the second when the Greens won office before they were a registered party.

The process of candidate selection was synchronized with the norms of internal party democracy written in the party law. According to the electoral law from 1969, membership vote is compulsory in candidate selection. Exceptions to this rule can only be made if the number of nominees does not exceed the maximum number of candidates permitted in every constituency. Usually, the number of candidates is big enough to find an internal consensus, and therefore a membership vote is not needed. However, many parties have utilized membership votes to recruit popular candidates. Furthermore, the party districts are given a free hand to organize the nomination process. If the party rules do not include anything about the process in the districts, parties have to follow the regulations in the law. In fact, most rules follow the intentions of the law, which gives the national party the right to change 1/4 of the nominated candidates. This option to change candidates is generally not used, except in cases of internal conflicts or cases of open discrimination.

In 1998, all electoral laws in Finland (Parliament, President, European Parliament, and Municipal Council) were brought together under one law, namely the Electoral Law (714/1998). The changes were mainly technical and the former laws remained almost unchanged. Some changes were discussed regarding a coming division of constituencies, but in the 1999 election the division mainly followed the old order (RP 48/1998).

An Act on Campaign Financing came into force in the year 2000. According to this law, candidates for Parliament, President, Municipal Government, and European Parliament elections are obliged to report their total campaign expenditures. The candidate has to report her/his own financial contribution and the external financial support given by the party, any other organization or donor (Komiteanmietintö 1999:6). The intention of the law is to gain a better insight into what financial connections the candidates are involved in during the campaign.

4. Electoral Laws and Their Consequences

The restrictions in the right to vote from 1906 (discussed above) have been gradually repealed. Voting age has decreased as follows: from 24 years in 1906 to 21 years in 1944, to 20 years in 1969, to "the age of 18 years before the election" in

1972, and "the age of 18 no later than election day" in 1995. The voting age regulations have been modified with the same motivation each time: because the present youth has demonstrated itself to be more mature than its predecessors, to enlarge suffrage is justified. This has not been a highly politicized matter. It has been treated more as a technical matter reflecting larger societal changes. It is noteworthy, though, that in 1944 the younger generation's right to vote was motivated not only by the standard rationale of earlier maturation, but also by the fact that the younger generation had fulfilled its duty to protect the country during the war. It was deemed unseemly that young people were expected to offer their lives for the country, but not given the right to vote.

Since 1969, there is no requirement of a voter's domicile in Finland. All Finnish citizens have franchise, regardless of their domicile. Also, those citizens who have permanently moved abroad retain the right to vote. They participate in advance voting at Finnish embassies or onboard Finnish ships. There are today somewhat more than 200,000 enfranchised persons living abroad, most of them in Sweden. The inclusion of those not domiciled in Finland has decreased the voting turnout, as a percentage of eligible voters, as most of them choose not to participate. Therefore, the degree of electoral participation is estimated with two percentages: one which includes all the enfranchised, and another where only the domiciled votes are calculated. The latter choice gives a result that is higher by approximately 3 per cent points. This is the most commonly used measure, even in official terms, though the result is manipulated.

Many of the rules disqualifying voters were removed by the Parliament Act of 1928. The Social Democrats and Communists heavily criticized the rule that disqualified those poor citizens who were dependent on public assistance. In 1944 this rule was revoked. In the same year, enfranchisement was also extended to those performing military service. With this latter reform, the number of enfranchised rose by about 40,000 people. According to estimates, between 13 to 15 per cent of all those who fulfilled the age criteria at the beginning of the 20th century were disqualified to vote (Tarasti 1998, 59-62). Now the proportion of disqualified can hardly be recognized.

The electorate has increased since the first elections in 1907 as follows:

Table 1: The Increase in the Electorate Since 1907

Year	Population	% of Population	Voting Turnout
1907	1.272.873	45.0	70.7
1919	1.438.709	45.9	67.1
1930	1.722.588	50.6	65.9
1945	2.284.249	61.1	74.9
1962	2.714.838	60.7	85.1
1970	3.094.359	67.0	82.2
1983	3.951.932	75.8	75.7
1999	4.152.430	80.5	65.8
Change N	+2.879.557		
Change %	+69	+35.5	-4.9

The expansion of the electorate is partly explained by population growth and partly by the enlargement of those enfranchised. In the 1999 election, the electorate was more than three times bigger than in 1907. However, in 1907 only 45 per cent of the population was entitled to vote, and now it is around 80 percent. Since then, the age structure has changed and the voting age has been lowered from 24 to 18. The revoked restrictions have also contributed to this development. However, the enlargement of those enfranchised has not automatically resulted in an increased voting turnout. The trend was increasing during the first decades after World War II; from the early 1980s, the turnout has been decreasing. The inclusion of those not domiciled in Finland, from 1975 onward, to some extent has contributed to the decline, but other political and social factors are important as well.

The main political actors in Finland have been organized around three poles of conflict since the first universal elections in 1907: labor and capital (the Social Democratic Party and the Conservative Party), the rural periphery, and the urban center (the Agrarian Party = the Center Party) (Rokkan 1987, 81-95). As these three fronts of parties, supplemented by the Liberal parties and the Communist parties, still vital in the 1960s, reflected old cleavages from the 1920s, Stein Rokkan called them frozen (Lipset and Rokkan 1967,· 50). Rokkan wondered how it was possible for these old parties to have survived fascism, world wars and profound changes in the social and cultural structure. Thirty years later, after deep economic, social and political changes such as the collapse of the Soviet Union and the entrance of Finland into the European Union, we are still concerned with whether the party system is frozen or whether it has been replaced by new cleavages and parties. In a European perspective, the frozen Scandinavian model, if still alive, is unique.

The Scandinavian democracies are commonly described as five-party systems (Berglund and Lindström 1978). During the initial period, the Liberal parties were among the most influential. Much of their former strength has faded, their organization has either been weak or has weakened, and the parties have suffered from internal splits. Nevertheless, they are included as one of the five. The parties to the left of the Social Democrats, except for in Finland, have never been included among the established ones. In addition, the variety of parties is large, as it includes old Communist parties (orthodox and non-orthodox) and various left-socialist parties with a Social Democratic heritage which appeared in the early 1960s. In the five-party model, only the Communist parties are included.

The five-party system discussed above is not complete, as many other parties, old and new, could be included. The former include the Swedish People's Party and the small Christian Party. From the early 1970s, a wide variety of new parties have emerged on the electoral arena in Finland. Given the change within parties and in their environment, the five-party conception is no longer a good illustration of the party system. Doubts have been raised as to whether the frozen party hypothesis is still valid. In a recent study comprising 18 European democracies, Jan-Erik Lane and Svante Ersson assert that the hypothesis has lost its validity and should be replaced by a new theory about the interaction between parties and the electorate (Lane and Ersson 1997, 179-196).

The freezing hypothesis is not put off that easily. Its defenders argue that the frozen party system hypothesis is wrongly understood. According to Peter Mair, a transformation of a frozen party system can only be determined by changes in the cleavage system and not by electoral volatility or the like. It is the change in the cleavage system which is the very essence of the freezing hypothesis and not the degree of electoral stability or instability (Mair 1997, 45-66). As a result, Mair argues that the West European party systems are still frozen, despite studies which claim the opposite.

The three-front party cleavage defined by Rokkan is not solely based on class cleavages. In the Norwegian case (which fits well with the rest of Scandinavia), the cleavage system, according to Stein Rokkan, is based on three basic economic dimensions: 1) the conflict between rural and urban economies 2) the class struggle in the primary economy, and 3) the class struggle in the secondary/tertiary sectors (Valen and Rokkan 1974, 332-335). In the first case, class is not even mentioned, as the cleavage is concentrated on a conflict between the center and the periphery. The agrarian center parties are the defenders of the rural periphery. As farming has declined, the rural economy has been more vulnerable and the migration to cities has been extensive. The center parties have responded by struggling to incorporate middle-class rural voters who are directly or indirectly dependent on the agrarian economy. This struggle, emphasized by Rokkan, has not vanished. As a result, the Agrarian parties have managed to retain their electoral strength without giving up the rural defense. In the 1994 EU referendum, the old conflict between the center and the periphery flamed up and the anti-EU response was compact in the Finnish northern periphery. Membership in the EU seems to have given more fuel to the defenders of the rural north against the national capitals and the EU bureaucracy in Brussels.

Most of the class struggle in the primary sector has vanished, as the marginal small holders have disappeared through the big structural transformation in agriculture. The struggle in the declining secondary sector of today is much focused on the conflict between the new populist right wing parties and the Social Democrats. Well-paid workers have been attracted by the populist appeal of low taxation and anti-immigrant stands. As our figures have shown, the struggle between Social Democrats and traditional Communist parties is history, today. Also, polls show that the non-socialist parties have won a small share of the working class votes from the first surveys conducted in the mid 1950s.

It is, however, the struggle within the vast middle class which has been the big challenge for the Social Democrats on the left, the Conservative parties on the right, and to some extent the Agrarian parties on the countryside. As the middle class is heterogeneous, the preferences among the different categories seem to diverge. This gives the class-struggling parties a chance to incorporate these categories, as the middle class *per se* so far has not produced a new societal cleavage between work and capital. Studies show that the middle class can be categorized in different ways. One is the division into old and new middle class.

The old middle class is mostly self-employed, whereas the new middle class consists of a heterogeneous group of salaried employees (Kerr 1990, 5-26; Kivinen 1989). Not surprisingly, it is among these the Social Democrats have succeeded to win votes. The middle class can also be hierarchically categorized into upper, middle, and lower levels. Studies show that the Conservatives are successful among the upper level voters and the Social Democrats among the lower middle-class voters (Sänkiaho 1996, 80-83).

The middle class can also be horizontally divided, according to whether they are public employees or not. This division has particular relevance in Scandinavia, where a considerable part of the middle class consists of public employees. In addition, most of the lower level employees are publicly employed, and a vast majority of those are women. Very few studies have been undertaken to systematically determine which party or parties are the main beneficiaries when the public employees' vote. There is no doubt among the voters that it is the main political actors (three-front parties) who decide the future of the public service sector. The Social Democrats are usually recognized as the founding fathers of the Scandinavian welfare system. Their defense of public service has successfully attracted those lower level public employees who are members of a labor union .

It is the heterogeneity of the middle class which opens the gates to successful competition between the three-front parties. This of course would not have been successful if the three parties had frozen their class appeal. The agrarian parties had almost vanished and the Social Democrats had been reduced to middle-sized parties. It is only the Conservatives who are a true class party. They have no need to appeal to workers, and only a minor (regional) stake in attracting farmers.

In addition, 47 per cent of the population in Finland (ages 15-74 years) were not employed in 1994. Those not employed comprise the unemployed, students, pensioners and those unable to work, those working at home, conscripts, and others (Yearbook of Nordic Statistics 1996, 78-79). This vast category of people outside the labor force cannot be placed in any settled way in the three-front cleavage structure. To be sure, this category of people is also heterogeneous, and some of them, especially the young, have given the parties considerable problems to incorporate them.

5. The Effects of the D'Hondt System

As the Finnish electoral system permits parties to enter electoral alliances, the d'Hondt system is only slightly less disproportional than the modified St. Laguë system. Only in pure forms is the difference between these two considerable (Laakso 1980, 249-264). Disproportionality, however, can be measured in different ways. One approach follows a formula developed by Douglas Rae, which measures the deviation in average (Rae 1971, 84). The formula has been criticized because it underestimates systems with many parties, as well as the disproportionality in relative proportional systems. These shortcomings are avoided in John Loosemore's and Victor Hanby's formula. In contrast to Rae's index, the total deviation is measured, not the average. But this system is not free from shortcomings, either. It tends to exaggerate the disproportionality in systems with many parties. A middle way between these two has been developed by Michael Gallagher (least-squares index LSq); it registers a few large deviations more strongly than many small ones (Lijphart 1994, 58-62). Both the latter systems are used in the following table. More attention is given, however, to Gallagher's index, as the number of parties in the Finnish electoral system is large.

In addition, the table includes the number of parties and their effective numbers in terms of votes and seats. The number of parties (in Parliament) can be counted one by one, without paying attention to their size. Following this approach, party systems can be categorized according to their degree of fragmentation, which is the same as the number of parties (Sartori 1976, 125-129). When party size is important, other measures must be used. Markku Laakso's and Rein Taagepera's "effective number of parties" is perhaps the best developed measure where size and numbers are combined. This index can be used on votes and on seats (Laakso and Taagepera 1979, 3-27). In Table 2, both types of application are measured.

Table 2: Disproportionality and fragmentation in Finnish elections since 1907

Year	Loosem. & Hanby	LSq	Eff. nr. of parties(v)	Eff. nr. of parties(s)	Number of parties
1907	5.15	3.23	4.00	3.57	6
1908	4.65	3.02	3.95	3.56	6
1909	2.65	2.18	3.90	3.64	6
1910	3.85	2.68	3.94	3.67	6
1911	3.70	2.50	3.94	3.65	6
1913	3.05	2.11	3.72	3.53	5
1916	4.70	3.41	3.42	3.07	6
1917	2.15	1.52	3.13	3.01	4
1919	3.45	2.25	4.18	3.96	6
1922	3.75	2.44	5.46	5.24	6
1924	2.75	1.85	5.14	4.92	6
1927	5.15	3.38	5.08	4.69	6
1929	6.05	3.80	5.02	4.46	6
1930	4.65	2.96	4.18	3.94	6
1933	5.75	3.74	4.23	3.81	7
1936	7.00	4.34	4.28	3.71	8
1939	7.80	4.84	4.05	3.50	7
1945	4.15	2.69	5.09	4.77	6
1948	4.45	3.08	4.90	4.54	6
1951	2.30	1.60	4.96	4.78	6
1954	3.20	2.16	4.98	4.71	6
1958	4.05	2.27	5.23	4.87	7
1962	7.60	4.18	5.86	5.09	8
1966	4.45	2.94	5.22	4.96	8
1970	5.65	2.91	6.17	5.58	8
1972	4.35	2.35	5.95	5.51	8
1975	6.70	3.26	5.90	5.32	11
1979	5.10	2.78	5.75	5.22	9
1983	3.90	2.19	5.49	5.18	10
1987	10.50	5.00	6.16	4.95	10
1991	6.40	3.07	5.92	5.25	10
1995	8.30	3.82	5.80	4.90	11
1999	7.40	3.85	5.87	5.15	10

The degree of disproportionality has been low, and stable, for 92 years. Also, the number of parties has increased and the effective numbers have only undergone a smooth change. Effects from the electoral reforms of 1944, 1954 or any other related reform cannot be found in the table. However, the increase in the number of parties means that the Finnish party system is more fragmented than ever before. Most of these parties are small, with limited influence. It is only the Christian League and the Greens who have been successful over time. Others, like the Finnish Rural Party, have vanished after two landslide elections in 1970 and 1983. As a result, the effective numbers in terms of votes and seats have only modestly increased. The number of parties has increased by 4, from 1907 to 1999, and the effective number of seats by 1.58 during the same period.

Although the disproportionality is low, the difference between the two measures is considerable. In addition, the difference seems to increase with a growing number of parties. Gallagher's LSq index is more stable, as the shift from one election to another is more moderate than in the Loosemore and Hanby index. The Gallagher index appears to be more appropriate in the Finnish context, where the number of small parties is high. Defined this way, no extensive change in the degree of disproportionality has emerged during the entire period. In addition, the noticeable shifts in disproportionality can hardly be linked to the electoral reforms discussed earlier in this paper.

6. Constituency Malapportionment

Studies show that district magnitude seems to have more effect on disproportionality than the electoral formula. Districts with a small magnitude tend to be more disproportional than the big ones (Kuusela 1995, 37-40). The number of constituencies has to some extent changed. More important, however, are the drastic changes in district magnitude. Finland is divided into a number of administrative counties. In elections, the constituency division follows the county borders. If the county is large, it has been divided into two and even three parts. From 1907 to 1938, the number of constituencies was unchanged (16). During this period, Lapland in the north was a one-member constituency. Single-member representation was replaced by multi-member representation when the county of Lapland was created. As the constituency was enlarged, a one-member solution could no longer be retained, and the apportionment of seats in Lapland grew to 7 (Törnudd 1968, 53-54 and 120).

For some years, all constituencies were multi-member districts, until 1947 when the Åland Islands in the far west was made a separate one-member constituency. This solution is still in force and it guarantees Åland one seat out of 200 in Parliament. From 1938, the number of constituencies remained unchanged at 15, although the bases for division and size shifted as a result of the war. In 1952, the capital of Helsinki became the 16th constituency. From the 1962 election, the number of constituencies was reduced again, and since then the number of 15 has remained unchanged (Tarasti 1998, 78-79; Törnudd 1968, 166-167). When the number of counties was reduced from 11 to 5 plus Åland, in 1997, a discussion of constituency size arose. However, in the amendment to a new constitution (2000), it is proposed that the country be divided into a minimum of 12 and a maximum of 18 constituencies, which follows the principles already adopted in 1906. In the 1999 election, the number of constituencies remained unchanged, but some names were changed to fit into the subdivision of counties in provinces.

Magnitude is more important than size and number in the apportionment of seats. The district magnitude is fixed through a formula where the population of the constituency, Pc, is divided by the population in the entire nation, Pn, and multiplied by the total number of seats in Parliament (- 1 for Åland).

$$\frac{Pc}{Pn} \times 199$$

The formula gives an advantage to those constituencies with a high rate of population under the age of 18. This bias was more pronounced earlier, when the voting age was 24. Lapland (until 1938) and Åland (from 1947) excluded, the district magnitude has shifted from 6 to 33. In the 1995 election, the magnitude ranged from 7 (North Karelia) to 31 (Uusimaa/Nyland). The electoral threshold in the former case was 12.5 per cent and in the latter case 3.1 perper cent cent (RP 48/1998, 11-12). Therefore, big parties have an advantage in constituencies with a low district magnitude and small parties have better prospects in constituencies with a high district magnitude. The proportionality between parties is better maintained than the geographical representation, in the former case; in the latter case, the proportionality between parties suffers and the geographical representation is well distributed.

In North Karelia, the Social Democrats got 39.4 per cent of the votes in 1995 and 57 per cent of the seats. The proportion between the remaining seats is much closer to the percentage of votes cast for the Center Party (2 seats) and the National Coalition (1 seat). On the Åland Islands, the winning voters' association got 61 per cent of the votes in 1995, and the payoff was the single seat, which corresponds to 100 percent. As a result, voting turnout in Åland is lower than average, and the trend was the same in Lapland when it was a single-member district before World War II. On the Åland Islands, voters' associations compete exclusively using party names, as the requirements for a registered party in the Party Act (by way of example, 5000 signatures) could hardly be filled. Until the 1979 election, the Coalition of Åland dominated the candidate selection and the elections. A tiny minority voted for candidates nominated by nationally organized parties. Since the 1983 election, voters' associations with party labels have replaced the Coalition of Åland. In the following table, three elections are chosen under a period when the districts (constituencies) are the same but the magnitudes have altered.

Table 3: Disproportionality at constituency level at the parliamentary elections 1966, 1979 and 1995 as measured by least-squares index

LSq index **District and magnitudes**	**1966**	**1979**	**1995**
Helsingfors stad-Helsingin kaup. (21,20,19)	3.44	6.81	5.75
Nylands l.-Uudenmaan l. (18,26,31)	2.80	4.98	4.57
Åbo l. södra-Turun l. etel. (16,17,17)	6.18	5.37	6.31
Åbo l. norra-Turun l. pohj. (13,13,11)	3.83	5.54	6.83
Tavastehus l. s.-Hämeen l. et. (14,15,13)	5.60	5.61	6.94
Tavastehus l. n.-Hämeen l. pohj. (12,13,16)	6.83	5.08	7.50
Kymmene l.-Kymen l. (15,15,13)	5.78	6.17	4.54
St. Michels l.-Mikkelin l. (10,9,8)	6.89	5.95	11.57
N. Karelens l.-Pohj.-Karjalan l. (9,7,7)	12.69	7.57	14.45
Kuopio l.-Kuopion l. (12,11,10)	6.14	6.78	8.43
Mell. Finlands l.-Keski-Suomen l.(11,10,10)	7.70	5.00	9.04
Vasa l.-Vaasan l. (20,18,18)	4.54	3.75	3.61
Uleåborgs l.-Oulun l. (18,17,18)	5.33	4.73	8.85
Lapplands l.-Lapin l. (10,8,8)	8.79	6.09	9.57
Åland (1,1,1)	3.70	1.50	35.36
Average from district results	5.60	5.39	9.55
Nationwide results	2.94	2.78	3.82

—

Through migration from north and east to southern urban areas, these constituencies have lost in district magnitude during this period. In the south, the constituency of Uusimaa/Nyland has increased in magnitude from 18 in 1966 to 31 in 1995. District magnitude is the most important determinant of disproportionality. The table shows that the nationwide disproportionality is constantly lower than the average from district results. This tendency is even more pronounced when the Loosemore and Handby Index is used (Kuusela 1995, 37-40). Disproportionalities on the district level tend to even out across the country and not to be cumulative when aggregated on the nationwide level. Differences in disproportionality between districts could otherwise give advantages to a single party.

The degree of disproportionality (Åland excluded) ranges from 2.80 in 1966 to 14.45 in 1995. As a rule, there is a strong tendency that small district magnitudes increase disproportionality and big magnitudes reduce it. Åland as a single-member district had the overwhelmingly highest disproportionality in 1995. Earlier, the disproportionality was extremely low, as the Coalition of Åland almost totally dominated in elections. In addition, North Karelia has a magnitude of 7 and scores highest when Åland is excluded, followed by Mikkeli/St. Michel and Lappi/Lappland. Uusimaa/Nyland is the biggest and one of the

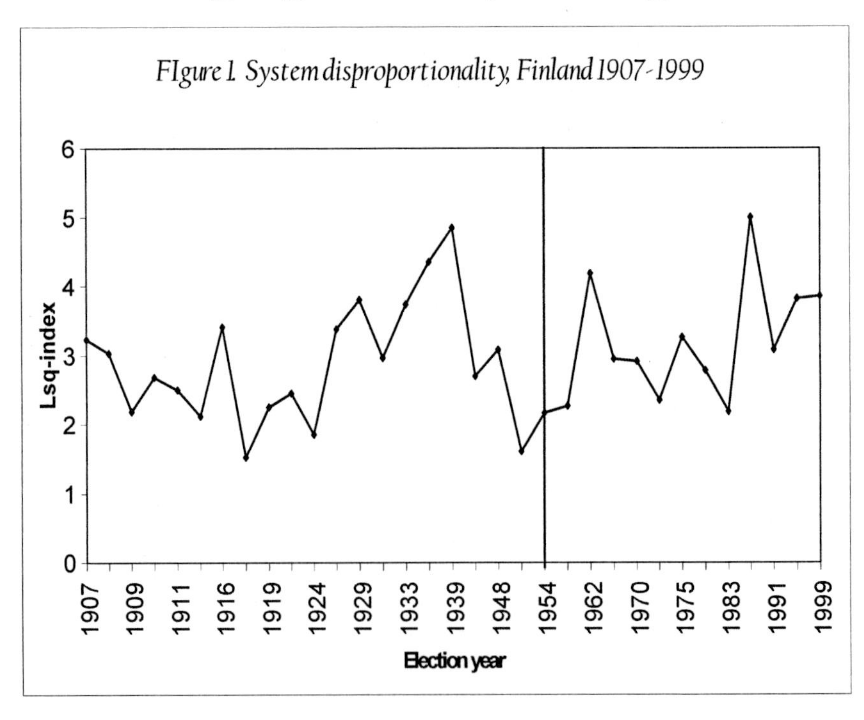

FIgure 1. System disproportionality, Finland 1907-1999

most proportional districts. There is no doubt that the disproportionality would be lower if the nation was formed into one single district, as it is in European Parliament elections.

7. Conclusions

In Finland, proportional elections have led to a political tradition in which governments are nearly always coalition governments with many parties. As no party clearly dominates, the Finnish system has been unstable. From the day of independence in 1917, a total of 67 cabinets have been formed, including the cabinet from April 1999 (Nousiainen 1998, 243-246). The frequent cabinet shifts cannot be associated with the moderate changes in the electoral laws. More generally, the proportional system has produced a party system with no dominant party. The period from 1917 to 1937 was characterized by a search for non-socialist majority cabinets, but the result was often a minority cabinet. From 1937 to 1987, the coalitions were built around the Social Democrats and the agrarian Center Party, filled with parties either from the right or the left. The inclusion of the Communists often resulted in crisis (Jansson 1992, 225-241). However, since the 1983 election, all cabinets have been in office for the entire electoral period.

The structure of the Finnish electoral system has been successful in the Finnish circumstances. A good indication of this is that the main solutions in 1906 concerning parliamentary elections are still in force today. And even now there is no major pressure for amendments to the electoral system. Although the new Finnish constitution was rewritten in 2000, no reforms were made in the electoral provisions. One strength in the present electoral system is that it is relatively simple.

The whole Finnish electoral system is quite uniform. Local elections in municipalities, and in many respects also elections to the European Parliament, take place following the lines of parliamentary elections. The presidential elections, however, differ from other general elections. The President of the Republic is elected by direct elections in two rounds. Plurality run-off is applied. Similarly, as in elections to the European Parliament, the entire nation forms one constituency in Presidential elections.

How accurate have actors been in anticipating the likely consequences of the changes in the electoral system that actually took place? This is a difficult question to answer because the reforms are never justified by using partisan arguments. Quite the contrary: partisan motivations, if there have been any, have been hidden in the legalistic formulations motivating the reforms. The linkage between suffrage changes and pressures for suffrage expansion and choice of electoral system has not been a salient issue in Finland. Factors related to party political tactics were not present in any of the texts the committee produced, in the preparation of the 1906 reform. This is commonly explained by referring to the fact that the party political representatives in the Hermanson Committee, which prepared the 1906 reform, did not have any realistic estimate of the political support of the parties among the electorate. But it would be wrong to claim that the specialists in the Hermanson Committee were naive idealists because they were not clever enough to focus on the political consequences of the design of the election system. In fact, they were experienced politicians, so we must assume that they also had political calculations in mind when they proposed or opposed certain ideas.

Appendix

Table A-1: Electoral systems in Finland since 1906

Electoral system	**1906 - 1954** **20 elections**	**1954 -** **13 elections**
District magnitude*	12.7	13.2
Electoral formula	d'Hondt	d'Hondt
Number of compensatory seats	No	No
Allocation of seats in multi member constituencies final	Yes	Yes
Legal thresholds (and effective thresholds)	No/ Effective threshold = 5.6%	No/ Effective threshold = 5.6%

* Number of seats in Parliament divided by the number of constituencies

Table A-2. Major Parties and Governing Coalitions in Finland 1919-2001

Period	Major Leftist (socialist and communist) parties	Major C enter parties	Major Right (Conservative) parties	Governing coalitions
1919-	Social Democrats	Center party	Conservatives	Center party supported by non-socialist parties
1926-	Social Democrats	Center party	Conservatives	-Social Democrats single party cabinet -Center Party single party cabinet -Liberals single party cabinet -Center party single party cabinet
1930-	Social Democrats	Center party	Conservatives	-Conservatives supported by non-socialist parties -Center party supported by non-socialist parties Liberals and Swedish People's Party -Center party and Liberals
1937-	Social Democrats	Center party	Conservatives	-Liberals together with Center party and Social Democrats
1939-	Social Democrats	Center party	Conservatives	Grand coalitions during the war
1944-	Social Democrats Communists	Center party	Conservatives	-Combinations of Center party, Social Democrats, Communists supported by Liberals and/or Swedish People's party -Social Democrats
1950-	Social Democrats Communists	Center party	Conservatives	-Combinations of Center party and Social Democrats supported or led by Liberals and Swedish People's party
1957-	Social Democrats	Center party	Conservatives	-Coalitions mainly led by the Center Party and supported by non-socialist parties -One short period of Social Democratic participation
1966-	Social Democrats Communists	Center party	Conservatives	-Coalitions either Communists led or supported by Social Democrats and Center party. Support altered or jointly with Communists, Swedish People's party and Liberals -One short period of Social Democratic rule
1966-	Social Democrats Communists/Left-Wing Alliance	Center party	Conservatives	-Coalitions either -Coalitions led by Communists/Left-the Social Democrats supported by Center party and other small non-socialist parties -Coalitions led by the Conservatives supported by the Social Democrats and other small non-socialist parties -Coalitions led by the Center party supported by the Conservatives and other non-socialist parties
1995-	Social Democrats Left- Wing Alliance	Center party	Conservatives	-Coalitions led by the Social Democrats supported by the Left-Wing Alliance from the left to the Conservatives on the right, except for the Center party

Table A-3: Parliament election results 1906-1999

Table A-3(a)
The pre-independence period

	1907	**1908**	**1909**	**1910**	**1911**	**1913**	**1916**	**1917**
Social Democrats								
Votes%	37.0	38.4	36.9	40.0	40.0	43.1	47.3	44.8
Seats %	40.0	41.5	42.0	43.0	43.0	45.0	51.5	46.0
Seats	80	83	84	86	86	90	103	92
Swedish People's Party								
Votes%	12.6	12.7	12.3	13.5	13.3	13.1	11.8	10.9
Seats%	12.0	12.5	12.5	13.0	13.0	13.0	10.5	10.5
Seats	24	25	25	26	26	26	21	21
Christian Labor Union								
Votes%	1.5	2.3	2.7	2.2	2.1	Labor 1.8	1.8	1.6
Seats%	1.0	1.0	0.5	0.5	0.5	-	0.5	-
Seats	2	2	1	1	1	-	1	-
Agrarian Union								
Votes%	5.8	6.4	6.7	7.6	7.8	7.9	9.0	12.4
Seats%	4.5	4.5	6.5	8.5	8.0	9.0	9.5	13.0
Seats	9	9	13	17	16	18	19	26
Young Finnish Party								
Votes%	13.6	14.2	14.5	14.4	14.9	14.1	12.5	*
Seats%	13.0	13.5	14.5	14.0	14.0	14.0	11.5	16.0
Seats	26	27	29	28	28	28	23	32
Finnish Party								
Votes%	27.3	25.4	23.6	22.1	21.7	19.9	17.5	30.2*
Seats%	29.5	27.0	24.0	21.0	21.5	19.0	16.5	12.0
Seats	59	54	48	42	43	38	33	24
Others								
Votes%	2.1	0.5	0.2	0.1	0.1	0.2	0.1	
0.2								
Seats%	-	-	-	-	-	-	-	-
Seats	-	-	-	-	-	-	-	-
Total								
Votes%	100	100	100	100	100	100	100	100
Seats%	100	100	100	100	100	100	100	100
Seats	200	200	200	200	200	200	200	200

*Young Finnish Party and Finnish Party nominated candidates on joint lists named United Finnish Parties.

Table A-3(b)
Independence and the first decades of democratic rule

	1919	1922	1924	1927	1929	1930	1933	1936	1939
Social Democrats									
Votes%	38.0	25.1	29.0	28.3	27.4	34.2	37.3	38.6	39.8
Seats %	40.0	26.5	30.0	30.0	29.5	33.0	39.0	41.5	42.5
Seats	80	53	60	60	59	66	78	83	85
Swedish People's Party									
Votes%	12.1	12.4	12.0	12.2	11.4	10.8	10.4	11.2	10.1
Seats%	11.0	12.5	11.5	12.0	11.5	10.5	10.5	10.5	9.0
Seats	22*	25*	23*	24*	23**	21*	21*	21*	18*
Christian Labor Union									
Votes%	1.5								
Seats%	1								
Seats	2								
Agrarian Union									
Votes%	19.7	20.3	20.2	22.6	26.2	27.3	22.5	22.4	22.9
Seats%	21.0	22.5	22.0	26.0	30.0	29.5	26.5	26.5	28.0
Seats	42	45	44	52	60	59	53	53	56
National Coalition									
Votes%	15.7	18.2	19.0	17.7	14.5	18.0	16.9***	10.4	13.6
Seats%	14.0	17.5	19.0	17.0	14.0	21.0	9.0	10.0	12.5
Seats	28	35	38	34	28	42	18	20	25
Patriotic People's Movement									
Votes%	-	-	-	-	-	-	***	8.3	6.6
Seats%	-	-	-	-	-	-	7.0	7.0	4.0
Seats	-	-	-	-	-	-	14	14	8
Progressive Party									
Votes%	12.8	9.2	9.1	6.8	5.6	5.8	7.4	6.3	4.8
Seats%	13.0	7.5	8.5	5.0	3.5	5.5	5.5	3.5	3.0
Seats	26	15	17	10	7	11	11	7	6
Socialist Workers' Party									
Votes%	-	14.8	10.4	12.1	13.5	1.0			
Seats%	-	13.5	9.0	10.0	11.5	0.0			
Seats	-	27	18	20	23	0			
Small Farmers' Party									
Votes%	-	-	-	-	1.1	1.8	3.4	2.0	2.1
Seats%	-	-	-	-	-	0.5	1.5	0.5	1.0
Seats	-	-	-	-	-	1	3	1	2
Others									
Votes%	0.1	0.1	0.2	0.4	0.4	1.0	2.0	0.8	0.1
Seats%	0.0	0.0	0.0	0.0	0.0	0.0	1.0	0.5	0
Seats	0	0	0	0	0	0	2	1	0
Total									
Votes%	100	100	100	100	100	100	100	100	100
Seats%	100	100	100	100	100	100	100	100	100
Seats	200	200	200	200	200	200	200	200	200

Includes one seat of the Swedish Left
** Includes two seats of the Swedish Left
*** National Coalition and Patriotic People's Movement nominated candidates on joint lists

Table A-3(c).
Working democracy in the shadow of the Iron Curtain

	1945	1948	1951	1954	1958	1962	1966	1970	1972
Social Democrats									
Votes%	25.1	26.3	26.5	26.2	23.2	19.5	27.2	23.4	25.8
Seats %	25.0	27.0	26.5	27.0	24.0	19.0	27.5	25.5	27.5
Seats	50	54	53	54	48	38	55	51	55
Swedish People's Party									
Votes%	8.4	7.7	7.6	7.0	6.7	6.4	6.0	5.7	5.4
Seats%	7.5	7.0	7.5	6.5	7.0	7.0	6.0	6.0	5.0
Seats	15*	14	15	13	14	14	12	12	10
Agrarian Union/Center Party									
Votes%	21.4	24.2	23.3	24.1	23.1	23.0	21.2	17.1	16.4
Seats%	24.5	28.0	25.5	26.5	24.0	26.5	24.5	18.5	17.5
Seats	49	56	51	53	48	53	49	37	35
National Coalition									
Votes%	15.0	17.0	14.6	12.8	15.3	14.6	13.8	18.0	17.6
Seats%	14.0	16.5	14.0	12.0	14.5	16.0	13.0	18.5	17.0
Seats	28	33	28	24	29	32	26	37	34
Progressive Party/Finnish Peoples Party/Liberal People's Party									
Votes%	5.2	3.9	5.7	7.9	5.9	5.9	6.5	5.9	5.2
Seats%	4.5	2.5	5.0	6.5	4.0	6.5	4.5	4.0	3.5
Seats	9	5	10	13	8	13	9	8	7
Small Farmers' Party									
Votes%	1.2	0.3	0.3						
Seats%	0.0	0.0	0.0						
Seats	0	0	0						
Finnish People's Democratic Union									
Votes%	23.5	20.0	21.6	21.6	23.2	22.0	21.2	16.6	17.0
Seats%	24.5	19.0	21.5	21.5	25.0	23.5	20.5	18.0	18.5
Seats	49	38	43	43	50	47	41	36	37
Liberal League									
Votes%	-	-	0.3	0.3	0.3	0.5			
Seats%	-	-	0.0	0.0	0.0	0.5			
Seats	-	-	0	0	0	1			
Social Democratic League									
Votes%	-	-	-	-	1.7	4.4	2.6	1.4	1.0
Seats%	-	-	-	-	1.5	1.0	3.5	0.0	0.0
Seats	-	-	-	-	3	2	7	0	0
Christian League									
Votes%	-	-	-	-	0.2	0.8	0.4	1.1	2.5
Seats%	-	-	-	-	0.0	0.0	0.0	0.5	2.0
Seats	-	-	-	-	0	0	0	1	4
Rural Party									
Votes%	-	-	-	-	-	2.2	1.0	10.5	9.2
Seats%	-	-	-	-	-	0.0	0.5	9.0	9.0
Seats	-	-	-	-	-	0	1	18	18
Others									
Votes%	0.3	0.5	0.3	0.1	0.5	0.7	0.0	0.2	0.0
Seats%	0.0	0.0	0.0	0.0	0.0	0.0	0.0	0.0	0.0
Seats	0	0	0	0	0	0	0	0	0.0
Total									
Votes%	100	100	100	100	100	100	100	100	100
Seats%	100	100	100	100	100	100	100	100	100
Seats	200	200	200	200	200	200	200	200	200

*Includes one seat of the Swedish Left

Table A-3(c) Continued

	1975	1979	1983	1987
Social Democrats				
Votes%	24.9	23.9	26.7	24.1
Seats%	27.0	26.0	28.5	28.0
Seats	54	52	57	56
Swedish People's Party				
Votes%	5.0	4.6	4.9	5.6
Seats%	5.0	5.0	5.5	6.5
Seats	10	10	11	13
Center Party				
Votes%	17.6	17.3	17.6*	17.6
Seats%	19.5	18.0	19.0	20.0
Seats	39	36	38	40
Liberal People's Party				
Votes%	4.3	3.7	*	1.0
Seats%	4.5	2.0	*	0
Seats	9	4	*	0
National Coalition				
Votes%	18.4	21.7	22.1	23.1
Seats%	17.5	23.5	22.0	26.5
Seats	35	47	44	53
Finnish People's Democratic Union				
Votes%	18.9	17.9	14.0	9.4
Seats%	20.0	17.5	13.5	8.0
Seats	40	35	27	16
Christian League				
Votes%	3.3	4.8	3.0	2.6
Seats%	4.5	4.5	1.5	2.5
Seats	9	9	3	5
Rural Party				
Votes%	3.6	4.6	9.7	6.3
Seats%	1.0	3.5	8.5	4.5
Seats	2	7	17	9
Constitutional People's Party				
Votes%	1.6	1.2	0.4	0.1
Seats%	0.5	0.0	0.5	0.0
Seats	1	0	1	0
Finnish People's Unity Party				
Votes%	1.7	0.3	0.1	
Seats%	0.5	0.0	0.0	
Seats	1	0	0	
Greens				
Votes%	-	-	1.4	4.0
Seats%	-	-	1.0	2.0
Seats	-	-	2	4
Democratic Alternative				
Votes%	-	-	-	4.2
Seats%	-	-	-	2.0
Seats	-	-	-	4
Others	-			
Votes%	0.8	0.2	0.1	1.8
Seats%	0.0	0.0	0.0	0.0
Seats	0	0	0	0

Table A-3(c) Continued

	1975	1979	1983	1987
Total				
Votes%	100	100	100	100
Seats%	100	100	100	100
Seats	200	200	200	200

*Liberal People's Party merged with the Center Party, for a period

Table A-3(d). Towards European integration and full EU membership

	1991	1995	1999
Social Democrats			
Votes%	22.1	28.3	22.9
Seats%	24.0	31.5	25.5
Seats	48	63	51
Swedish People's Party			
Votes%	5.8	5.5	5.5
Seats%	6.0	6.0	6.0
Seats	12	12	12
Center Party			
Votes%	24.8	19.8	22.4
Seats%	27.5	22.0	24.0
Seats	55	44	48
Liberal People's Party			
Votes%	0.8	0.6	
Seats%	0.5	0.0	
Seats	1	0	
National Coalition			
Votes%	19.3	17.9	21.0
Seats%	20.0	19.5	23.0
Seats	40	39	46
Left-Wing Alliance			
Votes%	10.1	11.2	10.9
Seats%	9.5	11.0	10.0
Seats	19	22	22
Christian League			
Votes%	3.1	3.0	4.2
Seats%	4.0	3.5	5.0
Seats	8	7	10
Rural Party/True Finns			
Votes%	4.8	1.3	1.0
Seats%	3.5	0.5	0.5
Seats	7	1	1
Constitutional Party			
Votes%	0.3		
Seats%	0.0		
Seats	0		
Greens			
Votes%	6.8	6.5	7.3
Seats%	5.0	4.5	5.5
Seats	10	9	11
Ecological Party			
Votes%	0.1	0.3	0.4
Seats%	-	0.5	0.0
Seats	-	1	0
Progressive Finnish Party			
Votes%	-	2.8	1.0
Seats%	-	1.0	0.0
Seats	-	2	0

Table A-3(d) Continued

	1991	1995	1999
Reform Group			
Votes%	-	-	1.1
Seats%	-	-	0.5
Seats	-	-	1
Others			
Votes%	3.2	2.9	2.4
Seats%	0.0	0.0	0.0
Seats	0	0	0
Total			
Votes%	100	100	100
Seats%	100	100	100
Seats	200	200	200

THE ICELANDIC ELECTORAL SYSTEM 1844-1999

BY
ÓLAFUR TH. HARDARSON
DEPARTMENT OF POLITICAL SCIENCE
UNIVERSITY OF ICELAND, REYKJAVÍK

1. INTRODUCTION

In 1845, Iceland's Althingi (founded in 930 and abolished in 1800) was re-established as a consultative assembly to the Danish king. This was in accordance with the wishes of the Icelanders, who did not want to take part in the Danish "Consultative Assemblies to the Estates," founded in the early 1830s, preferring to have an assembly of their own. While the new Althingi did not have legislative powers, it became an important forum for the political discussions of the Icelandic elite, and was extensively used to formulate demands for increased Icelandic independence.

In 1874 — when the Icelanders celebrated the 1000th anniversary of settlement — the king granted the Icelanders a constitution, giving the Althingi legislative and financial powers. The executive power remained in Copenhagen, and the king had an effective veto on legislation, which was used 93 times in 1874-1903.

In 1904 — after the breakthrough of parliamentarian rule in Denmark in 1901 — the Danish authorities granted Home Rule to the Icelanders, including an Icelandic minister and administration in Reykjavík. The minister was responsible to the Althingi — parliamentarian government was established. With Home Rule, the Icelanders largely received control over domestic affairs.

In 1918, Iceland became a sovereign state in a royal union with Denmark. Foreign affairs continued to be the responsibility of the Danish government. According to the treaty of the union, the Icelanders could dissolve the union in 25 years — which they did, founding the Republic of Iceland in 1944.

The Electoral Systems

The Icelandic election system has been characterized by frequent changes during the 150 years since the Althingi was re-established, especially in the 20th century. The major reasons for most of the changes were disproportionality between the parties and unequal weight of votes in constituencies (malapportionment). A transformation of the occupational structure, enormous migration to the towns and an unusually high concentration of the population in the center (the capital Reykjavík and the surrounding Reykjanes, see Tables A2 and A3) created great inequality of votes between parties and constituencies. Demands for increased equality were raised regularly, but as the champions of the periphery were able to avoid radical changes for a long time, bitter disputes on the electoral system continuously took place.

Both the longevity and magnitude of rural over-representation make the Icelandic case quite interesting. Of particular interest is the fact that this extreme over-representation was not only achieved through a special peripheral party and disproportionality *between* parties, but also through over-representation of rural MPs *within* each party — and this latter mechanism survived in the electoral system when simple disproportionality between parties was no longer tolerated.

Before 1874, electoral rules were simply set by the king (in fact, the Danish minister), but the opinion expressed by the consultative Althingi clearly had an effect. The constitution of 1874 did not include anything on the constituency system nor the electoral formula used: those were subject to electoral law only.[1] A constitutional change in 1915 however established majority vote in the constituencies as the major rule (without further specifying the electoral formula), and an amendment in 1920 allowed the introduction of PR in Reykjavík by electoral law. In 1934, the details of the constituency system were written into the constitution, as well as the number of supplementary seats. Since then, all major electoral reforms have required a constitutional change. In Iceland, constitutional amendments have to be passed in two consecutive sessions of the Althingi — with a fresh election in between. No increased majority is needed.

1. The radical proposal of introducing PR in multi-member constituencies, defeated in the Althingi in 1907, was for instance presented in a bill amending electoral law.

Arend Lijphart has suggested four criteria for distinguishing one electoral system from another. A change in the electoral formula at the decisive tier, or a 20% change in either district magnitude, the national legal threshold, or assembly size constitutes a significant change, marking the beginning of a new electoral system (Lijphart, 1994: 12-14).[2]

In this chapter, we distinguish ten electoral systems in Iceland in the 1845-1999 period, largely based on those criteria (see Table 1). A stringent application of the criteria might, however, result in collapsing Ice4 and Ice5 together in one system — and Ice9 and Ice10 would be considered one electoral system instead of two.

The electoral system adopted when the Althingi was re-established (Ice1) was a plurality system in single-member constituencies: each voter gave the name of two persons he wanted to vote for. The candidate with the most votes became an MP, the one coming second became his deputy. The new assembly consisted of 20 popularly elected MPs and 6 Royal Members.

In 1857, the electoral formula was changed (Ice2): instead of plurality, absolute majority in up to three rounds was introduced. The rationale for this change was that an increased majority was needed, as the suffrage was greatly extended.

Iceland obtained its first constitution in 1874. This was accompanied by a new electoral system (Ice3). While the electoral formula remained unchanged, assembly size increased from 27 to 36 (33%)[3] and district magnitude increased from 1 to 1.4 (40%), as some two-member constituencies were introduced.

With Home Rule in 1904, the electoral formula was changed from absolute majority to simple plurality (Ice4). The change was related to an increase of polling places: instead of one polling place and vocal voting in each constituency, secret voting and a polling place in each commune were introduced, making it impossible to conduct up to three rounds in one election meeting on the same day.

In 1915, the six Royal seats were abolished. Instead, six members were elected by PR (d'Hondt) in the country at large. The electoral system for the other 34 members remained unchanged. This constitutes a new electoral system (Ice5) if we consider this a change in electoral formula. While all six at-large members admittedly sat in the Upper House, it has to be borne in mind that

2. Here we use the criterion of the effective threshold (cf. Lijphart, 1994).
3. The number of popularly elected members increased from 21 to 30 (43%).

despite its two chambers the Althingi was not really a bicameral assembly, but rather a modified unicameral system — similar to Norway's. From 1874 to 1903, half of the members of the Upper House were elected in general elections along with all members of the Lower House, and simply chosen to sit in the Upper House by the United Althingi when it convened. After 1903, a majority of the Upper House was chosen in this manner — and since 1934 all MPs have been elected in the same general election. If the two houses could not agree, the matter could be solved by a joint meeting of the United Althingi (see Magnússon, 1987: 239-249). However, it could be argued that Ice5 should be lapsed together with Ice4.

In 1920, another change in the electoral formula was introduced (Ice6): the number of MPs for Reykjavík was increased from two to four, and those members were now elected by PR (d'Hondt), thus greatly reducing the electoral threshold in the capital.

A major change took place in 1934, when 11 supplementary seats were introduced to the electoral system (Ice7), thus making it a two-tier system, greatly reducing disproportionality. The electoral threshold in Reykjavík was also reduced, as the number of PR seats was increased from four to six.

Another important change was made in 1942 (Ice8), when PR (d'Hondt) was introduced in the six two-member constituencies, greatly reducing the over-representation of the Agrarian Progressive Party. This shows that a change in the electoral formula at the lower tier can indeed have major consequences. Besides, the increase of PR seats in Reykjavík lowered the effective threshold from 11.3 to 8.7 (23%).

In 1959, the electoral system was transformed by introducing PR (d'Hondt) in eight multi-member constituencies (Ice9) instead of the mixed system of single-member majority, two-member PR, and multi-member PR in Reykjavík. The number of MPs was increased from 52 to 60, while the 11 supplementary seats remained. As the number of MPs in Reykjavík was also increased, the effective threshold was lowered from 8.7 to 5.9 (32%). It is noteworthy that only the last change fulfills Lijphart's criteria for system change. A complete transformation of the electoral system at the lower tier does not necessarily mean system change, if the system at the upper tier remains unchanged. While this can of course be quite useful in systematic comparisons of electoral systems, Icelandic MPs would have been most surprised in 1959 if they had been informed that the only significant change made to the electoral system that year was the increase of members in Reykjavík!

In 1982-87, the number of MPs was increased to 63 and the number of supplementary seats to 13. The use of d'Hondt at the lower tier was replaced by LR-Hare, while d'Hondt was still used to divide the supplementary seats between the parties at the upper tier. The number of seats in Reykjavík was increased to 14, lowering the effective threshold from 5.9 to 5.1 (14%). None of the changes were thus significant, according to Lijphart's criteria (cf. Lijphart, 1994: 34). However, here we consider the 1987-1999 system a separate electoral system (Ice10). After an increase of Reykjavík seats in 1995, the effective threshold was down to 4.8. This constitutes a 19% decrease in the effective threshold compared to 1959, very close to the 20% criterion.[4] The combined effect of introducing LR-Hare at the lower tier and the two additional supplementary seats was the elimination of 1-2 bonus seats obtained by the Progressives compared to the other parliamentary parties in the previous system. This was a major objective of the change — and it worked as expected.

While Ice10 attained the purpose of increasing proportionality between the parliamentary parties, enormous malapportionment remained. The major aim of yet another electoral reform by a constitutional change in 1999 was to substantially reduce malapportionment, simplify the electoral system, and make further changes easier by removing parts of the electoral system from the constitution to electoral law.

Table 1: The ten Icelandic electoral systems 1844-1999

Electoral system	ICE-1	ICE-2	ICE-3	ICE-4	ICE-5	ICE-6	ICE-7	ICE-8	ICE-9	ICE-10
Elections included	1844-1852 (2)	1858-1869 (3)	1874-1903 (8)	1908-1914 (3)	1916-19 (2)	1923-33 (4)	1934-42 (3)	1942-59 (6)	1959-83 (8)	1987-99 (4)
Electoral formula at lower level	Plurality	Absolute majority - up to 3 rounds	Absolute majority - up to 3 rounds	First-past-the-post	First-past-the-post	First-past-the-post, PR-d'Hondt	First-past-the-post, PR-d'Hondt	First-past-the-post, PR-d'Hondt	PR-d'Hondt	PR-LR Hare
District magnitude	1	1	1.4	1.4	1.4	1.4	49	52	60	63

4. The effective threshold in 1959 was 5.93. The average threshold in 1987-99 was 4.96 (a reduction of 16%), as it was 5.12 in 1987-91 (a reduction of 14%) and 4.79 in 1995-99 (a reduction of 19%.) Here we calculate reductions in the effective threshold by comparing to the 1959 level. This however raises the general question of problems that may arise in the classification of electoral systems when a system changes gradually.

Table 1: (Continued) The ten Icelandic electoral systems 1844-1999

Electoral formula at higher level	NA	NA	NA	NA	NA	NA	d'Hondt	d'Hondt	d'Hondt	d'Hondt
"Extra" members	6 Royal mbrs	6 Royal mbrs	6 Royal mbrs	6 Royal mbrs	6 national mbrs elected at-large — PR-d'Hondt	6 national mbrs elected at-large — PR-d'Hondt				
Number of supple-mentary seats							11	11	11	13
Supple-mentary seats in percent							22	21	18	21
Allocation of seats in multi-member constitu-encies final?	NA	NA	NA	NA	NA	NA	Yes	Yes	Yes	Yes
Legal threshold (and effective threshold)	NA	NA	NA	NA	NA	NA	1 seat at lower level Effective threshold: 11.3	1 seat at lower level Effective threshold: 8.7	1 seat at lower level Effective threshold: 5.9	1 seat at lower level Effective threshold: 5.0
Average assembly size	26	27	36	40	40	42	49	52	60	63

Notes: The number of elections includes only general constituency elections. By-elections are omitted (including a special election for 4 new seats in towns 1904 and the first proportional election in Reykjavík 1921 (3 seats, including 2 new ones)), as well as the countrywide at-large PR-elections of the 6 national members 1916 (6 seats), 1922 (3), 1926 (3), 1926 (1 seat, by-election), and 1930 (3).
The basis for average assembly size is the total number of MPs after each general constituency election.
Effective thresholds are calculated on the basis of number of seats in Reykjavík (cf. Lijphart, 1994: 38).

The Party System

In the 19th and early 20th century, the question of Iceland's relationship with Denmark dominated Icelandic politics. While informal blocks (issue-groupings) could be observed concerning the independence question — and a few other policy areas — in the Althingi, no parties emerged during the 19th century. With Home Rule in sight, the first parties emerged at the turn of the century. Those parties were cadre parties, formed by rival political leaders and groups competing for the new ministerial power. The ideological differences between these parties, which frequently split and restructured, concerned mainly tactics in the independence struggle.

The independence question was largely resolved in 1918, and in the 1916-1930 period the party system was completely transformed. Economic and class-related issues became the focal point of politics, as four new parties emerged: the Social Democratic Party (1916), the Agrarian Progressive Party (1916), the Conservative Party[5] (1923-29), and the Communist Party (1930) — later to be succeeded by the United Socialist Party (1938) and the People's Alliance (1956). This four-party format came to dominate Icelandic politics ever since. In 1999, when the SDP and the left-socialist People's Alliance both joined in an electoral alliance[6] — which seems to be developing into a new social democratic party — the left-socialist banner was taken over by a new party, the Left-Greens, emphasizing classical radical left-wing policies along with environmentalism.

The SDP was founded as the political arm of the labor movement, and remained organizationally linked to the Icelandic Federation of Labor until 1942. The party represented reformist working-class politics, and grew steadily in strength during its first two decades, polling 21.7% in 1934. After 1942, however, the party was usually the smallest of the four parties, polling on average around 15% of the vote. This stands in stark contrast to the development of the Social Democratic parties in Scandinavia, where they became the largest parties in their countries. The SDP, however, frequently participated in government coalitions — but has only twice obtained the office of the Prime Minister. In 1999, the SDP entered a new social democratic alliance, which polled 26.8% of the national vote.

Since the formation of the four-party system the Progressive Party has usually been the second largest party in electoral terms, polling around 25% on average.[7] For decades, the party was over-represented in the Althingi in relation to its vote share. While the party has always been strongest among farmers and in the rural areas, it became quite successful in towns, especially in the 1960s and early 1970s. The party held the premiership continuously from 1927-42, and frequently took part in coalitions after that. Since 1971 the Progressives have only been out of government twice, in 1979-80 and in 1991-95.

---

5. The name of the Conservatives has been the Independence Party since 1929.
6. Along with the Women's Alliance and the People's Movement.
7. Since 1983 however, the Progressives have usually polled 18-19% of the national vote.

From the start, the Conservatives have always polled most votes in national elections, receiving on average around 40%. The party has combined elements of liberalism and conservatism, and emphasized nationalism and opposition to class conflict. In the 1930s, when the party was mostly in opposition, party policy was more strongly directed toward economic liberalism and private initiative, while after the war the Conservatives increasingly accepted the welfare state and participated in governments whose policies were strongly in favor of state intervention and protectionism. The party has always had a major working class following, in stark contrast to conservative and liberal parties in Scandinavia. In 1944 it became the natural party of government, being continuously in government from 1944-71, with the exception of the years 1956-59. While the party spent more than half of the 1971-91 period in opposition, it has now held the premiership continuously since 1991.

Table 2: Parties represented in the Althingi and Government 1845-1999

Electoral system	Parties in the Althingi	Government
ICE1, ICE2 (1844-1869)	No parties	Danish minister
ICE3 (1874-1903)	No parties (1874-1894) Home Rule Party (1900-03) Independence Party — old (1900-03)	Danish minister
ICE4 (1908-1914)	Home Rule Party (1908-14) Independence Party — old (1908-14) Independence Party — independents (1911) Union Party (1914)	Home Rule Party (1904-09, 1912-14) Independence Party — old (1909-12, 1914-15)
ICE5 (1916-1919)	Home Rule Party (1916-19) Independence Party — old (1916-19) Independence Party — along (1916) Independence Party — across (1916) Social Democrats (1916) Farmers' Party — old (1916) Independent Farmers (1916) Progressives (1919)	Independence Party — along (1915-17) Home Rule Party, Independence Party — old, Progressives (1917-20) Home Rule Party (1920-22, minority) Independence Party — across (1922-24, minority)
ICE6 (1923-33)	Social Democrats (1923-33) Progressives (1923-33) Conservatives (1923-33) Liberal Party (1927)	Conservatives (1924-27) Progressives (1927-32, minority) Progressives-Conservatives (1932-34)
ICE7 (1934-42)	Social Democrats (1934-42) Progressives (1934-42) Conservatives (1934-42) Communists (1937-42) Farmers' Party (1934-37)	Progressives-Social Democrats (1934-38) Progressives (1938-39, minority) Progressives-Conservatives-Social Democrats (1939-42) Progressives-Conservatives (1942) Conservatives (1942, minority)

Table 2: (Continued) Parties represented in the Althingi and Government 1845-1999

ICE8 (1942-59)	Social Democrats (1942-59) Progressives (1942-59) Conservatives (1942-59) Left Socialists (1942-59) National Preservation Party (1953)	Non-party government (1942-44) Conservatives-Social Democrats-Left Socialists (1944-47) Social Democrats-Conservatives-Progressives (1947-49) Conservatives (1949-50, minority) Progressives-Conservatives (1950-53) Conservatives-Progressives (1953-56) Progressives-Social Democrats-Left Socialists (1956-58) Social Democrats (1958-59, minority)
ICE9 (1959-1983)	Social Democrats (1959-83) Progressives (1959-83) Conservatives (1959-83) Left Socialists (1959-83) Union of Liberals and Leftists (1971-74) Social Democratic Alliance (1983) Women's Alliance (1983)	Conservatives-Social Democrats (1959-71) Progressives-Left Socialists-Union of Liberals and Leftists (1971-74) Conservatives-Progressives (1974-78) Progressives-Social Democrats-Left Socialists (1978-79) Social Democrats (1979-80, minority) (Conservatives)-Progressives-Left Socialists (1980-83) Conservatives-Progressives (1983-87)
ICE10 (1987-1999)	Social Democrats (1987-99) Progressives (1987-99) Conservatives (1987-99) Left Socialists (1987-99) Women's Alliance (1987-95) Citizen's Party (1987) Union of Regional Equality (1987) People's Movement (1995) Liberal Party (1999)	Conservatives-Progressives-Social Democrats (1987-88) Progressives-Social Democrats-Left Socialists (1988-89) Progressives-Social Democrats-Left Socialists-Citizens' Party (1989-91) Conservatives-Social Democrats (1991-95) Conservatives-Progressives (1995-99)

For parties classified under the banners of Conservatives, Progressives, Social Democrats and Communists/Left Socialists, see Table A1. Years showed for electoral systems and parliamentary parties refer only to election years, while the last column shows the actual period each government was in power.

The communist/left-socialist movement became stronger in Iceland than in most other Western European countries. The Communist Party, which was an orthodox party and a member of the Comintern, met with moderate success in the 1930s, winning three seats in the Althingi in 1937. After the SDP refused to join the Communists in a Popular Front, the left wing of the SDP broke off in 1938 to join the Communists in the United Socialist Party, which in its first election polled 16.1% of the votes, more than the SDP. In 1956 the SDP split again, and its left wing formed an electoral alliance with the United Socialist Party — the People's Alliance, which became a formal party in 1968, when the United Socialist Party was dissolved. While the United Socialist Party was not a Comintern member, the party was clearly pro-Soviet and most of its leaders had been prominent members of the Communist Party. The United Socialist Party took part in a coalition with the Conservatives and the Social Democrats 1944-47, but that coalition broke down due to disagreements over foreign policy. The United Socialist Party, and later the People's Alliance, strongly opposed the American base in Keflavík and Iceland's membership of NATO, mainly on a nationalistic platform. Since 1947 the left-socialists and the Conservatives have not joined forces in a government coalition.[8] The People's Alliance took part in a left-wing coalition with the Progressives and the Social Democrats in 1956-58. The party increasingly moved in a reformist direction, and became a more acceptable coalition partner in the 1970s, taking part in coalitions 1971-74, 1978-79, 1980-83 and 1988-91. The party has nevertheless never held the portfolios of Prime Minister, Foreign Affairs, and Justice, but was entrusted with the Finance Ministry for the first time in 1980. When the People's Alliance in 1999 joined a social democratic electoral alliance, its successor as a separate left-socialist party — the Left-Greens — obtained 9.1% of the national vote.

The four-party system had its heyday from the early 1940s until the 1970s. The political system became highly elitist and the parties dominated most spheres in society. While the parties had all adopted a formal mass organization in the 1930s, they nevertheless remained in fact "network parties" based on personal ties, or "cadre parties" strongly marked by tendencies towards patronage. The parties have been unprincipled on policy, and eager to take part in government coalitions, a necessary condition for success if the parties' aims are to distribute goods and favors rather than pursue policy. The party leaders were influential in the strongly state-regulated economy and the state banks, and they had strong ties with interest organizations. The administrative bureaucracy was weak and dominated by ministers. The press "did not constitute an independent sphere of influence; it was simply yet another arm of the party leadership" (Grímsson, 1976: 20). The party leaders also dominated the cultural sector.

On the whole, then, the parties were strong in the sense that party leaders were powerful, but they remained organizationally weak and weak on policy making.

Around 1970, the established power system started to show increasing signs of disintegration. The 1959-71 coalition of Conservatives and Social Democrats had introduced some liberal economic policies, especially regarding trade, and patronage in the economy became weaker as state regulation decreased. Increasing professionalization served to depoliticize the civil service and interest organizations became more independent of the political parties. Similarly, the parties' near-monopoly of political communication disappeared. Within the parties, the influence of the party leadership on nominations

8. Nevertheless, in 1980 Gunnar Thoroddsen, deputy leader of the Conservatives, supported by three other Conservative MPs, formed a coalition government with the People's Alliance and the Progressives, while the Conservative parliamentary group remained in opposition. From 1978, the People's Alliance did not make the removal of the US-base in Keflavík a precondition for government participation, thus making a coalition with the Conservatives a real possibility.

decreased, as (open) primaries were increasingly used to select candidates for party lists.

The increasing pluralism of the 1970s coincided with the old parties' loosening grip on the electoral market. The 1942-67 period had been marked with a remarkable electoral stability: net gain in elections (Pedersen's volatility index) was usually 2-6%. Since 1971, electoral volatility has been the norm. In seven out of eight elections in 1971-1995, net gain has exceeded 10% — in four out of eight elections net gain has exceeded 15%. In the elections of 1987, 1991 and 1995 around 1/3 of the voters switched parties between elections.

Since 1971, successful challenges to the four-party system in the form of new parties have also become more common. In the 1931-67 period, only two fifth parties managed to obtain seats in the Althingi, the Farmers Party in 1934 and 1937, and the National Preservation Party in 1953. Since 1971, five or six parties have been the rule in the Althingi. Most of the new parties have, however, been short-lived: the Union of Liberals and Leftists obtained representation in the Althingi in 1971 and 1974, the Social Democratic Alliance in 1983, the Citizens' Party in 1987, and the People's Movement in 1995. The Liberal Party, which obtained two seats in 1999, seems likely to suffer the same fate. Only one of the new parties — the Women's Alliance — survived in the Althingi for several terms, obtaining MPs in four consecutive elections 1983-95.

While class voting has probably always been weaker in Iceland than in Britain, Norway and Sweden, the parties nevertheless had a clear class basis in the electorate in the 1930s and 1940s. This class basis grew weaker with time, and when the first election surveys were carried out in the 1980s, class voting was found to be very weak indeed (the Alford Index was 11% in 1983, 10% in 1987). This weak class voting eroded still further in the 1990s (the Alford Index was 7% in 1991, 0% in 1995, 2% in 1999). In recent elections, regional differences in party support have been more important than class voting (Hardarson, 1995. Hardarson and Kristinsson, 2000).

However, the left-right ideological dimension is still by far the most important in the Icelandic electorate, just as is the case in Scandinavia. In the election studies 1983-99, most voters have been willing to rank themselves and the parties on a 0-10 left-right scale. In 1999, their ranking of the major parties was as follows, from left to right: the new left-socialist party, Left-Greens (2.4); the new social democratic party, the Alliance (3.7); Progressive Party (5.7); Conservatives (8.4)[9]. The self-placement of voters on the abstract left-right scale is clearly related to their choice of party, their liking and disliking of parties and party leaders, and their stands on conventional left-right issues, as well as foreign policy (Hardarson and Kristinsson, 2001).

An ideological center-periphery dimension is also of some importance among the voters. The ranking of the parties on this dimension is different from the left-right ranking: Progressive and left-socialist voters have been most pro-periphery, while SDP and Conservative voters have been most pro-center.

2. Suffrage

1843-1857: Strict Property Requirements (Icel)

In 1844, the first election for the new consultative Althingi took place. The suffrage rules, specified in the Danish king's directive from 1843, were quite strict (Lovsamling for Island, 1864: 499-501) and rather similar to the Danish electoral law for the Consultative Assemblies of the Estates (see chapter on Denmark). The franchise was confined to men 25 years and older who owned a farm of a certain value (10 *hundrud*), or a town house of certain value (1000 *ríkisdalir*), or had a life-long tenure on a state or church farm of a certain value (20 *hundrud*). Local officials were to make lists of such properties in their localities, on which the electoral register would be based. In addition, voters had to have an unblemished reputation and be financially independent. Only 2-3% of the population was enfranchised by those rules (Líndal, 1963: 36. Thorsteinsson, 1938: 82). One constituency — the Westman Islands — had no member elected to the Althingi until 1858, as nobody fulfilled the requirements for voting rights! (Arnórsson, 1945: 398).

A prospective candidate for the Althingi had to be at least 30 years of age, adhere to the Christian faith, be of unblemished reputation and be financially independent. He should have fulfilled the property requirements for voting for the last two years, be a subject of the Danish king and have had residence for the last five years in the king's countries in Europe. Furthermore, he could only stand in a constituency located in the region (*amt*) in which his property (but not necessarily his home) was located. Royal members of the Althingi were not eligible and heads of Election Boards could not stand in their own constituencies.

---

9. The left-right scores of the parties who formed the new social democratic party, the Alliance, in 1999 were as follows in 1995 election: the left-socialist People's Alliance (2.1), People's Movement (3.3), Women's Alliance (3.5), Social Democratic Party (5.2).

The strict franchise rules were harshly criticized in Iceland and among Icelandic intellectuals in Copenhagen (Arnórsson, 1945: 390, 393).

A Liberal Interlude: Election to the National Assembly 1851

In Denmark, the franchise was greatly extended in the 1848 electoral law for the popularly elected members of the Constituent Assembly. This body passed the 1849 Danish constitution, which gave the Danish parliament legislative powers and preserved the 1848 franchise rules for the election of the Danish Lower House (see chapter on Denmark).

Five Icelanders were appointed members of the Danish Constituent Assembly by the king. In 1848, 150 prominent Icelanders petitioned the king, asking for the five members to be elected in Iceland, and for a separate legislative assembly for Iceland. The king rejected the former request as too time consuming, but declared that no decision on the constitutional position of Iceland would be taken until the Icelanders had had the opportunity to express their wishes in a special meeting in their own country (Arnórsson, 1945: 461-462). Such a meeting, the National Assembly, took place in 1851 (instead of a regular meeting of the Althingi) — but did not pass any resolution, as the king's representative dissolved the meeting when it was clear that the Icelandic demands were totally unacceptable to the Danish authorities.

In 1849, the Althingi discussed a government bill on election rules for the National Assembly, suggesting liberal franchise rules, similar to those for the Danish Constituent Assembly.[10] The government, however, suggested a higher voting age of 30, and a method of indirect elections, as the removal of property qualifications for the franchise "makes it necessary to obtain by other means some hindrance against too rapid change" (AR, 1849 Vidbaetir A: 33). The Althingi accepted the higher age limits, but rejected indirect elections. In the subsequent 1849 law, the franchise was given to financially independent males of unblemished reputation, 30 years of age, who paid some commune tax and were not recipients of poor relief,[11] and were not dependents (or who were heads of household, commercial clerks or had finished a matriculation examination). Besides, voters should have been residents of the constituency for the last year, and be the king's subjects. Local officials had to prepare an electoral register of

10. In fact, the Althingi had already passed its own version when the government bill was introduced, as the ship taking it to Reykjavík did not arrive until at the end of the session. The Althingi however discussed the government bill, and rejected it (AR, 1849: 709, 714, 879, 938-944).

eligible voters. Candidates had to fulfill the voting requirements, except for residence, and they only had to be 25 years of age! (Arnórsson, 1945: 463. AR, 1853 Vidbaetir B: 25-26).

While those liberal rules obviously greatly extended the franchise, no information is available on the number of eligible voters for the National Assembly. And contrary to Denmark, the suffrage rules for the National Assembly did not become a part of electoral law for parliamentary elections.

1857-1903: Tax qualifications, especially in towns and villages — most farmers get the vote (Ice2 and Ice3).

A government bill presented in the National Assembly of 1851 suggested that the liberal franchise rules adopted in 1849 for the National Assembly should also apply in Althingi elections, while the strict 1843 property qualifications should be maintained for Althingi candidates (NAR, 1851: 483, 491-492). The committee dealing with the bill suggested that the voting age should be 25, and strongly protested the stringent qualifications for candidates (NAR, 1851: 526-535).

As the National Assembly was dissolved, no changes were made before the Althingi election of 1852. In a resolution to the king, the 1853 Althingi asked for a new government bill, reforming the 1843 electoral law which "right from the start created a strong disgust, and was considered both too narrow and badly suited to the state of the individuals' economic situation and enlightenment in this country." While the Althingi wanted the rules on franchise and eligibility for election to be liberalized, it did not want to make the "absolutely unlimited franchise" used in the election for the National Assembly the general rule for Althingi elections. The Althingi found it "frightening and impossible to give voting rights to all town cottagers and unmarried men in the densely populated fishing villages, who often find it most easy to attend the polling place, and thus easily can determine the election outcome for the whole constituency, or that can be done by individuals who want to get those voters to vote in their favor" (AR, 1853: 977). The Althingi suggested instead that the franchise should be

11. The phrase used in the Althingi bill was "not in debt for poor relief." That formulation was also adopted in the electoral law for the National Assembly and the 1857 electoral law for the Althingi, and remained in force until 1934. An amendment excluding this condition was voted down in 1849, 22-1. The 1849 government bill only made the requirement that a voter had not received poor relief during the last year, except he had paid it back (AR,1849: 560, 697-699. 1849 Vidbaetir A: 27. 1853 Vidbaetir B: 25. Arnórsson, 1945: 402).

given to all farmers, who paid some tax to "all classes" (i.e. to the state, church, clergyman and commune). Those taxes could be very low, so those qualifications would enfranchise all farmers except the very poor and those receiving poor relief (AR, 1853: 981-982. See also Arnórsson, 1945: 398-399). In the debate it was maintained that "almost every farmer, even the most poor, obtains this right" (AR, 1853: 409).

The Althingi also suggested that public officials, scientists, and town burghers (*kaupstadarborgarar*) who paid a certain amount (4 *ríkisdalir*) to the commune should get voting rights.[12] Those proposals were supported by an overwhelming majority. Franchise for town cottagers was more controversial. While the Althingi committee dealing with the issue had excluded this group, one member proposed the enfranchisement of those town workers who paid a high amount (6 *ríkisdalir*) to the commune — and this was passed by 13 votes against 7 (AR, 1853: 982). The Althingi also suggested that the eligibility of candidates should not be limited by any requirement of property or taxes — recipients of poor relief could, however, not stand. In order to compensate for the more liberal rules, the Althingi also suggested that an absolute majority was needed for the election of Althingi members.

This resolution of the Althingi is quite important. It shows that right from the beginning the rural farming community had strong tendencies to keep political power in its own hands, and was very skeptical of increasing the political influence of the emerging towns.

In 1855, the government presented a bill meeting those demands on voting rights, except it wanted to lower the tax criterion for town cottagers (from 6 *ríkisdalir* to 4) as the higher amount would "exclude most of them from the franchise" (AR, 1855 Vidbaetir: 39). In the debate, the member for Reykjavík claimed, that of cottagers in the town paying something to the commune, only 4% met the higher tax criterion, while 28% met the lower criterion. He found this unfair, as he estimated that 95% of other tax payers would be enfranchised (AR, 1855: 182-183). The Althingi however decided by 16 votes to 5 to suggest again the higher criterion (6 *ríkisdalir*) for town cottagers (AR, 1855: 306) — despite warnings from the king's representative against such an illiberal measure in such a liberal bill (AR, 1855: 191).

The government gave in on this issue. The 1857 electoral law gave the franchise to financially independent males of unblemished reputation, 25 years

12. A proposal enfranchising all burghers who paid something to the commune was voted down (AR, 1853: 522).

and older, who had had residence in the constituency for the last year, and were besides farmers paying some tax "to all classes," town burghers or cottagers paying a certain amount to the commune (4 and 6 *ríkisdalir* respectively), or public officials, — or had obtained degrees from the University of Copenhagen or the Clergymen's College. Excluded from the franchise were thus all women and dependents, the poorest farmers, most town cottagers, and all recipients of poor relief (Arnórsson, 1945: 398-402).

The 1857 electoral law also liberalized the eligibility qualifications. Candidates no longer needed to adhere to the Christian faith, and instead of the property requirements candidates only had to fulfill the general conditions for the franchise. However they had to be 30 years of age, be the subjects of the Danish king and have had residence in his countries in Europe for the last five years.[13] Heads of Election Boards were not eligible in their own constituency. Voters could only give their vote to a candidate living outside the constituency if it was proven that the candidate in question was eligible and was ready to accept an election in that constituency and no other (Arnórsson, 1945: 403-407).

The 1874 constitution — giving the Althingi legislative powers — did not substantially change the rules on franchise and eligibility.[14] In 1874-1903, 9-10% of the population had voting rights (see Table 3). This may also have been the case from 1857-1874, but figures from that period are not available.

While the 1874 constitution was unilaterally "given" to the Icelanders by the king, the Althingi had discussed government bills on the constitution introduced in 1867, 1869, and 1871, and amended those bills to such a degree that they were not acceptable to the government. The Althingi versions of those bills did not, however, substantially change the proposed requirements for voting and eligibility (AR, 1867: 15-16, 622-623. 1869: 24-25, 390. 1871: 11, 640-641).[15]

In 1881-1895, constitutional amendments were proposed in each Althingi session by the hard-liners in the independence struggle. Only two of those bills

13. In 1865, an elected member could not take his seat in the Althingi, as he had lived in England for the last five years, and also gone bankrupt (Arnórsson, 1945: 405).

14. The tax amount required for town burghers and workers (8 and 12 crowns respectively) was equivalent to the amount required in the 1857 electoral law (4 and 6 *ríkisdalir*) (AR, 1875 Vidbaetir: 387-388. See also Arnórsson, 1945: 483-489).

15. The same goes for a constitutional bill in the Althingi's petition to the king in 1873 (AR, 1873: 268-269). In 1867 the Althingi committee on the bill discussed if the franchise should be narrowed (property, indirect elections), but decided not to make such proposals (AR, 1867: 464). A proposal from one Althingi member, suggesting a high property requirement for eligibility (40 *hundrud*) was voted down, 20-1 (AR,1867: 574).

passed the Althingi (in 1885-86, and 1893-94)[16] — and were subsequently vetoed by the king. The other bills however, passed the Lower House, except in 1881. All those bills included proposals extending the franchise.

The 1881 and 1883 bills suggested that town burghers and cottagers should get the vote if they paid any taxes at all (AR, 1881: 371).[17] The bills in 1885-1895 all gave the vote to male heads of households paying any taxes at all (AR, 1885C: 400. 1887C: 294-295. 1889C: 562. 1891C: 294-295. 1893C: 247. 1895C: 331).[18]

In 1885, it was for the first time suggested to give women the vote for parliamentary elections: a farmer proposed in a bill that independent widows and unmarried women, fulfilling the requirements for men, should get the vote. The Speaker ruled that his bill could not be dealt with by the Althingi, as it was presented as an ordinary bill but not as a bill of constitutional change (AR, 1885C: 195). Later in the same session, however, two members of the Upper House proposed to enfranchise female heads of households. While this was not approved, the final version of the bill included a clause permitting the extension of voting rights to women, by law (AR, 1885C: 372, 400). A similar clause was included in all subsequent bills in 1887-1895. Bills on electoral law, accompanying the constitutional amendments and also passed by the Althingi in 1886 and 1994, used this constitutional provision, extending the vote to women "running an independent business or in some way independent, besides fulfilling the general requirements for the suffrage" (AR, 1886C: 63, 1894B: 105). The laws never did, of course, take effect, as the Althingi's constitutional amendments were vetoed.

A new group in the Althingi, more willing to compromise on Icelandic demands for independence, presented more moderate constitutional bills in 1897 and 1899, which did not pass the Althingi. Those bills contained no changes on the franchise and eligibility (AR, 1897C: 171, 269-270. 1899C: 184-185). The same group, on the other hand, had its bill passed in 1901. That bill gave voting rights to all independent males who paid at least 4 crowns in local taxes, and allowed the tax qualification to be abolished by law (AR, 1901C: 387-388). In the same session the minority — the emerging Home Rule Party — also introduced a

16. Extra sessions were held in 1886 and 1894 after fresh elections, in order to pass the constitutional amendments for the second time.

17. An amendment passed by the Lower House in 1883 gave the vote instead to all male heads of households, paying at least 10 crowns in taxes (AR, 1883C: 140, 393).

18. The bill introduced in 1885 limited the vote to heads of households paying at least 8 crowns in taxes, but the Althingi changed this to paying some tax.

constitutional bill including the lower tax limits, but also permitting the extension of the franchise to women by law (AR, 1901C: 187-188).The 1885-1895 bills all suggested the abolition of the six Royal seats in the Upper House. To compensate for this, a higher age of 35 was required for eligibility to the House, while the age limit for candidates to the Lower House was lowered to 25 years. All bills from 1887-1895 contained a clause extending eligibility to women by law.

1903-1915: Extended Suffrage for Town Workers and Fishermen (Ice4)

In 1901, the acceptance of parliamentarism brought a new government to power in Denmark. The new government was prepared to give Iceland more independence than previous administrations — and grant the Icelanders home rule with a minister in Reykjavík, responsible to the Althingi. Instead of re-introducing the constitutional bill that the Althingi had passed in 1901, it presented a new one in the 1902 session, giving the Althingi an opportunity to choose between the two bills. Both bills however contained similar suffrage rules. Not surprisingly, the Althingi passed the government bill in 1902, and again after fresh elections in 1903.

This constitutional change greatly extended the suffrage in towns and villages, as the tax qualifications were greatly reduced (from 8 and 12 crowns to 4 crowns). While the qualifications for farmers remained unchanged, all other males now obtained the franchise if they paid at least 4 crowns in local tax and were neither dependent as servants (including farm-laborers), or recipients of poor relief. As a result, the electorate grew by fifty percent: 14-15% of the population was entitled to vote in the elections of 1908-1914 (AR, 1903C: 2. Arnórsson, 1945: 483-489. Kosningaskýrslur, 1988: 40).

The constitutional change of 1903 did not extend voting rights to women. A private member bill presented — but not passed — in 1907 proposed suffrage for all men and women, except recipients of poor relief (AR: 1907A: 486).[19] In 1909 a government constitutional bill — that did not pass — included the 1907 suffrage proposals, but only for men: women, married and unmarried, could however be given suffrage and eligibility by law (AR, 1909A: 192[7]). In the government's comments with the bill it was suggested that women should receive the vote

19. Besides, voters had to fulfill the general requirements of unblemished reputation, residence in constituency for the last year, and being financially independent. Married women would get the vote even if not financially independent.

gradually, by age-groups, as including them all at once would be too rapid a change (AR, 1909A: 192[15]). The Lower House committee dealing with the bill supported giving voting rights and eligibility to women (AR, 1909A: 1117). This bill also suggested a higher age limit of 40 for suffrage and eligibility to the Upper House, as Royal Members were to be abolished.

In 1911, the Althingi passed a constitutional bill that included the 1907 suffrage proposals for both men and women: only recipients of poor relief would be excluded (AR, 1911A: 1170).[20] An amendment, proposing that women should obtain the franchise gradually by age groups did not pass (AR, 1911A: 462).[21] Interestingly enough, the committee dealing with the bill in the Upper House, while supporting franchise for women, opposed giving the vote to servants (AR, 1911A: 910-911).[22] The bill also proposed a 30 years age limit for suffrage and eligibility to the proportionally elected members of an Upper House without Royal Members.

In 1912, the extra Althingi session however decided not to confirm the 1911 bill, as further negotiations with the Danish authorities were to take place (AR, 1912A: 483).

1915-1920: Women and Servants Obtain the Vote: Special Age Qualifications (Ice5)

In 1913, the Althingi passed a new constitutional bill, abolishing the tax requirements from 1903, and extending the suffrage to women and servants, but not to recipients of poor relief (AR, 1913A: 1329-1330).[23] A special clause however set a higher age limit of 40 for women and servants, a limit that should be lowered by one year annually until the usual minimum age of 25 would be reached in 15 years' time. The special age limit was included on the recommendation of the majority of the committee dealing with the bill in the Lower House,

---

20. A new general condition was added in 1911: voters should be born in Iceland or had legal residence there for five years. Married women would get the vote, even if not financially independent.

21. A number of amendments on the franchise was introduced in the debate, for instance on a lower age limit of 21, to abandon the requirement of financial independence, to give the vote to recipients of poor relief, and to permit to add knowledge-requirements for the suffrage by law.

22. The committee proposal on this was voted down, as well as a proposal permitting to give the vote to servants by law — after a referendum on the issue.

23. Besides voters should fulfill the following general requirements: being born in Iceland or having had legal residence in the country for the last five years, be 25 years of age, have an unblemished reputation, had residence in constituency for a year, and be financially independent. The last requirement did however not exclude married women from the vote.

as it was considered unwise to increase the number of voters to such an extent in one step "that present voters are deprived of almost all power in national affairs" (AR, 1913A: 933). The committee dealing with the bill in the Upper House on the other hand found the special age limit for women "an unnatural limitation of the suffrage", but did not think the limitation serious enough to vote the bill down. The committee did not propose an amendment abolishing the age limits, as it did not expect that the Lower House would accept such a change (AR, 1913A: 1535-1536). The bill also abolished the Royal seats in the Upper House, and replaced them with six members proportionally elected in special elections in the country at-large. The age limit for suffrage and eligibility in the at-large elections was set at 35 years of age, while the eligibility for seats in general elections was lowered from 30 to 25 years. In 1914, the Althingi passed the bill unchanged, and it was ratified by the king in 1915.

This extension of the suffrage more than doubled the number of electors: the size of the electorate increased to 32-34% of the population in the 1916-1919 elections. Despite the special age limits, women constituted 43% of the electorate in 1916 (Kosningaskýrslur, 1988: 89).[24]

Table 3: Suffrage: Size of electorate as percent of population 1874-1999

Year	% pop	Reason for change
1874	8.8	
1880	9.1	
1886	9.2	
1892	9.5	
1894	9.2	
1900	9.4	
1902	9.5	
1903	9.8	
1908	14.1	Lower tax requirements for males
1911	15.4	
1914	15.3	
1916	31.7	Women and servants get the vote

24. Population figures (Jónsson and Magnússon, 1997: 124-127) indicate that in 1915 38-39% of women 25 years and older fell in the 25-39 age category. When the age limits were abolished in 1920, around 28% fell in the 25-34 category, then excluded from the franchise.

Table 3: (Continued) Suffrage: Size of electorate as percent of population 1874-1999

1919	34.3	
1923	45.2	Special age requirements for women and servants abolished
1927	44.9	
1931	46.4	
1933	46.7	
1934	56.4	Voting age lowered from 25 to 21. Recipients of poor relief get the vote
1937	57.1	
1942 (J)	59.7	
1942 (O)	59.7	
1946	59.0	
1949	58.7	
1953	58.4	
1956	56.8	
1959 (J)	55.3	
1959 (O)	55.2	
1963	53.9	
1967	53.9	
1971	57.6	Voting age lowered to 20
1974	58.8	
1978	61.6	
1979	62.6	
1983	63.8	
1987	70.0	Voting age lowered to 18
1991	70.8	
1995	71.8	
1999	72.8	

1920-1933: Special Age Limits for Women and Servants Abolished (Ice6)

After the agreement with the Danish authorities on Icelandic sovereignty in 1918, a new constitutional bill was introduced in the Althingi in 1919, abolishing the special age limits for women and servants (AR, 1919A: 97).[25] The Althingi passed the bill unchanged in 1920, and the new constitution was confirmed by the king. As a result, the electorate constituted 45-47% of the population in the 1923-1933 elections. An amendment, giving the vote to recipients of poor relief, did not pass (AR, 1919A: 416).

1933-1999: Suffrage for Recipients of Poor Relief and Lowering Age Limits (Ice7 to Ice10)

As a part of the 1933 electoral reforms, the minimum voting age was lowered to 21 years, and those who had received poor relief got the vote, increasing the size of the electorate to 54-60% of the population in the 1934-1967 elections. While the Social Democrats had mainly been fighting for those reforms, they were accepted by all parties without much controversy. In 1927, the Social Democrats had included those reforms in their unsuccessful constitutional bill on the introduction of PR with the whole country as one constituency (AR, 1927A: 165). In 1931, a constitutional bill that did not pass, presented by the Progressive government, included only lowering the age limits. When criticized by the Social Democrats, the Prime Minister explained that this was simply because he had not expected the Althingi to be ready to extend the suffrage to recipients of poor relief. The Upper House however passed a Social Democratic amendment to this effect by 9 votes to 2 (AR, 1931A (43. session): 159-160. 1931C (43. session): 564, 571). In a Conservative bill, presented later in the same year, both reforms were included (AR, 1931A (44. session): 182).

The age limit was further lowered to 20 years in 1968, and to 18 years in 1984. In the 1987-1995 elections, the electorate contained 70-72% of the population.

The extension of the franchise in Iceland did not give rise to any serious conflicts, and was not a result of a mobilization of the lower classes. When the Icelandic Federation of Labor — and its political arm, the Social Democrats — were founded in 1916, the major step towards universal suffrage had already been taken.

25. Icelandic citizenship was also made a condition for the franchise and eligibility, except for those already having voting rights.

3. The ten electoral systems

1844-1852 (Icel): Simple Plurality (20 members) in Single-Member Constituencies + 6 Royal Members

When the Icelandic Althingi was re-established by a royal decree in 1843 as a consultative body, the new unicameral parliament consisted of 26 members: 6 public officials were appointed by the king as Royal Members, while 20 members were elected for a six-year term in 20 single-member constituencies, consisting of the 19 counties and one town, Reykjavík. Each voter should give the names of two persons he wanted to vote for: the person obtaining most votes became an elected member, the person coming second became a deputy member (Lovsamling for Island, 1864: 498-499, 501, 507-508). Right from the start, the size of the electorate varied a great deal between constituencies: the population in the six most populous counties was 10-13 times larger than was the case in the least populous constituency (Grímsson, 1977: 2).

The new system was based on proposals made by a royal commission of public officials, which met in 1839 and 1841 in order to discuss Icelandic matters. While it was widely accepted that the counties should be the basis of the constituency structure,[26] it had been suggested in a periodical published by Icelanders living in Copenhagen that each constituency should elect one, two or three members according to size (Grímsson, 1977: 2. Fjölnir, 1844: 133-134). Some leading Icelanders in Copenhagen also wanted a larger body, consisting of 42-48 members. Indirect elections were also proposed — one argument against such a system was that direct elections would stimulate more interest in politics among the general public (Arnórsson, 1945: 389-390).

In 1849, a government bill was introduced in the Althingi concerning the electoral system to be used in an election for a National Convention on an Icelandic constitution, which was held in 1851 instead of a regular Althingi session. According to the bill, the Convention should consist of six Royal Members and 34 elected ones: the most populous constituency should elect three members, 11 constituencies should elect two members each, and 9 constituencies should elect one member each.[27] As the bill greatly extended the franchise, the government also proposed a method of indirect elections and to

26. The exception was a proposal by a leading Icelandic intellectual, that each quarter of the country should elect 12 members to the new Althingi, thus resembling the structure of the old Althingi, established in 930.

increase the minimum age for voting from 25 to 30 (AR, 1849 Vidbaetir A: 26-27, 33-34).

The 1849 Althingi increased the number of elected members to 40, and rejected indirect elections. Despite eloquent arguments from the king's representatives (*konungsfulltrúi* and *stiftamtmadur*) on more equal weight of votes — even discussing the idea of making the whole country one constituency — the Althingi suggested that each constituency should elect two members, regardless of the size of the electorate. The major arguments put forward were that the National Convention was to discuss national issues, but not the issues of individual constituencies; that perfect equality could not be obtained if the counties were to remain as constituencies; and that it would be difficult to agree on a different but fair number for individual constituencies (AR, 1849: 559, 566-567, 572-585, 661-714, 786-797, 792-801, 835-879, 938-944). A proposal giving the most populous constituency (with 5159 inhabitants) three members and the least populous (with 398 inhabitants) only one member was voted down 21-2 (AR, 1849: 697). Thus it was clearly stated that the Althingi did not consider equal weight of votes an important right — a position that was to be remain strong — albeit in a milder form — to the present day.

The government accepted the Althingi proposals in the electoral law for the National Convention (AR, 1853 Vidbaetir B: 25-29), but that electoral system was only used on this one occasion.

A government bill presented in the National Convention of 1851 suggested that the number of elected Althingi members should be increased to 30, elected in 9 two-member constituencies, and 12 single-member ones, while the six Royal Seats would remain unchanged. Explaining the reasons for the bill, the government admitted that in this system great inequality of votes would remain, and outlined a more fair proposal of 21 constituencies, not based on the counties, electing one, two or three members each (NAR, 1851: 482-483, 489-491). The committee dealing with the bill emphasized that the counties should remain as boundaries for the constituencies, and suggested 2 members for each county, except the two least populous ones, elected in single-member and two-member constituencies. The committee also wanted to increase the number of elected members to 36, and to abolish the Royal Seats (NAR, 1851: 529-530).

---

27. Explaining the reasons for the bill, the government points out, that the population of individual counties ranges from 398 to 5159. According to its proposal, the smallest constituency would of course have one member elected for its 398 inhabitants, but in all other constituencies inhabitants per member would range from 961 to 2388, thus greatly equalizing the weight of votes (AR, 1849 Vidbaetir A: 33).

1858-1869 (Ice2): Absolute Majority (up to 3 rounds) in 21 Single-Member Constituencies + 6 Royal Members

In a petition to the king, the 1853 Althingi asked the government to propose a bill widely extending franchise and eligibility. However — in order to "ensure good elections" — the Althingi also suggested that instead of single majority, an elected member should have an absolute majority in his constituency. If no candidate obtained an absolute majority in the first two rounds, a third and decisive round was to be held to decide between those two having received the most votes. The same rules applied to deputy members, but now they were to be elected separately (AR, 1853: 975-982. Arnórsson, 1945: 415).

In 1855, the government presented a bill in accordance with the Althingi's wishes. Absolute majority became the rule. The constituencies remained the same, except that one constituency was divided into two single-member constituencies, thus increasing the number of elected members to 21 (AR, 1855 Vidbaetir A: 32-33, 41-43).[28] The Althingi passed the bill, and it subsequently became electoral law (AR, 1855: 303-307).

1874-1903 (Ice3): Absolute Majority (up to 3 rounds) in Single-Member and Two-Member Constituencies (30 members) + 6 Royal Members

The government introduced constitutional bills in 1867, 1869 and 1871. Those bills did not become law as the Althingi made amendments that were unacceptable to the Danish authorities. The disputes between the Althingi and the government, however, did not concern the electoral system.

In 1867, the government presented a bill on the relationship between Iceland and Denmark, and a new constitution. The bill made no changes to the electoral system (AR, 1867: 15).[29] However, the Althingi amended the bill,

28. The division of Skaftafellssýsla into two constituencies — which Althingi had also recommended in 1853 — was necessitated by the fact, that due to extremely difficult travel conditions, two polling places had been operated in this county. This constituted no problems when the simple majority rule was used — votes could simply be gathered from the two polling places and counted. With absolute majority in three rounds this became impossible, as votes had to be counted between rounds, in order to decide if more rounds were needed.

29. The bill however suggested, that instead of letting the king appoint six public officials as Royal Members, the individuals occupying certain offices would automatically become Royal Members. The Althingi rejected this proposal, preferring to keep the appointment for Royal Members (AR, 1867: 464-465, 622).

suggesting to increase the number of elected members to 30 and to divide the Althingi into two houses, a Lower House consisting of 24 of the 30 elected members, and an Upper House consisting of the six Royal Members and six of the elected members — 40 years or older — chosen by the Althingi to sit in the Upper House (AR, 1867: 622-623).[30] The Althingi also recommended that the same constituencies were to remain, but the most populous ones should elect two members each (AR, 1867: 639).

The 1869 government constitutional bill accepted the 1867 Althingi proposals, except for the age limit for the elected members to the Upper House — the government pointed out the possibility that no elected member had reached forty years of age! (AR, 1869: 40-41). The Althingi passed those sections of the bill unchanged (AR, 1869: 389).

The 1871 bill contained the same proposals concerning the composition of the Althingi and the electoral system. The Althingi passed those proposals, except it now wanted not only the number of elected members, but also the numbers of Royal Members and the numbers of members in both houses, to be subject of law only (AR, 1871: 640).

No government bill on the constitution was presented in 1873, but the Althingi passed a petition to the king, asking for abolition of the Royal seats. Instead, the Althingi should consist of 36 elected members. 14 of the most populous constituencies should elect two members each, the remaining ones one each (AR, 1873: 268, 276).[31]

The 1874 constitution — unilaterally set by the king — largely accepted the Althingi proposals on the composition of the Althingi and the electoral system — except for the proposal of abolishing the Royal seats. The Althingi now consisted of six Royal Members[32] and 30 elected members. The number of elected members could be changed by law. The Royal Members and six of the elected members, chosen by the Althingi, should sit in the Upper House. The numbers of MPs in the Lower and the Upper House could be changed by law. A provisionary clause decided that until a new electoral law would be passed, 11 counties should elect two members each,[33] while the remaining ones and

30. Althingi also suggested that the number of elected members could be changed by law.

31. The Althingi also suggested that the numbers of Althingi members and the numbers in each House, could be changed by law.

32. But now they did not have to be public officials.

33. Voters in the two-member constituencies voted for two candidates. Both elected members needed an absolute majority, as this was required by electoral law (but not the constitution).

Reykjavík should elect one member each. Deputy seats were abolished (AR, 1875 Vidbaetir: 387, 393).

In 1877 the Althingi passed a government bill, splitting two two-member constituencies into two single-member constituencies each, thus decreasing the number of two-member constituencies to nine, while the number of Althingi members remained unchanged. The requirement of an absolute majority also remained unchanged (AR, 1877: 509-510, 512). This electoral system was to remain until Iceland obtained home rule in 1904 — except that in 1902 the two-member constituency of Ísafjarðarsýsla was divided into two single-member constituencies.

Various changes on the electoral system were however discussed in this period, and indeed proposed in the hard-liners' constitutional bills presented in every Althingi session in 1881-95, as well as in bills changing the electoral law.

The first of those proposed changes was the abolition of the Royal seats in the Upper House. The 1881 and 1883 bills — not passed by the Althingi — however only suggested to reduce the number of Royal seats to four. In 1883, the version that was passed in the Lower House had been amended, and suggested that the six seats should remain (AR, 1881: 371. 1883C: 139, 392) .

All the bills introduced from 1885-95 proposed the abolition of the Royal seats, both those passed by the Althingi in 1885-86 and 1893-94 — which were subsequently vetoed — as well as the bills that were passed by the Lower House in 1887, 1889, 1891 and 1895.[34]

All those bills proposed that the Althingi should continue to consist of 36 members. 24 of those, elected in constituencies, should sit in the Lower House. 12 should sit in the Upper House. The numbers of Althingi members and those sitting in each chamber could now be changed by law.

Various ideas were proposed on the election of the Upper House. The constitutional bills — including both the bills that were passed by the Althingi — usually just said that the 12 members of the Upper House should be elected with the whole country as one constituency, according to rules further specified in electoral law (AR, 1885C: 399-400. 1887C: 204. 1889C: 181. 1891C: 294. 1893C: 247. 1895C: 140). Two systems seemed to be the major alternatives: either

34.I n 1889 the committee dealing with the bill in the Lower House suggested that for the first time after the abolition of the Royal seats, the proposed new Governor should appoint four members of the Upper House. The Upper House committee suggested that all 12 members of the Upper House should be Royal Members. When passing the bill, the Upper House however reduced the number of Royal seats to four. The Lower House was not ready to accept the amendments made to the bill by the Upper House (AR, 1889: 265, 349-350, 446-447, 561, 571-574).

electing the members of the Upper House by PR — or let them be elected by regional governments.

While the original 1885 constitutional bill had suggested PR for the Upper House, it was amended by the Althingi, leaving the method of election open. In an accompanying bill on electoral law, passed by the Althingi in 1886 — but vetoed along with the constitution — it was decided to elect all 12 members by PR, using lists for the whole country as one constituency (AR, 1886C: 66-68).[35] The bill easily passed both chambers. Its supporters emphasized the fairness of PR, giving substantial minorities representation (AR, 1886A: 51, 123, 218. 1886B: 452). One member, arguing for indirect election to the Upper Chamber along Danish lines, maintained that PR in multi-member constituencies should rather be used in elections to the Lower House (AR, 1886A: 126). The National Governor (*landshöfdingi*) objected to letting voters elect lists instead of individuals — he also pointed out that ten years earlier a government proposal to elect Althingi committees by PR had been rejected, but "what in 1875 was considered too complicated for Althingi members in committee elections only, now is considered easy and good in all respects for the general public" (AR, 1886B: 377). The problem of numerous minor parties was also discussed (AR, 1886A: 123-124) — but members did not seem particularly worried, suggesting a system that seemed to presuppose party lists — in a country where no political parties existed. One supporter of the bill pointed out that PR was a novelty — not only in Iceland but the world — and "it is natural that people think that there are defects in this arrangement, as in all things people are not used to, but those imagined defects disappear when the experience shows that they do not create problems" (AR, 1886B: 447). In any case, the Althingi members of course knew that passing the bill was only a theoretical exercise — the bill would be vetoed.

When the Althingi next passed a constitutional bill in 1893-94, the accompanying bill on electoral law that was passed — but vetoed — suggested that the 12 members of the Upper House should be elected by members of county and town councils by simple plurality vote (AR, 1894B: 106-107). The member introducing the bill explained that while PR was the most proper system, giving all parties their fair share, this did not apply in Iceland, as no

35. A candidate was allowed to be on more than one list. The basic allocation rule was that the number of valid votes was to be divided by the number of members elected (12), thus constituting a quota. The number of valid votes for each list, divided by the quota, should determine the number of members elected from each list.

parties really existed. Besides, PR would make the system more complex. Therefore the 1886 proposals were not re-introduced in this bill (AR, 1894A: 103).

Several other aspects of the electoral system were also discussed in the last 25 years of the 19th century. In 1884, Indridi Einarsson, an economist educated in Copenhagen and Edinburgh, published an impressive essay on suffrage and elections, comparing the Icelandic system to that in several other countries. Einarsson harshly criticized the unequal weight of votes between constituencies and proposed a system adding counties into seven constituencies, electing 1, 4, 5, 6 or 7 members each. He also recommended polling places in each commune and the abolition of absolute majority. Einarsson explained how PR could be used to elect members, either in multi-member constituencies or in the country as a whole. While he emphasized the fairness of such a system, especially to minorities, he also pointed out that due to primitive communications and lack of organization it might be difficult to implement in Iceland (Einarsson, 1884).

In the following 1885 Althingi session, a bill was introduced suggesting a system of eight constituencies, electing three or four members each. The bill was rejected. In the debate it was maintained that large constituencies would lead to decreasing interest in elections and worse representation of the interests of individual constituencies. Besides, multi-member constituencies without PR would simple increase the tyranny of the majority (AR, 1885A: 207-212, 307-309. 1885B: 490-492, 921-928). A bill giving the two most populous constituencies 3 members each was rejected in 1889 and 1891 (AR, 1889C: 451, 1891C: 227). The great inequality in the weight of votes between constituencies remained.

The fact that there was only one polling place in each constituency made voting extremely difficult in many places as the journey could take several days, even up to a week (NRA, 1851: 191. AR, 1891A: 86). The low turnout in Althingi elections — varying between 20 and 30 percent in 1874-1894 — was clearly related to this fact. In 1880, the turnout was 47% in communes with a polling place, while it was only 21% in communes without a polling place (Einarsson, 1884: 26). Turnout was below 30 percent in only 16% of the communes with a polling place, while this was the case for 74% of the other communes (Grímsson, 1970: 297).

The electoral bill rejected by the Althingi in 1885 had proposed an increase of polling places and simple plurality instead of absolute majority (AR, 1885C: 209, 212, 308). In 1889, 1891 and 1893, bills were introduced suggesting a polling place in each commune and simple plurality (AR, 1889C: 154-156. 1891C: 116-119.

1893C: 172-175). None of those bills was successful. The objections were mainly of two kinds. Some members did not want to abolish the absolute majority rule, and maintained that a polling place in each commune would make elections more expensive, especially if many rounds were needed on separate days. The other main argument was that this would make it more difficult for candidates to express their views, as they could no longer make speeches and answer accusations at the polling place on election day (see e.g. AR, 1889C: 488-489. 1891B: 1352. 1891C: 303).

However, the electoral bill passed by the Althingi in 1894 included the simple majority rule, and allowed up to three polling places in each constituency. As only one Election Board would administer the election meetings in each constituency, those meetings would not take place at the same time. Candidates could thus continue to be present at all election meetings and make their views known (AR, 1894B: 109-111). But as this bill was vetoed, along with the constitution, absolute majority and one polling place in each constituency remained the rule.

The disputes during the 19th century on suffrage and the electoral system were mainly based on the personal views of individual members, perhaps influenced by factors like their education and the type of constituency they represented. No political parties, however, existed. That changed, around the turn of the century. When home rule with an Icelandic minister and parliamentarism were on the horizon, political parties became a necessity. Gradually, two main parties emerged, the Home Rule Party and the party of its opponents, which used different names but became the Independence Party (old) in 1908.In the last quarter of the 19th century the abolition of the two-member constituencies was also discussed. In the electoral bills passed by the Althingi in 1886 and 1894 — which were subsequently vetoed — all 24 members of the Lower House were to be elected in single-member constituencies, constituted of the counties and the towns (AR, 1886C: 68. 1894B: 109).[36] The bill introduced in 1886 suggested that the 24 constituencies would not follow county boundaries, thus increasing the equality of votes, but the Althingi chose to keep the counties as boundaries (AR, 1886C: 11-12, 37).

36. In 1886, the most populous county should however elect two members for the time being, as the combined number of counties and towns was only 23. One of those two members should go to a new county or town when established. According to this bill, the towns of Akureyri and Ísafjördur would have become separate constituencies. The 1894 bill however solved the problem by splitting one county, Bardastrandarsýsla, into two constituencies.

The parties had hardly entered the political stage when party political considerations started to influence disputes concerning the electoral system. In 1901, Hannes Hafstein, the emerging leader of the Home Rule Party and later the first Icelandic minister, presented a bill suggesting only that his own two-member constituency, Ísafjardarsýsla, should be split into two single-member constituencies. His bill passed the Lower House, 11-10, but was defeated in the Upper House, 6-5 (AR, 1901C: 496, 619. 1901B: 1221. 1901A: 509). In 1902 the bill was reintroduced. In the debate — which was clearly party political — it was maintained that the reasons for splitting this particular constituency was in general to help the Home Rule Party winning one of the two seats, and in particular to enable Hafstein to recapture his seat which he had lost in the 1902 election (AR, 1902C: 207. 1902A: 76-97. 1902B: 77-112).[37] Now the bill was passed. In 1902 the Home Rule Party had a comfortable majority in the Althingi, which had not been the case in 1901 (Kjartansson, 1996: 39-40).

1908-1914 (Ice4): First-Past-the-Post in Single-Member and Two-Member Constituencies (34 members) + 6 Royal Members

A constitutional amendment passed by the Althingi in 1902 and 1903 introduced home rule, an Icelandic minister, parliamentarism, and an increase of elected members of Althingi from 30 to 34. The six Royal seats in the Upper House remained, but the number of members in that House was increased from 12 to 14 (AR, 1903C: 1-3).[38]

A bill on electoral law presented by the Danish government and passed by the Althingi in 1903 introduced major changes on the electoral system: secret ballot, polling places in every commune, same election day for the whole country, and first-past-the-post instead of absolute majority (AR, 1903C: 293-302). The old election meetings at the polling place, in which the candidates could take part in discussions with the electorate, were now abolished (see AR, 1902C: 243). The government bill largely reflected private members' bills that had been discussed in 1901 and 1902 (AR, 1901C: 686, 782-793. 1902C: 298-309). The 1902 bill had actually been passed, but vetoed, as the government considered

37. The two members for Ísafjardarsýsla had been leading opponents of the Home Rule Party, Sigurdur Stefánsson since 1886 and Skúli Thoroddsen since 1892. In 1900 Hafstein captured Stefánsson's seat, while in 1902 their fortunes were reversed. In 1903 — when the constituency had been split in two — the Home Rule Party did indeed win one of the two new constituencies. Hafstein was however not the candidate — he got elected for another constituency.

38. The number of members in each chamber could be changed by law.

some aspects of it ill-suited and contrary to the constitution — it mainly objected to the Althingi's decision to demand a 50 crown deposit[39] only to be returned to candidates receiving 1/3 of the number of votes needed to be elected. The deposit was intended to limit the numbers of candidates, now that absolute majority was abolished. The Upper House committee dealing with the bill in 1903 accepted the government's verdict, while still maintaining that the idea of a deposit was both proper and constitutional. In order to compensate, the committee increased the number of supporters needed for each candidature from the 4 suggested to 12 (AR, 1902C: 301. 1903C: 214-215, 296. Hardarson, 2001).

Making changes to the constituency system proved a more difficult task. Because of migration and population changes, the unequal weight of votes had still increased (Grímsson, 1977: 4). In 1902, a proposal was rejected, suggesting a system of single-member constituencies only — thus dividing the counties, which many members strongly opposed (AR, 1902C: 40-42).[40] Instead, the Althingi passed a resolution asking the government to gather proposals from regional governments and prepare a comprehensive legislation on the constituency system (AR, 1902C: 296). In the bill passed in 1903, the old single-member and two-member constituencies simply remained. The four new seats were allocated to Reykjavík — which now became a two-member constituency — and to the towns of Ísafjördur, Akureyri and Seydisfjördur, electing one member each. Suggestions of dividing instead the four new members between the regional *amts* were rejected, as it was considered natural that the new and growing towns with different occupational structures should have their own representation. A proposal giving Reykjavík three members at the expense of Seydisfjördur — which had very few inhabitants — was voted down (AR, 1903C: 246, 276, 285, 313-314, 330-331, 406).

The first Icelandic minister, Hannes Hafstein, presented a government bill on the electoral system in his first Althingi session in 1905. The main aim of the bill was to reduce the great inequality in weight of votes between constituencies. In 1904, the voter-per-member ratio was almost six times greater in the most populous constituency than in the least populous one. Constituencies containing 34% of the voters elected half of the members.[41] The government explained that it was not possible to use the recommendations gathered from

39. This amount was roughly equivalent to a worker's monthly wage in Reykjavík (see Jónsson and Magnússon, 1997: 608).

40. Reykjavík was to be divided into two single-member constituencies.

41. Those figures are calculated on the basis of a table presented in AR, 1905A: 168.

regional governments in accordance with the Althingi resolution from 1902, as their recommendations would only increase the number of Althingi members without correcting the present inequality. There was simply no way of dividing the country into 34 single-member constituencies without widely dividing and joining counties.

Instead, the government proposed to introduce PR (d'Hondt) by party lists in seven multi-member constituencies, electing four, five or six members each. The seven constituencies — geographically, remarkably similar to the system finally adopted in 1959 — mainly joined counties: in three cases, however, counties were divided between constituencies. This system would almost perfectly equalize the weight of votes between constituencies (AR, 1905A: 162-181).

The bill was not put to a vote in 1905: the Minister said he only wanted to introduce the new ideas to the Althingi and the nation, but he expected the bill to be voted on in the next Althingi session in 1907. The idea of using PR in Althingi elections was a radical one, even though PR had been adopted for the Althingi procedures in 1890 and local elections in towns in 1903. Many MPs argued that the introduction of PR was premature, as the party system was still too volatile. It was also argued that the new constituencies would be too large: ties between voters and MPs would become weaker, and power would be moved from the rural areas to the towns. Besides, the old constituencies based on the counties represented a national tradition of dividing the country into regions, a tradition that could be traced back many centuries. Some MPs wanted to delay all changes until the Royal seats would be abolished (AR, 1907A: 198-201, 836, 838-840. 1907B: 2090-2168. Grímsson, 1977: 5).

In 1907, the government bill was rejected in the Lower House, in a close vote indeed, 12-11. The minister maintained that the Opposition had made the issue a party matter, while he had not wanted to ram his proposal through by making the passing of the bill a cabinet question (AR, 1907B: 2107, 2109). The roll call seems to confirm this: 10 members of the minister's Home Rule Party supported the bill, while 5 opposed it. Only one member of the Opposition voted for the bill, 7 opposed it, and 2 abstained (AR, 1907B: 2168).[42] Party interests clearly played a part here, as the Home Rule Party tended to be electorally stronger in towns and central areas, while the Opposition was stronger in the over-represented peripheral constituencies (see Kristinsson, 1991: 58-60).[43] As

42. For party affiliation of individual members, see Althingismannatal 1845-1995, 1996.

an amendment to the bill, making all constituencies single-member, was also voted down (14-8), the constituency system remained unchanged (AR, 1907A: 836-838. 1907B: 2121-2122).

In 1914, the outgoing minister — Hafstein again — tried once more to decrease the inequality of votes, arguing that now when the suffrage was being extended with the aim of giving all individuals — men and women — equal opportunities to influence the legislation and government of the country, it was particularly ill-suited to maintain an electoral system which gave some votes seven times greater value than others. He now proposed a system of 34 single-member constituencies — disregarding county boundaries. Reykjavík was to have four members instead of two, elected in four single-member constituencies with equal number of voters; the constituency boundaries in the capital should be redrawn every four years. According to those proposals, most constituencies would have 300-400 voters. Reykjavík was, however, still most under-represented with 581 voters per member, while the least populous constituency only contained 259 voters (AR, 1914A: 6-49).

Hafstein's proposals were solidly defeated in the Lower House. Five members of his own party were in favor, while four voted against. 14 members of the Independence Party opposed the proposal, while only one — a member from Reykjavík — supported it. The opponents argued that the bill had not had enough preparation, and it was unclear if it enjoyed support among the public. It was strongly emphasized that the counties were important units with separate interests. Generally, it was argued that it was simply inapplicable and wrong to base the constituency system on simple head counts, and in particular it was considered unnecessary to give Reykjavík more members, as the Althingi was situated in the town so it was easy for the inhabitants to make their views known to MPs — and besides, many MPs lived in the capital. The supporters of the bill mainly emphasized the fairness of equality, but argued also that dividing the counties would have the extra advantage of decreasing pork-barrel politics (AR, 1914A: 508-512. 1914B: 43-98).

The constituency system thus remained unchanged once again. Hafstein's attempts to increase equality of votes had been rejected twice: first in the form of PR, then in the form of single-member constituencies. The Althingi simply

43. In 1916, the Home Rule Party obtained 40% of votes and 35% of the seats — in 1919 46% of votes and 38% of seats. In 1916, the three splinters of the Independence Party jointly obtained 30% of votes and 38% of seats. In 1919, the party obtained 25% of votes and 32% of seats. Exact figures for previous elections are not available.

rejected the demand of one vote — one value. Party interests, along with perceived interests of farmers and the periphery, had prevailed.

1916-1919 (Ice5): First-Past-the-Post in Single-Member and Two-Member Constituencies (34 members) + PR (d'Hondt) in a Special Country At-Large Election (6 members for a 12-year term)

In a constitutional amendment confirmed in 1915, the Royal seats were finally abolished — a demand that had been on the Althingi's agenda for decades. Instead of the six Royal Members, six members of the Upper House were now to be elected in a country at-large special election, using PR (d'Hondt) with party lists — and with a higher suffrage and eligibility age limit of 35 years. The term of those members was 12 years. Such elections should, however, be held every sixth year, electing three members each time (AR, 1914A: 757-758, 760). This of course meant that the threshold was extremely high in the special elections.

Various constitutional amendments had been discussed in the Althingi sessions from 1907-1914. While there was a general agreement on the abolition of the Royal seats, different ideas were proposed on how to replace them. Suggestions were made that all 14 members of the Upper House should be elected in the special PR at-large election (AR, 1909A: 192. 1911A: 240, 401, 403, 620, 1116-1117. 1913A: 933), which would have been some compensation to voters in under-represented constituencies. Leading members of the Independence Party proposed on the other hand that no PR at-large elections should take place: the United Althingi should simply elect a part of the members to sit in the Upper House (AR, 1907A: 486. 1911A: 217-218, 477. 1913A: 278). Compromises suggesting 10, 8, 7 and 6 members to be elected at large by PR were also introduced. While a compromise accepted in 1911 proposed 10 PR members, the number was reduced to six in the final version passed in 1913-14 (AR, 1911A: 676, 1117, 1169. 1913A: 939, 1081, 1329). The Upper House committee dealing with the final version in 1913 commented that the proposed arrangement of six PR members elected for a 12 year term, which could not be dissolved, along with the higher age limit, introduced a strong enough conservative element to the Althingi — and also had the advantage that there was no need to change the constituency system, which would prove extremely difficult (AR, 1913A: 1536).

While the introduction of PR into the electoral system must be considered of a major importance, the Althingi had guaranteed — for the time being — that its impact would be extremely limited, not really disrupting the existing political and regional power relations and preserving the great inequality in the weight of votes.

1920-1933 (Ice6): First-Past-the-Post in Single-Member and Two-Member Constituencies (32 members) + PR (d'Hondt) in Reykjavík (4 members) + PR (d'Hondt) in a Special Country At-Large Election (6 members for a 8-year term)

Following Icelandic sovereignty in 1918, a government bill on constitutional amendments was passed by the Althingi in 1919 and 1920. The electoral term for general elections was shortened from 6 to 4 years, and from 12 to 8 years for the members elected in the country at-large PR elections. Proposals of increasing the number of PR elected members to 12, 10 and 8 were not accepted. On the other hand, the Althingi added to the bill a provision making it possible to introduce PR in Reykjavík by law (AR, 1919A: 96-97, 1090, 1194, 1197, 1247, 1592).

In 1920, a government bill suggested to increase the number of MPs in Reykjavík from 2 to 6, elected by PR (d'Hondt). The value of votes in the least populous constituency in 1919 was tenfold compared to the rapidly growing capital — 17% of the electorate now lived in Reykjavík, but they elected only 6% of the constituency MPs. The Lower House found an increase to six MPs too generous — pointing out once more that the Althingi was situated in Reykjavík and many MPs lived there — but accepted an increase to four. The Upper House tried to reach a compromise on five members, but to no avail.

The introduction of PR in the capital seems to have been uncontroversial. In the debate, several members pointed out that by making Reykjavík a multi-member constituency with PR, the growing working class would get an opportunity to elect its own MP — and that no one group would be able to elect all four (AR, 1920A: 91-96, 136-138, 199, 245, 289, 293. 1920B: 76-168).

In 1922, the two-member farming constituency of Húnavatnssýsla was divided into two single-member constituencies without much controversy (AR, 1922A: 182-183, 197, 297, 344, 409. 1922B: 670-682). In the following Althingi session of 1923, a similar split of Eyjafjardarsýsla between the primarily farming south and the predominantly fishing north was however defeated (AR, 1923A: 279-280, 464-465. 1923C: 93-105). A bill suggesting to add one member to the Althingi by giving the fishing town Hafnarfjördur one MP was also defeated in 1922 and 1923, even though the number of inhabitants in Hafnarfjördur had surpassed the population of the towns Ísafjördur and Seydisfjördur, which both had their own MPs. The supporters of the bill pointed out the different occupational and class structure of the town as compared to the rest of the constituency, but its opponents did not want to increase the number of MPs, especially as the government was supposed to be working on proposals for a comprehensive revision of the electoral system (AR, 1922A: 187-188, 266-267, 269. 1922C: 240-253. 1923A: 309. 1923C: 34-36).

While party interests had influenced the debate on electoral reforms, as we have seen, in the 1920s party considerations became completely dominant along with a continued emphasis on protecting the overweighting of votes in the periphery. This followed the formation of the new party system in 1916-1930. Shortly after the foundation of their party in 1916, the Social Democrats started demanding a better deal for the growing towns — not surprisingly, as their following was mainly among the working class and the party was greatly underrepresented in the Althingi. The agrarian Progressives were generally against all changes, as the system greatly benefited them. Views among the Conservatives were divided: many — especially MPs from towns — wanted electoral reforms, while Conservatives from the periphery were more cautious in their approach.

In 1927, the Social Democrats introduced a constitutional bill proposing to reduce the number of Althingi members to 25, but electing all of them by PR with the whole country as one constituency. This would be more democratic, they argued — all disproportionality would be history, the working class would achieve fair representation, and old-fashioned pork-barrel politics would disappear. Both the Progressives and the Conservatives completely rejected the SDP proposals (AR, 1927A: 164-171. 1927C: 1146-1161).

The Social Democrats also tried to increase the representation of towns within the existing constituency system. Their proposals in 1921 and 1923 to increase the number of Reykjavík MPs from four to seven were defeated — despite support from Reykjavík Conservatives (AR, 1921A: 531-532. 1921C: 167-171. 1923A: 308. 1923C: 31-34). In 1926 and 1927, Social Democratic bills to separate the two-member constituency of Gullbringu and Kjósarsýsla into two single-member constituencies of the county and the fishing town Hafnarfjördur were also defeated. The Conservatives strongly opposed this in a debate largely concerned with party interests (AR, 1926A: 179, 245, 257. 1926C: 187-216. 1927A: 247, 325-326, 329-330. 1927C: 146-167). In the 1926 local elections, the Social Democrats had obtained majority in the town council, and could be expected to win a seat if the town was a separate constituency — at the expense of the Conservatives.

In the 1927 constituency elections, the Progressives got 17 members elected with 29.8% of the vote, the Conservatives 13 members with 42.5%, and the Social Democrats 4 members with 19.1%.[44] The Progressives formed a minority government, enjoying neutrality from the Social Democrats.

In 1928, the Social Democrats re-introduced their bill on Hafnarfjördur, and now the Progressives secured its passing. The debate was long and rough: the Conservatives maintained that the Progressives' support for the bill was the price paid for the Social Democrats' neutrality towards their government. The Conservatives pointed out that both the Social Democrats and the Conservatives were under-represented, so it was blatantly unfair to correct the lot of the Social Democrats at the expense of the Conservatives, rather than the greatly over-represented Progressives. While admitting that the Conservatives were split on the issue of electoral reform, they also threatened that the Conservatives might in the future join the Social Democrats in radical changes of the electoral system. It was now obvious that political considerations and narrow party interests were out in the open and that electoral reforms would be subject to political deals between the parties. A compromise attempt by the Conservatives, giving Hafnarfjördur an MP by adding one member to the Althingi, was voted down (AR, 1928A: 179, 237, 267, 353, 386, 494, 521-522, 575. 1928B: 2943-3136).

In 1930, the Social Democrats introduced a parliamentary resolution asking the government to prepare a bill on electoral reforms, securing equal weight of votes in all regions of the country. While the party still preferred PR with the whole country as one constituency, the SDP was ready to compromise on five multi-member PR constituencies. If that was not possible, the party was ready to accept the continued use of single-member constituencies, if supplementary seats would be introduced in order to increase proportionality. While the leader of the Conservatives accepted the need of electoral reform, and was prepared to increase the number of MPs in Reykjavík, he was not ready to accept the absolute equality principle of the resolution. The Progressives bluntly opposed any change (AR, 1930A: 1209. 1930D: 299-314). In the same session a bill from two Conservative Reykjavík MPs on increasing the number of Reykjavík members to seven was voted down, as some rural Conservatives did not support it (AR, 1930A: 300-301, 1930C: 1-2).

In the 1931 Althingi session, the Progressive minority government presented a constitutional bill abolishing the countrywide at-large PR elections

---

44. Others obtained two seats.

and thus simply decreasing the total number of MPs to 36. While the Social Democrats and the Conservatives were prepared to abolish the at-large elections, they were not ready to accept an unchanged constituency system. The SDP presented electoral bills increasing the number of MPs in Reykjavík to nine and giving two towns new MPs. A compromise between the SDP and the Conservatives increasing the number of MPs in Reykjavík to five passed the Lower House. The two parties also amended the government constitutional bill in such a way that PR could be introduced in all constituencies by electoral law. The Progressives were furious, and the Prime Minister maintained that a new political alliance was forming: if those new constitutional provisions were accepted and confirmed after a fresh election, the Social Democrats and the Conservatives were going to adopt a system of 5-6 multi-member constituencies with PR, simply by changing electoral law. He accused the Conservatives of having joined hands with the Social Democrats with the aim of taking political power from the farmers and the rural areas — an accusation that obviously made some rural Conservative MPs uneasy (AR, 1931A (43. session): 159-160, 660-661, 774-776, 794-795, 893, 908-909, 938-939, 946, 963, 1000-1001. 1931C (43. session): 550-574, 1074-1115).

No changes on the electoral system were, however, made during this session. When it was clear that a no-confidence motion against the government would be passed by the Conservatives and the Social Democrats, the Prime Minister dissolved the Althingi and called for a fresh election in order to avoid changes on the electoral system. The opposition considered the dissolving of the Althingi unconstitutional, and emotions ran high — the foundation of a republic was suggested. In the election, the Progressives were victorious: they received 35.9% of the votes and won 21 (58.3%) of the 36 contested seats. However, the dissolving of the Althingi did not apply to the six MPs elected in the countrywide elections — those seats were thus not contested in 1931. As two of those MPs were Progressives, the party had an absolute majority (23 out of 42) in the Althingi — but not a working majority, as the party did not have a majority in the Upper House.

In a special summer session after the 1931 election, debates on the electoral system continued in the Althingi. The Conservatives presented a very open constitutional bill, simply saying that the number of MPs allocated to each party in Althingi elections should be in accordance with the total number of votes received. An electoral system fulfilling this requirement should be designed in electoral law. The bill of course did not pass, but a commission of all three parties was elected to try to make proposals for the next Althingi session (AR, 1931A (44. session): 182-183, 742-743. 1931C (44. session): 334-340. 1931D (44. session): 15-91).

The commission could not agree on any proposal. The Conservatives suggested a system of single-member constituencies, PR in Reykjavík, and supplementary seats numerous enough to secure overall proportionality. If any two-member constituencies were to remain, PR should be introduced there. The Social Democrats suggested PR with the whole country as one constituency. Both the Conservatives and the Social Democrats seemed prepared, however, to accept a system of six multi-member constituencies with PR. The Progressives basically wanted an unchanged system, but were ready for some minor concessions.

In 1932, the Social Democrats and the Conservatives re-introduced the open constitutional bill that the Conservatives had suggested in the summer session of 1931, confirming the proportionality principle, but leaving all details for electoral law. The bill passed the Upper House, but in the Lower House the Progressives made amendments, preserving the present system while increasing the number of Reykjavík MPs to eight, and allowing the introduction of up to five supplementary seats in electoral law (AR, 1932A: 198-245, 548, 619-620, 761, 771-789, 849-850, 1072-1074, 1104, 1134-1136. 1932C: 1420-1609). A deadlock thus remained. In June 1932, however, the Progressives and the Conservatives formed a coalition government. The solution of the deadlock became a part of a general agreement and political deals on government formation (Grímsson, 1977: 11).

1934-1942 (Ice7): First-past-the post in single-member and two-member constituencies (32 members) + PR (d'Hondt) in Reykjavík (6 members) + 11 supplementary seats (PR — d'Hondt)

A constitutional amendment was passed in two Althingi sessions in 1933 — with a general election in between. While the Conservatives had only wanted the constitution to include general principles, leaving details to electoral law, the constituency system and the exact number of MPs now became part of the constitution. The existing system of 32 seats in single-member and two-member constituencies with simple plurality remained — two-member constituencies could, however, be split into two single-member constituencies by law. The number of Reykjavík members, elected by PR, was increased from four to six. And finally — and most important — up to 11 supplementary seats were added in order to achieve greater proportionality between the parties (AR, 1933A (47. session): 1-2).

According to new electoral law, also passed in 1933, the supplementary seats were to be allocated to parties that had obtained at least one constituency member, by dividing their total number of votes nationally by already-obtained Althingi seats (d'Hondt). In order to maintain the strong position of the periphery, however, the following rules were set for deciding which of each party's unsuccessful candidates would take the party's supplementary seats:

1. A party's first supplementary seat would go to the candidate (not yet elected) with the highest number of votes in a constituency.

2. A party's second supplementary seat would go to the candidate (not yet elected) with the highest proportion of votes in a constituency.

3. A party's third supplementary seat would go to the candidate (not yet elected) at the top of the party's nationwide ranked party-list (if the party had chosen to present such a list).

4. A party's fourth supplementary seat would be allocated by Rule 1, etc.

5. Each party was only allowed one supplementary seat in each constituency (AR, 1933A (47. session): 485-488).

Rules 2 and 5 were particularly important, as they gave some of the supplementary seats to constituencies already over-represented.[45]

The electoral reforms of 1933 were a messy compromise — a mixture of different principles. The Progressives had to accept increased proportionality between parties by introducing supplementary members — of which they could not expect to have any — but they managed to keep the single-member and two-member constituency system and secure the continued overweighting of the periphery. They also avoided the introduction of PR in two-member constituencies — despite demands to that effect from the Conservatives — and they made further changes more difficult by including the constituency system into the constitution. The Conservatives gained from increased proportionality. However, many of their MPs would have liked to see a greater increase in the number of Reykjavík members, while others were quite happy with the

45. An illustration of this can be taken from the 1949 election. Then the Socialist candidate in Seydisfjördur became a supplementary member with 66 votes (16% of the votes in the constituency). The Socialist candidate in South-Thingeyjarsýsla did not obtain a supplementary seat, despite his 255 votes, as he only obtained 13% of the votes in his constituency. The third candidate on the ranked Socialist party list in Reykjavík became the party's first supplementary member with 2711 votes (but only 9.5% of the total votes in Reykjavík). Rule 5 of course excluded the fourth candidate on the party list in Reykjavík, despite his 2033 votes.

continued overweighting of the periphery. While the Social Democrats were still not satisfied, the new system greatly reduced their under-representation — it also opened the way for the Communist Party to have members elected to the Althingi (Grímsson, 1977: 12. AR, 1933B (46. session): 2720-2870).

1942-1959 (Ice8): First-past-the post in 21 single-member constituencies + PR (d'Hondt) in six two-member constituencies (12 members) + PR (d'Hondt) in Reykjavík (8 members) + 11 supplementary seats (PR — d'Hondt)

By yet another constitutional change in 1942, the number of MPs was increased from 49 to 52. Two of the new seats were allocated to Reykjavík, and the town Siglufjördur became a separate single-member constituency. The most important change however, was that PR was introduced in the two-member constituencies. While the Progressives usually had obtained both members in those constituencies under simple plurality, the Conservatives would in most cases be able to obtain one of the two under PR.

In 1939 the Progressives, the Conservatives, and the Social Democrats formed a national coalition government, leaving only the communists (now the United Socialist Party) in opposition. Due to unrest in the labor market, the Social Democrats left the coalition in 1942.

The Social Democrats — now in opposition — soon proposed a change in the electoral system. The Progressives believed they had had a promise from the Conservative leadership that their coalition partner would not support any electoral reforms during the electoral term. When it became clear that the Conservatives were ready to join the Social Democrats and the United Socialist Party in supporting electoral reforms, the Progressive leaders accused the Conservative leadership of betraying their gentlemen's agreement — and dissolved the government coalition. Party leader Ólafur Thors, on the other hand, maintained that he had only promised that the Conservatives would not *present* a bill on electoral reforms during the term — he had never promised not to *support* a bill presented by the Social Democrats![46] Whatever the truth is (still a matter of some dispute in Iceland), one Conservative MP bluntly joked: "When six geese fly into your mouth — fully fried — that's simply an offer you cannot refuse!" — referring to the introduction of PR in the six two-member constituencies.

Only the Progressives suffered from these changes — and they suffered badly. Their over-representation was such that even if the party were to lose six of their 20 constituency members obtained in the last election before the change (in July 1942), the party would still be over-represented and thus not qualify for a supplementary seat. The political importance of the change is clearly indicated by the fact that the Progressives, who had headed all governments in the 1927-42 period, now lost their dominant role. Since 1942, the Conservatives have held the Prime Ministership for a longer period than any other party (Grímsson, 1977: 13-14).

An unexpected and unintended consequence of the 1942 electoral system was that it opened the possibility for the Conservatives to obtain an absolute majority in the Althingi with less than 40% of the votes. In 1949, the party only needed around 300 more votes — correctly distributed in eight constituencies — to win an overall majority. In 1953 around 350 additional votes — correctly distributed in six constituencies — would have given the party an overall majority. This led to informal discussions between the Progressives and the Social Democrats on electoral reform — but the result was that those two parties decided to use the disproportionality of the system for their own advantage.

A special committee of all parties had been working on a revision of the Constitution from 1944, but its work came to a close in 1952 as the representatives of the parties failed to reach any agreement — disputes on electoral reforms were one of the major reasons. While the Conservatives declared themselves ready to either divide the whole country into single-member constituencies[47] or introduce PR in multi-member constituencies, the Progressives rejected both solutions (AR, 1958A: 727).

Progressive leader Hermann Jónasson was not a minister in the Conservative-Progressive government 1953-56. He was, in fact, preparing a coalition government with the Social Democrats, behind the scenes. An integral part of the plan was to use the electoral system to obtain an absolute majority in the

46. This incident — the case of the broken oath — led to a mutual distrust between Progressive leader Hermann Jónasson and Conservative leader Ólafur Thors that played an important role in government formations for many years to come and made the formation process difficult. A non-party government held office from 1942-44. Neither of the party leaders served as ministers for their parties in the SDP-Conservative-Progressive coalition 1947-49. When a Progressive-Conservative coalition was formed after great difficulties in 1950, both party leaders became ministers, but neither of them was Prime Minister. When Thors became Prime Minister in the Conservative-Progressive coalition formed in 1953, Progressive leader Jónasson did not serve as one of his party's ministers.

47. Dividing Reykjavík into several single-member constituencies could have meant that the conservatives would have obtained all seats in the capital.

Althingi for those two parties, even though they would receive less than 40% of the votes.

In 1953, the Social Democrats introduced an amendment bill on electoral law, allowing formal electoral alliances between two or more parties. Votes for one party could be transferred to the other in order to maximize their representation (apparentement). This, they argued, would lead to the formation of blocks, increasing stability and giving voters a possibility to choose between alternate government possibilities. They pointed out that electoral alliances had been allowed in Norway and Sweden, even though that system now had been replaced by the introduction of St. Laguë — which also had the effect of strengthening the position of middle-sized parties against big ones.

The Conservatives strongly opposed the bill, maintaining that it was a direct attack on their party. They pointed out that if this system had been at work in the 1953 election, an alliance of the Progressives and the Social Democrats would have obtained a majority in the Althingi with only 37% of the votes. The Social Democrats argued that since the Conservatives could in fact be able to obtain a majority with 39% of the votes, it was only fair that an alliance of smaller parties had the same opportunity! The Progressives did not take part in the debate, but some party newspapers supported the bill. The bill was never reported from a committee (AR, 1953A: 389-392. 1953C: 381- 447. Grímsson, 1977: 14-15).

Without formal rules of apparentement, an electoral alliance was difficult — but still possible. The parties would simply not put up candidates against each other in any constituency. Social Democrats in the rural areas would be asked to vote for the Progressive candidate while Progressive voters in Reykjavík and the towns were asked to vote for the SDP. If successful, this would lead to a huge over-representation of the Progressives — and the votes borrowed from the Progressives in the towns would come in handy for the Social Democrats when the supplementary seats were allocated. Such an electoral alliance was formed before the 1956 election — nicknamed "the Alliance of Fear," by its opponents — presenting a joint program and aiming at an overall majority.

The strategy almost worked, but the joint vote of the two parties in 1956 was 33.9% — down from 37.5% in 1953. The parties got 25 MPs elected (48.1%) — two MPs short of a working majority. The new left-socialist People's Alliance had to be included in the coalition formed after the election.[48] It had become abundantly clear, however, that the electoral system could be manipulated —

and that both the Conservatives and an electoral alliance of smaller parties could realistically expect to win an overall majority with less than 40% of the vote.

1959-1983 (Ice9): PR (d'Hondt) in eight multi-member constituencies (49 members) + 11 supplementary seats (PR — d'Hondt)

In 1959, the number of MPs was increased from 52 to 60 by a constitutional change, and the electoral system was completely restructured as the old single-member and two-member constituencies were abolished. Instead, PR (d'Hondt) was introduced in eight multi-member constituencies. The number of constituency seats was as follows: Reykjavík 12 seats, the North East and the South 6 seats each, Reykjanes, the West, the West Fjords, the North West and the East 5 seats each. While this change greatly increased proportionality for the parties, the less populous constituencies remained greatly over-represented. As the rules for allocating the 11 supplementary seats remained unchanged (except that ranked nationwide party-lists were abolished), some of the supplementary seats would end up in over-represented constituencies.

This radical change took place after the fall of the left-wing coalition in 1958, as the Conservatives, the Social Democrats and the left-socialists joined hands in reducing once more the over-representation of the Progressives. An added incentive for the Conservatives and the Social Democrats was that new possibilities for a cooperation of those two parties in government had emerged. The Social Democrats — disappointed by the disastrous results of the left-wing coalition's economic policy — decided to follow the example of many European social democrats and abandon their old socialist policies in favor of a more market-oriented approach. They now wanted to change the Icelandic economy, which for a long time had been over-politicized, heavily state-regulated and strongly protected by tariffs and bans on imports. This meant a change of partners: abandoning their old ally, the Progressives, and joining forces with their old enemy, the Conservatives. However, it was very unlikely that those two parties would obtain an overall majority in the Althingi in an unchanged electoral system, despite an overall majority among the voters. Electoral reforms were thus a necessary condition for their coalition. After the 1959 elections, those parties formed the longest-lasting government in Icelandic history — the

48. While the Progressive vote was down from 21.9% in 1953 to 15.7% in 1956, the party obtained 17 MPs in 1956 compared to 16 in 1953! The SDP vote was up to 18.3% in 1956 from 15.6% in 1953 — and the party had 8 MPs elected compared to 6 in 1953.

coalition was in power until 1971 — greatly liberalizing trade and having Iceland join EFTA and acceding to GATT (Kristinsson et.al., 1992. Hardarson, 1995).

The Progressives fought fiercely against the electoral reforms and made various counterproposals, but to no avail. The major arguments they presented in the debate were the following: The electoral reforms this round were only a prelude to the final aim, which was to make the whole country one constituency. Abolishing 27 constituencies deprived them of their historical and traditional right to a separate representation in the Althingi — a right that had been observed since the re-establishment of the Althingi in 1845. Population changes could be accommodated into the old system, as had been done previously. The counties were administrative units, and as such were a natural basis[49] for constituencies. Single-member constituencies had served to strengthen the ties between voters and MPs and increase the personal responsibility of the MPs; now, impersonal party power would grow. The job of the MPs would become still more difficult in the new constituencies. The new order would increase the number of parties and make it more difficult to form stable government coalitions. Voters had not demanded any electoral reforms (Grímsson, 1977: 15-18. AR, 1958A: 643-644, 727-730, 810-817, 1052-1057, 1064. 1958B: 1254-1689. 1959A (79. session): 1, 43-47, 89-91. 1959B (79. session): 21-365). The arguments in the long and heated debate in the Althingi in 1959 were familiar. The supporters of electoral reform emphasized that it was fair that the Althingi should reflect the will of the nation and only PR would achieve this. However, the interests of the rural areas would be protected: those areas would still have some over-representation, and their absolute number of MPs would not decrease. Small nations had had favorable experiences using PR-systems. The impact of the ordinary voter would increase. The counties did not really have any historical right to have their own representation — in fact, the new constituencies had boundaries quite similar to the regional *things* of the Icelandic commonwealth founded in AD 930. Larger constituencies would increase healthy cooperation between local communities. Voters' chance of having access to an MP from their own party would increase. The party organizations in the regions would be in a stronger position vis-à-vis the central party organizations in Reykjavík.

49. In the Icelandic commonwealth (930-1262) each quarter of the country had its own regional assembly (*thing*) while Althingi was the superior assembly for the whole country.

The new constituencies soon became important units. The parties established new constituency organizations. MPs from different parties — but from the same constituency — formed informal groups in the Althingi in order to further the interests of their constituents. The administrative system was to some extent adapted to the new constituency system (Grímsson, 1977: 19).

1987-1999 (Ice10): PR (LR-Hare) in eight multi-member constituencies (50 members) + 13 supplementary seats (PR — d'Hondt)

While the 1959 electoral reforms greatly reduced disproportionality for the parties, the Progressives still benefited from the system, obtaining 1-2 extra MPs in most elections. Migration and population changes however steadily increased malapportionment, measured as the ratio between the number of votes per seat in the least and most populous constituencies.[50] In 1982, all four parties introduced a constitutional bill on electoral reform, which was passed in 1982 and 1983 (AR, 1982-83A: 2329-2357, 2704, 3093). An accompanying bill on electoral law — including the electoral formulae used — was passed in 1983, but was never actually used as it was amended before the 1987 election (AR, 1983-84A: 1293-1324, 3136, 3298. 1986-87A: 501-508, 3073-3094, 3181-3193, 3334-3335, 3387-3389, 3504).[51] The major aims of the reforms were to obtain proportionality between the parties and reduce malapportionment to the 1959 level. This was to be obtained without a great increase in the number of MPs.

In the new electoral system, the number of MPs was increased from 60 to 63. While the constituency boundaries remained unchanged, the number of seats in constituencies and the rules for allocating seats were changed.

All seats except one were now fixed to a particular constituency before each election (including the supplementary seats). There were 54 seats fixed to a particular constituency by the constitution, specifying the minimum number of seats for a constituency, and 8 seats were to be allocated to constituencies before each election, on the basis of the number of registered voters in the last election.

50. In the last election before the 1959 reforms the weight of votes ratio between the least and most populous constituencies was 1:19.2. In the first election after the reforms this ratio was down to 1:2.92, while in 1979 it had increased to 1:4.80 (see Skýrsla um breytingar á kjördæmaskipan og tilhögun kosninga til Alþingis, 1998: 12).

51. In 1983-84, 5% of the national vote was made a condition for obtaining a supplementary seat. In 1986-87, this was replaced by the old condition of a party having obtained at least one constituency member. Other changes mainly concerned thresholds for allocating constituency seats and computations for the allocation of each party's supplementary seats.

One of the supplementary seats, nicknamed "the vagabond," could, in principle, end up in any constituency whatsoever, depending on the overall results.

On the face of it, the 8 seats allocated to constituencies on the basis of population should function as a barrier to further malapportionment. However, already in the 1987 election, 7 of those seats ended up in the two constituencies greatly under-represented in the system, Reykjavík and Reykjanes, while 1 seat was allocated to the North East. Because of population changes, this one seat was moved to Reykjanes in 1995.

The total number of seats in each constituency was to be divided into constituency seats and supplementary seats. The number of constituency seats was the least integer greater than or equal to 3/4 of the total number of seats in the constituency; the rest were supplementary seats. The constituency seats were allocated by LR-Hare. Only parties whose vote exceeded 2/3 of the Hare quota (based on the votes of all parties) could participate in seat allocations. If any parties were eliminated, the quota was recomputed in terms of the votes of qualifying parties only.

As the total number of constituency seats became 50, the remaining 13 became supplementary seats. Those 13 seats were allocated to the parties on the national level by d'Hondt on the basis of the total number of votes obtained nationally and the seats already won in the constituencies. A party had to win at least one constituency seat in order to qualify for the allocation of supplementary seats. Quite complex rules were used to decide which of each party's unsuccessful candidates would obtain the party's supplementary seats.

In 1987 and 1991, the seats were distributed as follows: Reykjavík had 18 seats (14 fixed [minimum] seats + 4 allocated seats) including 4 supplementary seats, Reykjanes had 11 seats (8 fixed + 3 allocated) including 2 supplementary seats, the North East had 7 seats (6 fixed + 1 allocated) including 1 supplementary seat, the South had 6 seats (all fixed), including 1 supplementary seat, the West, the West Fjords, the North West, and the East had 5 seats each (all fixed), including 1 supplementary seat in each constituency. While "the vagabond" could in principle end up in any constituency, his home turned out to be in the already highly over-represented constituencies both in 1987 and 1991 (the West and the West Fjords).

In 1995, the North East lost its allocated seat to Reykjanes. By a change in electoral law, it was possible to give "the vagabond" a permanent home in Reykjavík (AR, 1994-95A: 3871-4000). This meant that Reykjavík obtained 19 seats (including 4 supplementary seats), Reykjanes 12 seats (including 3 supplementary seats) and the North East 6 seats (including 1 supplementary seat).

While the 1983-87 compromise on electoral reforms was supported by the four major parties and passed by a large majority in the Althingi, many MPs were not really happy (AR, 1982-83B: 2287-2351, 2592-2670, 2673-2688, 2699-2742, 2750-2757, 2769-2785, 2880-2882, 3095-3097. 1983-84B: 2238-2239, 2345, 3363-3374, 3456-3475, 3639-3656, 6185-6207, 6260-6291, 6297-6305, 6414-6431, 6556-6557). The Social Democrats still wanted to make the whole country one constituency — a position not shared by any other party. Some Conservatives however agreed that in principle the weight of all votes should be equal, even though that step had not been achieved in this round. The Progressives — while arguing that some overweighting for parties in the periphery was not in any way unnatural — were ready to abandon the overweighting of their party, but strongly emphasized the continued overweighting of the periphery.

Many MPs disliked abandoning the d'Hondt rule for allocating constituency seats, but seemed to accept the argument that LR-Hare was better suited to ensure proportionality among parties in the small constituencies with 5-6 members, and also made it easier to obtain overall proportionality without greatly increasing the number of supplementary seats (AR, 1982-83A: 2340. 1982-83B: 2294). An important part of the deal was the continued use of d'Hondt in local elections.[52]

A common complaint of MPs in the Althingi debates was that the new system was too complicated — it was impossible for ordinary voters to understand the system and make their own calculations by hand. The more technical aspects of the system were hardly discussed at all in the debate. Various alternative suggestions made by the experts preparing the bills (for instance, on the possible use of St. Laguë or LR-Droop, see AR, 1983-84B: 6187. 1986-87B: 83) were hardly mentioned. It was known, however, that during the preparatory stage, many MPs had studied in detail computer simulations showing how different alternatives would have distributed seats in past elections — thus telling them what systems would have secured their own seats in the Althingi.

The new system secured proportionality between the major parties, but great malapportionment remained — and only increased as time went by. In

52. The Conservatives had several times obtained a majority in the Reykjavík town council with less than 50% of the votes because of using d'Hondt rather than e.g. St. Laguë or largest remainder.

1999, the voters living in the Reykjavík and Reykjanes constituencies (68% of the total electorate) elected 31 MPs, while voters in the six regional constituencies (32% of the electorate) elected 32 MPs.

New Century — New System: Decreasing (but Remaining) Malapportionment

Major changes in the electoral system were introduced by a constitutional change in 1999 and subsequent changes of electoral law in 2000. Those changes are quite important, as they greatly reduced malapportionment in the electoral system. In the next Althingi election — due in 2003 — the majority of voters living in the urban South West will for the first time elect a majority of MPs (33 out of 63). However, the regional constituencies, now containing around 38% of the voters, will still elect 48% of the MPs.

The major aims of the 1999 changes were to reduce the over-representation of the countryside and to simplify the electoral system. Future improvements were also made easier, as some important aspects of the electoral system no longer require constitutional change. While the new system is outside the time period covered in this chapter, a short description of its major features nevertheless follows here.

The following aspects of the electoral system are now specified by the constitution: The number of MPs (63), proportionally elected for a four-year term, is unchanged. Instead of eight constituencies with constitutionally defined boundaries, the number of constituencies is reduced to six or seven; their exact number and boundaries are to be decided by law. Each constituency shall have at least six seats, allocated on the basis of constituency results. Supplementary seats are to be allocated in order to make each party's number of seats proportional to the party's share of the national vote. However, a party now must obtain at least 5% of the national vote in order to obtain supplementary seats — before, parties could obtain supplementary seats if they had at least one member elected in a constituency. After each election, the National Election Board shall calculate the number of registered voters per seat in each constituency (including supplementary seats). If this number turns out to be half (or less) of any other constituency, the National Election Board shall change the number of seats in these constituencies in order to decrease the discrepancy — except if a constituency is down to the minimum of six seats. Changes of constituency boundaries and allocation rules can now be amended by electoral law, but only by an increased majority of 2/3 in the Althingi. It should be noted however that a simple majority in the Althingi can by law reduce the number of seats in any constituency to six, if it so chooses.

According to the electoral law passed in 2000, the number of constituencies shall be six. Three of these are in the urban South West: two Reykjavík constituencies, and the South West Reykjavík suburbs. The number of constituencies in the countryside is reduced from six to three: the North West, the North East, and the South. The boundaries are defined by law, except the boundaries between the two Reykjavík constituencies: when an election is called, the National Election Board shall draw those boundaries in such a way that the number of voters per seat in both constituencies is approximately equal.

The law also decides that 54 of the 63 seats shall be allocated on the basis of constituency results. The nine remaining seats are supplementary seats, fixed to particular constituencies. All six constituencies obtain nine constituency seats. The two Reykjavík constituencies and the South West Reykjavík suburbs each also obtain two supplementary seats, while each of the three constituencies in the countryside obtains one such seat.

The allocation rule in constituencies has been changed. Before the 1987 election, the d'Hondt rule had been replaced by LR-Hare, in order to increase the chance of small parties obtaining one of the four or five seats on offer in the regional constituencies, and thus reducing the need for supplementary seats. As all constituencies now contain nine constituency seats, this was no longer deemed necessary and the d'Hondt rule was adopted again. For the same reason, only nine supplementary seats — instead of thirteen, before — are thought sufficient to secure proportionality between the parties. The allocation of the supplementary seats between the parties is based on the d'Hondt rule as before (Hardarson and Kristinsson, 2000: 417-418).

4. IMPACT OF THE ELECTORAL SYSTEMS

According to Duverger's famous thesis, simple majority electoral systems lead to the formation of two-party systems. As the Icelandic electoral system was basically a simple majority system from 1908-1933 — despite the introduction of PR elements in the at-large elections 1916-1930, and PR in Reykjavík from 1921 — we should expect the formation of two parties. While it is clear that the logic of the system worked in the expected direction, this did not quite happen. In 1933 — the last election before the introduction of supplementary members — the four parties that were to dominate the Icelandic party system for the rest of the century had emerged, even though only three of them had members elected to the Althingi.

The initial formation of a party system in the beginning of the 20th century was in accord with Duverger's thesis. Two cadre parties emerged, competing for the new ministerial post. Those parties presented two reasonably clear alternatives in the elections of 1900, 1902, 1903 and 1908, even though party labels of candidates and MPs were sometimes in doubt and were changeable. The alternatives were much less clear in the elections of 1911 and 1914, as parties and party groups frequently split and united (Kjartansson, 1996). In the 1916 general election, seven "parties" had members elected to the Althingi, according to the official records. The origins of two of the modern parties can be traced to this election: the Social Democrats fielded candidates for the first time, and two farmers "parties" formed the Agrarian Progressive Party after the election. Most MPs however belonged to the Home Rule Party and the old Independence Party, which now was split into three groups.

The days of the parties of independence politics were, however, numbered. The Home Rule Party and the old Independence Party — now in one part — participated for the last time in the general election of 1919 and the country at-large PR election of 1922. In addition to the Social Democrats and the Progressives, a large Conservative party was forming during the 1920s. When the Communist Party was formed in 1930, the four major parties in modern Icelandic politics had entered upon the stage.

The new parties had clear ideological and socio-economic bases, reflecting three of Stein Rokkan's famous cleavages: workers-employers, center-periphery, and reformist-revolutionary working-class politics. The Social Democrats and the Communists were representatives of reformist and revolutionary socialism respectively, while the Progressives presented themselves as the defenders of farmers' interests and the periphery. The Conservatives opposed the new class-parties and claimed to represent the interest of all classes — emphasizing market solutions and nationalism. Their appeal was successful: the Conservatives became the largest party by far, enjoying large working-class following and strong support in the periphery, even though the capital was always their major stronghold.

This transformation of the party system in 1916-1930 took place in electoral systems (Ice5 and Ice6) which were mainly based on the majority principle. The electoral system did not prevent the formation of the new cleavage-based parties — but it had great effect on their success at the parliamentary level.

From the start, the Progressives and the Conservatives had no difficulty having members elected in the majority system, even though the system greatly favored the Progressives. The Social Democrats on the other hand had a rough ride. Nevertheless, they managed to break through and obtain representation in the Althingi.

The introduction of PR in Reykjavík helped the Social Democrats. While they had managed to obtain their first MP in the capital in 1916 as one of the two plurality members elected, this was exceptional. One of the two SDP candidates probably got some votes from supporters of the Independence Party (across), which did not present candidates, and the votes for the candidates of the Home Rule Party and the Independence Party (along) split favorably for the SDP. In 1919, the Social Democrats lost their member in Reykjavík — and with the conservative forces united in the 1920s, the SDP would not have been able to win a seat in the capital under plurality rules. However, in a by-election in 1921 they had one member out of three elected in Reykjavík under PR, two out of four in the 1927 election, and one out of four in the elections of 1931 and 1933.

The Social Democrats were also able to win plurality elections in some single-member constituencies in towns. They had a member elected from the towns of Ísafjördur in 1927, 1931 and 1933, Akureyri in 1927, and Seydisfjördur in 1931 and 1933. They also managed to win a seat in Nordur-Ísafjardarsýsla in 1933, a constituency with a mixed electorate of farmers, workers and fishermen.

The PR country at-large elections did not help the Social Democrats much, as only three members were elected each time.[53] They had no members elected in 1916 (6.8% of the vote), 1922 (17.2%) and 1930 (20.3%) — while the 22.7% obtained by the party in 1926 secured one seat.

The predominantly majoritarian electoral systems in 1916-1933 thus allowed three new parties to enter the parliamentary arena. The fourth actor, the Communist Party, however, did not manage to break through in the 1931 and 1933 elections, with 3% and 7.5% of the national vote. In 1934 — after the introduction of supplementary members and the lowering of the electoral threshold in Reykjavík (Ice7) — the Communists still did not receive representation with 6.0% of the vote, as they did not win seats in any constituency.[54] The new rules finally gave them three seats (including two supplementary seats) with 8.4% of the national vote in 1937, as they had one constituency member elected in Reykjavík.

The two-tier system clearly increased small parties' chances of having MPs elected. However, the four-party format proved very stable. From 1942 to 1967, a fifth party managed only once to have a member elected, in 1953. Since 1971, however, five to seven parties have always been represented in the Althingi, except after the election of 1978.

53. All six members were however elected in 1916, the initial country at-large election.

54. The new Farmers' Party — a splinter from the Progressives — however obtained three members (including two supplementary members) with 6.4% of the national vote in 1934. In 1937 the Farmers' Party obtained two seats (including one supplementary seat) with 6.1% of the vote.

Figure 1. Effective number of parties in Iceland 1916-1999

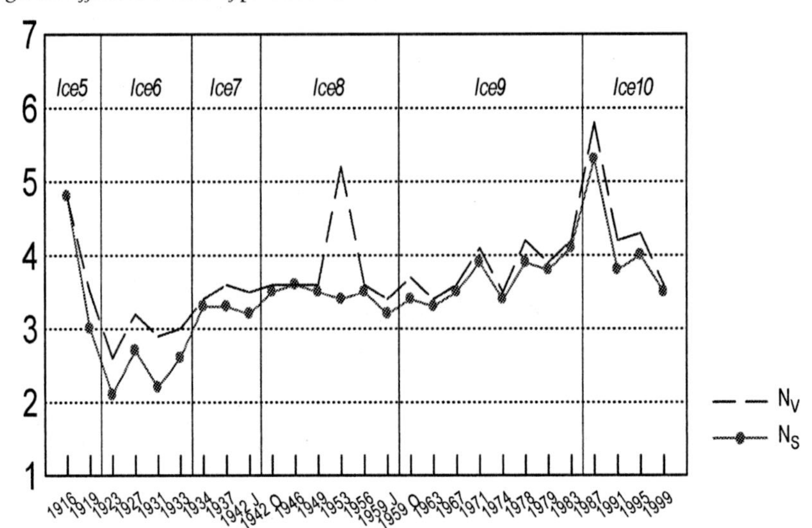

The general relationship between electoral systems and the party system can be observed in Figure 1, showing the effective number[55] of both elective parties (parties fighting elections, N_V) and parliamentary parties (obtaining a seat in the Althingi, N_S) in 1916-1999. The average number of effective parliamentary parties in Ice5 (1916-1919) is 3.9 — despite the system's majoritarian features. The lower electoral threshold in Reykjavík in Ice6 (1923-1933) notwithstanding, the average goes down to 2.4, as the parties of independence politics are replaced by the Progressives, the Conservatives and the Social Democrats. A sharp increase in the effective number of parliamentary parties (by 38%) takes place in Ice7 (1934-1942) as the average goes up to 3.3 — a result of the entrance of the Communists to the Althingi and a more proportional representation for the Social Democrats. Increasing proportionality and the growth of the left-socialists explain why the average is 6% higher (3.5) in Ice8 (1942-1959). Another slight increase (5%), to an average of 3.7, can be observed in Ice9 (1959-1983). Figure 1 shows, however, that no change takes place in 1959-1967: the increase starts in 1971, when the virtual monopoly of the four old parties in the Althingi comes to an end. The average number of effective parliamentary parties still goes up by 14% (to 4.2) in Ice10 (1987-1999). This higher average in Ice10 is solely the result of the exceptional 1987 election. The number of effective parliamentary parties in the elections of 1991, 1995 and 1999 is similar to that in Ice9. It

55. Taking into account not only the number of parties, but weighting also their size (cf. Lijphart, 1994).

is clearly not only the electoral system that has been influencing the effective number of parliamentary parties in the last 40 years.

Disproportionality between parties has had considerable effect on the Icelandic party system. Figure 2 shows disproportionality in the six electoral systems from 1916-1999, measured by Gallagher's least square index.

While existing electoral statistics do not allow us to exactly calculate disproportionality in 1900-1914 — the first years of Icelandic parties — it is clear that the electoral system favored the Independence Party (old), as explained in Section 3. In Ice5 (1916-19) — when the transformation from independence politics to modern politics got under way — the average disproportionality on Gallagher's index is 8.8. In Ice6 (1923-33) — when three new parties became dominant in the Althingi — disproportionality greatly increases: the average is 14.6. As we have seen (Section 3), the major aim of all subsequent changes on the electoral system was to decrease disproportionality. This aim was gradually achieved: average disproportionality goes down to 9.8 in Ice7 (1934-42), to 6.6 in Ice8 (1942-1959), to 2.9 in Ice9 (1959-83), and to 2.1 in Ice10 (1987-99). This amounts to a reduction in the Gallagher Index of 33% in both Ice7 and Ice8, of 56% in Ice9, and of 28% in Ice10. The slow step-wise process indicates the strong opposition to the equality principle — champions of the periphery had to give in, but they fought every inch of the way. It is also noteworthy that there are systematic variations in disproportionality in Ice7, Ice8 and Ice9: disproportionality tends to increase as time goes by within each system.

Figure 2. Gallagher's least-squares disproportionality index for parties 1916-1999

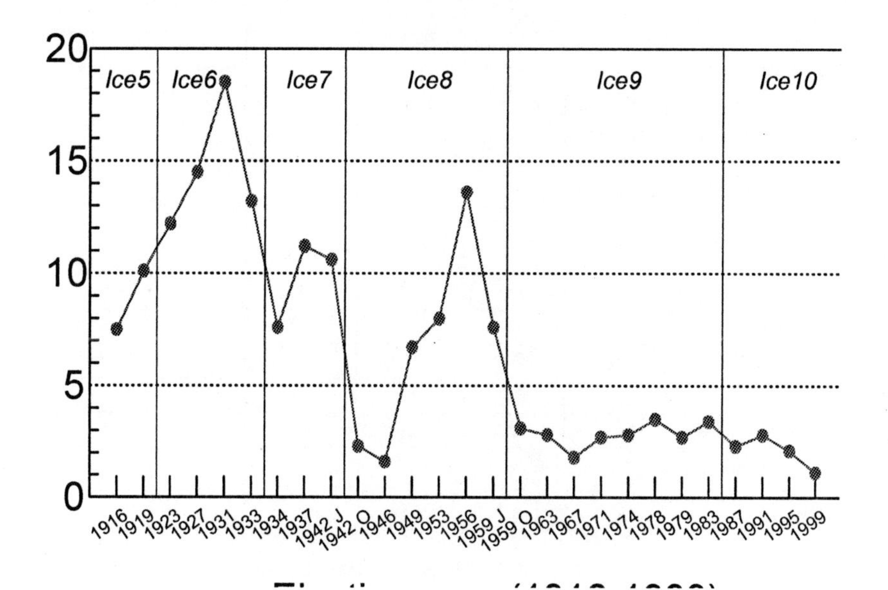

Table 4: Disproportionality for individual parties in the Althingi 1916-1999

Election	Gallagher's least square index	Loosemore-Hanby's index	Disproportionality for individual parties				Others, obtaining MP	Others, obtaining no MP
			Conservatives	Progressives (agrarian)	Communists/ left-socialists	Social Democrats		
Ice5	8.8	15.0		6.0		-5.3	2.9	
1916	7.5	15.6	-	4.7	-	-3.8	6.2	-7.1
1919	10.1	14.3	-	7.2	-	-6.8	-0.5	-
Ice6	14.6	18.6	-4.0	16.1		-9.3		-1.5
1923	12.2	15.8	4.7	9.6	-	-13.4	1.5	-2.4
1927	14.5	19.4	-6.4	17.4	-	-7.9	-1.1	-2.0
1931	18.5	22.4	-10.5	22.4	-3.0	-7.8	-	-1.2
1933	13.2	16.8	-0.8	15.0	-7.5	-8.1	1.8	-0.3
Ice7	9.8	12.3	-4.3	11.9	-4.1	-2.4		-0.7
1934	7.6	9.8	-1.5	8.7	-6.0	-1.3	0.8	-0.7
1937	11.2	13.9	-6.6	13.9	-2.3	-2.7	-2.0	-0.2
1942 (J)	10.6	13.2	-4.8	13.2	-4.0	-3.2	-	-1.2
Ice8	6.6	8.6	-1.8	8.0	-1.7	-2.1		
1942 (O)	2.3	2.9	-0.1	2.3	0.7	-0.7	-	-2.2
1946	1.6	1.9	-1.0	1.9	-0.3	-0.5	-	-0.1
1949	6.7	8.2	-3.0	8.2	-2.2	-3.1	-	-
1953	8.0	12.1	3.3	8.9	-2.6	-4.1	-2.2	-3.3
1956	13.6	17.1	-5.8	17.1	-3.8	-2.9	-	-4.5
1959 (J)	7.6	9.3	-4.0	9.3	-1.8	-1.0	-	-2.5
Ice9	2.9	3.8	-0.1	3.2	-0.4	-0.5		-1.8
1959 (O)	3.1	3.6	0.3	2.6	0.7	-0.2	-	-3.4
1963	2.8	3.4	-1.4	3.4	-1.0	-0.9	-	-0.2
1967	1.8	2.7	0.8	1.9	-0.9	-0.7	-	-1.1
1971	2.7	3.5	0.5	3.1	-0.5	-0.5	-0.6	-2.0
1974	2.8	3.5	-1.1	3.5	0.0	-0.7	-1.3	-0.4
1978	3.5	5.5	0.6	3.1	0.5	1.3	-	-5.5
1979	2.7	3.9	-0.4	3.4	-1.4	-0.8	0.5	-1.3
1983	3.4	4.3	-0.3	4.3	-0.6	-1.7	-1.1	-0.5
Ice10	2.1	3.5	1.8	1.2	-0.2	0.3	-0.6	-2.5
1987	2.3	4.4	1.4	1.7	-0.7	0.6	0.0	-3.1
1991	2.8	4.8	2.7	1.7	-0.1	0.4	-0.4	-4.3
1995	2.1	3.1	2.6	0.5	0.0	-0.3	-0.9	-1.9
1999	1.1	1.8	0.5	0.7	0.2	0.4	-1.0	-0.8

For parties included in each category, see Table A1.

Table 4 shows disproportionality for individual parties in the simple form of percentage difference between share of seats and votes for each party. Those figures can be directly compared to the Loosemore-Hanby's index, which shows the total percentage difference of seats and votes for all over-represented (or under-represented) parties. For comparison, we also include Gallagher's index of disproportionality.[56]

The results in Table 4 are striking indeed. Almost all disproportionality in 1923-59 (Ice6 to Ice8) is simply due to the over-representation of the Agrarian Progressives, and most of the disproportionality in 1959-83 (Ice9) can be attributed to the same source. Just like overall disproportionality, the over-representation of the Progressives was reduced gradually. In 1923-33 (Ice6) the party gained on average 16.1% more seats than votes. In 1934-42 (Ice7), the party's over-representation was down to 11.9%, and in 1942-59 (Ice8) it was further reduced to 8.0%. A dramatic decrease took place when the single-member and two-member constituencies were abolished in 1959 (Ice9) — Progressive average over-representation went down to 3.2%, usually reflected in 1-2 bonus members in the Althingi. Since 1987 there has been no over-representation to speak of — the Progressives even managed to get their first supplementary members ever in the election of 1999.

Another interesting feature in Table 4 is that the Conservatives — by far the largest party, electorally — did not gain from the electoral system. In 1923-1942 (Ice6 and Ice7), the party was in fact on average under-represented by some 4 percentage points. This under-representation was greatly reduced when PR was introduced in the two-member constituencies in 1942 (Ice8), and it was eliminated from 1959 (Ice9 and Ice10).

The Social Democrats suffered badly from the electoral system in their first years. Their average under-representation in 1916-19 (Ice5) was 5.3%, increasing to 9.3% in 1923-33 (Ice6). The supplementary members introduced in 1934 (Ice7) greatly improved their lot; however, they continued to be under-represented until 1959.

The new rules of Ice7 also opened the way for Communist representation in the Althingi in 1937. Like the Social Democrats, the Communists/left-socialists suffered from some under-representation until 1959.

The most obvious example of the political impact of Progressives' overweighting in the electoral system was their continuous hold on the premiership from 1927 to 1942, despite that fact that the Conservatives always were a much larger party, electorally. And disproportionality may however have

56. While the Loosemore-Hanby's index gives higher values than Gallagher's index, both indices show the same trend. The correlation between the two is 0.98.

had more lasting effects on the Icelandic party system. In 1942, the party system "froze," despite fluctuations since 1971, and the strength relations of the four major parties were strikingly stable for sixty years (see Table A1). Those strength relations clearly deviated from the Scandinavian pattern, as the Icelandic agrarians were comparatively strong, the Social Democrats very weak, and the left-socialists relatively strong. At the time of the "freezing," the Progressives were an established major party, while the Social Democrats were still very much a minor party. In 1934, the Progressives and the Social Democrats both obtained around 22% of the national vote: the Progressives, however, obtained 15 seats compared to 10 for the Social Democrats. Those parties subsequently formed a coalition government in which the Social Democrats were very much the junior partner. In the next years, the relatively weak Social Democrats were unable to successfully fight the Communist challenge. The disproportionality of the Icelandic electoral system may thus be one of the explanations why the Icelandic party system came to deviate substantially from the Scandinavian pattern.

5. Malapportionment

Malapportionment was a major feature of the Icelandic electoral system right from the start, as the votes/seats ratio varied greatly between constituencies (see Section 3). The enormous disproportionality in 1923-33 (Ice6) was largely due to malapportionment.

Table 5 shows malapportionment in 1916-1999. The Loosemore-Hanby's Index for constituencies shows the total percentage difference in votes and seats (supplementary seats included) for over-represented (or under-represented) constituencies. For comparison, the Loosemore-Hanby's Index of disproportionality between parties is also included in the table.

The table reveals a very interesting development. While disproportionality has been gradually reduced, and largely eliminated, average malapportionment from Ice6 to Ice10 has remained at the same very high level. The defenders of the interests of the periphery have managed to secure their continued over-representation in the Althingi — not by an overweighting of the parties of the periphery, but by an overweighting of MPs from the periphery within the parties.

A striking example of this can be taken from the 1995 election. While there was hardly any disproportionality between parties, a majority of MPs was elected from the six regional constituencies containing only one third of the electorate. The Progressives obtained 15 seats, roughly proportional to their national vote. Malapportionment however greatly influenced the distribution of the party's seats. While almost half of the national vote for the Progressives came from the constituencies of the center (Reykjavík and Reykjanes), they only had four members elected — while the other half of Progressive voters — located in the six regional constituencies — had 11 representatives in the Progressive parliamentary group.[57] It does not come as a surprise that in recent years Progressive MPs from the center have for the first time joined those demanding equal weighting of votes in the Icelandic system!

Malapportionment can have wide-ranging political consequences — even though no disproportionality between parties is present in the electoral system. If the views and policies of MPs *within* each party differ by region, the skewed power balance within the parliamentary groups becomes important, especially if those groups are powerful as has been the case in Iceland.

An elite study of Icelandic parliamentarians, conducted in 1996, shows that in some areas — especially concerning regional policy — there are great differences in the views of MPs from the center and the periphery. To some extent, this is also the case with the opinion of the voters. Emphasis on working with problems of individual voters and advocating interests of their own region is significantly stronger among MPs from the periphery than from the center. For example, opposition to Icelandic membership in the European Union is stronger both among MPs and voters in the periphery than in the center (Valen et. al., 2000).

57. This was also the case for the other major parties. Althingi members from the periphery constituted 48% of Conservative MPs (with 28% of the party's national vote), 43% of Social Democratic MPs (with 25% of the party's vote), and 56% of the left-socialist MPs (with 37% of the party's vote).

Table 5. Malapportionment: Loosemore-Hanby´s Index for constituencies and parties 1916-1999

Election	Loosemore-Hanby's index for constituencies	Loosemore-Hanby's index for eight regions (the 1959 constitu-encies)	Loosemore-Hanby's index for parties
Ice5	16.8	12.6	15.0
1916	16.4	11.8	15.6
1919	17.1	13.3	14.3
Ice6	18.5	15.1	18.6
1923	15.3	12.1	15.8
1927	17.1	14.3	19.4
1931	19.9	17.7	22.4
1933	21.7	16.4	16.8
Ice7	20.6	17.2	12.3
1934	21.4	19.3	9.8
1937	18.8	13.8	13.9
1942 (J)	21.6	18.5	13.2
Ice8	23.7	20.8	8.6
1942 (O)	17.6	14.6	2.9
1946	20.8	16.1	1.9
1949	25.2	21.4	8.2
1953	24.9	22.6	12.1
1956	26.2	24.5	17.1
1959 (J)	27.4	25.6	9.3
Ice9	20.1	20.1	3.8
1959 (O)	16.9	16.9	3.6
1963	17.8	17.8	3.4
1967	19.7	19.7	2.7
1971	20.0	20.0	3.5
1974	20.8	20.8	3.5
1978	22.2	22.2	5.5
1979	23.8	23.8	3.9
1983	19.4	19.4	4.3
Ice10	17.1	17.1	3.5
1987	16.2	16.2	4.4
1991	18.3	18.3	4.8
1995	16.8	16.8	3.1
1999	18.8	18.8	1.8

The number of constituencies on which the figures in Column 1 are based differ by periods: 1916-1919 (N=25), 1923-1927 (N=26), 1931-1942 (J) (N=27), 1942 (O)- 1959 (J) (N=28), 1959 (O) - 1995 (N=8).

In column 2, individual constituencies are aggregated into the eight constituencies adopted in 1959 — thus making the figures for the whole period comparable.

In recent decades, Icelandic regional policy has been very expensive, but largely unsuccessful, as migration from the periphery towards the center has continued (Kristinsson et al., 1992). Patronage has been a major characteristic of Icelandic politics and much stronger than in most other countries in northern Europe (Kristinsson, 1996). The parties seem less ideologically concerned than parties in Scandinavia and have some characteristics of cadre parties (Kristinsson, 1991; Hardarson, 1995). Weight of votes is clearly correlated to public expenditure per capita in individual constituencies (Kristinsson, 1999).[58] There seems little doubt that malapportionment — despite the withering away of disproportionality — has had important consequences in Icelandic politics.

6. Conclusions

The origins of the Icelandic electoral system in 1844 can be traced to Denmark. Already in the first sessions of the consultative Althingi, it became clear that Icelandic politicians did not regard equality of votes important. Instead, they strongly emphasized the right of the counties for a separate representation, as suggestions from the Danish authorities on increased equality of votes were rejected. This emphasis led both to great disproportionality between parties in the 20th century — not eliminated until 1987 — and enormous malapportionment — which has remained to this day.

Apart from the Althingi's decision to introduce absolute majority instead of simple majority when the franchise was widely extended in 1857, extension of the suffrage was not related to other changes in the electoral system. Suffrage reforms were generally not debated in party political terms.

Disproportionality and malapportionment continued, not because reforms were not suggested. The Althingi debates show that at least some MPs were quite familiar with various types of electoral systems and understood their consequences. PR was discussed already in the 1870s. In 1907, a government bill introducing PR with almost perfect equality of votes between constituencies was rejected. Proposals to introduce a system of single-member constituencies with more equal weighting of votes were also rejected. The political will for reforms was simply lacking among the majority in the Althingi. Perceived interests of the periphery and party political self-interest prevailed.

58. The correlation also holds when controlling for several other variables (e.g. population size).

However, disproportionality was gradually reduced from the 1930s to the 1980s, in four major steps (Ice7 to Ice10). The introduction of a two-tier system with supplementary seats in 1934 was very important, as well as the continued lowering of the effective threshold — a result of increasing the number of MPs for Reykjavík. Changes at the lower tier were also of major importance. The introduction of PR in the two-member constituencies in 1942 and the transformation of the constituency system into multi-member constituencies with PR in 1959 greatly reduced disproportionality. The latter change was actually the largest step, reducing the Gallagher's Index by 56%. In 1987, the introduction of LR-Hare in the constituencies along with some increase in the number of supplementary seats also reduced disproportionality.

A major peculiarity of the Icelandic system is that disproportionality was eventually abolished without reducing malapportionment. In general, electoral reform did not move seats from the periphery to the center. Instead the number of seats in the center — and thus the total number of MPs — was increased. A much greater increase of seats would, however, have been necessary if equal weighting of votes was to be obtained. The periphery thus continued to be greatly over-represented in the Icelandic system — not in the form of an over-representation of the major party of the periphery, but in the form of over-representation of the periphery within the major parliamentary parties. As discussed in Section 5, this kind of malapportionment has probably had some very important consequences in Icelandic politics.

The electoral reforms of 1933-34, 1942 and 1959 were a result of bitter disputes and political deals among the parties. While party political self-interest was present in debates on electoral reforms right from the very beginning of political parties in Iceland, it became dominant in the 1920s. Most of the disproportionality in the Icelandic system was simply due to the over-representation of the second largest party, the Agrarian Progressives. Understandably, they fought hard against reforms — even though they were partners to the deal made in 1933, as no other option seemed possible.

Abolishing disproportionality was in the interest of all other parties. Why was it not done earlier? The major answer must be the ambivalent attitude of the Conservatives. While always stronger in the center, the party was still the main competitor of the Progressives in the periphery. Many Conservative MPs from the center wanted to eliminate malapportionment, but their rural colleagues did not share their view. Compromises, reducing disproportionality but maintaining malapportionment, were the solution. Besides, a first-past-the post system, giving the party a chance of absolute majority in the Althingi, has always been attractive to some Conservatives.

The reduction of disproportionality served the interests of the Social Democrats and the left-socialists, but they were not able to make any changes without the help of the Conservatives. The Social Democrats — always the most vocal proponents of equal weight of votes and PR — were also quite ready to put the disproportionality of the system to their own use when it suited them in their electoral alliance with the Progressives in 1956.

Gradually, the tolerance for disproportionality seems to have been decreasing. The Progressives were partners to the electoral reforms of 1982-87, which mainly aimed at reducing their over-representation. The view that considerable disproportionality can be a normal feature of a PR system does not have many spokesmen any longer. Some interest in introducing first-past-the-post remains, however, but has not been seriously on the political agenda for a long time.

The tolerance for malapportionment has, on the other hand, survived. Arguments emphasizing the necessity of an over-representation of the periphery are still commonly heard in Icelandic politics. Nevertheless the major aim of the 1999 electoral reforms was to substantially reduce malapportionment — and a major step was indeed taken in that direction. But despite the reforms, voters in the periphery will elect 30 members of the Althingi in the 2003 election, instead of the 24 members they would obtain if the weighting of votes were equal. Malapportionment still gives the periphery six bonus members (out of a total of 63) in the beginning of the 21st century.

The electoral system did not create the party system that has dominated Icelandic politics since the 1930s. The four major parties, based on ideology and social cleavages, were founded in 1916-30 under electoral systems in which majority vote was the main rule, and three of them obtained representation in the Althingi.

The electoral system was, however, a very important factor during the formation period of the parties and has greatly influenced their fortunes. The majoritarian features of the system may have contributed to the formation of a united and strong Conservative party in the 1920s. The great under-representation of the Social Democrats early on may partly explain why they never managed to become a large party like their counterparts in Scandinavia. The great over-representation of the Agrarian Progressives helped them maintain their status as one of the two major parties.

The introduction of the two-tier system in 1934 greatly improved the lot of the Social Democrats and opened the way for Communist representation in the Althingi. Consequently, the average number of effective parliamentary parties in 1934-42 (Ice7) was 38% higher than in 1923-33 (Ice6). In 1942, the party system "froze" — and ever since, the strength relations of the four major parties have been remarkably stable. Increasing of proportionality and lowering of the effective threshold may have contributed to the continued presence of one or two "extra" parties in the Althingi since the 1970s. The major reasons for their presence however are likely to be other political factors. In any case, the increase in the effective number of parliamentary parties in the last decades must be regarded as quite modest.

The electoral system has played a large role in Iceland, indicating an unusual strength of the periphery in national politics. It is worth remembering that radical reforms of introducing PR in multi-member constituencies were defeated by only one vote in 1907. A different result on that occasion would almost certainly have greatly altered the subsequent political development in Iceland.

Appendix

Table A1. Votes and MPs 1916-1999

	Conservatives			Progressives (Agrarian)			Social Democrats			Communists/ left-socialists			Others		
	Votes	MPs		Votes	MPs		Votes	MPs		Votes	MPs		Votes	MPs	
	%	%	N	%	%	N	%	%	N	%	%	N	%	%	N
1916	-	-	-	12.9	17.6	6	6.8	2.9	1	-	-	-	80.3	79.4	27
1919	-	-	-	22.2	29.4	10	6.8	0	0	-	-	-	71.0	70.6	24
1923	53.6	58.3	21	26.6	36.1	13	16.2	2.8	1	-	-	-	3.7	2.8	1
1927	42.5	36.1	13	29.8	47.2	17	19.1	11.1	4	-	-	-	8.6	5.6	2
1931	43.8	33.3	12	35.9	58.3	21	16.1	8.3	3	3.0	0	0	1.1	0	0
1933	48.0	47.2	17	23.9	38.9	14	19.2	11.1	4	7.5	0	0	1.4	2.8	1
1934	42.3	40.8	20	21.9	30.6	15	21.7	20.4	10	6.0	0	0	8.1	8.2	4
1937	41.3	34.7	17	24.9	38.8	19	19.0	16.3	8	8.4	6.1	3	6.4	4.1	2
1942 J	39.5	34.7	17	27.6	40.8	20	15.5	12.2	6	16.2	12.2	6	1.2	0	0
1942 O	38.6	38.5	20	26.6	28.9	15	14.2	13.5	7	18.5	19.2	10	2.2	0	0
1946	39.5	38.5	20	23.1	25.0	13	17.8	17.3	9	19.5	19.2	10	0.1	0	0
1949	39.5	36.5	19	24.5	32.7	17	16.5	13.5	7	19.5	17.3	9	-	-	-
1953	37.1	40.4	21	21.9	30.8	16	15.6	11.5	6	16.1	13.5	7	9.3	3.8	2
1956	42.4	36.5	19	15.6	32.7	17	18.3	15.4	8	19.2	15.4	8	4.5	0	0
1959 J	42.5	38.5	20	27.2	36.5	19	12.5	11.5	6	15.3	13.5	7	2.5	0	0
1959 O	39.7	40.0	24	25.7	28.3	17	15.2	15.0	9	16.0	16.7	10	3.4	0	0
1963	41.4	40.0	24	28.2	31.7	19	14.2	13.3	8	16.0	15.0	9	0.2	0	0
1967	37.5	38.3	23	28.1	30.0	18	15.7	15.0	9	17.6	16.7	10	1.1	0	0
1971	36.2	36.7	22	25.3	28.3	17	10.5	10.0	6	17.1	16.7	10	10.9	8.3	5
1974	42.7	41.7	25	24.9	28.3	17	9.1	8.3	5	18.3	18.3	11	5.0	3.3	2
1978	32.7	33.3	20	16.9	20.0	12	22.0	23.3	14	22.9	23.3	14	5.5	0	0
1979	35.4	35.0	21	24.9	28.3	17	17.4	16.7	10	19.7	18.3	11	2.5	1.7	1
1983	38.7	38.3	23	19.1	23.3	14	11.7	10.0	6	17.3	16.7	10	13.3	11.7	7
1987	27.2	28.6	18	18.9	20.6	13	15.2	15.9	10	13.4	12.7	8	25.3	22.2	14
1991	38.6	41.3	26	18.9	20.6	13	15.5	15.9	10	14.4	14.3	9	12.6	7.9	5
1995	37.1	39.7	25	23.3	23.8	15	11.4	11.1	7	14.3	14.3	9	13.9	11.1	7
1999	40.7	41.3	26	18.4	19.1	12	26.8	27.0	17	9.1	9.5	6	5.0	3.2	2

Conservatives: Citizen's Party (1923), Conservative Party (1927), Independence Party (1931-99).
Progressives: Independent Farmers and Farmers' Party (1916), Progressive Party (1919-99, including Progressive independents in 1919).
Social Democrats: Social Democratic Party (1916-95), The Alliance of Social Democrats, People's Movement, People's Alliance and Women's Alliance (1999).
Communists/left-socialists: Communist Party (1931-37), United Socialist Party (1942-53), People's Alliance (1956-95), Left-Greens (1999).
[See note on following page.]

Note to *Table A1. Votes and MPs 1916-1999*

Percentage of votes and number of seats for other parties obtaining an MP or receiving at least 2% of the national vote:

1916: Home Rule Party 40.0 (12), Independence Party — across 15.7 (7), Independence Party — along 7.0 (3), Independence Party 7.6 (3), independent candidates (obtaining seats) 4.1 (2).
1919: Home Rule Party 45.8 (13), Independence Party 25.3 (11).
1923: An independent candidate 1.3 (1).
1927: Liberal Party 5.8 (1), an independent candidate 0.8 (1)
1933: An independent candidate 1.0 (1).
1934: Farmers' Party 6.4 (3), an independent candidate 0.9 (1).
1937: Farmers' Party 6.1 (2).
1942O: Commonwealth Party 2.2 (0).
1953: National Preservation Party 6.0 (2), Republican Party 3.3 (0).
1956: National Preservation Party 4.5 (0).
1959J: National Preservation Party 2.5 (0).
1959O: National Preservation Party 3.4 (0).
1971: Union of Liberals and Leftists 8.9 (5), Candidature Party 2.0 (0).
1974: Union of Liberals and Leftists 4.6 (2).
1978: Union of Liberals and Leftists 3.3 (0).
1979: An independent conservative 1.2 (1).
1983: Social Democratic Alliance 7.3 (4), Women's Alliance 5.5 (3).
1987: Citizen's Party 10.9 (7), Women's Alliance 10.1 (6), Union for Regional Equality 1.2 (1).
1991: Women's Alliance 8.3 (5).
1995: People's Movement 7.2 (4), Women's Alliance 4.9 (3).
1999: Liberal Party 4.2 (2).

Table A2. Population by industry 1845-1990. Percentages

	1845	1880	1901	1920	1930	1950	1970	1990
Agriculture	84.5	77.0	59.9	39.1	36.4	25.7	12.4	4.9
Fishing, fish processing	6.5	12.2	17.4	18.3	20.4	16.0	14.4	11.8
Manufacturing, construction	1.2	2.3	5.7	11.0	12.4	24.4	26.6	23.2
Services	7.2	6.8	13.9	30.6	30.5	33.3	45.2	54.9
Other industries	0.7	1.7	3.2	0.8	0.3	0.6	1.4	4.9
Total	**100**	**100**	**100**	**100**	**100**	**100**	**100**	**100**

Source: Jónsson and Magnússon, 1997: 217 (Table 3.8).

Table A3. Population changes 1890-2000, in Percentages

	1890	1901	1910	1920	1930	1940	1950	1960	1970	1980	1990	2000
Inhabitants in Reykjavík and the surrounding Reykjanes	14	15	21	26	34	39	49	56	59	59	63	68
Inhabitants in towns (pop. 200+)	12	21	34	44	57	65	76	81	85	88	91	92
Inhabitants in Reykjavík and the surrounding Reykjanes living in towns	46	63	78	85	91	95	96	98	99	100	100	100

Source: Jónsson and Magnússon, 1997: 120 (Table 2.9), 123 (Table 2.10). Iceland in figures, 2002:6.

ELECTORAL SYSTEMS IN NORWAY[1]

BY
BERNT AARDAL
INSTITUTE FOR SOCIAL RESEARCH, OSLO
AND DEPARTMENT OF POLITICAL SCIENCE,
UNIVERSITY OF OSLO, NORWAY

1. INTRODUCTION

The year 1814 stands out as a dramatic turning point in Norwegian history, signifying if not the birth then at least the conception of the modern state.

After being ruled from Denmark for more than 400 years, Norway was ceded to Sweden as a result of Denmark's alliance with the losing side in the Napoleonic wars. In the wake of the dissolution of the Danish-Norwegian union, the Norwegian elite seized the opportunity to call a Constitutional Assembly before the Swedish authorities were able to intervene (Steen, 1964). Thus, the Norwegians were able to establish a semi-independent state, although the further nation-building process took place within the realm of a personal union with Sweden until 1905.[2] Then, the Norwegian Parliament *(Storting)* in a peaceful coup d'état declared Norway independent of Sweden. In August 1905, a national referendum concurred in the decision with an overwhelming majority. Another referendum, in November 1905, established Norway as a constitutional monarchy.

An important part of the 1814 Constitution was the formulation of specific rules regarding elections to a new national assembly.[3] The origin of the

1. Professor Aanund Hylland at the University of Oslo deserves special thanks for valuable and instructive comments and recommendations.

2. Norway and Sweden shared the same (Swedish) king and Foreign Service.

Norwegian electoral system can, in other words, be traced back to the very beginning of the modern state. Moreover, the inclusion of electoral rules into the Constitution has been a characteristic feature of the Norwegian electoral system ever since. As a consequence, electoral reform has often been a cumbersome process contingent upon broad-based consensus among legislators.

Although the history of electoral systems in Norway has been one of successive changes and adaptations, we may distinguish five different eras, each representing a different arrangement of electoral procedures and rules. The system introduced in 1814 was based on indirect elections. The voters elected members of Electoral Colleges — one in each district — which in turn formally elected Members of Parliament. Indirect elections lasted until 1905, covering a total of 31 elections. When direct elections finally were introduced, a plurality/runoff procedure was implemented. This system, however, was used in only 5 elections. In 1920 plurality was replaced by PR, using the d'Hondt formula for transforming votes into seats. This formula was used in 8 national elections. In 1952 it was replaced by the modified Sainte-Laguë formula. At the same time district boundaries were redrawn. The last major reform took place in 1988, when adjustment (compensatory) seats were introduced. Table 1 summarizes the most important aspects of the particular election systems and the election periods covered.[4]

Table 1: Electoral Systems in Norway since 1814

Electoral system	NOR-I	NOR-II	NOR-III	NOR-IV	NOR-V
# Elections included	1815-1903 (31 elections)	1906-1918 (5 elections)	1921-1949 (8 elections)	1953-1985 (9 elections)	1989- (3 elections)
Electoral formula at lower level	Indirect, plurality	Majority, runoff	PR d'Hondt	PR Modified St. Laguë	Modified St. Laguë
District magnitude	2.6	1	5.2	7.8	8.7
Electoral formula at higher level	NA	NA	NA	NA	PR Modified St. Laguë

3. Local self-government and local elections, however, was not introduced until 1837.

4. The move from varying to a fixed number of representatives in 1859 may also be considered an important system change, although not included in my classification of electoral systems.

Table 1: (Continued) Electoral Systems in Norway since 1814

Number of compensatory seats	NA	NA	NA	NA	8
Compensatory seats in per cent	NA	NA	NA	NA	5
Allocation of seats in multi-member constituencies final?	NA	NA	NA	NA	Yes
Legal thresholds	NA	NA	NA	NA	4% of valid national vote for compen-satory seats
Average assembly size	103.6	123.6	150	152.4	165

Before we present the various election systems that have been used — and the reasons why they came into being — we need to give a brief presentation of the principal agents in any discussion of electoral reform — namely the political parties.

2. Party System and Cleavage Structure

The history of electoral systems in Norway spans a period of almost 200 years. Needless to say, the social and political fabric of Norwegian society has undergone major transformations in this period. The first formal parties were established in 1884. Since then a number of parties have entered the arena, and faded into the background, while new parties have taken on more prominent positions.

The Rokkan/Valen Cleavage Model

Space does not allow us to go into detail about the historical processes involved. Nevertheless, the well-defined cleavage model developed by Stein Rokkan and Henry Valen sums up the major political conflicts in Norwegian history (Rokkan & Valen, 1962; 1964; Rokkan 1967; Valen & Rokkan, 1974).[5] The model basically consists of five conflict dimensions or cleavages:

A territorial conflict, between the capital (*center*) and provinces (*periphery*).

A sociocultural conflict, between a Europe-oriented urban elite and a more nationally-oriented rural population. The opposition between defenders of the Danish-influenced urban language and the dialect-based "new Norwegian" epitomizes the underlying sociocultural conflict.

A religious conflict, between the orthodox lay movement and the more secular urban population. This conflict also involved the struggle for control of the Lutheran State Church.

An economic conflict in the *commodity market*, between producers and consumers of produce from the primary sector, mainly agriculture.

An economic conflict in the *labor market*, between employers and employees. This is the classical conflict between capitalists and wage earners.

The numbering of the cleavages indicates a historical sequence, where new cleavages did not necessarily replace the old, but rather supplemented them in a crosscutting pattern. Even more important is the close link between the structuring of political cleavages on one hand and the development of the party system on the other.

The territorial cleavage made its impact when the first electoral system was formed in 1814. The distinction between urban and rural districts (see the discussion of the "peasant clause" later in this chapter) is directly related to this conflict. Furthermore, the persistence of the territorial conflict is demonstrated in the strong support for maintaining the over-representation of peripheral areas even today. The sociocultural differences between the urban and the rural population were decisive when the opposition challenged the entrenched elite in the 1870s and 1880s. When the parties eventually were officially established in 1884, the Left (or Liberal) party represented the rural periphery with strong attachments to the "new Norwegian" language phalanx, while the Right (or Conservative) party defended the interests of the urban elite.[6] The religious conflict surfaced in the late 1880s, and found its first political expression when the Left Party was split in 1888. The Moderate Left Party (*Moderate Venstre*), the

5. Interestingly, analyses of Norwegian politics formed the initial basis for the more general model presented by Lipset and Rokkan in their seminal book *Party Systems and Voter Alignments* (Lipset & Rokkan, 1967).

6. In order not to confuse the reader I will be using the literal translations "Left" and "Right" throughout this chapter, instead of "Liberal" and "Conservative" which are used in more contemporary translations.

result of this split, usually is seen as an early predecessor of the Christian People's party. The attempts by various pressure groups (e.g. the so-called "Church Party") to influence the election process in the runoff elections between 1906 and 1919 underscores the importance of the religious cleavage. Industrialization came relatively late in Norway and the industrial proletariat was small and did not expand until after the turn of the century.[7] In the first decades of the 20th century, however, the conflict in the labor market not only polarized the political debate, but steadily increased the support of the Labor party as well.[8] In the last part of this period, the conflict in the commodity market became manifest as can be demonstrated in the electoral success of the Farmers' Association in the 1918 election and subsequently the establishment of the Agrarian Party in 1920. The emergence of several new parties was closely linked to rapid changes in the economic and social structure of Norwegian society. The rise of the Labor party, for instance, was contingent upon the increasing industrial working-class situated in urban centers, although its first electoral success took place in the rural fisheries districts of Northern Norway.[9]

In terms of voter alignments, the party system had found its form around 1920, *before* the introduction of PR and before the new electoral system had been able to make its impact. Moreover, the balance between cleavage structure and party system would turn out to be remarkably stable over time. Even though the party system has changed, the parties established around 1920 still are important players in terms of popular support and parliamentary presence (see Table A1). All in all, Rokkan and Lipset's statement that "*the party system of the 1960s reflects, with few but significant exceptions, the cleavage structure of the 1920s*" was particularly appropriate for Norway (Rokkan & Lipset, 1967: 50). (Tables 2a and 2b present a condensed summary of the major parties and government coalitions in Norwegian politics from the late 1880s up until today).

7. As table A2 shows, the secondary sector (industry, manufacturing) employed only about 25 per cent of the economically active population around 1900.

8. In the elections between 1900 and 1918, Labor increased its electoral support from 5.2 per cent to 31.6 per cent.

9. See Table A2 regarding the relative size of economic sectors over time, and Table A3 for the increasing urbanization..

Table 2a. Parties represented in the Storting 1882-1997

Party Name	Elections contested	Number of elections
Liberals (Venstre, the Left)	1882ff	33
Conservatives (Høyre, the Right)	1882ff	33
Moderate Left (Moderate Venstre)	1888-1903	6
Labor party (Det norske Arbeiderparti, DNA)	1894ff	29
Worker Democrats (Arbeiderdemokratene), from 1921 Radical People's	1906-36	11
Liberal Left (Frisinnede Venstre)	1909-36	10
Farmers' Association (Landmandsforbundet), from 1920 the Farmers' Party	1915ff	22
Communist Party (Norges Kommunistiske Parti, NKP)	1924ff	18
Christian People's Party (Kristelig Folkeparti, KrF)	1933ff	16
The Society Party (Samfunnspartiet)	1933-49	4
Socialist People's Party (Sosialistisk Folkeparti), since 1975 Socialist Left	1961ff	10
Anders Lange's Party (Anders Langes parti), renamed to Progress Party	1973ff	7
New People's Party (Det Nye Folkepartiet), renamed Liberal People's Party	1973-1985	4
Future for Finnmark (Aune-lista, Framtid for Finnmark)	1989	1
Coast Party (Kystpartiet, Tverrpolitisk folkevalgte)	1997	1
Red Electoral Alliance (Rød Valgallianse)	1973	7

Table 2b: Governing Parties in Norway 1884-1997

Governing period	Party (-ies)
1884-1889	Left
1889-1891	Right
1891-1893	Left
1893-1895	Right
1895-1898	Right + Moderate Left + independent left
1898-1903	Left
1903-1905	"Unification party" (Right + Moderate Left + liberals)
1905-1907	Left +Right + Moderate Left + Liberals
1907-1908	Independents + Left
1908-1910	Left
1910-1913	Liberal Left + Right
1913-1920	Left

Table 2b: (Continued) Governing Parties in Norway 1884-1997

1920-1921	Right + Liberal Left
1921-1923	Left
1923-1923	Right + Liberal Left
1923-1924	Liberal Left + Right
1924-1926	Left
1926-1928	Right + Liberal Left
1928-1928	Labor
1928-1931	Left
1931-1933	Farmers' Party
1933-1935	Left
1935-1945	Labor
1945-1945	Unification government (interim)
1945-1963	Labor
1963-1963	Right + Left + Center + Christian
1963-1965	Labor
1965-1971	Right + Left + Center + Christian
1971-1972	Labor
1972-1973	Christian+ Center + Left
1973-1981	Labor
1981-1983	Right
1983-1986	Right + Left + Christian + Center
1986-1989	Labor
1989-1990	Right + Christian + Center
1990-1997	Labor
1997-	Left + Christian + Center

Notes: The Left and the Right were not formally established as parties until 1884, but ran as *de facto* in 1882. The Conservatives were known as the Unification party (Samlingspartiet) between 1903-1913.

3. Suffrage Extensions

The cleavage structure and the party system provide an important background for the analysis of changes in electoral systems. This also applies to expansions of the suffrage, being a basic precondition for democratic electoral politics.

Liberal franchise rules in 1814

According to the 1814 Constitution, franchise was given to three different groups: 1) civil servants, 2) peasants who owned their own land, or who had rented registered land for at least five years, and 3) urban residents who owned property valued above a certain limit. The franchise was furthermore restricted to adult males who were at least 25 years old and who had lived in Norway for a minimum of 5 years. An estimated 45% of the adult male population qualified (Kuhnle, 1972). This amounts to between 10-11% of the overall population (Rokkan, 1967: 379); but far from all qualified voters made use of their rights. Only 6.7% of the population actually registered to vote at the 1815 election (Kuhnle, 1972: 388).[10] Nevertheless, no other Western European nation seems to have reached such a high level of enfranchised voters this early, and Norway even managed to stay on at that level (Rokkan, 1967: 379; Kuhnle, 1972: 389).[11] Norway was the first of the Nordic countries to introduce a wide suffrage (Rokkan, 1967: 379). The liberal franchise rules in 1814 were a result of an alliance between peasant groups and urban elites, and represented in many ways a continuation of old traditions with respect to equal representation.[12] Some conservative safeguards were, however, included in the Constitution. It was, for instance, mandatory for qualified voters to register before being allowed to vote.[13] The registration procedure demanded that the voter pledged allegiance to the Constitution, and that his name was written into the official list of registered voters. The distinction between "qualified" and "registered" voters was not removed until 1898 (Danielsen, 1964: 65). Figure 1 depicts the number of eligible (registered) voters as a percentage of the total population from 1815 until 1997.

10. Data on eligible voters, or rather qualified voters who had registered, from the period 1815-1826 is based on estimations (Utheim, 1895; Kaartvedt, 1964: 13). Because the number of electors (members of the Electoral Colleges) was directly linked to the number of eligible voters, it is fairly straightforward to estimate the number of voters in each constituency.

11. In England about 20 per cent of adult men were enfranchised in 1833. In Denmark about 3 per cent of the population was enfranchised in 1834, while in Sweden the comparable figure was 5 per cent in 1866 (cf. Kuhnle, 1972: 388).

12. It should be noted that the basis for representation at the Constitutional Assembly itself was even more widespread (democratic) than the rules regulating the franchise after 1814.

13. J. Utheim (1895: 5) emphasizes the need to pledge alliance to the Constitution in addition to the formal qualifications in order to be included in the public record of eligible voters.

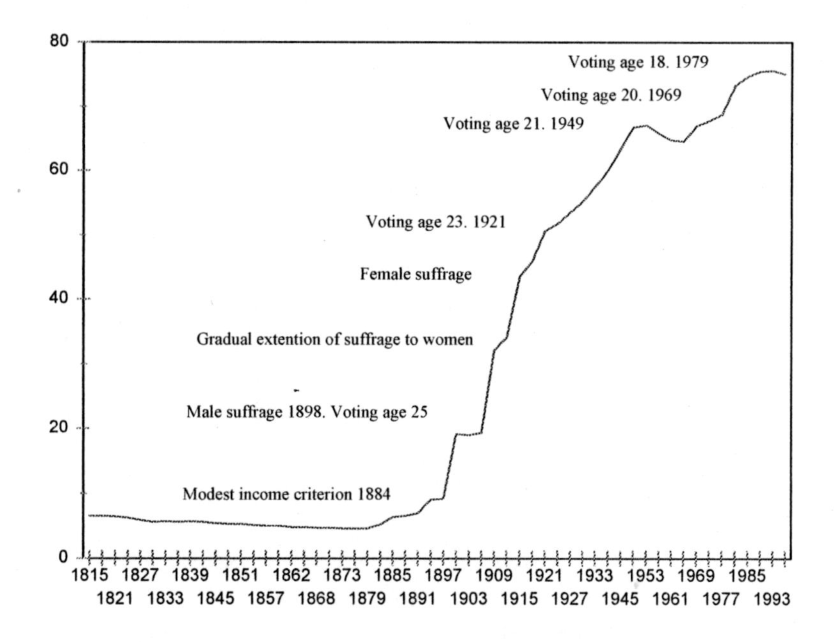

Figure 1. Eligible voters as a percentage of total population Norway 1815-1997

At the time, the 1814 Constitution was recognized as one of the most democratic constitutions in the world. Although it did not give voting rights to all citizens, it did give them to a major proportion of adult males. More important, the most numerous class of Norwegian society — the peasants — was also the dominant group among the enfranchised voters. Consequently, the potential for radical change of the political structure was embedded in the Constitution itself. The most "deviant" part of the Norwegian franchise compared with other European nations was the voting rights given to peasants. The Norwegian peasants have traditionally been very independent and not subservient to land-owning masters. Hence, as the largest social group, the enfranchised peasants represented a potential "time bomb" against the *ancien regime*. The peasants, however, used the new political rights only to a limited extent to promote their own interest in the first decades after 1814 (Valen, 1981: 34). Instead, the peasants voted for their "superiors." The first wave of rural protest came in 1832, but the rural population was not fully mobilized until the end of the 19th century (Rokkan, 1967: 370; 379-389).

As demonstrated in Figure 1, the suffrage remained at about the same level for most of the 19th century, although with a downward trend towards the late 1870s due to increasing urbanization (Rokkan, 1967: 380). From around 1870, however, the extension of suffrage became a hot topic not the least within the leftist opposition. Being a socially heterogeneous group, the left alliance was far from united with respect to the question of extending the suffrage to new groups. Several proposals were put forward, but none won the support of the two-third majority needed to change the Constitution. In the mid-1870s, some "Leftists" that previously had supported suffrage extensions became more skeptical as newly enfranchised groups, in particular the working class, became more radical and militant. In the early 1880s, however, they supported further extension of the suffrage as a means of increasing the potential for more Left voters in urban areas (Seip, 1981: 187-190). Eventually a reform was implemented in 1884, giving voting right to citizens above a certain income level. As the income criterion was quite modest, it resulted in a sudden increase in the number of eligible voters, in particular among the urban working class (Rokkan, 1967: 383). Secret voting was also implemented in 1884, something which necessitated a change from oral voting to written ballots, although this change had been in the making for some time (Danielsen, 1964: 57).[14] Moreover, increasing economic growth and prosperity contributed to increasing the size of the electorate. Elected representatives were also given a more prominent role in the local electoral boards overseeing the elections. Both the increase of the electorate and the democratization of election administration paved the way for wider participation (Danielsen, 1964: 61).

The sudden influx of voters from the lower classes made the peasants fear that they might lose their political influence (and majority). This obviously contributed to a more positive attitude vis-à-vis reforms of the electoral system. Manhood suffrage (for those 25 years old or more) was implemented in 1898, and this of course increased the potential threat of new challengers — not the least represented by the Labor Party. But, the extension of the suffrage in this period was linked to the main political conflict — the question of national independence from the union with Sweden, and not to the class struggle. Interestingly, manhood suffrage was introduced *before* the proletariat was fully mobilized. As noted earlier, the liberal franchise rules of 1814 were based on an

14. The use of written ballots was also connected to the increased writing skills among the lower classes. Furthermore, fewer voters now signed their ballots.

alliance between peasants and urban middle class groups. This was also the basis for further extensions of the suffrage in the 1800s. Thus, Rueschemeyer et al.'s argument that the working class movement played a decisive role in the extensions of the suffrage only holds for the last part of the 19th century (Rueschemeyer et al., 1992: 91). In the late 1880s, however, the working class movement contributed to what may be called "the final push for suffrage."

The introduction of manhood suffrage in 1898 more than tripled the number of eligible voters (cf. Figure 1) and the suffrage qualifications did not exclude all women, either. Females owning property and with a certain income from 1907 on qualified for the vote, and an increasing number of women reached this stage. The first female Member of Parliament, for instance, was elected as an alternate in 1909 and won her own seat in the Storting in 1911. As demonstrated in Figure 1, the extension of the suffrage continuously expanded the pool of voters until 1913, when universal suffrage finally was implemented.[15] The number of eligible voters has increased considerably even after the introduction of universal suffrage. This has to do with the fact that universal suffrage normally means giving voting rights to citizens above a certain age. The increase after 1913 can be explained by changes in this threshold. In 1921, the voting age was reduced from 25 to 23, in 1949 it was reduced from 23 to 21, in 1969 it was reduced from 21 to 20, and finally it was reduced from 20 to 18 years of age in 1979.[16] In the last elections, the proportion of eligible voters has stabilized around 75% of the overall population. The average turnout since 1945 in national elections is around 80%.

4. Electoral System Eras

In the next paragraphs, we will analyze the five electoral systems in detail. First, we start with the period starting just after the Constitutional Assembly in 1814.

1814-1905: Indirect, plurality elections

The first elections in Norway were held as indirect, plurality elections in single- and multimember districts. Urban and rural areas were organized in

15. Universal suffrage at local elections was implemented in 1910.

16. In the 1970s the definition was changed from reaching the specified age at the date of the election to reaching that age in the election *year*.

separate electoral districts. The number of MPs elected by the cities varied, with a maximum of 5, compared to maximum of 4 in the rural districts (Utheim, 1895: 166-169; Mjeldheim, 1984: 290-292). The average district magnitude for the whole period was 2.6 (see Table 1). The voters did not vote directly for Parliament (*Storting*) candidates, but rather for members of Electoral Colleges that later elected the actual representatives.[17] Formally organized political parties were unknown at the time of the Constitutional Assembly. The Electoral College was intended to make sure that the general will would prevail over narrow self-interest in the selection of candidates (Kristvik & Rokkan, 1966: 4).

Although the voting rights were quite democratic, the electoral rules to a large extent modified the influence given to the enfranchised peasants. In particular, the drawing of constituency boundaries and the distribution of representatives on constituencies were advantageous for the established elite. The division of electoral districts in *amt* (province) and *kjøpstad* (city) was based on existing administrative units, but at the same time it secured socially homogenous districts. This, in turn, secured representation from the two most important social classes: peasants and the urban middle class (Kristvik, 1953: 3). The number of *electors* (members of the Electoral College) was directly linked to the number of enfranchised voters within the boundaries of each electoral district. The cities had one elector per 50 voters, compared with one elector per 100 voters in the rural areas. The electors in urban districts then selected ¼ of their own number to be *Storting* representatives, while the rural electors only selected 1/10 of their number as representatives. This clearly favored the urban districts, and an additional clause stated that if the number of representatives from the cities was more — or less — than one third of all representatives, the number of urban versus rural representatives should be fixed at a 1:2 ratio.[18] Considering the fact that the rural areas dominated over the cities both in terms of population and number of enfranchised voters with a ratio of about 10:1, this setup gave a relative advantage to the urban elite. According to Kristvik (1953: 5), the main motive behind the meticulous allocation of members to the Electoral Colleges and subsequent designation of representatives elected to the *Storting*

17. This was also the system employed when the Constitutional Assembly was called in 1814. The indirect method was modeled after the French Constitution of 1791 (Stortingsproposisjon nr. 76 (1903-1904): page 11). Some representatives were actually directly elected in 1814, but the vast majority was indirectly elected.

18. The number of members of the electoral colleges and of the *Storting* was in other words flexible (until 1859). Even at the Constitutional Assembly in 1814 the number of urban versus rural representatives reflected the 1: 2 ratio.

was to secure the interest of urban residents against "unfortunate" consequences of the enfranchisement of the rural population. Thus, the Constitutional Assembly combined more democratic franchise rules with compensatory measures from the entrenched elites.[19]

The "Peasant Clause"

As the number of cities as well as the urban population increased, the balance between urban and rural representatives came under pressure. In order to maintain the ratio between urban and rural representatives, the total number of representatives might exceed the maximum limit of 100. This called for changes in the electoral rules. Actually, the distribution of seats and constituency boundaries was a recurring theme, and adjustments were implemented in 1816, 1830 and 1842.[20] In 1859, the peasant representatives in the *Storting* considered abolishing the 1:2 ratio, as the cities were still heavily over-represented. Eventually, they decided to keep the clause — even making it more precise and binding — as it guaranteed rural areas a sizable representation even if the population structure should change in favor of urban areas (Bergsgård, 1964: 148). The number of electoral districts, the district boundaries, and the number of representatives in each district were included in the Constitution, "*with particular attention paid to the ratio between urban and rural districts.*" It explicitly gave the peripheral districts a relatively larger number of representatives than the central areas. The 1:2 clause was not removed until 1952, an illustrative example of the inertia embedded in many electoral systems.

An Electoral System Under Pressure

Indirect elections made the representatives independent of the voters. The idea of Electoral Colleges was indeed to "*secure general interests and counter narrow group interests*" (Kristvik, 1953: 13). Michael Birkeland presented a more blunt view in 1869: "*Through direct elections the large masses' ignorance, prejudices and passions are given a direct expression. Through indirect elections... the election is more narrow, intelligence and level-headedness will prevail to a larger extent in the smaller electoral corporation*" (as quoted in Seip, 1974: 116-117). Birkeland conceded that indirect elections presupposed a "*certain political innocence, that seemingly is disappearing.*"

19. But, the elite did not succeed in institutionalizing other conservative safeguards, like a two-chamber system — into the Constitution (see Steen, 1964: 24-32).

20. Stortingsproposisjon nr. 76 1903-1904, Bilag 2: Historisk Oversigt.

However, the advent of organized political parties gradually undermined the idea of indirect elections. This, in particular, was caused by the linking of a rigorous plurality principle to the indirect method. Although political parties were not formally established until 1884[21], political affiliation gradually became the most important criterion for electing members to the Electoral Colleges (Mjeldheim, 1984: 291). Hence, party political differences reduced the legitimacy of the indirect system, while at the same time the electoral system contributed to increased political polarization. Due to the indirect system, a party could win all representatives in a constituency even if another party had won most of the votes (Kristvik, 1953: 13). In the 1894 election, for instance, the Left Party won a majority of the *Storting* seats from the urban constituencies with less than half of the votes. In the years 1882 to 1903, a minority party won a number of elections in different parts of the country. This was possible only in rural districts or in urban districts consisting of several smaller cities or towns.[22] Adding to the frustration of the "unfairness" of the electoral system was the fact that quite often it was the same party that reaped the benefits in consecutive elections. Because smaller urban areas were linked to larger cities in the same electoral district, some towns lost all influence with respect to electing *Storting* representatives. As a consequence, the electoral system was facing growing criticism and even voter boycotts![23]

The critique of the 1814 system can be summed up as follows (cf. Kristvik, 1953: 23):

1.) The biggest party won too big a proportion of the representatives compared to their strength among the voters.

2.) A minority of the voters in an electoral district could be represented in the *Storting*, while the majority in the same district was not.

3.) A relatively large number of voters were never represented in the *Storting*. Adding to this was the gradual decline of enfranchised voters, due to changes in the population structure. As the population increased, more and more

21. The first parties that were formally established was the Left (Venstre) party and the Right (Høire) party.

22. This was particularly the case in the cities in Finnmark, our northernmost region. In the elections of 1891, 1894 and 1897 the Conservative party won more electoral college members than the Liberal party, despite the fact that the Liberal party received more votes (see Kristvik, 1953: 21b).

23. In the town of Sandefjord, for instance, no voters showed up at the 1900 and 1903 elections, while 2 voters voted in Haugesund in 1888 — none in 1900 (Kristvik, 1953: 23).

people moved from the countryside to the cities, where they were not entitled to vote (Rokkan, 1967: 380).[24]

Partisan Dispute about Electoral Reform

The emergence of distinct political parties in the 1880s was closely linked to a growing polarization between the entrenched political elite, represented by the Swedish king and his Norwegian officials on the one hand, and an alliance between radical-democratic intellectuals in the cities and national-populist peasants on the other (Rokkan, 1967: 371-372). The Right party represented the ruling elite, while the Left Party voiced the concerns of the opposition. In the 1885 election the Left received 63% of the votes, compared to 37% for the Right. This raised serious concerns, particularly among leaders of the Right party. In the 1883-96 period several proposals were presented, suggesting alternative forms of proportional representation. But the idea of PR was heavily politicized: the Left Party opposed it, while the Right party endorsed it. In 1896, however, PR was implemented as optional in local elections.[25] One fifth of the eligible voters in a community could demand PR elections. Eventually, in 1919, PR became common for local elections (Opheim, 1997: 7).[26] This reform was, however, not particularly controversial. In most local communities (*communes*) a plurality system would give all the representatives to one party. Because most communes constituted one electoral district, the only way to accommodate disparate interests was to introduce a PR system. In addition, party alignment was less important at the local level (Kristvik, 1953: 37). The system used in local elections was the largest remainder with the Droop quota (Hagenbach-Bischoff's method). This method was presented as a simplified version of the d'Hondt method (Opheim, 1997: 6).[27] This method is still being used in local elections in Norway.

---

24. Even though the percentage of enfranchised voters decreased, it did not fall lower than 33 per cent (in 1865) (Rokkan, 1967: 380).

25. See Aars (1998) for an overview of the electoral systems used at local elections.

26. In some instances local elections may even today be held as majority elections if no lists are presented to the voters, or if only one list is presented or accepted.

27. Originally, in 1886, H. E. Berner (MP) proposed STV with Hare's quota. In 1896, A. Quam (MP) who found the Hare quota somewhat less desirable because of the "accidental" distribution of remaining seats revised the proposal. Quam favored d'Hondt's method "as it gave the most just distribution", but he proposed to use the Hagenbach-Bischoff's method instead. (see *Dokument nr.1, 1896: 7*). The algorithm based on Hagenbach-Bischoff's method was simpler to calculate, thus saving time and resources. This was, of course, a consideration caused by the technological limitations at the time.

The debate about using PR in national elections blended into the struggle between the opposition and the establishment. Eventually, Parliamentarism was introduced in 1884 after a rather dramatic confrontation ending in Court of Impeachment proceedings.[28] Parliamentarism to some extent presupposed the existence of separate political factions, as well as it encouraged further acceptance of a party system (Kristvik, 1953: 26). Interestingly, for the victorious Left Party the argument *against* a proportional electoral system was consistent with an argument in *favor* of Parliamentarism: i.e. the insistence upon majority rule. The Left Party also feared that PR could prevent the necessary majority needed for Constitutional reform. In addition, the Left explicitly argued against a system that would benefit the Right (Kristvik, 1953: 54). All in all, a PR system might erode the basis for the Left Party's governmental position (Solberg, 1964: 162). The Right party, on the other hand, needed institutional safeguards to protect themselves against the dominant Left Party.

Interestingly, a prominent conservative, T. A. Aschehoug, in 1874 proposed a two-chamber system, where the upper chamber should protect the right of the (conservative) minority even if government power slipped out of their hands. The upper chamber should have its own elections, with restricted suffrage (Nerbøvik, 1973: 84-85). The idea did not catch on, neither among competing factions in the conservative camp nor in the efforts to build alliances with conservative-minded peasants (Seip, 1981: 220-222). There is an interesting link between the two parties' views on electoral systems and the extension of the suffrage. The income criterion introduced in 1884 created a gradual expansion of the electorate in a period of economic growth (Rokkan, 1967: 384). The Right party feared that this would reduce its political influence within a system of plurality elections at the *national* level. The Left Party on the other hand argued in favor of PR in *local* elections using the same arguments. Hence, the two parties favored different systems at local and national elections — depending on which system benefited them the most. Bjørn Kristvik underscores the partisan perspective in his analysis of the election debates in the 1880s and 1890s by stating that: "*From 1885 and throughout most of the 90's the debate was characterized by a mutual suspicion and an absolute lack of will to accept any of the opponent's arguments. The Right would secure its position as a minority party by introducing proportional representation. As a countermove the Left demanded large extensions of the suffrage, so that they could secure their position as a majority party*" (Kristvik, 1953: 159).

28. Historians emphasize, however, that full support for parliamentarism only developed in the years after 1884 (Nerbøvik 1973: 104).

The End of Indirect Elections

The immediate breakdown of indirect elections was caused by the dramatic increase in the number of members elected to Electoral Colleges. This increase was in turn linked to the increase in the number of enfranchised voters. The ballot of each voter should contain as many names as the number of electors to be elected, plus alternates. In 1903, a record of 815 electors had to be elected from the capital area (Kristiania, Hønefoss & Kongsvinger). This represented a formidable burden both for voters and for those administering the election.[29] In addition, many who were qualified to vote did not bother to register. For minority groups, registration was of no use, as it would not give them any influence over the election outcome. There was also a growing democratic concern about putting voters under "guardianship" by not allowing them to vote directly for their own representatives (Aasland, 1965: 267; Valen, 1981: 35). Direct elections would, by contrast, "educate" the voters (Kristvik, 1953: 136).

Table 1 sums up the major characteristics of the various election systems used in Norway. The indirect system covers the longest time period of any particular system in Norway with a total of 31 parliamentary elections — spanning almost 90 years. The average assembly size for the whole period was 103.6 seats, which is lower than in any of the other electoral eras.

Majority Runoff Elections 1906-1918

In 1900, an Electoral Reform Commission started drafting a new electoral system, taking note of the concerns raised about the deficiencies of the indirect system. A constitutional amendment of May 15th, 1905, introduced direct elections in single-member constituencies. In 1906, additional laws concerning district boundaries and electoral procedures were introduced. There were 41 urban electoral districts and 82 rural districts, each electing one representative to the *Storting*. The ballots contained both the name of the representative to be elected and his alternate.[30] If no candidate reached absolute majority in the first ballot, a runoff election was needed. In the second ballot (runoff), the winner

29. This fact was acknowledged by the Government in its proposal to change the system: "universal suffrage has increased the number of eligible voters and thus also the number of electors to the extent that it is almost impossible for individual voters to be knowledgeable about the proposed electors, and the counting of votes takes a long time and causes great problems" (Stortingsproposisjon nr. 76, 1903-1904, Om grundlovsbestemmelse..)

only needed a plurality of the votes. The number of candidates in the second ballot was *not* limited to a fixed number of candidates. Even candidates who did not run in the first ballot could to run in the second! (Mjeldheim, 1955: 22; Helland and Saglie, 1997).[31] The idea of this system was to encourage cooperation and negotiations between the parties. The call for a majority of the votes in the first round was implemented in order to reduce the risk that a minority of the voters would win the election — as happened in the old system.[32]

The idea of having a relatively large number of electoral districts was partly that this would bring the representative closer to his constituency. It also made it possible to give representation to smaller towns, which previously had to be represented by a person from a nearby city. Because the parties already had different geographical bases, the new system would also lead to better proportionality among parties in the *Storting*. On the other hand the Electoral Reform Commission feared that single-member constituencies would lead to a skewed social representation. Hence, the boundaries between the constituencies were deliberately drawn in such a way as to include disparate social groups and economic sectors (Kristvik & Rokkan, 1966: 10).

To really understand the new electoral system of 1905-1906, one must take into consideration both the system it replaced, the political situation in which it emerged, and the political development after its initiation (Solberg, 1964: 161). The debate about the new system was influenced by a reaction against political parties as such. Around 1905, the political cleavages became more diffuse than they had been around the turn of the century (Kristvik & Rokkan, 1966: 10; Blom, 1974: 43; Nordby, 1983: 26ff). A strong drive among moderates and conservatives focused on a program of national unification — above and beyond political parties. Some even hoped that the new candidate-centered electoral system would make the parties less important and contribute to a fundamental

---

30. If the elected representative became ill, or died, the alternate automatically would succeed the representative, without a by-election. This was also the procedure used during indirect elections.

31. Mjeldheim refers to one candidate (Wollert Konow (SB)) who was defeated in the first round in one constituency (Voss), and who then ran as a second round candidate in another constituency (Midt-Hordaland), where he subsequently was elected. Helland and Saglie refers to another case in 1918 in the *Smålenene* constituency where the Right party in conjunction with the Liberal Left Party withdrew their own candidate from the first round and in the second run supported a candidate from the Farmers' Association that did not run in the first round.

32. Indst. S. XXXXIII, 1904-1905, page 16.

change in the party system itself (Solberg, 1964: 161). From the late 19th century until 1905 the major constituent cleavage between the Left and the Right was the dispute about the union with Sweden. Before the *Storting* election of 1906, leading politicians on both sides argued that future party alignments would not follow traditional patterns (cf. Nordby, 1983). Thus, the deliberate efforts of undermining the party system complicate the question of what effects the change of electoral system had on party alignments. We will return to this question later.

Despite a pronounced skepticism towards political parties in the elite circles, the old parties did not wither away. The voters obviously put more emphasis on issues and promotion of self-interests than evaluations of the personal qualities of candidates (Kristvik & Rokkan, 1966: 10). In addition, the established parties faced the challenge by reorganizing at the local level, thus revitalizing and consolidating their position in the local communities (Mjeldheim, 1978: 168). Nonetheless, the new system gave the pressure groups considerable influence. Usually they "negotiated" with the parties, in order to find out which candidate supported their group's views. If they were not satisfied with the candidates presented in the first round, they would "offer" their voters to the candidate most sympathetic to their cause in the second round. Or they could threaten the established parties that they would run in the second round, and thus take voters from an "unsympathetic" candidate (Furre, 1972: 45-46; Mjeldheim, 1978: 135-36).[33] The transition to single-member constituencies narrowed the competition to one candidate. At the same time the replacement of Electoral Colleges with runoff elections increased the opportunities of pressure groups to obtain influence by wheeling and dealing with the parties (Blom, 1974: 44). On the other hand, the political parties were not particularly well organized. Hence, they could reap benefits from cooperating with well-run groups like the Language, Teetotaler and Missionary organizations (Blom, 1974: 43; Mjeldheim, 1978: 195ff). Adding to this, the governments in the first part of this period had a very weak parliamentary basis (Blom, 1974: 44), making ample room for strategic maneuvering. Interestingly,

33. The most active of these pressure groups, cum "parties", were the Christian Lay Movement, the Teetotaler Movement, as well as groups representing both sides of the Language conflict.

the first round in many instances used a *primary* election (*prøvevalg*) where voters quite freely could display their candidate preferences (Aasland, 1965: 275; Mjeldheim, 1978: 135ff).

The Threat of the Labor Party

Although the Left lost its *Storting* majority in 1918, the party was still highly over-represented (Kristvik & Rokkan, 1966: 11; Furre, 1972: 163). Within the Labor party anti-democratic, or at least anti-parliamentary, forces were struggling for control over the party. The unfair election system certainly did not boost the faction that wanted to use democratic methods in their struggle for the rights of the working class. In this perspective it is important to recall that the suffrage had been extended *before* the final mobilization of the rural proletariat and the industrial workers. The radical-agrarian Left had defeated the old establishment, but was not willing to lower the thresholds of representation to meet the demands of the labor movement. On the contrary, the Left helped raise the threshold by introducing the two-ballot system in 1906. Stein Rokkan argues that "*there is little doubt that this contributed greatly to the radicalization and alienation of the Norwegian Labour party*" (Rokkan, 1970: 158). Within the Labor party the negative feelings towards the election system were intense (Valen, 1981: 36). In addition, the provision that voters that had received public assistance or were in bankruptcy proceedings temporarily lost their right to vote represented a stigma of poverty that had deep symbolic implications (Rokkan, 1967: 385).

The deadlock was a classical one: the upcoming Labor party was systematically discriminated against by the electoral laws, while the established party (parties) won more than the fair share of the seats. But, the system properties which were advantageous for the established parties in one setting could prove disastrous under new circumstances. An important impetus for change was actually embedded in the system itself. As a result of universal suffrage, the number of potential Labor voters had increased significantly. After a while Labor might be able to win almost all seats, leaving only a few to the nonsocialist parties! The ideological mobilization and radicalization of the working class added to the perceived threat against the established parties. Actually, the Norwegian Labor party was the only social-democratic party in Western Europe to join the Moscow-dominated Third Communist International (although only for a brief period in the 1920s). On this background it is easy to understand that the reforms of the electoral system was also seen as part of a "containment" strategy where the nonsocialist parties hoped to encourage the moderate factions within the radical Labor party and thus tip the balance in a less militant direction (see Danielsen, 1984: 57ff).[34]

The time was ripe for reform, if not revolution as in other parts of the world. In 1917, the *Storting* appointed a new commission, and instructed it to present proposals to reform the electoral system (see Greve, 1964: 5-7). The Commission conceded that "*the transition to some kind of proportional elections has become a political necessity*" (Kristvik & Rokkan, 1966: 12). The *Storting* election of 1918 divided the electorate in three equally sized groups: the conservative Right party (including *Frisinnede Venstre*), the Left Party (including the Labor-Democrats) and the Labor party. The two-party system (or rather 2+) was definitely a thing of the past (Furre, 1972: 163). In more general terms, the mobilization of the peasantry was the basis for the struggle between the two oldest parties, the Left and the Right. The decisive cleavages were territorial and cultural. The mobilization of the workers, on the other hand, caused by emerging economic cleavages, brought the Labor party into the forefront of national politics (cf. Rokkan, 1966: 76-77).

In sum, the majority runoff system was at work in a total of 5 national elections (see Table 1). The average assembly size increased from 103.6 in the previous system to a total of 123.6, while the district magnitude was reduced from 2.6 to 1.

Proportional Elections — the d'Hondt Method 1919-52

The call for PR systems was widespread in a number of countries after the turn of the century. Norway was no exception, but was representative of a broader trend (Lijphart, 1994: 54). Karl Braunias identified two distinct phases in the spread of proportional representation: first, the "minority protection" phase before World War I, and second, the "antisocialist" phase just after the war (as quoted in Rokkan, 1970: 157; see also Rokkan, 1968). It was no surprise that the move towards PR first came in some of the most heterogeneous European countries. "In linguistically and religiously divided societies majority elections could clearly threaten the continued existence of the political system. The introduction of some element of minority representation came to be seen as an essential step in a strategy of territorial consolidation" (Rokkan, 1970: 157). Later the demand for proportional systems was also heard in culturally more

34. For the Right party the reform was also viewed as an opportunity to revitalize the party organization (Danielsen, 1984: 58-59).

homogenous countries. Usually, the introduction of PR was a result of both pressures from below and above. This certainly was the case in Norway. From below, the growing working class represented by a radical and militant Labor party, wanted to lower the thresholds of representation. From above, the old parties wanted protection from the growing number of new voters made possible by universal suffrage (Rokkan, 1970: 157). Tensions between urban and rural areas, directly linked to political antagonisms between the Right and the Left, impeded a joint nonsocialist alliance against the rising Labor party, making amendments to the electoral system even more pertinent. As the Left and the Right parties were unwilling, or rather unable due to political differences, to merge into a broad national coalition, they preferred a proportional system (Valen & Rokkan, 1970: 325). For the dominant Left Party, the acceptance of a new electoral system was motivated "not (by) a sense of equalitarian justice but (by) the fear of rapid decline with further Labour advances across the majority threshold" (Rokkan, 1970: 158; see also Solberg, 1964: 162).

Increasing Proportionality

The 1917 Electoral Reform Commission presented its recommendations in April 1919. The majority of the Commission recommended a system of proportional representation with list elections in multimember constituencies (Greve, 1964: 5).

The ensuing *Storting* debate was fragmented and technically complex as the number of proposals and alternatives was very high (Greve, 1964: 6). A proposal to remove the "peasant clause" was rejected by a large majority, even though a majority in the Commission had proposed it. Furthermore, the choice between list election in multi-member versus single-member constituencies was controversial, as well as the drawing of district boundaries.

On November 29th, 1919, the *Storting* passed a new constitutional bill, introducing proportional representation in multimember constituencies. The final bill was passed on the 17th of December, 1920. The calculation of seats from votes was to be done according to the d'Hondt largest averages method.[35] At the time, this was a frequently used method in Europe (Rokkan, 1970: 158). As the method favors the largest party and does not lower the threshold very much in small constituencies electing few representatives and with few party lists, it

35. In addition, the voting age was reduced from 25 to 23 years.

certainly appealed to the established parties. The d'Hondt system was also familiar, as it had been used in local elections since 1896.

The new electoral system was not only opened up for the Labor party. It secured representation from minority groups as well. While the inclusion of the Labor party reduced the tensions in terms of class conflict, PR and systematic over-representation of some regions and rural areas secured the future of the old parties. In this respect introduction of PR was an essential element in a strategy of territorial consolidation (Rokkan, 1970: 157).

Adapting to the Political Circumstances

As the d'Hondt method presupposes clearly defined party lists, the new election laws also included provisions for procedures concerning the setup of such lists, registration of party names et cetera. However, the opportunity to influence the choice of candidates on the list was limited. Voters could delete names on a list, but this would only affect candidate selection if at least half of the party's voters made exactly the same change. The same system exists even today for parliamentary elections, making the opportunity for a personal vote limited, if not totally extinct.[36] However, new reforms recently have been proposed by the Government. If implemented, they will give voters a decisive influence on the selection of candidates even in national elections.

The introduction of PR was motivated by a need to adapt the electoral system to a changing environment. The political parties received a legal status that corresponded to their factual influence in politics. But, at the same time, the new system contributed to an intensification of the cleavages between the parties, thus influencing the party system as a whole (Kristvik & Rokkan, 1966: 22). Despite the fact that the d'Hondt formula resulted in a more proportional system, it gave a considerable bonus to larger parties at the expense of smaller parties. If the same party were advantaged in several constituencies, this would give it a major over-representation in seats. The 1917 Commission was aware of this phenomenon, and suggested that the parties could join forces in electoral cartels or apparentement (*listeforbund*). The voter casts his/her vote for the individual party list, but the allocation of seats is based on the total sum of votes cast for the participating parties. Then the seats are distributed proportionally

36. Local elections, however, are more open to voter preferences with respect to candidate selection. New reforms proposed by the Government in the spring of 2002, however, introduce personal vote in parliamentary elections as well.

to the individual parties (Lijphart, 1994: 134).[37] This proposal was, however, defeated in the *Storting* in 1920. But the proposal was reintroduced at a later stage, and it was passed by the nonsocialist parties in 1930. The electoral advances of the Labor party, in particular at the local elections of 1928, were seen as pre-warnings of a potential Labor majority victory in the 1930 election. The nonsocialist parties countered the threat by introducing apparentement (Furre, 1972: 211). The Labor party opposed apparentement, as they thought it would give the nonsocialist parties an unfair advantage at Labor's expense. Apparentement was used in the elections of 1930, 1933, 1936 and 1945.[38] The "combined" lists won a total of 24 seats, most of which were taken from the Labor party (Greve, 1964: 27-28). In 1949, Labor succeeded in getting rid of apparentement, although by a very narrow margin (the *Storting* president's deciding vote).[39] A proposal to replace the d'Hondt method with the largest remainder method was defeated with the same narrow margin (Greve, 1964: 29).

In general, the influence of political parties was strengthened after the transition to multimember constituencies. The Nomination Act of 1920 increased the parties' position vis-à-vis the voters.[40] The parties were given sole control over the nomination of *Storting* candidates. However, this control was placed in the hands of the provincial parties and not the central party elite (Valen, 1988).

Adjustment Seats — Not Yet

The new system was actually intended only for one election — in 1921 — and the idea was to change it in due time before the next election (Nissen, 1945:

37. In 1985, however, the procedure was somewhat different as the voters could reserve their vote to be valid only for the specific party list and not for the linked lists. This means that the cooperating parties receive a number of seats calculated *either* from their combined number of votes, *or* from the number of votes given to the individual parties — depending on which procedure that will give the parties the highest number of seats (see Overå & Dalbakk, 1987: 90-91). Even though it was possible to make a reservation in the 1930-45 period as well, all votes cast for a party in the *listeforbund* was automatically transferred to the allied parties — disregarding possible reservations (Valen, 1994: 319).

38. A total of 74 list alliances ran for election in the 1930-1945 period (Greve,1964: 27)

39. This was in the lower chamber (Odelstinget). In the upper chamber (Lagtinget), the vote was 20 against, and 18 for.

40. At the time Norway was one of the few countries where the authorities regulated the nomination procedure. The Nomination Law put down several requirements with respect to the nominations. The parties were, however, not obliged to follow the Nomination Law, although it was mandatory in order to receive financial support for nomination meetings. The Nomination Law and the Electoral Law was merged into one law in 1985.

17). Nobody was entirely satisfied, for instance, with the drawing of the district boundaries.[41] After 1930, the decreasing degree of proportionality and the increasing over-representation of the largest party (Labor) became an additional concern for the smaller parties (see Figure 2). In the 1920-49 period, several proposals were put forward in order to amend the system, but none received the necessary support in Parliament (see Nissen, 1945: 17-30; Eide, 1998: 4). The idea of adjustment or compensatory seats was one of the many proposals presented. The *Storting* appointed a new electoral reform commissions both in 1927 and in 1935, but their proposals did not carry the floor and, thus, did not bring about any major changes in the system (Nissen, 1945: 19-28). The only major change was the extension of the election periods from three to four years, in 1938. Then the threatening international situation in the late 1930s shifted the political focus away from national controversies, and reduced the interest for electoral reform (Furre, 1972: 281).

After World War II, the debate about electoral reforms started again. In 1948 the *Storting* discussed twelve different proposals of constitutional amendments with several hundred alternatives.[42] None of the proposals was approved, but the *Storting* decided to appoint yet another electoral reform commission. The main objective was to draft a system that provided better proportionality than the old one. The disproportionality of the old system was particularly pronounced in the 1945 and 1949 elections. Labor won more than half of the *Storting* seats, without obtaining more than 41 and 45.7%, respectively, of the votes (Kristvik & Rokkan, 1966: 24-25; Valen, 1981: 36).

The majority of the Electoral Reform Commission recommended a system with adjustment seats. The Labor party, however, preferred another alternative: to keep the present formula, but to change the district boundaries so that they followed the administrative boundaries of the provinces. The minority group in the *Storting* committee wanted to have adjustment seats, and to replace the d'Hondt method with the largest remainder method. The L-R method would significantly improve the seat/vote ratio, but the Labor party opposed this. In the *Storting* debate, Labor MPs explicitly argued that an executive bonus for the largest party was not undemocratic but necessary in order to provide stable

41. In particular, the combination of cities from different provinces into one electoral district was unpopular (Greve, 1964: 7).

42. This illustrates the formidable challenge politicians are faced with when they try to understand the political implications of a large number of electoral amendments.

government. One Labor MP emphasized that *"we must have an electoral system that makes it possible to 'do politics'"* (Greve, 1964: 14).

To sum up, the d'Hondt method was used in a total of 8 national elections. The average district magnitude in this period increased from 1 to 5.2 and the average assembly size increased from 123.6 to 150 (see Table 1).

Redistricting and the Sainte-Laguë Method 1953-88

In the wake of World War II, the Labor party in 1945 consented to reform the electoral system, in order to make the *Storting "a best possible expression of the public will"* (*Fellesprogrammet*, see Valen, 1981: 36).[43] In order to change the system, it was necessary to reach a compromise between Labor and the opposition parties. Every system seems to have its own threshold of tolerance with respect to imbalances or deviations from the ideal of *"one vote, one value."* In the early 1950s it was clear that many Norwegians, not the least within the opposition parties, felt that this threshold was being stepped over. The 1949 election gave Labor 85 seats in the *Storting*, compared to 65 for the opposition parties, despite the fact that the latter parties received almost 40,000 more votes than Labor! (Langslet, 1989: 109).

Abolishing the "Peasant Clause"

Labor was not very eager to change the electoral system and made it perfectly clear that if they were to consider supporting a reform, it was absolutely necessary to abolish the "peasant clause." The urban and rural vote did not have equal weight, something that was a clear disadvantage for the Labor party because of their strength among urban workers. The majority of the Electoral Reform Commission of 1948 particularly emphasized the need to increase the number of representatives from the capital (Oslo) region. At the same time it did not want to increase the total number of *Storting* representatives. The only way to accomplish this was either to reduce the number of representatives from other cities, or to abolish the "peasant clause" (Kristvik & Rokkan, 1966: 27). The final vote took place on November 26th, 1952. A majority in the *Storting* abolished the dreaded clause, which in turn necessitated the drawing of new district boundaries. It was not only the Labor party that wanted to get rid

43. *Fellesprogrammet* was a common political platform for all the political parties after World War II.

of the "peasant clause." The conservative Right party had seen a significant change in its electoral basis after 1945. The party lost ground both among peasant voters and in the rural electorate more generally (Espeli, 1983: 43). The Right party feared that it would not be properly compensated for the gains among urban voters in the future due to the peasant clause. The explicit motive of John Lyng, one of the conservative leaders, was to introduce an electoral system, which reduced the over-representation of the Labor party — after the prohibition of apparentement ahead of the 1949 election. But, because Labor did not want adjustment seats, the Right sided with the other parties in the constitutional committee defending the "peasant clause." Mr. Lyng, however, considered an electoral reform to be absolutely necessary in order to bring about a change in the present political regime (Langslet, 1989: 111). When there was a complete deadlock in the ensuing *Storting* debate, he urged Labor to consider a change in the first divisor (1.4) if the "peasant clause" was removed simultaneously. When Labor eventually agreed to do this, the Right changed its position on this clause, although with a narrow margin within the conservative group.[44] Among the conservatives, 14 voted in favor of abolishing the clause, while 9 voted against. Traditionally, the agrarian faction had been quite strong within the Right party. Those who wanted to keep the clause feared that the party would lose rural votes if they agreed to abolish it (Espeli, 1983: 43-48).

New Electoral Districts

The administrative regional units (*fylker*) now became the new electoral districts, and the old distinction between urban and rural constituencies was removed.[45] The number of representatives elected from each district was, as before, written into the Constitution. The old over-representation of peripheral areas was maintained. Although the capital, Oslo, was given twice the number of seats as it had before, it still took two votes in the capital to balance one vote in the peripheral districts (Rokkan, 1967: 389). The regional cleavage once again prevailed over the principle of equal value for all votes, regardless of geographical location. Representation was obviously not only of party and population, but of *territory* as well. There was, however, no attempt at attaching a fixed formula to the weight given to each electoral district (Rokkan, 1967: 387).

44. Even within the Labor group the margin in favor of changing the first divisor from 1.5 to 1.4 was very narrow (Eide, 1989: 67). Consequently, the argument that the modified divisor of 1.4 was some kind of a social-democratic "invention", must be modified.

45. Only the two largest cities, Oslo and Bergen, formed separate electoral districts.

With respect to the electoral formula, the Electoral Reform Commission argued that the largest remainder method would yield the best proportionality between the parties. In addition, the Commission proposed a system of adjustment seats on a regional or national basis, and a minimum threshold of three per cent in order to win such a seat (Kristvik & Rokkan, 1966: 28). The majority of the *Storting*'s constitutional committee, however, did not support the largest remainder method and instead suggested a modified version of Sainte-Laguë's method. The intention behind an increased first divisor was to maintain a high threshold against small parties. At the same time the change from d'Hondt to Sainte-Laguë reduced the over-representation of the largest party. In 1949, Labor had an over-representation of 11 percentage points, in 1953 this was reduced to 4.6 percentage points.

Stabilizing the Party System

The modified Sainte-Laguë formula, as well as the other changes in the electoral system, obviously was part of a compromise between the established parties. In Stein Rokkan's words: "*This formula fitted the established power constellations as closely as any procedure at this level of simplicity could ever be expected to. It had all the appearance of a universal rule, but in fact it was essentially designed to stabilize the party system at the point of equilibrium reached by the early 1950s*" (Rokkan, 1970: 161). Interestingly, the modified Sainte-Laguë system was introduced in Denmark and Norway shortly after it had been introduced in Sweden (Särlvik, 1983: 122). It is reasonable to think that there was a "contamination" effect here, as the governments in all three countries belonged to the same social-democratic party family and maintained close relations with each other. In addition, the growing support for the Communist party after World War II in particular troubled the social-democratic parties. By reducing the over-representation of the largest party, the middle-sized nonsocialist parties were strengthened. But, this was also a strategic advantage for the governing party as it reduced the pay-offs of strategically motivated cooperation among the opposition parties. The number of joint lists by opposition parties consequently dropped from 8 in 1949 to only 1 in 1953. And, not the least, the new system helped all the established parties by discouraging splinters and new parties (Rokkan, 1970: 160).

Demands for More Proportionality

Despite the fact that middle-sized parties fared better after the 1952 reform, the smaller parties were not satisfied. Compared with other Western systems, the Norwegian system was still less proportional. In particular, the Labor party was over-represented, albeit much less so than under the previous electoral regimes. On the other hand, increases in the degree of disproportionality, although small in a historical perspective, may receive a lot of attention. This was exactly what happened in Norway in the 1960s and 1970s. In the 1970s the overall disproportionality of the system increased (see Figure 2).[46] In addition, new parties experienced difficulties obtaining representation in the *Storting*. The Socialist People's Party, established in 1961, won two seats both in 1961 and 1965. In 1969, however, the party received almost 80,000 votes (3.4%) and no seat. The formation of the Socialist People's Party was a result of increasing tensions within the Labor party about foreign policy, particularly the question of Norwegian membership in the NATO alliance and opposition to nuclear weapons. Prominent laborites were excluded from the Labor party, and eventually formed their own party.[47] The political antagonism between the two parties added to the intensity of the debate of the specific electoral arrangement that prevented the Socialist People's Party from being represented in the *Storting* in 1969.

The fate of the old Left Party that dropped out of the *Storting* in 1985 also revived the debate about electoral reform. For the first time after the Left Party was established in 1884, it did not win a single seat. The same thing happened in 1989.[48] As both these parties suffered setbacks in terms of popular support, it was not totally unfair that they were unrepresented. On the other hand, the psychological and political effect was that they became preoccupied with the specific mechanisms that barred their representation. The modified divisor of 1.4 was a natural target for their attacks (Valen, 1981: 42-44). If the first divisor had been reduced, the Socialist People's Party would have won a seat in 1969. Likewise, the Left Party would have won a seat in 1985.[49]

---

46. The increase from 1969 to 1973 and 1977 is more pronounced using the simpler Loosemore-Hanby's index than the more sophisticated Gallagher's index.

47. The Socialist People's party was merged into the Socialist Left Party in 1975, after the first referendum on membership in the European Community. The new party consisted of former members of the Socialist People's party, the Communist party, former Laborites and some "independent" socialist. The majority of members and voters, however, came from the Socialist People's party.

48. The Left Party received only 3,1 per cent (1985) and 3,2 per cent (1989) of the votes.

49. A first divisor of 1,2 would have given the Left Socialist party 1 seat in 1969, while a divisor of 1,1 would have given the party 2 seats (simulations done by the author). Although the party won two seats in 1965, this represented an under-representation of almost 5 percentage points.

Contributing to the uneasiness about the existing electoral procedures was also the fact that the majority constellation in the *Storting* quite often was at odds with the majority constellation in the electorate. The divide between socialist and bourgeois parties has been decisive with respect to government formation for most of the postwar period. Thus, in five out of seven elections between 1965 and 1989, the *Storting* majority was different from the majority constellation in the electorate (Rommetvedt 1994: 102-106).

Using Apparentement as Reform Leverage

The Labor party was not interested in changing what they considered to be a lasting compromise embedded in the 1952 reform. From Labor's point of view, the consequences of lowering the threshold would be a further fragmentation of the party system, to the disadvantage of effective government. As the election formula was not part of the Constitution, it did not need a 2/3 majority to be changed. But, a broad consensus was preferred. To add pressure on the Labor party to accept new reforms, the nonsocialist parties reinstated the system of apparentement before the 1985 election. The explicit justification was that because Labor did not want to contribute to a fairer electoral system, apparentement was reinstated on a *temporary* basis, until a new system could be introduced. This procedure was preferred instead of changing the first divisor (Innst. O. Nr. 36-1984-85: 13). The Labor representatives claimed that apparentement was introduced "*as a result of purely political considerations by the present governing parties, with the intention of providing themselves continued government power*" (Innst. O. Nr. 36-1984-85: 13). Apparentement particularly hurt the Labor party, which lost 6 seats, while the smaller opposition parties won a total of 8 seats (see Valen, 1994 for an in-depth analysis of apparentement in the 1985 election).[50] Interestingly, the introduction of apparentement not only affected the outcome of the election in terms of seats for each party, but also contributed to a long-time instability in the *Storting*. This was due to the fact that the populist Progress party (with only two seats) controlled the balance between the socialist and the nonsocialist block (Valen, 1994: 317).[51]

In sum, the 1952 election system was used in a total of 9 national elections. The district magnitude varies somewhat during the 1953-85 period, as

50. In addition, the Right party lost 2 seats, while the Christian People's party won 5 seats, and the Center party won 3 seats.

51. Just one year after the election the Progress party actually was instrumental in bringing the nonsocialist government down.

the total number of seats increased from 150 to 155 in 1973 and then to 157 in 1985 (giving an average of 152.4). This gives an average district magnitude of 7.5 for the 1953-69 elections, 8.2 for the 1973-81 elections and 8.3 for the 1985 election. On average for the whole period the district magnitude was 7.8 — compared to 5.2 in the previous era.

The 1988 Reform: Two-Tier Districting, 8 Adjustment Seats

1.) The Labor party primarily wanted to maintain status quo, except that it wanted to abolish apparentement. In addition, the party wanted to take prohibition of apparentement, as well as maintaining the first divisor of 1.4, into the Constitution (something that would necessitate a two thirds majority to change).The question of amending the Election Laws had been raised several times since 1953, but to no avail. The Labor party opposed any changes. The "punishment" of apparentement, introduced in 1985, finally made the party more accommodating. A private [52]proposal by MPs from all of the opposition parties, in addition to one MP from the Labor party, finally was brought before the *Storting* in 1988. The Committee for Foreign and Constitutional Affairs had prepared the proposal before the *Storting* debate. The main change affected the introduction of adjustment seats. Although the Committee was unanimous with respect to the introduction of these seats, it disagreed with regard to the number of such seats and the specific threshold needed to win them. Three different factions could be identified in the committee (Hoff, 1995):

2.) The Right party wanted 10 adjustment seats with 4% threshold (only for adjustment seats), and it wanted the first divisor of 1.4 and prohibition of apparentement brought into the Constitution.

3.) The Christian People's party, the Center party and the Socialist Left Party wanted 10 adjustment seats and a threshold of 3%, and would not take the first divisor into the Constitution. The three parties did, however, agree that prohibition of apparentement could be taken into the Constitution.

The rhetoric in the *Storting* debate was quite harsh by Norwegian standards. The Labor party was concerned with the stability and governability of the system, while the opposition parties accused Labor of being "greedy" and

52. The introduction of two-tier districting with a threshold of 4 per cent blends into a more general trend in the same way as the change from d'Hondt to Sainte-Laguë in 1952 (Lijphart, 1994: 54).

"arrogant." Kjell Magne Bondevik, representing the centrist parties, complained that "*the Labor party has a sad history with respect to electoral reforms. The party has single-mindedly resisted reforms that would give a better correspondence between voter support and representation in the Storting. Labor has now given up this fight only because apparentement was introduced, and forced Labor to give in*" (Stortingsforhandlinger 1987-88, nr. 31: 3253). Gunnar Skaug, representing the Labor party, on the other hand accused the centrist parties of manipulating the electoral system to their own advantage in 1985. He even referred to apparentement as a kind *of "political prostitution based on tactical considerations*" (Stortingsforhandlinger 1987-88, nr. 31: 3252; 3254). Despite accusations of tactical maneuvers, several parties emphasized that they supported changes without expecting benefits in terms of seats. Both Labor and the Right party supported adjustment seats, although they did not foresee that they could win any of them. In the case of the Right party, this was a clear miscalculation. In the 1989 election, the party actually won one adjustment seat.[53] On the other hand, the centrist parties, benefiting from the 1985 apparentement, agreed to abolish it in future elections. The intensity of the debate and the reciprocal accusations of "undemocratic" behavior was, however, not consonant with the qualitative differences in the various proposals in terms of seats,[54] that is, for parties represented in the *Storting* at the time. For the Left Party, however, the threshold was of ultimate importance because the party was just above the 3.0% level and below the 4.0% level.[55] Nevertheless, the need to ventilate accumulated frustrations should not be underestimated in debates on electoral reform!

The Labor party and the Right party controlled a two-third majority of the representatives in the *Storting* debate. Hence, it was no surprise that their harmonized proposal carried the floor. Nevertheless, the final vote was unanimous — for the first time in Norwegian electoral history. The new electoral system added 8 adjustment seats to the previous 157 district seats. The adjustment seats would be distributed on the basis of total discrepancies between votes and seats brought by the initial district distribution, in order to improve the overall proportionality of the system. Parties that were over-

---

53. If 10 adjustment seats had been added — as was proposed — the Right party would have won two of these in 1989 (simulations done by the author).

54. Simulations done by Hoff (1995) gave small differences in terms of seats for the parties represented in the *Storting*.

55. The Left Party received 3,1 per cent of the votes in 1985 and 3,2 per cent in 1989. A 3,0 per cent threshold would have given the Left 5 seats in 1989, all adjustment seats.

represented in the initial allocation would keep their seats, and no seats were taken away from the electoral districts. As the Conservative leader, Jan Petersen, aptly observed in the debate: "*The characteristic trait of the new system is that it keeps all the old rules, but supplements them with adjustments seats which makes the end result more fair. All districts and parties that win seats with the old system, will keep these seats*" (Stortingsforhandlinger 1987-88, nr. 31: 3252; 3256).

The adjustment seats would go to districts were the under-represented parties had the largest remaining quotas in terms of votes. In effect, this would give the more densely populated regions more seats than before. The Labor party, which traditionally has been quite strong in rural as well as in urban areas, voiced some concern about this effect. The Right party, which usually receives more votes in urban than in rural areas, argued that this was an advantage rather than a disadvantage (Stortingsforhandlinger 1987-88, nr. 31: 3252; 3256-3257). Despite the small corrections of the malapportionment made by the adjustment seats, nobody wanted to make any fundamental change in the over-representation of the peripheral areas. Jan P. Syse (Conservative) summed up the essential elements of any electoral reform, saying that: "*An electoral system must be a compromise between desires for the best possible degree of proportionality, regional representation and the need for a parliamentary situation that can give stable governments*" (Stortingsforhandlinger 1987-88, nr. 31: 3252; 3274).

In addition to these changes, the prohibition of apparentement and the electoral formula (Sainte-Laguë with a first divisor of 1.4) were taken into the Constitution.

The Present Electoral System

The present Norwegian electoral system can be summarized as follows (see also Table 1):

- 157 seats are allocated in 19 districts, following the administrative province boundaries.
- 8 adjustment seats are allocated among parties who have received at least 4.0% of the national vote, giving the parties a number of seats that corresponds to their share of the votes as much as possible.
- The parties who have won one or more adjustment seats will win these seats in the district (districts) where they have the largest number of remaining votes (after divisions for district seats). This means that the adjustment seats go to the most densely populated districts.
- Allocation of seats is in all instances done by the modified Sainte-Laguë method with 1.4 as the first divisor.

In the three first elections after the 1988 reform the district magnitude increased from 7.8 in the previous period to 8.7, while the assembly size increased from 152.4 to 165 seats. The 8 adjustment seats amounts to 5% of the total seats in the *Storting*, which is considerably less than in, for instance, Sweden and Denmark.

The Battle Goes On…

Despite the consensus reached when adjustment seats were introduced, the smaller parties were not satisfied with the balance between adjustment seats and district seats. Therefore, they have repeatedly proposed amendments of the electoral system. But until now, Labor and the Right have turned them down. However, in October 1997 the Government appointed a new Electoral Reform Commission with the mandate to simplify and revise the electoral system. Based on proposals from this Commission, the Norwegian Government presented several reform proposals to the *Storting* in the spring of 2002. If implemented, the number of adjustment seats would increase from 8 to 19 — thus increasing the overall proportionality of the system. This would increase the total number of seats from 165 to 169. Furthermore, a new allocation of seats on the electoral districts is proposed, reducing the over-representation of peripheral areas. The third major reform proposal is to introduce personal vote also in national elections.[56]

5. Electoral Laws and Their Consequences

In the preceding sections we have dealt with electoral system change in a historical, sequential manner. We will now more specifically address the consequences of the various reforms and changes. Arend Lijphart argues that the ideal situation to study changes in election rules is "*one in which, in the same country, two successive electoral systems differ with regard to only one dimension, because this allows us to gauge the influence of this one dimension with the knowledge that neither the other dimensions nor other background variables could have had a substantial effect on the outcome*" (Lijphart, 1994: 78). A different, but supplementary and more direct approach would be to run computer simulations of historical elections, where the element of interest is systematically manipulated.[57] This has been done for all elections after World War II.[58] Let us first examine the links between electoral system type (and change), and the party system.

56.See http://www.odin.dep.no/krd/norsk/publ/otprp/016001-050016/index-inn001-b-n-a.html for a detailed description of the proposal (in Norwegian).

Consequences for the Number of Parties

1906-18: For the majority, runoff system of the 1906-1918 period, Duverger's thesis that "*simple-majority systems with second ballot . . . favors multipartyism*" obviously is of particular interest (Duverger, 1954: 239 as quoted in Cox, 1997: 14). Norway was actually one of the empirical cases upon which Duverger based his hypothesis. Tertit Aasland (1965) has reanalyzed the five elections between 1906 and 1918 with Duverger's thesis in mind.[59] First of all, one has to take into consideration that the party system at the start of this period was not only diffuse; it was also undergoing a fundamental change. This makes it difficult to put party labels on various voter groupings. Moreover, it is not very accurate to describe the party system in the preceding period as a "two-party system" (Aasland, 1965: 272). To answer the question of how many new parties emerged after 1906 is also difficult. Apart from several small "parties" which actually were more or less well-organized interest groups (e.g. the "Teetotaler party" and the "Church party"), the major difference was the growth of the Labor party (established in 1887). Aasland concludes that the change from a simple plurality system to majority runoff elections did *not* replace a two-party system with a multiparty system (Aasland, 1965: 272; 274). Indeed, the effective number of parliamentary parties in the 1906-1918 period varied between 2.2 and 2.9 with an average value of 2.4 (see Figure 2 and Tables A4 and A5). In the last election of this era, in 1918, the number of parties was actually higher than in the first elections.

57.One caveat is, of course, that voters were not influenced by the manipulated electoral rules when casting their vote. In other words, we presuppose that their votes were sincere and not strategically motivated. Following Cox's argument that "*strategic voting ought to fade out in multimember districts when district magnitude gets much above five*" (Cox, 1997: 100ff), we believe that simulation of these elections represent a valuable supplement to the historical analysis as the average district magnitude vary between 7.5 and 8.3. In order to simplify the analyses we have not simulated the effects of interactions between individual elements, although it would be possible to study at least some interaction effects with the computer program I have used.

58.The simulations have been carried out using a computer program developed and written by the author. This program — called *Celius* — is commercially available from the Norwegian Data Archives (NSD) in Bergen, Norway (http: //www.nsd.uib.no/skoleveven/materiell/celius). Computer simulations of historical elections are not often used, but they represent a valuable data source for systematic studies of electoral systems.

59.Aasland argues that Duverger's information and knowledge of the countries he is referring to is not always convincing (Aasland, 1965: 269; 296). One example is that Duverger mistakenly registers renaming of an old party, as a new party. See Kuhnle (1987) for a critical perspective on Duverger's law.

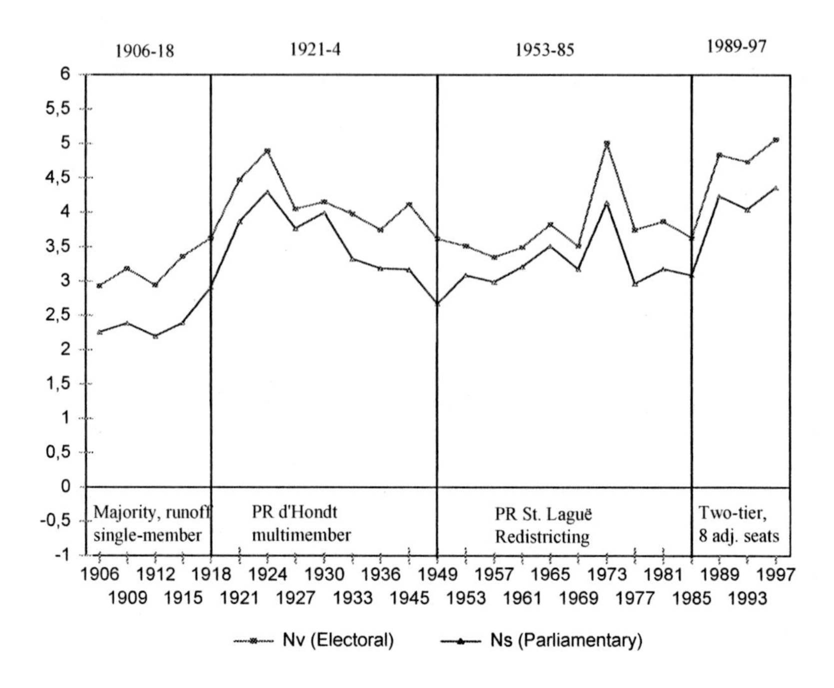

Figure 2. Effective Number of Parties. Norway 1906-1997

Aasland concludes that she did not find that the second ballot system resulted in intimate alliances between the parties to the extent claimed by Duverger. His claim that the Left and the Right parties in particular joined forces in order to block the Labor party in the second round, is not substantiated as a *general* trend (Aasland, 1965: 287). In some elections, in particular in 1915, the two parties did, however, coordinate their efforts in the second ballot — against Labor (Aasland, 1965: 287). For some other parties which did cooperate closely (e.g. *Høire* and *Frisinnede Venstre*), Aasland argues that the second ballot was unnecessary, as the parties had joined forces already in the first round (Aasland, 1965: 289). In the five elections during which the system was at work, an average of 3.4 candidates ran for election in the first ballot, compared to an average of 2.7 candidates in the second. A second ballot was used in about half of the constituencies throughout the period. This means that although fewer candidates ran in the second round than in the first, the reduction in number was relatively small.[60]

1921-49: In the 1921 to 1949 period, after the introduction of PR, the number of parties varied considerably. The average number of parliamentary parties was 3.5, but it varied between 2.7 and 4.3 (see also Tables A4 and A5). Despite the widespread belief that a PR system is conducive to an increase in the number of parties compared with non-PR systems, Figure 2 demonstrates that the effective number of parties actually *decreased* from 1924 to 1949, after an increase in the first two elections after the reform. In the last election with the d'Hondt method (1949) the effective number of parliamentary parties was actually *lower* than in the last election with majority elections (1918), while the effective number of electoral parties remained the same.

1953-85: The effect of replacing the d'Hondt formula with the modified Sainte-Laguë in the1953 to 1985 elections can be studied in Figure 2. The change of formula did not result in major changes in the party structure. The effective number of parties was about the same as before 1953. The average number of parliamentary parties was 3.3 with a low of 2.9 in 1977 and a high of 4.1 in 1973 (see also Tables A4 and A5). However, the 1973 election stands out and warrants an explanation. In 1972, Norway said no to membership in the European Economic Community (EEC), in a dramatic referendum. The EEC debate created tensions and splits both within and between parties. As a direct consequence of the EEC conflict, the Socialist Left Party — representing the victorious "no to EEC" side — increased its representation from 1 to 16 seats at the 1973 election.[61] In addition, the EEC issue split the old Left Party, giving both the new and the old party seats in the *Storting*. Unrelated to the EEC debate a totally new party, the Progress Party, was also represented in the *Storting* after the 1973 election.[62]

60.The extent of strategic coordination from the first to the second ballot has been analyzed in an unpublished paper by Leif Helland and Jo Saglie, Department of Political Science, University of Oslo (1997). They find support in election return data from the 1909-1918 elections for the equilibrium theory. But, did only applies to Left and Right voters, and not for Labor voters nor for candidates in general (Myerson & Weber, 1993; Cox, 1997: 123-138).

61.Actually the Socialist Left Party (or the Socialist People's Party as it was called then) did not win a seat of their own in the 1969 election. However, one MP (Arne Kielland) defected from Labor to the Socialist Left Party after the 1969 election.

62.One of the two new parties, the DLF was a split-off from the Left Party — caused by internal EEC differences.

The effective number of parliamentary parties has been estimated through simulations for the 1953 to 1985 elections, keeping all factors constant, except the formula by which votes are transformed into seats (see Table A6).[63] On average, the introduction of the Sainte-Laguë formula increased the effective number of parliamentary parties with 0.40 or 14% as compared to d'Hondt. Thus, the simulations corroborate the findings in Figure 2: the change of formula had a limited effect on the number of parties. Actually, the modest increase in the number of parties is consistent with Cox's argument that "*increasing the proportionality in an electoral system in a homogenous society does not proliferate parties*" (Cox, 1997: 25).

1989-97: The last major reform, the inclusion of compensatory seats in 1988, had a sizeable impact on the number of parties as seen in Figure 2. The effective number of parliamentary parties increased from 3.3 for the 1953-85 period to 4.2 for the 1989-97 period (see Table A6). This amounts to an increase of almost 30 compared to the previous era. Thus, despite the relatively low number of adjustment seats, the reform did have a significant impact upon the number of parties. Simulations show that the over-representation of Labor, as the largest party, dropped from 6 percentage points to 4 percentage points — a drop of more than 30%.

Consequences for Ideological Structure and Formation of New Parties

Majority elections in single-member districts in the 1906-18 period severely impeded the chances for smaller parties to be represented in the *Storting*. At the same time new political conflicts were surfacing. This obviously created a mismatch between the party system and the political environment. To a large extent the introduction of PR in 1919 made the electoral system compatible with the existing political situation, but this did not prevent the new electoral system from being conducive to the formation of more parties. *Landmandsforbundet* (The Farmers' Association), for instance, had participated in elections since 1906 as a pressure group. The Farmers' Association even won three *Storting* seats in 1918, two years before the *Bondepartiet* (literally the Farmers' Party) was formally established (Blom, 1974: 50). Politically speaking, the Farmers' Party cut across the dominating cleavage between the Right and the Left. An economic conflict in

63.As the system was changed before the 1989 election, the elections in the 1953-85 period are more directly comparable.

the commodity market had been channeled into the party system. In the beginning, the boundaries between the interest group and the party were diffuse, but eventually the Agrarian Party developed into an ordinary party, although closely linked to the Farmers Association (In 1959, the party changed its name to the present Center Party). After internal rifts within the Labor movement, the Norwegian Communist party was established in 1923.[64] The next party was established in 1933, namely the Christian People's Party. At first it was located only in the *Hordaland* province, but it became a nationwide party in 1945.[65] Like the Farmer's Party the Christian People's Party was a split-off from the Left Party. And like the Agrarian Party, the new party had a predecessor in the majority, single-member era. *Kirkepartiet* (the Church "party") was formed in 1907 as a result of tensions between orthodox and liberal theological groups within the Lutheran State church (Blom, 1974: 42). As mentioned earlier, the split of the Left Party in 1888 was also linked to religious differences. Although the formation of new parties was caused by deep-seated conflicts in the Norwegian society, proportional representation gave these parties a prominent status in the *Storting*. The Agrarian Party won a handsome representation in the Storting in 1921 with 17 seats,[66] and the small Communist party won 6 seats in 1924.[67] Even the Christian People's party won one seat in 1933, running in only one district.

After the formative years of the 1920s, the party system had found its form. In Lipset and Rokkan's term, the party system was "frozen." Ironically, just after Lipset and Rokkan had published their famous book, *Party Systems and Voter Alignments* (in 1967), the system was beginning to thaw. The debate about membership in the European Community had a profound fragmenting impact upon the Norwegian party system. The Left Party was split on the European issue in 1972, after the referendum. In 1973, the remaining Left Party won 2 seats, down from 13 in the previous election. The splinter party, the Liberal People's Party, also won a seat.[68] A rightwing populist tax-protest party named Anders

64.When the Labor party joined the Third International in 1919, a dissenting group left the party and eventually formed the Norwegian Social Democratic Party in 1921, but this party was reunited with the Labor party in 1927. Labor left the Third International in 1923.

65.Several other parties, which later disappeared, were also established in 1933: Samfunnspartiet (The Society Party) and Nasjonal Samling (the National Socialist or Nazi party).

66.The Agrarian Party received 13.1 per cent of the votes in this election.

67.The Communist party won 6.1 per cent of the votes in this election.

68.This was the only period the Liberal People's party was represented in the *Storting*. In 1988 the two parties merged, keeping the name of the Left Party.

Lange's Party[69] (later renamed the Progress Party) was also established in 1973. Anders Lange's Party benefited from general unrest and frustration generated by the European debate, but was not directly linked to the issues raised in this debate. Rather, the Progress Party voiced anti-welfare sentiments that had not previously been represented by the established parties.

In the 1970s, new issues penetrated the political agenda in Norway much in the same way as they did in other Western countries. The most prominent new issues were environmental protection and gender equality. In many ways the scene was set for a generational conflict. The pre-war generation defended the "old" way of doing politics, while the post-war generation was fighting for "new" politics. Concomitant with the generational divide one found differences with respect to issue preferences and modes of political participation (Barnes, Kaase et al. 1979). Grassroots organizations with widespread support among young voters attacked the established channels of representative democracy. Ronald Inglehart framed the social transformations from industrial to postindustrial society in a theory of a cultural shift where materialist values gradually were supplanted by postmaterialist values due to generational replacement (Inglehart 1977; 1987; 1997).

Gender equality was subject to a similar development. The established parties opened up for female activists and succeeded in bringing more women into prominent positions within the parties and as members of local and national political bodies (Skjeie, 1992; 1997). The number of female *Storting* representatives rapidly increased from 9.3% in 1969 to 39.4% in 1993, being among the highest in any parliament in the world.[70] The main point is that this process took place *within* the realms of the already established parties and without any changes in the electoral rules. Thus, it underscores the importance of the opportunity structure implicit in a PR list system. On the other hand, it also sheds light on the necessity of political *mobilization* in order to increase the representation of new groups. Without the gender equality movement in the 1970s, the parties would probably not have been so eager to introduce gender quotas when composing their candidate lists. And without the gender quotas, the increase in female representation would have been much slower.[71] For the

---

69.The official party name was (in translation) "Anders Lange's party for strong reductions in taxes, tariffs and public interventions ."

70.In the 1997 election the per cent of women dropped a little to 36.4 per cent.

71.All parties, except the Right party and the Progress party, have a rule declaring that an electoral list must include at least 40 per cent women and 40 per cent men. The parties introduced gender quotas voluntarily.

established parties, the new issues and modes of participation represented a considerable challenge. Environmentalism and gender equality was neither related to the traditional cleavage structure nor decisive for the emergence of the established parties. Thus, the question was whether these new trends would lead to formation of new parties or not, and to what extent they would bring about a disintegration of the electoral bases of the old parties. Even though a Green Party *was* established in Norway (in 1988), the electoral fortune of the party was meager at best.[72] Instead of seeing new parties being born, the established parties to a large extent opened up for new issues and agendas. The Left Party and the Socialist Left Party adopted environmental protection as their new ideological platform. In addition, the other parties went through a process of gradual assimilation of ecological ideas and environmental concern. There was, in other words, no vacant spot in Norwegian politics for the Green Party (Aardal, 1990a; 1993). On the other hand, the barriers against small parties embedded in the electoral system did not improve the Green Party's chances of being represented in the *Storting*. This underscores the point that political cleavages and electoral systems tend to interact (Cox, 1997: 23-27).

In many ways the debate about Norwegian membership in the European Community served as a catalyst for new issues. This might be explained not least by the establishment versus anti-establishment character of the debate. It is also important to note that the anti-establishment side won the referendum in 1972. Rather than being a revolt from the outside, it was a revolt from the inside where the established parties fought each other. There were major rifts inside the parties as well. The pattern repeated itself in connection with the new referendum about membership in the European Union (EU) in 1994. Once again, the anti-establishment side won, and once again the struggle was fought between parties inside the system. In the 1990s, the effects on the party system were less significant than in the 1970s. No new parties emerged as a result of the last EU-debate, and none were split.

However, this did not preclude new parties from winning *Storting* seats. In the 1989 election, a regionally based protest list from the northernmost province of Finnmark won one seat, in 1993 the tiny Red Electoral Alliance won a seat from the Oslo region, and finally another regional list won a seat from the Nordland province in 1997. The first two lists did not have any impact on the national political agenda, and they did not win reelection.[73] In the most recent

---

72.In the 1989 election the Green party won 0.5 per cent of the votes. In 1993 it won 0.3 per cent, and in 1997 only 0.2 per cent of the votes.

elections, more than 20 registered parties have been running. Most of them have received only marginal support by the voters.

The long-term consequence of the political turmoil of the 1970s was an increase in the number of volatile and disloyal voters (Aardal & Valen, 1995). Although the system returned to a more "normal" situation after the 1972 referendum, this did not benefit the largest party (Labor) as much as it did the Right Party and the Progress Party. The "swing to the right" in the early 1980s, in particular the growth of the Progress Party, destabilized both the parliamentary and the party system (Aardal & Valen, 1995). Whether or not we are witnessing a process of *dealignment* or *realignment* is still a matter of scholarly debate, but political parties are obviously facing the challenges of a new society (see Strøm & Svåsand, 1997, in particular Urwin, 1997). At present, many parties are struggling hard to increase or even maintain their representation in the *Storting*. Not surprisingly, institutional gatekeepers — in the guise of electoral rules — are as salient as ever. The interesting thing, however, is that the changes in the party system and the emergence of new political issues took place without major changes in the electoral system. Within the institutional boundaries the system showed an impressive adaptability where "new" politics blended in with "old" politics. Lipset and Rokkan's "thesis" of frozen cleavages is often interpreted to imply a static, never-changing party system. Taking into account the historical character of their approach, not the least based on Norwegian experiences, this interpretation is a clear misunderstanding (see the discussion in Aardal, 1994). Again, the Norwegian case is illuminating. Despite the fact that Norway displayed all the properties of a frozen party system up until the 1960s, the system has adapted to changing circumstances. Far from being static and unresponsive, the system has shown a great deal of flexibility and dynamism *within* a relatively stable institutional framework (Aardal & Valen, 1995).

Consequences for System Disproportionality

1906-18: Going back to the single-member, majority, runoff system of 1906-18, the most pronounced aspect was the discrepancy between the voters'

73.Interestingly, the 1989 Finnmark list was not formally registered as a political party. In order to register a party you need at least 5000 signatures. But, to run for election you only need 500 signatures in the district where you are running. The Red Electoral Alliance received only 1.1 per cent of the votes in 1993, but because its support was heavily concentrated in one district with many seats (Oslo), it managed to win one seat. In 1989 the *Aune-list* won one seat from the Finnmark province. Although they received only 0.3 per cent of the total vote, they received 21.5 per cent of the votes in Finnmark. In 1997 the *Coastal Party* won one seat from the province of Nordland. This list won only 0.4 per cent of the total vote, but 6.2 per cent of the Nordland vote. In 2001 the Coastal Party MP, Steinar Bastesen, managed to be reelected, increasing his local support to 10.9 per cent.

preferences and the allocation of seats. In Figure 3 we see that this discrepancy was twice as big in 1915 as in 1906 (as measured by Gallagher's least square index; see also Tables A4 and A5).[74]

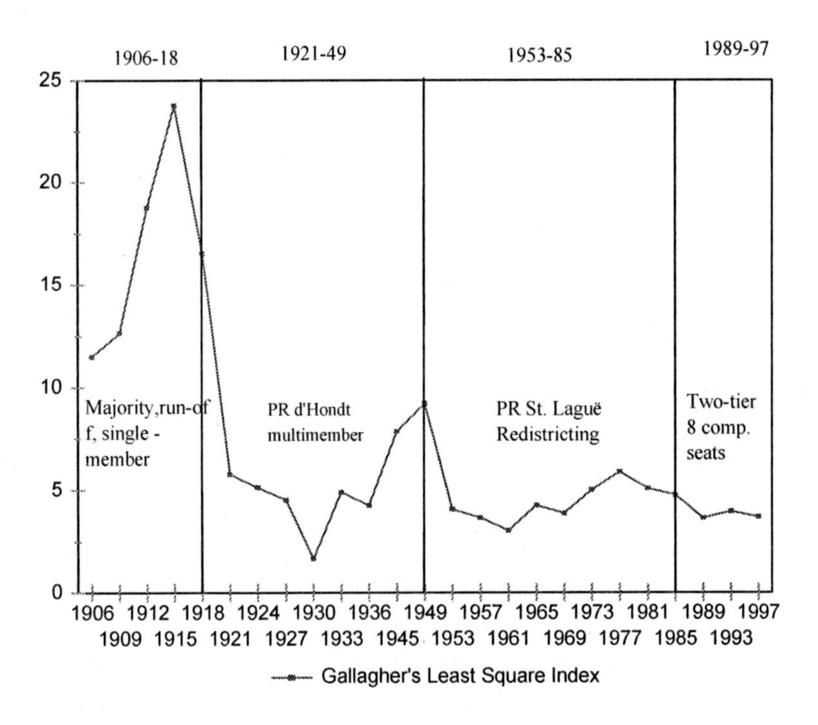

Figure 3. System disproportionality. Norway 1906-1997.

Deviations from mathematical proportionality probably would have been more acceptable if they gave one party an advantage at one election and another party an advantage at the next. In Norway, however, the losing party consistently was the growing and radical Labor party (Kristvik & Rokkan, 1966: 11). At the 1915 election, the Labor party won 32% of the votes but only 15% of the *Storting* seats. A considerable increase in terms of votes was accompanied by a loss of four seats! (Furre, 1972: 101). The Left Party, on the other hand, won 60% of the seats with only 33% of the votes. The over-representation of the largest

74.This index is calculated by squaring the vote-seat differences for each party and add them. This total is divided by 2, and finally the square root of this value is taken (see Lijphart, 1994: 61)

party (the Left) was particularly high in this election, although it was also high in 1912.[75]

1921-49: The introduction of PR in 1920 dramatically decreased the system disproportionality, as demonstrated in Figure 3.[76] The average index value went down from 16.6 in the 1906-18 period to 5.4 in the 1921-49 period — a decrease of almost 70%! But, it is important to note that the disproportionality varied considerably during the eight elections the system was at work. In the first years after the change, disproportionality went down, but after 1930 it increased. The 1930 election stands out as a deviant case and requires an explanation: the largest party (Labor) had a negative balance between its share of seats versus share of votes; consequently, the disproportionality index was very low. An important factor behind this was the fact that the four "largest" parties were quite similar in size. None of the parties was able to extract an executive bonus out of the system.[77] The introduction of apparentement in 1930 to a large extent explains this outcome. In the last election of this period (1949), however, the over-representation of Labor was almost as high as it had been in some elections during the previous era. The effective number of parties was also on par with pre-PR elections.

1953-85: The 1952 replacement of the d'Hondt formula with Sainte-Laguë's had an immediate impact on overall disproportionality. The index value went down from 9.2 in 1949 to 4.1 in 1953. On average for the whole 1953-85 period the index value was 4.4, down from an average of 5.4 in the preceding period, i.e. a reduction of almost 20%. Compared to the decrease in disproportionality going from a majority to a PR system, this decrease is less dramatic, but still significant. However, the electoral reform of 1952 not only changed the electoral formula, it also abolished the "peasant clause" and introduced new district boundaries. How can we be sure that the actual changes in index values are caused by the change in only on one of these factors, namely the formula? The effects of changing the formula can be measured more precisely by simulating election outcomes using the two methods for the same elections. If

75.Actually, the over-representation of the largest party closely follows the curve of the overall disproportionality of the system.

76.The average district magnitude in the 1921-49 period was 5.2, not 7.5 as stated in Lijphart, 1994: 22 (150 seats and 29 districts).

77.Labor won 31.4 pct. of the votes and 31.3 pct. of the seats. The Right party won 27.4 pct. of the votes and 28 pct. of the seats. The Left Party won 20.2 pct. of the votes and 22 pct. of the seats, and the Agrarian Party won 15.9 pct. of the votes and 16.7 pct. of the seats.

the seats had been distributed using the old d'Hondt formula instead of Sainte-Laguë's, the average index value would have been 7.9, compared to 4.4 for the latter formula (see Table A7). This means that the replacement of the d'Hondt formula with Sainte-Laguë's decreased the overall disproportionality by almost 40%! This is mainly due to major reductions in the over-representation of the largest party (*in casu* Labor) (see Table A4). Labor's over-representation on average would have been 9.3 percentage points with d'Hondt's method, compared to 4.1 with Sainte-Laguë's. Consequently, the change of formula reduced the over-representation of the largest party with more than 50%. Compared to the index values, as shown in Figure 3, the simulations demonstrate that the change of formula actually had a significant impact on the disproportionality of the system. The reduction of disproportionality did, however, not preclude the smaller parties from wanting even better opportunities for representation in the *Storting*.

1989-97: The last election period, starting in 1989, covers the introduction of adjustment seats. As seen in Figure 3, disproportionality decreased somewhat after adjustment seats were introduced. The index value went down from 4.4 to 3.8, a reduction of about 14%. A simulation of the three last elections demonstrates that this decrease was directly linked to the introduction of adjustment seats (see Table A8). The net effect on overall disproportionality was a reduction of 30% (from an average index value of 5.5 *without* adjustment seats, to 3.9 *with* adjustment seats). Once more, the reduction of the over-representation of the Labor party is the main reason behind the overall decrease in disproportionality. Without adjustment seats, Labor would have had an over-representation of six percentage points, compared to four percentage point with adjustment seats (see Table A9).

It is interesting to note that the extent to which an election system is considered to be legitimate is more a political-psychological than a technical question. Bo Särlvik emphasizes that "*proportional representation, once established, creates a dynamic of its own — fairness always seems to demand that it should be taken one step further*" (Särlvik, 1983: 142). This obviously has been the case with respect to the tolerance for disproportionality in the Norwegian system. What was accepted as an executive bonus for a large party in one period may be considered illegitimate in the next. Hence, the definition of a "fair" election system may change over time.

Variations within Electoral Eras

In most comparative analyses of electoral systems, effects of change as well as system properties are measured in terms of *average* values for several elections sharing the same characteristics. What Figures 2 and 3 have demonstrated, however, is the fact that these values may vary considerable from one election to the next, depending on a number of factors other than the properties of the electoral system itself. The complex interplay between old and new ideological structures and issues on one hand and the success or failure of parties and leaders on the other is often more important than specific aspects of the electoral system. Nevertheless, parties may adapt to changing institutional frameworks (*in casu* electoral systems) after a while and try to neutralize negative effects. With respect to overall disproportionality, we have not found any evidence of conscious efforts of "undermining" the new system in order to reestablish old advantages for the largest parties in the Norwegian case. There is, for instance, no systematic pattern of initial reductions in disproportionality being followed by increasing disproportionality.

Stable Government

An interesting topic when discussing the effects of electoral systems and system change is the consequences not only for individual parties, but also for the forming of government alternatives and for government stability. In Norway, many governments since World War II have been minority governments. In addition, the general trend with respect to changes of the electoral system has been to reduce the executive bonus of the larger parties. A reasonable hypothesis is that this would lead to a great deal of governmental instability. Indeed, the conventional wisdom about minority governments has been that they are more unstable than majority governments. However, this does not hold true for Norway. As Kaare Strøm has demonstrated, minority governments may even be superior to majority coalitions in some respects, not least because minority governments may enhance system responsiveness and accountability (Strøm 1985; 1990). However, this does not prevent changes in the electoral system from having an impact on government formation. The 1952 reform, for instance, to some extent adjusted the balance between the governing party and the opposition parties. Even with the modified Sainte-Laguë method, Labor would have won a majority of the *Storting* seats in the previous election (1949). In 1945, however, Labor would have lost its majority even if apparentement had been removed. This does not preclude the possibility that the Labor party was over-represented even with the new electoral formula.[78] But, the long-term consequence of the change is significant. Labor's loss of a *Storting* majority at the 1961 election would not have happened if the d'Hondt formula had been used. Simulations show that the same applies to the 1969, 1977 and 1985 elections. In this perspective the change from d'Hondt to Sainte-Laguë signifies an important shift in favor of proportionality at the expense of executive bonus to the largest parties. It has also been argued that the introduction of adjustment seats in 1988 probably will affect future attempts at establishing majority governments as well. The chance that one party will be able to win an absolute majority in the *Storting* — as Labor did in the 1950s — has been severely diminished with the introduction of adjustment seats (Aardal, 1990b).

When designing an electoral system the balance between proportionality ("fairness") and effective and stable government ("executive bonus") is hard to strike. Often the debates take the form of smaller parties advocating increasing proportionality "for the sake of democracy", while larger parties are more concerned with the "effective ruling of the country." In Norway, these contradictory concerns were particularly visible in the *Storting* debates in the mid-1980s regarding adjustment seats. Both arguments are perfectly valid from a democratic perspective. The problem is to find the balance that benefits both the individual parties and the system as a whole. To the extent we may discern a general trend in electoral reforms in Norway, it seems to tip in favor of proportionality. Nevertheless, the present Norwegian system still is *less* proportional than in the neighboring countries of Sweden and Denmark.

6. Malapportionment

As mentioned earlier, malapportionment has been an important and a long-lasting characteristic of Norwegian electoral systems. The rationale behind this principle was to compensate for the geographical distance to the power circles in the capital. The most explicit justification of the skewed influence of voters in different parts of the country was presented by the Electoral Reform Commission of 1917. They explained the logic of geographical over-representation in this way: "*Although the Commission shares the opinion that it would be desirable to allocate more seats to Kristiania* (the capital, now named Oslo), *the perception is that*

78. In 1949 Labor would have won 81 seats with the modified St. Laguë method, an over-representation of 12 seats (+8 pct), compared with 16 extra seats (+11 pct.) with d'Hondt. In 1945, however, Labor would have won 70 seats (6 short of majority) instead of 76 seats with d'Hondt. This applies both to a situation with and without apparentement in 1945 (according to simulations done by the author).

this city as the capital has access to political and parliamentarian influence which cannot be neglected. As the seat of the most influential newspapers in the country, of all political parties, of economic and professional organizations, and of central financial and administrative institutions, the capital holds a particular position, implying that it cannot to the same extent as other constituencies demand representation proportional to the size of its population or its electorate" (as quoted in Kristvik & Rokkan, 1966: 27).

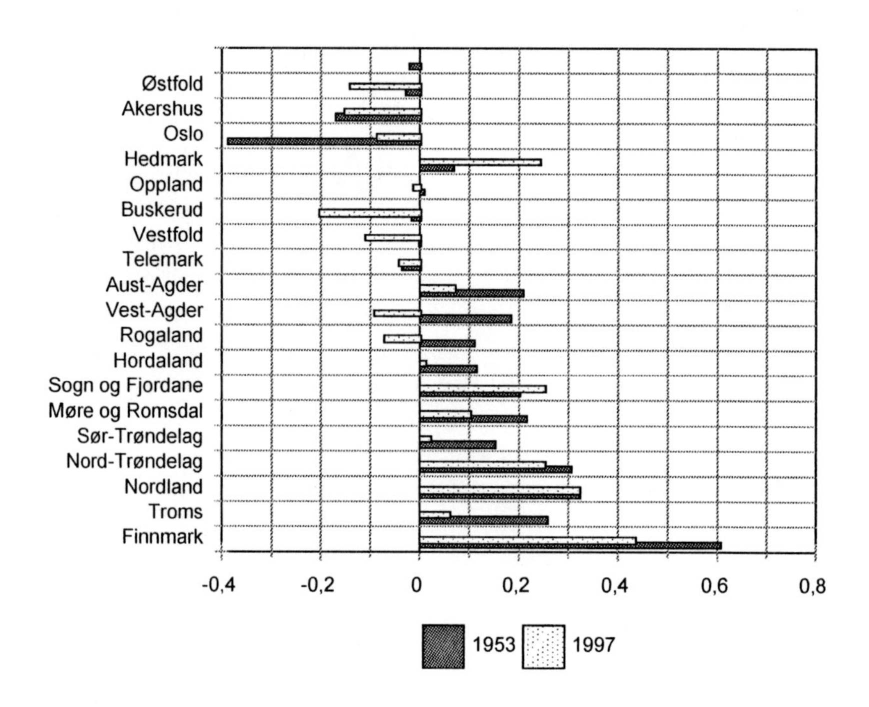

Figure 4. Malapportionment in Norway 1953 and 1997

Figure 4 illustrates the extent of malapportionment in Norway at the district levels for the 1953 and 1997 elections. The starting point of these comparisons is the average number of eligible voters per *Storting* representative for the whole country. The average number of eligible voters per seat in each constituency is weighted against this standard, giving the result as deviations from the national average (negative to the left and positive to the right). We see, for instance, that the average weight for voters living in Oslo was 39% *lower* than the national average in 1953 and 9% lower in 1997. In the northernmost district of Finnmark, the average weight of each voter was 60% *higher* than the national average in 1953, and 43% higher in 1997. The topmost regions in Figure 4 are the geographically most central districts, while the regions toward the bottom are located in the more peripheral part of the country. Hence, we clearly see that the distribution of seats favors the periphery and disadvantages the central areas. However, we also see that the most extreme deviations in both directions have been reduced from 1953 to 1997. Although the introduction of adjustment seats has reduced the under-representation for some districts, it has not removed the overall malapportionment in the system.[79] One obvious reason for not reversing this system is the persistent strength of the center-periphery cleavage. As to direct consequences for the distribution of seats on parties, malapportionment seems to plays a lesser role than many Norwegians think. A simulation of the last three elections shows that only a limited number of seats are affected by malapportionment, i.e. when counting the total number of seats for each party.[80] Nevertheless, the over-representation of the peripheral areas enjoys widespread support, although some alternative voices are heard.[81] In view of the revitalized center-periphery conflict, as witnessed in the recent debate on membership in the European Union, a fundamental change in the regional allocation is unlikely. A further increase in the degree of party proportionality may also — depending on the specific rules — negatively affect the regional distribution, thus representing conflicting interests for the parties involved.

7. Parties Behaving Strategically

Although apparentement in the form of *listeforbund* was abolished in the 1988 reform, this does not prevent parties from merging their lists into *joint lists (felleslister)*. The difference between these two types of strategic cooperation is that while *listeforbund* gave the parties the opportunity of either counting the votes separately or jointly, depending on which method gave the highest number of seats, *felleslister* means that two or more parties decide to run on the

79.The fluctuating location of the adjustment seats from one election to the next leads to variation in the degree of malapportionment for some districts.

80.We have eliminated malapportionment by redistributing the seats to each constituency in proportion to the number of eligible voters in the district. The simulations show that Labor would have lost 3 seats in 1989, while the Christian People's party, the Right party and the Progress party would have gained one seat each. In 1993 Labor and the Center party would have gained one seat each, at the expense of the Christian People's party and the Right party. In 1997 the Christian People's Party and the Coast Party would have lost one seat each, while the Center party and the Liberal party would have gained one seat each.

81.The Progress party is the only party that supports a change in the regional allocation of seats, based on population size.

same list. By doing this they hope to improve their chances of winning a district seat (see Cox, 1997: 39). Typically, the largest party will get the top position on the list, while the next largest party will get the next position, and so on. This kind of cooperation has been very common in Norwegian politics, and it illustrates that strategic behavior is inherent also in PR systems (see Cox, 1997: 31). Between 1949 and 1981 an average of 5.9 joint lists (counted on the district level) participated in the elections, winning an average of 5.6 seats. The interesting thing, however, is that *no* such lists have been established after 1988. The obvious reason is that the parties fear that joint lists might impede their chances of winning adjustment seats, because they cannot know in advance what the exact margins with respect to district or adjustment seats will be. An intended consequence of introducing adjustment seats was that no vote should be "wasted" as long as your party receives at least four per cent of the total votes. If the party does not win a seat in your district, your vote is transferred to the national pool of votes. Even if your party does not win a single district seat, it may compete for adjustment seats. But there is an important catch. If you vote for a party that has joined another party in a joint list, your vote will *not* be transferred to the national adjustment pool of your party, thus possibly spoiling your party's chance of winning an adjustment seat. The high volatility among Norwegian voters increases this uncertainty. The implication is that the parties are not able to take advantage of the strategic potential that is actually embedded in the new system. Simulations show that several parties could have reaped an extra bonus in the last three elections if they had cooperated in joint l[82]ists. This may be an example of the need to learn how the system works before you can utilize its full capacity. Conversely, it may also demonstrate that the stakes can be too high for a party to take advantage of the potential gains embedded in an electoral system.

8. Conclusions

Although the electoral system has been changed several times since 1814, there are also elements of institutional stability. The inclusion of electoral rules into the Constitution — needing cumbersome and lengthy procedures to change

82.For instance: even if the Center party and the Christian People's party would have lost some of their adjustment seats by entering joint lists, their net bonus would have been 3 seats in 1989, 2 seats in 1993 and 3 seats in 1997. An additional uncertainty is of course that a party may lose some votes if it aligns itself with a party some of its voters do not like.

them — is a typical example of institutional inertia.[83] The introduction of direct elections in 1905 and proportional representation in 1920 in many ways stand out at the most fundamental changes of the Norwegian electoral system. As we have seen, however, specific electoral setups have undergone numerous amendments and extensions.

How do we explain both the origin and the changes of electoral systems in this country? First of all, each system must be understood in its historical context. Even though the founding fathers were aware of electoral systems in other parts of the world, and borrowed heavily from them, they made an effort to adapt electoral rules to fit the national political situation. Moreover, the extensive use of broadly based electoral reform commissions not only contributed to informed decisions about which system, or parts of a system, to use, but also opened up the process to differing views even before the final parliamentary debate took place. Hence, with minor exceptions the parties have been able to foresee the consequences of changes in the electoral system.

A recurring theme in the Norwegian debate on electoral amendments has been the balance between party and group representation on one hand and representation of geographical entities on the other. To the extent that various electoral setups represent an innovation or at least a characteristic trait, this must be it. First and foremost, this applies to the skewed distribution of seats in the individual districts. This was not only a concern in the Constitutional Assembly in 1814, but has been so ever since. Thus, Rokkan's conclusion is particularly valid for Norway: "*Even in the most 'proportionalized' of democracies, the electoral arrangement still reflect tensions between three conceptions of representation: the numerical, the functional* (economic), *and the territorial*" (Rokkan, 1970: 165). However, the interaction between a particular electoral arrangement and the socio-economic and ideological environment is a complex one, and does not warrant simple and straightforward causal inferences (see Lipset & Rokkan, 1967: 30). A well-functioning system seems to be totally dependent upon its congruence with basic societal and political structures. This has been demonstrated with respect to extensions of the suffrage in the 1814-1913 period, the transition from indirect to direct elections around 1905, and the introduction of proportional representation around 1920, to mention but a few examples. In all these cases, change has come as a result of pressures both from above and

83.The reforms proposed by the Government in the spring of 2002, however, significantly reduce the number of electoral rules included in the Constitution.

from below. The extensions of the suffrage in the late 19th century directly affected both the workings of the indirect system and the electoral opportunities for old and new parties. Similarly, the mobilization of radical workers in the first decades of the 20th century made the established parties more susceptible to electoral reforms ending in the introduction of proportional representation. Nevertheless, it is important to note that calls for electoral reform usually have not originated among ordinary voters (Nissen, 1945: 34). This brings political tactics into the picture. The positions and the arguments of the parties cannot be properly understood if one does not take into consideration the strategic interests involved. The best example of this is perhaps the parties' different attitudes toward PR in local elections on the one hand and in national elections on the other — as presented in the pre-1920 period — but this does not preclude parties from consenting to changes that significantly reduce their parliamentary influence, as Labor did in the 1952 reform. Thus, although self-interest plays an important role (cf. Eide, 1998), it does not provide an exhaustive explanation of system change.

As we have seen in this chapter, the initial legitimacy of an electoral arrangement may erode over time. The 1917 Electoral Reform Commission's statement that proportional representation had become a "necessity" illuminates this point. However, decreasing legitimacy alone does not guarantee that the system will be changed. A willingness to *compromise* is a precondition not only for change, but probably also for its acceptance and legitimacy among the general public. In this perspective the consensus-building tradition embedded in Norwegian political culture may explain why conflicting interests eventually find a common ground when deciding on new electoral systems. Historically, the absence of a strong institutionalized elite — as demonstrated by the lack of an upper chamber — is important in order to explain how major reforms could be implemented despite the objections of the old establishment. Although a bicameral *Storting* was desired by some elites both in 1814 and in the 1870s, the idea did not catch on even within the conservative group itself. Although "inclusive government" does not explain why particular changes were implemented at a particular point in time, it does explain how important changes could be implemented with the consent of those parties that stood to lose most from them.

At the same time, compromises imply that we do not have a "winner take all" game. Even the "loser" gets something out of a change in the electoral framework. Thus, electoral change incorporates a complex mix of containment, adaptation and "revolt." Often the impetus for change is embedded in the system itself. Not disregarding the importance of social and political structure, we have seen that changes in electoral arrangements do have important implications for system properties such as number of parties and proportionality. Evidently, electoral systems *do* matter (see Cox, 1997: 14ff).

Appendix

Table A.1. Election results 1973-1997

Year/ Votes/ Seats	Red Electoral Alliance	Socialist Left Party	Labor Party	Liberal Party	Christian People's Party	Center Party	Conservative Party	Progress Party	Others
1973									
Votes %	0.4	11.2	35.3	3.5	12.3	11.0	17.4	5.0	3.9
Seats %	0	10.3	40.0	1.3	12.9	13.5	18.7	2.6	0.6
Seats	0	16	62	2	20	21	29	4	1
1977									
Votes %	0.6	4.2	42.3	3.2	12.4	8.6	24.8	1.9	2.0
Seats %	0	1.3	49.0	1.3	14.2	7.7	26.5	0	0
Seats	0	2	76	2	22	12	41	0	0
1981									
Votes %	0.7	5.0	37.1	3.9	9.4	6.6	31.8	4.5	1.0
Seats %	0	2.6	42.6	1.3	9.7	7.1	34.2	2.6	0
Seats	0	4	66	2	15	11	53	4	0
1985									
Votes %	0.6	5.5	40.8	3.1	8.3	6.6	30.4	3.7	1.0
Seats %	0	3.8	45.2	0	10.2	7.6	31.9	1.3	0
Seats	0	6	71	0	16	12	50	2	0
1989									
Votes %	0.8	10.1	34.3	3.2	8.5	6.5	22.2	13.0	1.4
Seats %	0	10.3	38.2	0	8.5	6.7	22.4	13.3	0.6
Seats	0	17	63	0	14	11	37	22	1
1993									
Votes %	1.1	7.9	36.9	3.6	7.9	16.7	17.0	6.3	2.6
Seats %	0.6	7.9	40.6	0.6	7.9	19.4	17.0	6.0	0
Seats	1	13	67	1	13	32	28	10	0
1997									
Votes %	1.7	6.0	35.0	4.5	13.7	7.9	14.3	15.3	1.6
Seats %	0	5.4	39.4	3.6	15.2	6.6	14.0	15.2	0.6
Seats	0	9	65	6	25	11	23	25	1

Table A.2. Economically active population by sector of employment, as a percentage

	1875	1890	1900	1910	1920	1930	1946	1950	1960	1970	1980	1990
Primary sector	51.9	49.3	40.8	39.0	36.9	35.8	29.8	25.9	19.5	11.6	7.8	6
Secondary	18.2	22.1	26.8	25.6	29	26.5	32.6	36.4	36.6	37.3	33.8	30.6
Tertiary sector	25.3	27.3	30.3	32.2	33.7	37.4	36.7	37.1	43.6	50.9	57.8	63.2

Source: Historical Statistics 1994 (Table 9.2; see page 227 for a definition of "economically active"), NOS C188, Oslo: Statistics Norway, 1995.

Table A.3. Per cent of population living in urban areas 1815-1996

1815	1835	1845	1865	1890	1900	1920	1946	1950	1960	1970	1980	1990	1996
9.8	10.8	15.6	19.6	31.3	35.7	45.3	50.1	52.2	57.2	65.9	70.3	72.4	74.0

Sources: Historical Statistics 1994 (Table 3.1), NOS C188, Oslo: Statistics Norway, 1995 and Statistical Yearbook 1997 (table 36), Oslo: Statistics Norway, 1997. Note: the distinction between urban and rural areas in this table is not identical to the urban-rural divide implemented in the peasant clause.

Table A.4. Indices of disproportionality and effective number of parties in Norwegian Storting elections 1906-1997

	I	D	LSq	PWI	Nv	Ns	r	OvL
1906	5.6	13.9	11.5	8.9	2.9	2.3	22.9	14.0
1909	6.9	17.3	12.6	9.3	3.2	2.4	25.0	10.6
1912	8.6	21.6	18.8	15.1	2.9	2.2	25.4	21.6
1915	11.3	28.2	23.8	17.6	3.4	2.4	28.8	26.9
1918	7.2	21.5	16.5	11.9	3.6	2.9	19.6	13.0
1921	2.6	9.2	5.8	3.5	4.5	3.9	13.4	4.6
1924	2.2	8.7	5.1	2.9	4.9	4.3	12.3	3.5
1927	1.9	7.7	4.5	2.8	4.0	3.8	6.8	2.5
1930	0.7	2.5	1.7	0.6	4.2	4.0	3.8	0.7
1933	1.5	7.3	4.9	2.9	4.0	3.3	16.4	5.9
1936	1.5	7.3	4.3	2.6	3.7	3.2	14.9	4.2
1945	2.8	9.7	7.9	4.9	4.1	3.2	22.8	9.7
1949	3.4	12.0	9.2	6.2	3.6	2.7	26.1	11.0
1953	1.6	4.9	4.1	2.6	3.5	3.1	12.1	4.6
1957	1.5	5.1	3.7	2.3	3.3	3.0	10.6	3.7
1961	1.2	4.7	3.0	1.6	3.5	3.2	8.0	2.5
1965	1.9	6.5	4.3	1.8	3.8	3.5	8.2	2.2
1969	1.4	5.7	3.9	1.9	3.5	3.2	9.6	2.8
1973	2.0	9.2	5.0	2.6	5.0	4.1	17.4	4.7
1977	2.3	10.2	5.9	3.8	3.7	3.0	20.8	6.7
1981	1.9	8.5	5.1	3.2	3.9	3.2	17.8	5.4
1985	1.8	8.8	4.7	2.8	3.6	3.1	14.9	4.4
1989	1.0	5.1	3.6	1.6	4.8	4.2	12.5	3.9
1993	1.3	6.4	4.0	2.0	4.7	4.0	14.7	3.7
1997	1.2	6.1	3.7	2.0	5.1	4.4	13.9	4.4

I: Rae's index
D: Loosemore-Hanby's index
LSq: Gallagher's index (minus "other" parties, cf. Lijphart, 1994: 61)
PWI Li's party weight index
Nv: Effective number of electoral parties
Ns: Effective number of parliamentary parties
r : difference (in per cent) between effective number of parties in the electorate and in parliament
OvL: over-representation of largest party

Table A.5. Indices of disproportionality and effective number of parties in Norwegian Storting elections 1906-1997 (average values)

	I	D	LSq	PWI	Nv	Ns	r	OvL
NOR I: 1906-18	7.9	20.5	16.6	12.6	3.2	2.4	24.4	17.2
NOR II: 1921-49	2.1	8.0	5.4	3.3	4.1	3.5	14.6	5.1
NOR III: 1953-85	1.7	7.1	4.4	2.5	3.8	3.3	13.3	4.1
NOR IV: 1989-97	1.2	5.9	3.8	1.9	4.9	4.2	13.7	4.0

I: Rae's index
D: Loosemore-Hanby's index
LSq: Gallagher's index (minus "other" parties, cf. Lijphart, 1994: 61)
PWI Li's party weight index
Nv: Effective number of electoral parties
Ns: Effective number of parliamentary parties
r : difference (in per cent) between effective number of parties in the electorate and in parliament
OvL: over-representation of largest party

Table A6. Effective number of parliamentary parties 1953-85

	1953	1957	1961	1965	1969	1973	1977	1981	1985	Average
D'Hondt	2.8	2.5	2.7	3.2	2.7	3.7	2.6	2.8	2.7	2.9
St. Laguë	3.1	3.0	3.2	3.5	3.2	4.1	3.0	3.2	3.1	3.3
Difference	0.3	0.5	0.5	0.3	0.5	0.4	0.4	0.4	0.4	0.4

Table A7. Overall disproportionality 1953-85 (Gallagher's least square index)

	1953	1957	1961	1965	1969	1973	1977	1981	1985	Average
D'Hondt	6.9	8.2	7.3	5.9	7.9	8.3	9.5	8.7	8.7	7.9
St. Laguë	4.1	3.7	3.0	4.3	3.9	5.1	6.0	5.1	4.8	4.4
Difference	2.8	4.5	4.3	1.6	4.0	3.2	3.5	3.6	3.9	3.5

Table A8. Overall disproportionality 1989-97 (Gallagher's index)

	1989	1993	1997	Average
Plus 8 adjustment seats	3.7	4.1	3.8	3.9
Minus 8 adjustment seats	4.9	5.9	5.8	5.5
Difference	1.2	1.8	2.0	1.6

Table A9. Over-representation of largest party (Labor) 1989-97 as a percentage

	1989	1993	1997	Average
Plus 8 adjustment seats	3.9	3.7	4.4	4.0
Minus 8 adjustment seats	5.8	5.8	6.4	6.0
Difference	1.9	2.1	2.0	2.0

Table A10. Effective number of parliamentary parties 1989-97

	1989	1993	1997	Average
Plus 8 adjustment seats	4.2	4.0	4.4	4.2
Minus 8 adjustment seats	4.0	3.8	4.0	3.9
Difference	0.2	0.2	0.4	0.3

PARTY AND ELECTORAL SYSTEM IN SWEDEN

BY
BO SÄRLVIK*
DEPARTMENT OF POLITICAL SCIENCE
UNIVERSITY OF GOTEBORG, SWEDEN

* *The initial version of this paper, authored by Professor Särlvik, was presented at the international conference on "Electoral and Party Systems in the Nordic Countries" held in Laguna Beach, California in December 1998 under the auspices of the University of California, Irvine Center for the Study of Democracy. After Professor Särlvik's untimely death, his former students, Peter Esaiasson and Ola Jodal, revised somewhat the tables and figures that Professor Särlvik had prepared and added a number of others that were needed to parallel the format of the companion chapters in this volume. Also, some very minor copy editing to integrate the old and new material was provided by Bernard Grofman. However, the chapter's basic contents and structure are the work of Professor Särlvik.*

Ever since Sweden's old Four Estate *Riksdag* (Parliament) was abolished and a new Two-Chamber parliament was established in 1866, party system and electoral system in Sweden have developed and changed in a sequence of interactions. Each change in the election system has had consequences for the party system (Särlvik, 1983; Lijphart, 1994). At every stage, however, changes in the electoral system have come about in a conjuncture of political forces that determined both the purposes of the change in electoral law and the further shaping of the party system. We show in Table 1 what we have identified as the six major electoral eras of Swedish politics, using what we regard as a major change in either electoral system (e.g., a change in average district magnitude, assembly size, or national legal threshold of more than 20%, or a change in the electoral formula) to delineate the boundaries between electoral eras. For comparison purposes we also introduce two other historical charts that we will refer to in the text below: Table 2, showing party strengths in the second chamber from the fourth through the sixth electoral eras, and identifies the parties formally in the government,[1] and Table 3, showing electoral participation rates (and information about changes in suffrage) for all six electoral eras. Additional historical information is provided in tables in the Appendix, including Table A1, which provides complete vote and seat information for all elections held between 1911 and 1998.

1. In many instances, there was informal support from other parties. During a great deal of the 2000 century there has existed two political blocks in Sweden, one socialistic (Social Democrats and Left Party) and one bourgeoisie (Conservatives, Center Party, Peoples Party and the Christian Democrats) block. The importance of these cleavage are not illustrated when just the formal governments are shown. In Table 6, however, where the focus is on governance, we do show both formal and informal coalitions.

Table 1: Electoral system eras and the details of system usage. Sweden 1866 - 1998

Electoral system	SWE-I	SWE-II	SWE-III	SWE-IV	SWE-V	SWE-VI
Elections included	1866 - 1887 (9 elections)	1890 - 1908 (7 elections)	1911 - 1920 (5 elections)	1921 - 1948 (8 elections)	1952 - 1968 (6 elections)	1970 - 1998 (10 elections)
Electoral formula at the decisive (higher) level[a]	Majoritarian formula, Plurality (FPTP). Direct or indirect elected members.	Majoritarian formula, Plurality (FPTP). Direct or indirect elected members.	PR, d'Hondt	PR, d'Hondt	PR, modified Sainte-Laguë	PR, modified Sainte-Laguë
District magnitude[b]	1.14	1.18	4.11	8.21	8.26	11.07
Electoral formula at the non-decisive (lower) level[c]	No	No	No	No	No	PR, modified Sainte-Laguë
Number of compensatory seats	No	No	No	No	No	39.2
Compensatory seats as a percentage	No	No	No	No	No	11.2
Allocation of seats in multi-member constituencies final?	Seats partially allocated in multi-member constituencies and partially allocated in single-member constituencies.	Seats partially allocated in multi-member constituencies and partially allocated in single-member constituencies.	Yes	Yes	Yes	Yes
Legal threshold (and effective threshold[d])	No legal threshold. (Effective threshold = 35%)	No legal threshold. (Effective threshold = 35%)	No legal threshold. (Effective threshold = 15.9%)	No legal threshold. (Effective threshold = 8.5%)	No legal threshold. (Effective threshold = 8.4%)	4% of the valid national vote (N) or 12% in 1 constituency. (Effective threshold = 4%)
Average Assembly Size	204.6	229.4	230	230	231.7	349.2

a. The principle for allocation of seats at the level which decides how proportional the allocation is. (Lijphart, p. 32)

b. The number of seats in the parliament divided by the number of constituencies.

c. The principle for allocation of seats at the first level when a two-tier system is used.

d. Effective threshold means the practically needed minimum share of votes a party needs to gain representation in the national parliament. To measure the effective threshold the following equation was used: (50% / district magnitude + 1) + (50% / (2 * district magnitude)) (Lijphart, p. 25 — 27). According to Lijphart the equation doesn't works well for plurality and majority systems. The same estimation has been done for the Swedish electoral eras when Sweden had a majority system.

Table 2: Parties in the second chamber, their seats in percent and the formal governing coalitions categorized in majority and minority governments based on their strength in the second chamber 1911 - 1998

SWE III

Year	Party Left Party[a] (LP)	Soc. Dem.[b] (S)	Cent.[c] (C)	Peopl. Part.[d] (PP)	Cons.[e] (Con)	Chr. Dem.[f] (CD)	Green Party[g] (G)	New Dem.[h] (ND)	Government Minority	Majority
1911	-	27.8		44.3	27.8	-	-	-	PP	
1914(I)	-	32.1	-	30.4	37.3	-	-	-	Temporary non party politician government	
1914(II)	-	37.8	-	24.7	37.4	-	-	-	(I): Temporary non party politician government (II): Con	
1917	4.8	37.4	6.1	27.0	24.8	-	-	-	(II): S	(I): S, PP
1920	3.0	32.6	13.0	20.4	30.9	-	-	-		Temporary non party politician government

a. The party was founded in 1917 as a separatist group of the Social Democrats. In 1921 a group who supported the Russian regime separated to form an own party. In 1924 and 1929 the party was split again. The separatist organization from 1924 later connected to the Social Democrats. The separatist group from 1929 later connected to the original party. From 1921 and up to 1967 the party's name was Swedish Communist party. In 1967 they changed the name to Left Party — the Communists. After the fall of the Eastern Europe communist regimes the word communists abandoned and their name changed to the Left Party.

b. 1889, the Social Democratic labor party was founded. During the years, small groups have separated and other groups have connected but in the whole they have been solid.

c. During the first two chamber period two groups were founded represent the agricultural population. In 1921 this organizations were united to one party. 1957 the party took their present name, the Center Party.

d. The party was founded as a liberal party in 1900. 1923 they split in two parts. When they united again in 1934 they took their present name, Peoples Party.

e. The Conservative Party was formed by a landowner party and in steps with two national parties in the early part of the twentieth century. It got its present name in 1969.

f. The party was founded in 1964. In 1991 they managed for the first time to pass the threshold to the national parliament and since then they have managed to stay.

g. The Green Party was founded in 1981 as a development from the organization which worked against nuclear energy at the popular vote in 1980. 1988 they managed to pass the threshold to the national parliament for the first time but they didn't manage to stay at the next elections. In 1994 they recaptured their seats in the parliament and they have managed to stay since.

h. New Democracy was founded as a dissatisfaction party before the elections in 1991. In their first election they got 6.7% of the votes and managed to pass the threshold to the national parliament, but already in the next election they lost their place in the parliament with only a vote share of 1.2%.

Table 2 (Continuation)

SWE IV

Year	Party Left Party (LP)	Soc. Dem. (S)	Cent. (C)	Peopl. Part. (PP)	Cons. (Con)	Chr. Dem. (CD)	Green (G)	New Dem. (ND)	Government Minority	Majority
1921	5.6	40.4	9.1	17.8	27.0	-	-	-	(II): S (II): Con	
1924	2.2	45.2	10.0	14.3	28.3	-	-	-	(I): S (II): PP	
1928	3.5	39.1	11.7	13.9	31.7	-	-	-	(I): Con (II): PP	
1932	3.5	45.2	15.7	10.4	25.2	-	-	-	(I): S (II): C	
1936	4.5	48.7	15.7	11.7	19.1	-	-	-		(I): S, C (II): Grand Coalition
1940	1.3	58.3	12.2	10.0	18.3	-	-	-		Grand coalition
1944	6.5	50.0	15.2	11.3	17.0	-	-	-	(II): S	(I): Temporary non party politician government
1948	3.5	48.7	13.0	24.8	10.0	-	-	-	(I): S	(II): S, C

SWE V

Year	Party Left Party (LP)	Soc. Dem. (S)	Cent. (C)	Peopl. Part. (PP)	Cons. (Con)	Chr. Dem. (CD)	Green (G)	New Dem. (ND)	Gov't Minority	Majority
1952	2.2	47.8	11.3	25.2	13.5	-	-	-		S, C
1956	2.6	45.9	8.3	25.1	18.3	-	-	-	(II): S	(I): S, C
1958	2.2	48.1	13.9	16.5	19.5	-	-	-	S	
1960	2.2	49.1	14.7	17.2	16.8	-	-	-	S	
1964	3.4	48.5	15.5	18.5	14.2	-	-	-	S	
1968	1.3	53.6	16.7	14.6	13.7	-	-	-		S

Table 2 (Continuation)

SWE VI

Year	Party Left Party (LP)	Soc. Dem. (S)	Cent. (C)	Peopl. Part. (PP)	Cons. (Con)	Chr. Dem. (CD)	Green (G)	New Dem. (ND)	Government Minority	Majority
1970	4.9	46.6	20.3	16.6	11.7	-	-	-	S	
1973	5.4	44.6	25.7	9.7	14.6	-	-	-	S	
1976	4.9	43.6	24.6	11.2	15.8	-	-	-	(II): PP	(I): C, PP, Con
1979	5.7	44.1	18.3	10.9	20.9	-	-	-	(II): C, PP	(I): C, PP, Con
1982	5.7	47.6	16.0	6.0	24.6	-	-	-	S	
1985	5.4	45.6	12.3	14.6	21.8	0.3[a]	-	-	S	
1988	6.0	44.7	12.0	12.6	18.6	-	5.7	-	S	
1991	4.6	39.5	8.9	9.5	22.9	7.4	-	7.2	Con, PP, C, CD	
1994	6.3	46.1	7.7	7.4	22.9	4.3	5.2	-	S	
1998	12.3	37.5	5.2	4.9	23.5	12.0	4.6	-	S	

a. 1985 had the Center Party and the Christian Democrats formed an electoral alliance. One Christian Democratic Member of parliament was elected.

Table 3: Electoral participation as a percentage of adults eligible to vote. The expansion of suffrage is shown in footnotes

Electoral system	Election year	Electoral participation	Average / era
SWE I (9 elections)			
	1866[a]	18%	
	1869	18%	
	1872	19.1%	
	1875	19.5%	
	1878	20.3%	
	1881	23.7%	
	1884	25.2%	
	1887 A[b]	48.1%	
	1887 B	35.9%	25.3%
SWE II (7 elections)			
	1890	38,5%	
	1893	42.4%	
	1896	45.3%	
	1899	40.3%	
	1902	47.2%	
	1905	50.4%	
	1908	61.3%	46.5%
SWE III (5 elections)			
	1911[c]	57.0%	
	1914 A[d]	69.9%	
	1914 B	66.2%	
	1917	658%	
	1920[e]	55.3%	62.8%

a. Only men over 21 years of age had the possibility to vote. Furthermore, an income of 8000 SEK a year or owner of a house assessed to 1000 SEK or leasing of a house assessed to 6000 SEK was demanded.

b.After dissolution of the Second Chamber there was election for the reminding part of the election period.

c.General suffrage for men over 24 years of age was introduced. However, a person would lose his right to vote under certain conditions: unpaid taxes, bankruptcy, dependence of poverty relief, being placed in ward and failure to undergo the national military service.

d.After dissolution of the Second Chamber there was election for the remaining part of the election period.

e.After dissolution of the Second Chamber there was elections for the remaining part of the election period. Furthermore, the election periods were extended from three to four years.

Table 3: (continued) Electoral participation as a percentage of adults eligible to vote. The expansion of suffrage is shown in footnotes

SWE IV (8 elections)			
	1921[a]	54.2%	
	1924	53.0%	
	1928	67.4%	
	1932	67.6%	
	1936	74.5%	
	1940[b]	70.3%	
	1944	71.9%	
	1948	82.7%	67.7%
SWE V (6 elections)			
	1952	79.1%	
	1956	79.8%	
	1958[c]	77.5%	
	1960	85.9%	
	1964	85.9%	
	1968[d]	91.2%	83.2%
SWE VI (10 elections)			
	1970[e]	89.7%	
	1973	92.0%	
	1976	94.1%	
	1979	93.1%	
	1982	92.8%	
	1985	92.8%	
	1988	85.2%	
	1991	88.1%	
	1994[f]	86.8%	
	1998	81.4%	88.3%

a. Women got the right to vote. There was a general suffrage for men and women over 24 years of age. The demand of paid taxes was abolished, but still a person lost the right to vote at bankruptcy, being placed under ward and failure to undergo the national military service.

b. The voting age was lowered to 21 years of age. The last part of the poverty bar was abolished.

c. After dissolution of the Second Chamber there was election for the remaining part of the election period.

d. The voting age was changed to 20 years of age.

e. The voting age was further reduced to 18 years of age. Furthermore the election period was decreased from three to four years.

f. The election period was expanded from three to four years.

Source: Esaiasson, P., *Svenska valkampanjer 1866 - 1988*, Allmänna Förlaget, Göteborg, 1990 and Hadenius, S., *Svensk politik under 1900-talet — konflikt och samförstånd*, Tidens förlag, Jyväskylä, 1995

The primary focus in this chapter is on the Swedish election system after the adoption of proportional representation (i.e., beginnings in 1911: see Table 1). We begin, however, by looking at the context in which the change to a proportional system was introduced as part of a broad political compromise that involved both general suffrage for men and the new electoral system.

1. From Four-Estate Parliament to Two-Chamber Parliament: The First Two Electoral Eras in Sweden

Until 1866, the Four Estates of the Realm (Parliament) consisted of four "chambers" of representatives for the four Estates: the Nobility, the Clergy, the Burghers and the Peasants. It is worth noting that there was a large social stratum of enfranchised peasants (who owned their farms or had permanent possession through a lease of Crown or former nobility land). The peasantry had the right of political representation through the Peasants Estate in the parliament. An estimated 16% of all adult males (21 years of age) had the right to vote.

The new *Riksdag* had two chambers, one of which — the *Second Chamber* — was elected in general elections by enfranchised citizens, while the other was elected by county councils and cities outside the counties. The right to vote in Second Chamber elections was restricted, however. Only those who met fairly stringent property or income qualifications were enfranchised. Yet, many independent farmers fulfilled the property requirement and they made up a strong majority of the electorate. About 22% of all adult (at least 21 years of age) men held the right to vote (provided that they did not owe unpaid tax); as real incomes increased a larger proportion became eligible to vote and by 1908 around 35% of the male population over 21 years of age had the right to vote.

In elections to the Second Chamber there could be either direct elections by enfranchised citizens or indirect elections by electors who themselves had been elected in the constituencies. In the first elections to the New *Riksdag* in 1866 a majority of the constituencies held indirect elections, but then a change to direct elections occurred in most constituencies and gradually the number of constituencies with indirect elections dwindled. Only one remained in the last election before the suffrage reform. (See Andrén, 1937, p. 211 and Table A2 in the Appendix.) Voting was by secret ballot in direct elections.

Open voting seems to have occurred to some extent in elections of electors, but the electors' voting was always by secret ballot. Most constituencies were single member constituencies but some larger cities that sent more than one representative to the *Riksdag* had multi-member constituencies. Electoral participation was low during the first decades of the two-chamber system (less than 20% in 1866) but increased gradually to 61% in 1908 (70% in the cities and 57% in the countryside). (Studies of the 19th century electorate and voting procedures are presented in Andrén, 1937; and Wallin, 1961.)

The right to vote in county council and city elections was restricted both by property and income requirements. In addition the suffrage was graduated by income and property; that is, the more wealthy, the more votes the voter could cast. Eligibility to be elected to the First Chamber was severely restricted by stringent wealth and income prerequisites. It has been estimated that only 6000 persons were eligible to be elected to the First Chamber. (Metcalf, 1987, p. 194). First Chamber members were elected for nine years under rules that entailed successive renewal of the Chamber.

The two chambers had equal powers. The standing parliamentary committees were joint for the two chambers, and half the committee membership was elected by each chamber. If the two chambers failed to agree on a budgetary bill, the decision was made by a joint vote. This gave the Second Chamber a certain advantage, since its membership was somewhat larger than that of the First Chamber.

The Second Chamber had at first 190 members, later increased to 230; while the First Chamber had 125 members, later increased to 150. In the 1950s and 1960s the membership of the Second Chamber increased to 233 and that of the First Chamber to 151 as consequences of constitutional changes which were intended to ensure that the number elected in each constituency would not fall below a certain minimum number.

In the old pre 1876 *Riksdag* the Estates themselves had been channels of interest articulation and representation of their constitutionally recognized segments of the population. Interest representation was in fact also built into the two new chambers. In the new *Riksdag*, he First Chamber represented wealth and social prestige. Its membership consisted largely of big estate owners, the higher levels of the bureaucracy and owners of large businesses. The chamber included a large proportion of members of the nobility (which still existed, albeit without a separate political channel of representation). Yet the First Chamber was a plutocratic rather than an aristocratic constitutional body (Andrén, 1937: 222).

In the Second Chamber farmers formed the largest occupational category, even though the towns were over-represented as a result of the apportioning of constituencies to countryside and urban areas (see Table A3 in the Appendix). Around or nearly half of the membership were farmers (including a small contingent of estate owners). As one constitutional historian has observed it was almost as if the farmers Estate had moved into this chamber to become its largest component.

In the Four Estate parliament, factions of like-minded members had played some role, especially in the House of the Nobility, but to some limited extent also in the other estates. They had been loose and transient formations which, however, could broadly be seen as forming a conservative, a center and a liberal tendency. In contrast, from the first meeting of the new *Riksdag* in 1867, a party system began to emerge. In that year the Agrarian Party (*Lantmannapartiet*) was formed. The party was primarily based on the farmers but it included also a component of urban representatives and became the largest party in the Second Chamber. Liberal and conservative groups were also formed. The First Chamber was the preserve of the right, but divided into a majority group of the most conservative wing and a more moderate and moderate-liberal tendency. (Thermænius, 1935.)

There were important political cleavages in the *Riksdag*, notably relating to the issues of taxation on farm land, the need for a strengthened defense, the controversy over free trade vs. protectionism (which caused a split in the Agrarian party), and the liberal striving to extend the suffrage, which ultimately became a demand for enfranchisement with equal voting right for all (men). Towards the end of the century the suffrage issue formed the ideologically most potent dividing line between left and right.

The party system underwent changes. In the first years of the 20th century a three party system consisting of Conservatives, Liberals and the still tiny group of Social Democrats had emerged in the Second Chamber. The Conservative party was formed by a merging of most of the remaining Agrarian party and a parliamentary faction on the right. Liberal groupings had existed right from the beginning but the Liberal party in its new form was a broad-based political force with its roots in the free-trade tendency and, both ideologically and organizationally, in the movement for extended suffrage; it also had important bases in the "free churches" (dissenters) as well as in the temperance movement. The Social Democrats had started outside the parliament already in 1889 as a national political movement with close ties to the trades union movement. The party did not win more than a few seats in the parliament until the franchise had been extended. A Liberal national organization was formed in 1902, and two years later a Conservative national organization was founded. In 1909, on the eve of the change to general suffrage for men and proportional representation, the division of strength in the Second Chamber has been estimated as follows on the basis of formal membership of parties supplemented by data on the Members stands on key policy issues: Conservatives, 91 seats; Liberals 105 seats, and Social Democrats 34 seats. In the First Chamber The first Chamber (protectionist) Right, 101 seats; Moderate conservatives and some moderate liberals, 49 seats. (Metcalf 1987, p 212).

Extension of the Suffrage With Proportional Representation as a Conservative Guarantee

Extension of the suffrage was an increasingly important goal for the liberals, and around the turn of the century this had become a demand for general suffrage for men. Conservative governments put forward modest reform plans, but these were rejected by the Second Chamber, and a proposal associated with moderate Liberals that offered something less than general male suffrage met the same fate. It was only when the Liberals and the Social Democrats achieved a majority in the Second Chamber, in the election of 1905, that leading Conservatives realized that the time had come when concessions acceptable to the Liberals were necessary. True, the First Chamber had defeated a bill presented in 1906 by the new Liberal government, which proposed general suffrage and single-member constituencies. Already in 1908 a Conservative government was ready to lay before the *Riksdag* a suffrage reform bill which in their view contained conservative guarantees. All men at least 24 years of age were to have the vote in the Second Chamber elections and county council and city elections. However, a person would lose his voting right under certain conditions: unpaid taxes, bankruptcy, dependence on poverty relief, being placed in ward, and failure to perform national military service. These requirements were not politically insignificant. In the election of 1911, 21% of those otherwise enfranchised lost their voting rights on one or another of these grounds.[2]

It was proposed that both chambers should be elected in proportional elections, in multi-member constituencies for the Second Chamber, and for the

---

2. For more general comparisons see Table 3.

First Chamber by county councils and the city councils of cities that did not belong to a county. The d'Hondt method for allocation of seats was to be applied both in the Second Chamber and First Chamber elections. It was a compromise, but it was grudgingly accepted by both left and right.

In elections to the Second Chamber, the voting right was equal for all eligible voters. In county and city council elections, however, an income grading of the vote was retained, with a maximum at 40 votes. Elections to the commune councils and the county councils were to be proportional, with the use of the d'Hondt formula.

The wealth and income requirements for entitlement to be elected to the First Chamber were reduced, but these requirements were still restrictive. Entrance of common people into the First Chamber was facilitated, however, by the fact that First Chamber members were now to receive salaries like the ones Second Chamber members already had. The election period for the First Chamber was reduced from nine to six years, and the councils were to be grouped so that one sixth of the Chamber was to be elected each year.

After new elections to the Second Chamber (required because the reform involved amendments to the constitution), the final decision to change electoral rules was taken in 1909. (For accounts of the political developments and analyses of party strategies, see: Timelin, 1928; Nyman, 1966; Lewin, 1984; Stjernquist, 1966.)

Why, it may well be asked, did the Conservatives insist on a proportional election system? The reason was, essentially, that the Conservative leaders feared that with general suffrage the Conservative party in the Second Chamber would be more or less extinguished under a first-past-the post system. In reality, of course, it was the Liberal Party that was squeezed by the Social Democrats while the Conservative survived the challenge of general suffrage. In all likelihood this would have happened also if the single-member constituencies had been retained. Yet the Conservatives could certainly not be expected to have had the prescience to predict that outcome.

There may also have been another reason, however. Because of the income-graduated vote in council elections, the Conservative had good grounds to expect that they would get a strong majority in the First Chamber. If the two chambers were to disagree on budget matters, the *Riksdag's* decision would — as before — be taken in a "joint vote" in which votes in the two chambers would be counted together. Relying on a strong majority in the First Chamber and substantial minority support in the Second Chamber, the Conservatives could well hope to win such joint votes. The Conservatives had good reason to opt for an election system under which they could expect to be represented according to electoral strength in the Second Chamber. When the Conservatives at a late stage on the way to suffrage reform came to support proportional elections also for the First Chamber, this is probably to be seen as a concession to those who were opposed to the conservative guarantees in the construction of that chamber. Yet the Conservatives, as expected, held a majority in the First Chamber until the income-graduated vote was abolished. A contributing factor

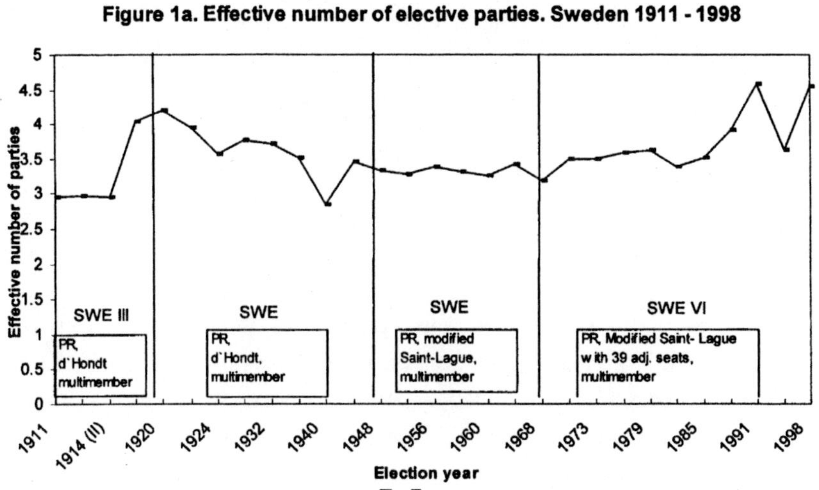

Figure 1a. Effective number of elective parties. Sweden 1911 - 1998

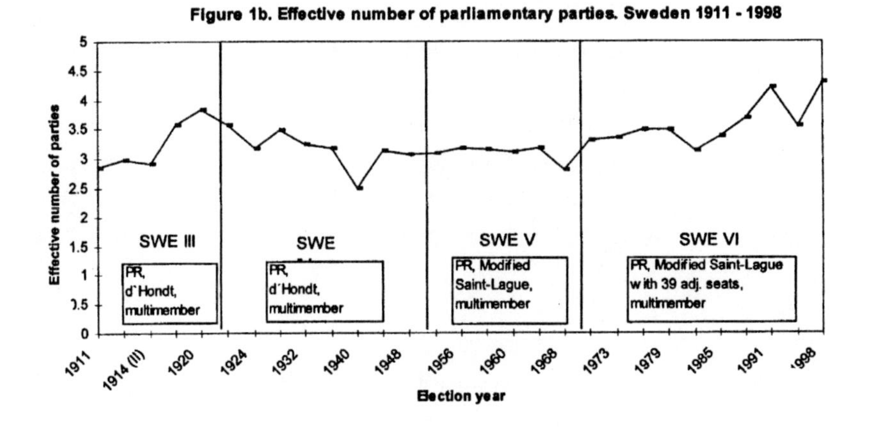

Figure 1b. Effective number of parliamentary parties. Sweden 1911 - 1998

was that the d'Hondt system, as will be discussed later, is favorable to a large party, especially when the number of seats to be filled is small.

The proportional system, it is important to note, was not introduced as a result of any deliberate adoption of proportionality as a principle of representation. The key issues were the general suffrage and the Conservatives' determined efforts to bring elements of guarantees against unfettered majority rule into the new constitutional settlement. The three-party system was thus not the result of proportional elections. It already existed in the electorate, and under general suffrage the Social Democrats were bound to become a major political force also in the parliamentary arena. The necessary compromises concerning the suffrage and the character of the two-chamber system within the Conservative — Liberal — Social-Democratic three-party system interacted and jointly caused the change to proportional representation.

2. Proportional Representation in Practice: Second Chamber Elections in the Third Electoral Era, 1911-1920

The Second Chamber elections were held in 56 constituencies with 3-7 seats (later the largest constituency increased to 11 seats). The number of seats in each constituency was determined by population size; the variation with regard to the population/seats ratio was rather modest. For the Second Chamber the election period was, as before, three years.

Parties could form electoral alliances by using a common label but nevertheless presenting separate candidate lists under that label. This meant that seats would be allocated first to the alliance and then amongst the candidate (party) lists within the alliance. A party could also present more than one candidate list in the election. A special procedure, basically by application of the d'Hondt formula, was used to merge the rank ordering of the candidates.

Figure 1 shows the effective number of parties in each of the elections, using the Laakso-Taagepera (1977) Index (see endnotes to Figure 1). Figure 2 shows the degree of disproportionality in translating votes into seats each of the elections, using the Gallagher least-square index of disproportionality (see endnotes to Figure 2).[3]

3.A full reporting of both seat and vote shares is given for the reader's convenience in Appendix Table A1.

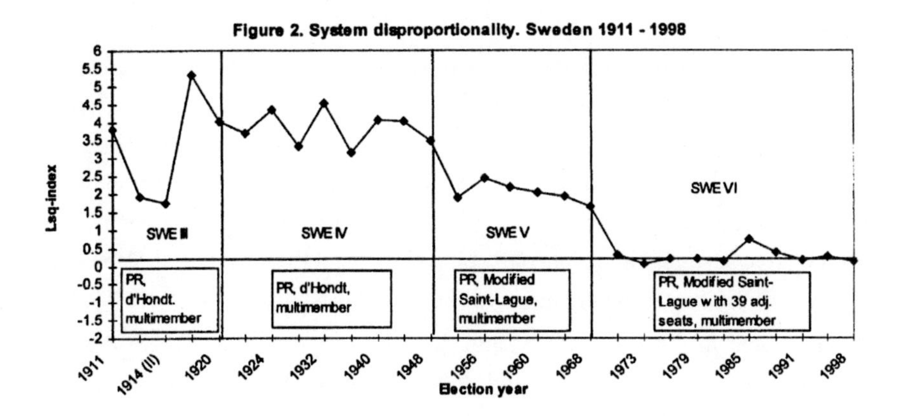

As is well known, the d'Hondt method tends to over-represent larger parties at the expense of small parties. It does so to a larger extent if the constituency magnitude is small. The purpose of the alliances was to reduce the disadvantage for smaller parties. In the first elections under the proportional system, most constituencies had 3-5 mandates. To some extent the possibility of forming electoral alliances thus affected the actual working of the system. In the first election under the new system, the Liberals and the Social Democrats formed alliances in 15 constituencies.

In the election of 1911, the party division of the seats actually came quite close to overall proportionality (see Figure 2).

In the subsequent two elections — both held in 1914 — the balance of strength changed owing to a decline for the Liberals and increase for the Social Democrats. The Liberals declined to 32% in the spring 1914 election and to 27% in the autumn election of that year. In these elections, the Social Democrats increased first slightly to 30% and then to 36%. (The election in the spring of 1914 was held after dissolution of the Second Chamber, but the election period for the newly elected chamber comprised only the remaining part of the ordinary election period. Therefore, ordinary elections were held already in the autumn 1914.)

The party system scene was changed in the 1917 election because of the split off from the Social Democrats of a Left-Socialist party as well as the formation of two farmers' parties, which later merged to form one party, the Agrarian Union. This increased fragmentation of the party system was accompanied by somewhat less proportionality in the distribution of seats (see Figures 1 and 2).

The three-party system was already in existence when proportional representation was introduced. What the architects of the new election system probably had not expected was that the secured representation of smaller parties through proportional representation would also entail formation of new parties. At the 1917 election, a five-party system had effectively emerged. One of the new parties was the result of a split off to the left of the Social Democrats. The other signaled the reemerging of the country-urban cleavage which had been so prominent in the 19th century, and drew its support from farmers who had previously been Conservative and Liberal voters. The old Agrarian Party (*Lantmannapartiet*) had become submerged in the Conservative Party and to some extent in the Liberal Party. Yet the country-urban cleavage had never really ceased to exist, and now it came out into the open again. The two new farmers' parties had different regional bases but soon merged into one party, the Agrarian Union (*Bondeförbundet*) This five-party system (not counting various splits on the extreme left) came to provide the framework for Swedish politics until the 1980s when the mold was broken by the Greens and the Christian Democrats as well as a short-lived phenomenon in the form of an extreme-right party.Although the outcome was less proportional than in 1911, the degree of disproportionality was still fairly modest. The only substantial deviation consisted in the over-representation of the Social Democrats. One factor at work was the operation of the d'Hondt formula when the constituency magnitude is comparatively small. The average number of seats per constituency was 4.1. At least as important, as a countervailing factor, was the formation of party alliances under a common label (but still with separate candidate lists). Such alliances, of one kind or another, were formed in 52 of the 56 constituencies. The Conservatives and one of the two farmers' parties formed alliances in 29 constituencies (the farmers' parties did not both present lists in any constituency), while Social Democrats and Left-Socialists had a common label in 44 constituencies (of which 5 also included the Liberals), and Liberals and Social Democrats had common labels in 5 constituencies.

Constitutional Democratization and Electoral System Change

Towards the end of the Great War, discontent with the way the country had been governed during the war was widespread. The wartime conservative government was held responsible for an economic policy which entailed declining living standards for ordinary people while a few made fortunes through speculation. The government was also accused of having caused food shortages through the way in which it had pursued a neutrality policy, which was seen as biased in favor of German interests.

The Second Chamber election in 1917 gave Liberals and Social Democrats a majority, reinforced by the newly formed Left-Socialist party. A Liberal and Social Democratic coalition was formed, thereby confirming the final recognition of a parliamentary system of government in Sweden. The First Chamber remained as a conservative bastion, however. The downfall of the German, Austrian and Russian empires radicalized public opinion and called forth demands for a profound democratization of the system of government. The Liberal and Social Democratic coalition government announced that it intended to lay before the *Riksdag* a program for democratization of voting rights and eligibility to be elected Member of both the chambers of the *Riksdag*, and to give women the right to vote. The Conservatives, both in the First and the Second Chamber, found it impossible to resist the demand for democratic reform; apparently both the Conservatives and the king feared that a revolutionary situation could arise if concessions were refused.

The democratization was completed through a sequence of legislative measures during the years 1918 -1921. For the Second Chamber, restrictions on the voting right that consisted in the loss of eligibility to vote for recipients of poverty relief were made less severe and for those who owed taxes the disqualification rules were also made less stringent, albeit not abolished altogether. The proportion of voters who had reached the voting age who lost their voting rights because of such restrictions fell from around 20% to around 2%.

The basis of the First Chamber was also democratized: through the abolishing of the income-graded vote in county council and local government district elections; each voter was to have one vote. For the First Chamber the income and wealth requirements for eligibility to be elected were also abolished. And women gained the right to vote.

Small concessions were made, however, by the Left: voting age for Second Chamber elections was increased to 23 years (reached in the year before the election, and the voting age for county council elections (and special elections of First Chamber 'electors' in cities outside the counties) was increased to 27 years.

The election period for the First Chamber was increased from six to eight years, which might also be seen as a change that strengthened the upper chamber's distinctive role as a component of the parliament that guaranteed a measure of continuity. One eighth of the chamber was to be elected each year; for this purpose the councils etc. that elected First Chamber Members were divided into eight groups. The election period for the Second Chamber was also lengthened, from three to four years.

For the First Chamber, the effect of the democratization was drastic. Party division of seats and votes in the first chamber for the period 1917-25 is shown in Table 4. The Conservatives lost their majority in 1919 and the Social Democrats became the largest party in the First Chamber, as they were in the second chamber.

Table 4: Party Division of Seats in the First Chamber: 1917-1925

	Seats			
Party	1917	1919 *	1922	1925
Conservatives	88	38	41	44
Agrarian Union **	-	19	18	18
Liberals**	45	41	38	.
Liberal Party	.	.	.	13
Liberal People's Party	.	.	.	22
Social Democrats	17	49	50	52
Left Socialists	-	3	2	-
Communists****	.	.	1	1
Total	150	150	150	150

* After dissolution of First Chamber in 1919
** In 1919, 8 belonged to the Farmers' National Association and 11 to the Agrarian Union. Later the two parties were merged.
*** The Liberal party was split into two parties in 1923 of which Liberal People's Party was a pro-temperance party.
**** The Left Socialist party was split into a Left-Socialist and a Communist party.

Consequences of the d'Hondt Formula in the Fourth Electoral Era, 1921 - 1948

As part of the reform of the election system, the division into constituencies was also changed. In order to increase the degree of proportionality in the distribution of seats in the Second Chamber, the number of constituencies was reduced from 56 to 28. This meant, of course, a considerable increase in constituency magnitude, from an average number 4.1 seats per constituency to 8.1 seats. After the reform, most constituencies were comprised of one county, although one was divided into two constituencies; two constituencies consisted of big cities and one constituency comprised four cities in the south of Sweden. It should, however, be kept in mind that the possibility for parties to form alliances had helped to improve proportionality already in the preceding elections, and such alliances could be formed also under the new order (from 1924, collaborating parties could have both a cartel label and a party label on the ballot.)

As can be seen from Figure 2, the degree of proportionality in the elections in the fourth electoral era (1921-1948) varied only slightly from election to election. Yet, when taken together, the increased constituency magnitude and electoral alliances contributed to enabling small parties to win seats. The farmers' parties thus formed alliances with the Conservatives. On the left of the party system, electoral alliances were facilitated by the fact that the Social Democrats used "The Labor Party" as a label on the ballots, and the Left-Socialists simply used the same label but put forward their own candidate list; for this, they did not have to obtain any formal permission from the Social Democrats. As we have already noted, the multi-party system in Sweden was not caused by proportional representation; yet the proportional system clearly contributed to the transformation of a three-party system into a five-party system.

From 1924 until 1948, the last election in which the d'Hondt formula was used in Second Chamber elections, the basic electoral system was on the whole unchanged, but there were some noteworthy election rule changes at various levels of government (Stjernquist, 1996: 100-112). The higher voting age in county council and city elector elections was abolished in 1937. The voting age for Second Chamber elections as well as county and city council elections was lowered to having reached 21 years in the year before the election (1945). The loss of eligibility to vote because of being taken in community care due to poverty was abolished. This was all that remained of the old "poverty bar," most of which had been abolished already through the reforms in the early twenties, and as has been noted previously — it had affected only a small percentage of the electorate.

Other changes in the election law were also politically important. The use of a "cartel" label which was to be placed above the party label on the ballot, and even a third — "fraction" — label beneath the party label had been formalized already in 1924. From 1935, however, cartels could only be formed by means of a formal registration by the participating parties. The parties' right to protect their party labels was also strengthened in other ways. Parties could now register their party labels, and if they did so they could also register candidate names on their official ballot. As before, it was possible for citizens to put forward a candidate list under one of the party labels, but a new restriction was introduced. Any "unofficial" candidate list had to have at least one of the candidate names that the party had registered as the first name. Various splinter groups would rarely be able to get more than one candidate elected, so this provided a bar against a smaller group's "poaching" a seat for someone not nominated by the party by using the party label of one of the bigger parties. In practice, these changes meant that the Communists could no longer gain anything by presenting a candidate list of their own under the "Labor Party" label.

By this time, the party cartel formation had become politically frozen. Electoral alliances between the Social Democrats and any of the bourgeois parties virtually disappeared in the course of the twenties. The cartel form was used by the three non-socialist parties (Conservatives, the liberal People's Party — reunited in 1934 — and the Agrarian Union) who normally formed a cartel all over the country. Under the new rules, this cartel had a common cartel label on the ballot and, beneath it, a party label. The Social Democrats did not enter any cartel, but the small parties on the far left sometimes did so. The effect was that the d'Hondt formula's tendency to over-represent bigger parties was weakened since the Social Democrats alone and the non-socialist parties in cartel were both "big parties" of roughly equal size. There was one politically significant exception, however: the small Communist parties were under-represented (even when they used the cartel option), though not eliminated.

Figure 2 only shows an overall measure of disproportionality in the relationship between seat share and vote share. However, if we look at the data at a more disaggregated level (see Appendix Table A1) we see evidence of differing degrees of equity of representation for different parties. In particular, the Communists were systematically under-represented — on average by 7.4 — seats, and the *Socialdemokrats* were consistently over-represented, also by 7.4 seats on average.

By and large the Social Democrats won the seats the Communists lost because of the combined effects of the d'Hondt system and cartel practice. Taken as a bloc, the non-socialist parties achieved very close to a proportional share of the vote, or sometimes a few seats in excess. Within that bloc the Conservatives tended to be slightly over-represented, while the Liberals — both before and after their reuniting in one party in 1934 — were slightly under-represented. This seems to reflect the fact that the d'Hondt formula was used also for the allotting of seats within the bourgeois cartel. The Agrarian Union, however, fared better and was — very slightly — over-represented in most elections. It is also noteworthy that the People's Party actually became over-represented in 1948 while the Conservatives were under-represented; by that time the People's Party had become the largest in the bourgeois bloc.

The Social Democrats came to power, although in a minority government, in 1932 and held office until 1936. The parliamentary base of the minority government was secured by a pact with the Agrarian Union concerning economic policy under the depression years. After a short interregnum in the summer before the election in 1936, the Social Democrats came back to office in a coalition with the Agrarian Union. In 1939, a national coalition government (including all parties except the Communists) was formed under a Social Democratic prime minister. In the ensuing election in the autumn of 1940 the Social Democrats won an overall majority in the electorate as well as in the Second Chamber. The outcome was widely interpreted as a vote of popular confidence in the Social Democratic prime minister. The national government came to an end in 1945 and the Social Democrats again formed one-party government. Although they did not have an overall majority, they could rely on the Communists to support the government when its continued existence was at stake, and in that sense the Social Democrats governed in effect as a majority party.

Elections to the First Chamber

To complete the picture of the Social Democrats' parliamentary basis of government in the fourth electoral era, one must also look at the balance of strength in the First Chamber (see Table 5.)

Table 5: Party Division in the First Chamber 1929 - 1968

Year*	Conservatives	People's P. incl Liberals	Center P. (Agrarian Union)	Social Democrats	Communists	Total
1929	49	31	17	52	1	150
1933	50	23	18	58	1	150
1937	45	16	22	66	1	150
1941	35	15	24	75	1	150
1945	30	14	21	83	2	150
1949	24	18	21	84	3	150
1953	20	22	25	79	4	150
1957	13	30	25	79	3	150
1959**	16	32	22	79	2	151
1961	19	33	20	77	2	151
1965	26	26	19	78	2	151
1969	25	26	20	79	1	151

* The table shows the party division in the First Chamber in the year after each Second Chamber election during the period.
(The election period for the Second Chamber commences with the year after the election.
** The Second Chamber was dissolved in 1958.

The Social Democrats had a much weaker position in the First Chamber than in the Second Chamber when they came to office in 1932. Together with the Agrarian Union, they could just barely count on a majority in the First Chamber in 1933. As the effects of increasing strength in county and city councils slowly worked their way, the Social Democratic strength in the First Chamber grew, but it was not until 1945 that they achieved an overall majority in that chamber. From then on, however, the First Chamber took on a new role, namely that of a Social Democratic rather than Conservative guarantee.

From the end of World War II and until the end of the two-chamber system, the Social Democrats held a majority in the upper chamber. This reflected the fact that the Social Democrats did very well in several county and city council elections, but it was to some extent also an effect of the use of the d'Hondt formula in the councils' elections of members of the First Chamber.

For the Social Democrats, the changing composition of the First Chamber did more than eliminate the risk of setbacks in the upper chamber. As has already been mentioned, if the two chambers came to different decisions in budget matters, the disagreement was resolved through a "joint vote" of both chambers. The First Chamber majority certainly strengthened the Social Democrats' hand in the post-war years when they governed without an overall majority. This was of course of less importance during the coalitions with the Agrarian Union (first in 1936-1939 and then 1951-57), but it certainly strengthened the Social Democrats' bargaining position in the parliamentary arena.

3. Proportional Representation Without Electoral Cartels: The Modified Sainte-Laguë Formula Replaces d'Hondt in the Fifth Electoral Era, 1952-1968

The Swedish political landscape underwent a change in October 1951. A new balance of political forces in the *Riksdag* was created when the Social Democrats and the Agrarian Union (later the Center Party) announced that they had agreed to form a coalition government. The new coalition had a strong majority base in both chambers of the parliament and it was hoped that the foundation had been laid for a prolonged period of political stability. (See Ruin, 1968.)

For the Agrarian Union, the new political combination entailed a quite intricate tactical problem. In elections in the past, the party had joined with the Conservatives and the People's Party under a common cartel label. As mentioned above, this protected the bourgeois parties from the tendency of the d'Hondt method to under-represent smaller parties. It would hardly be possible for the Agrarian Union to join the same kind of cartel in next year's parliamentary election. Despite the coalition, it was also deemed politically unfeasible to form a cartel with the Social Democrats. Without a change in the electoral rules of the game, the Agrarian Union might suffer a serious loss of seats in the election if it were to stand alone as a small party.

As it happened, a committee of inquiry with a brief to look into the possibilities of election system reform had been at work since 1950, although the

Social Democrats had shown only lukewarm interest in the matter. Now, haste was required and a proposal for a new election system was laid before the *Riksdag* so that it could be employed in the 1952 election.

What the coalition parties needed was an election system that would enable the Agrarian Union to do without a cartel. That clearly required the system to treat small parties more favorably than the d'Hondt system did. On the other hand it was feared that a fully proportional system might be too favorable for even smaller parties than the Agrarian Union and, perhaps, lead to a fragmentation of the party system. The solution espoused by the government parties was to construct an election system that attained the same degree of proportionality as the d'Hondt system — but without the need for medium-sized parties to form any cartel.

The solution found was to replace the d'Hondt formula with a modified version of the Sainte-Laguë formula. The Sainte-Laguë formula — like the d'Hondt one — is a so-called divisor formula. In each step of the allocation of seats under the d'Hondt (or "highest average") formula, a party's number of votes is divided by a number that is equal to the number of seats it has received in previous steps, plus one. One thus obtains a series of divisors which is equal to whole numbers (1, 2, 3, etc). The quota thus obtained is the party's "comparison number" for that stage, and the seat goes to the party that has the highest comparison number. In effect this means that — at each step — the seat goes to the party that will have the highest number of votes per seat if it receives the seat to be allocated. With the Sainte-Laguë formula, the divisor series consists instead of only the odd numbers, i.e. 1, 3, 5, etc. The effect is that the comparison numbers of the larger parties are reduced more rapidly in the course of the allocation of seats than under the d'Hondt formula. As a result, the Sainte-Laguë formula provides for a more proportional representation of smaller parties. This would relieve the Agrarian Union of the need to join any cartel.

There was a snag, however. The Sainte-Laguë formula is favorable also to very small parties, smaller than the Agrarian Union (i.e., the Communists). But that was not the intention. The solution was to use a modified version of the Sainte-Laguë formula in which the first divisor was to be 1.4, rather than 1.0 as in the original formula. This meant that a very small party — which normally could hope to win at most one seat in a constituency — would have its number of votes divided by 1.4 just to qualify for its first seat. In effect, that meant that in many instances they would have gotten no seat at all when all the seats in the constituency had been allocated. Hence very small parties (read, "the Communists") would be under-represented even henceforth. This is what was meant by the pronouncement that the election system should give the same measure of proportionality as before but without any need for cartels.

The thus modified Sainte-Laguë formula was adopted together with a provision in the electoral law which prohibited electoral cartels. The same formula was included in the election law for local government elections.

The new electoral formula performed as expected (see Appendix Table A1 and Figure 2). The Communists continued to be under-represented. Other parties won shares of the seats very near proportionality but with a slight over-representation caused by the under-representation of the Communists. On balance the gain from the Communists tended to be divided between the Social Democrats and the three non-socialist parties taken together, although with a slight advantage for the Social Democrats. (For the last two elections in the period comparisons are complicated by the fact that bourgeois parties presented joint lists in two constituencies.) It is worth noting that the Social Democrats had fared a little better under the old system.

The divisor of 1.4 has no well-defined mathematical ground; it does not define any threshold of representation that is consistent across constituencies and it does not specify any clear criteria with regard to proportionality. It was chosen because calculations on previous election results indicated that it would give the desired result. Yet it served certain political purposes. Interestingly, it was retained even when the election system was changed later by the introduction of additional seats and an entirely different type of threshold.

Elections to the First Chamber and the Operation of the Two Chamber System

The Swedish two-chamber system was rather unusual for several reasons. One was that, after the various constitutional reforms, the electoral bases of the two chambers had become equally democratic and virtually identical. True, the First Chamber was indirectly elected, but the number of elected Members in the First Chamber constituencies reflected the population size of each constituency in much the same way as the Second Chamber constituencies. The party system and the cleavage lines were identical in the parliamentary and county council elections. National politics in fact entirely dominated in both kinds of elections. In the *Riksdag*, bills were considered simultaneously in the two Chambers and in joint committees composed of an equal number of Members from both chambers. In case of disagreement between the two chambers, the matter (in all budgetary issues) was decided in a "Joint Vote" in which the votes cast in the chambers were counted together. That the members of the First Chamber had longer election periods and that members of county councils were strongly represented in the chamber was undoubtedly of some importance in certain fields of legislation. Arguably, it also made some difference that members of the First Chambers were not — like those in the Second Chamber — required to live in their constituencies. With some justification one could nevertheless take the view that the two chambers functioned much like two components of a unified parliament, which was comprised of two components elected under different election systems and with a delayed effect of changes in electoral opinion on one of the chambers.

Table 6: The Social Democrats' Parliamentary Bases in the Two Chambers, 1932-1970

Year	Second Chamber		First Chamber		"Joint Votes"	
	SocDem Major.	SocDem+C omm. Major.	SocDem Overall Major.	SocDem+ Comm. Major.	SocDem Overall Major.	SocDem+C omm. Major.
1932-36						#
1937-40		X				
1941-44	X		X	X	X	
1945-48		X	X		X	
1949-52		X	X		X	
1953-56		#	X		X	
1957-58*			X			X
1958-60*		X	X			X
1961-64		X	X		X	
1965-68		X	X		X	
1969-70	X		X		X	

X indicates a Social Democratic or a Social Democratic + Communist majority. At times the Social Democrats strengthened their parliamentary base through collaboration with the Center (Agrarian) Party. In 1933-1935 the Social Democratic minority government was supported by a pact with the Agrarian Union. During the years 1936-1939 and 1951-1957 there were coalition governments of Social Democrats and the Agrarian Union; the coalition governments had majority bases in the two chambers as well as in "Joint Votes" During 1939-1945 there was a National Coalition government with participation of all parties except the Communists.

Social Democrats + Communists and the Bourgeois parties were evenly balanced.

* The Second Chamber was dissolved in June 1958. The newly elected Second Chamber was elected until the end of 1960, that is for the remainder of the ordinary election period.

As we have seen, the First Chamber ceased to be a conservative guarantee when the Social Democrats achieved a perennial majority in the chamber. In practice, it became a component of the Parliament that helped to secure the Social Democrats' hold on the role as the party of government since the late 1930s.

Table 6 presents in a compact form the parliamentary bases for Social Democratic governing — alone and in coalitions — from 1932 to 1970. The table shows for each time period whether the Social Democrats had an Overall Majority or a Majority together with the Communists in the Second Chamber, First Chamber and in "Joint Votes," respectively. The time periods refer to the balance of strength after each election to the Second Chamber, i.e. in the first year after the election. A newly-elected Second Chamber assembled in January in the year after the election held in September the preceding year. In the course of a Second Chamber election period, some changes in the composition of the First Chamber would occur as a result of the annual election of one eighth of its membership. It should be kept in mind that there were Social Democratic-Agrarian two-party coalitions 1936-1939 and 1951-1957 and a national coalition government which included all parties except the Communists 1939-1945.

As is seen from the table, the Social Democrats had in fact an overall majority in the Second Chamber only during 1941-1944 and 1969-1970, and the first of these periods was during the national coalition government. With the support of the Communists, the Social Democrats commanded a Second Chamber majority throughout the period 1936-1970 with exception for the years 1953-1956, when there was an even balance, and 1957-1958 when there was a bourgeois majority in the Second Chamber. The Social Democrats' strong position — i.e. over-representation — in the First Chamber was a very significant factor in stabilizing their stay in office. The party held an overall majority in that chamber during the whole of the 1945-1970 period. In "Joint Votes," the Social Democrats had an overall majority 1941-1956 and 1961-1970, and with the support of the Communists they could count on a majority in such votes also in the years 1957-1960.

The role of the Communists as a support-force for the Social Democrats was always ambiguous since they often took a very critical view of Social Democratic policies. Nevertheless, they affected the parliamentary balance of strength in a crucial way during these years, because they could be counted upon not to join with the bourgeois parties to defeat a Social Democratic government and, moreover, would cast their strength behind the Social Democrats when the bourgeois parties did not hold an overall majority. Even so, the Social Democrats avoided becoming legislatively dependent on the support of the Communists. To that end, they formed a political pact with the Agrarian Union, as early as 1933-1936, and then government coalitions with the Agrarian Union during two periods. The collaboration with the Agrarian Union also, of course, served another purpose, namely to split the bourgeois bloc.

In one short period, 1957-1958, the Social Democrats' position in government was in real danger. After the Agrarian Union had left the coalition in 1957, there was a bourgeois majority in the Second Chamber. Although the Social Democrats held on to a majority in the First Chamber, they could win "Joint Votes" only with the support of the Communists. The Conservatives and the People's Party did indeed attempt to entice the Agrarian Union to join a three-party government. The attempt failed because the Agrarian Union leader, Mr. Hedlund, refused; as his reason for this decision he pronounced that it would be too inconsistent for his party to shift immediately from one coalition to another. Of course, the fact that there was still a Social Democratic-Communist majority in Joint Votes may have been a factor that he took into account.

4. The Sixth Electoral Era, 1970-1998

Constitutional Reform: A One-Chamber Parliament and Increased Proportionality through Additional Seats

In the late 1960s and first part of the 1970s, the Swedish constitution underwent a profound change which occurred in two stages. The first was a partial constitutional change in 1969. The old two-chamber system was abolished and replaced by a one-chamber *Riksdag* with 350 members; the number was later reduced to 349.

The new unicameral *Riksdag* was to be elected under an election system that provided for virtually full proportionality for all parties that passed the threshold of having received at least four percent of the total national vote. 310 seats are "fixed constituency seats," which were to be allocated to the same 28 constituencies as before. (Since then, the number of constituencies has been increased to 29.) The number of seats for each constituency is determined by the size of the electorate. As a complement there are 39 *additional* seats (at first the number was 40, but this has been reduced by one). In the first stage of the allocation of seats to parties, the modified Sainte-Laguë formula is applied within constituencies and an appropriate number of candidates on each party's list are declared elected. In the next stage, the modified Sainte-Laguë formula is applied on the national vote for those parties who have passed the four-percent threshold. The purpose is to determine how many seats each party is entitled to nationally out of the total number of seats. When the sum of a party's number of fixed constituency seats is less than what it is entitled to nationally, it receives a sufficient number of additional seats. These additional seats are then distributed within the party. A party gets additional seats in the constituencies where it — in comparison with the party's vote in other constituencies — is nearest to deserving increased representation (according to the Sainte-Laguë formula). Those elected are the candidates whose names on the party list follow after those who were elected for fixed constituency lists on the party list.

A party whose share of the national vote falls below the four-percent threshold can win seats only in constituencies where its share of the constituency vote amounts to 12%. Where this happens, the party retains the seat(s) in the constituency (or constituencies) where it passed the constituency threshold but wins no other seats. In practice, however, no party has gained any seat in this way.

The election period was shortened from four to three years. Parliamentary elections were to be held on the same day as the elections for county council elections and local government district elections, which were also to be held every third year.

The election period for the parliament elected in 1968 was shortened so that new elections for the unicameral *riksdag* could be held in 1970.

The new *Riksdag* met for the first time at the beginning of 1971. The process of constitutional change was completed in 1974 when the *Riksdag* adopted an entirely new constitution to replace the old "Form of Government" of 1809 and the constitutional laws, which were also part of the old constitution. The new constitution came into effect from the beginning of 1975.

The constitutional reform process thus completed had had a long period of gestation. A commission with representatives from all the four main parties with a brief to review all major aspects of the constitution was appointed in the mid-1950s and presented its proposal for a new constitution in 1963. Both the Social Democrats and the bourgeois parties, however, were dissatisfied with the proposal and therefore a new commission was appointed. They presented a revised proposal; on the whole, it was this proposal that was enacted as the new constitutional laws of 1974-1975. (See: Statens offentliga utredningar, 1972:15, Grundlagberedningen, *Ny regeringsform. Ny riksdagsordning.*)

The parts of the constitutional change that directly bear upon the subject of this chapter were the new election system and the unicameral *Riksdag*. At the outset of the long preparatory phase, the Social Democrats had actually striven hard to win support for an electoral system that would give a measure of over-representation for a large party — ostensibly in order to ensure that governments with a strong parliamentary basis could be formed. (In the first of the above mentioned commissions, some Social Democratic and one Liberal members even expressed a sympathy for the first-past-the post system, although they supported the version of a proportional system the was proposed by the commission majority.) The election system that the commission proposed was, however, not the one that was subsequently adopted in the later phases of the constitutional reform process.

The Social Democrats had also been of two minds about the consequences of abolishing of the First Chamber. In particular the Prime Minister, Mr. Erlander, argued strenuously for the need for a "communal connection" between national and local politics. The First Chamber could be seen as a way of making the "communal connection" an integral part of the political system, and it was argued that a new constitution ought to comprise such a connection in some form.

In the end, the Social Democrats accepted a highly proportional system, although with a threshold of representation as a safeguard against a fragmentation of the party system. The Social Democrats also gave their support to the abolishing of the two-chamber and the establishing of a unicameral parliament. Yet the Social Democrats insisted on a common election day for parliamentary and local elections as the means to retain a "communal connection."

One can think of several explanations for this outcome. One reason may have been that in a country in which proportional representation of parties had become part of the political culture, arguing for something less than full proportionality was actually politically difficult. With regard to the two-chamber system, it became increasingly difficult to resist the argument that it had become obsolescent. Indeed, it was the predominant view in the Social Democratic Party as well that a new constitution should have a unicameral parliament.

The very severe setback that the Social Democrats suffered in the 1966 local elections added weight to the conviction of those in the party who wanted to do away with the two-chamber system. The effect of the 1966 setback was that the party could look forward to a decline of strength in the First chamber; thus it was no longer a certain political asset.

That the Social Democrats came to accept full proportionality — above a fairly low threshold of voting support — can also be understood in strategic terms. Although the Social Democrats refused any formal collaboration with the Communists, this party had in fact always been assumed to be included in the party's parliamentary base. That is, if Social Democrats and Communists together were to have a majority in a unicameral *Riksdag*, the Social Democrats would form the government, whereas the bourgeois parties could form the government if they together had a majority. Therefore, the Social Democrats had to take into account that if they could not get an election system that ensured a bonus for the largest party — which they could not — then under-representation for the Communists might diminish the chances for a "socialist majority" in the *Riksdag*. The threshold was in fact set at a level which the Communists were likely to surpass. And if they did not, the resulting weakening of the left side would probably be offset by the "leak" of voting support for the bourgeois parties to the Christian Democrats.

Given that the Christian Democrats at that time were deemed unlikely to pass a four-percent threshold, the prospects did not look too bad for the Social Democrats. Yet it is indeed noteworthy that the Social Democrats ended up agreeing to an election system which — given the "normal" balance of strength in the electorate — made it an uphill task for them to win an overall majority, and would give the Communists considerably more parliamentary weight. Of course, the Social Democrats won an electoral majority in the 1968 election. But this had been achieved in a situation that was marked by a crisis in international politics that happened to strengthen the Social Democrats. Few could have expected that the feat of the 1968 election could be repeated under more normal circumstances. (The complex series of tactical maneuvers by the Social Democrats as well as other parties that led to this result are investigated in von Sydow, 1989.)

The Social Democrats had thus, in fact, agreed to changes that both diminished the their chances of forming governments with a strong parliamentary base and increased the likelihood of minority government parliamentarism. For the bourgeois parties, both the abolishing of the First Chamber and the increase in proportionality were gains of great political significance. There would no longer be a First Chamber to prop up the Social Democrats when they suffered a setback in a national parliamentary election. If the number of Communist seats increased as a result of increased proportionality, it would likely be harder than before for the Social Democrats to win more seats than the bourgeois parties taken together; in that case, a Social Democratic government could not win a vote merely by relying on the Communists to abstain, as had sometimes happened in the past. The prospects for transitions of power had undoubtedly become brighter.

The Ice Thaws and Breaks Up at the Edges: New Parties Pass the Threshold, Uncertain Coalitions, and Minority Governments

The effects of the new electoral system and a decline in the Social Democratic party's electoral support combined to set the scene for an era of unstable parliamentarism, which still endures. With the new electoral system, it is only the proportion of votes cast for parties that do not attain the four-percent threshold level that affects the overall level of proportionality. As we shall see, however, the existence of small parties that hover around that threshold can cause erratic shifts in the party division in the *Riksdag*.

The Social Democrats' decline was not large, but it was politically significant: in the 1950s and 1960s the Social Democrats' "normal support" was in the range of 46-48% of the voters, while from the 1970s it has rather been in the range of approximately 43-45%. For the remainder of the era under the new election system, the goal of attaining an overall majority of their own has been out of reach for the Social Democrats. (See Table 1.)

After the 1970 election, the Social Democrats continued in office as a minority government with a precarious parliamentary base which depended on the somewhat unreliable support of the Left (the former Communists). Through the 1973 election, parliamentary uncertainty reached an almost surrealistic height with the *Riksdag* being evenly divided between the Social Democrats and the Left, on the one hand, holding 175 seats and the three non-socialist parties an equal number between them. The Social Democrats continued in office as a minority government. (This was possible because a vote of non-confidence would have required an absolute majority of the members of parliament, i.e., 176 seats.) When the number of votes for and against a proposal is equal in the *Riksdag*, the outcome is decided by lottery. Given that the socialist parties stood against a united bourgeois front on many issues and given the strong cohesiveness of the parliamentary parties, a "lottery situation" did indeed occur on a number of occasions. For the next election period, the number of seats in the *Riksdag* was reduced to 349 in order to avoid this kind of predicament. (The number of additional seats was reduced from 40 to 39; see above.)

The 1976 election brought a non-socialist majority to the *Riksdag*. This was not unprecedented in the old Second Chamber, but this time there was neither a First Chamber nor a coalition with one of the bourgeois parties to protect the Social Democrats' hold on office. The three non-socialist parties — Conservatives (Moderates), People's Party (Liberals) and the Center Party — formed a coalition government with a majority base. The stability did not last, however. In 1978 the three-party coalition fell apart because of disagreement over the nuclear power issue, with the Center Party being opposed to nuclear power in general and the starting of new reactors in particular. The People's Party formed a minority government; the Social Democrats facilitated this surprising outcome by abstaining in the decisive investiture vote; the party was apparently intent on acting in such a way as to break up the alliance between the People's Party and the Conservatives. After the 1979 election the bourgeois parties attained a majority of one in the parliament and, again, attempted to govern in a three-party coalition. In 1981, that coalition collapsed when the Conservatives left, because the Center Party and the People's Party reached a compromise with the Social Democrats on the issue of a reform of the tax system.

In the 1982 election the Social Democrats came back to power for a period of minority government — supported by the Left party — which lasted until the party's defeat in the 1991 election.

The 1985 election did not cause a change in government but it was notable for another reason. Although the electoral system did not allow for the forming of "cartels" — i.e. the arrangement when two or more parties agree on a "cartel label" placed above the party's own party label on the candidate list ballot paper — it was perfectly possible for a party to present more than one party list under its own party label. This has indeed happened fairly frequently. A party has, for example, presented one list of candidates for the countryside part, and another for the urban part of a constituency, or it has resolved a within-party candidate competition by presenting two different candidate lists, often differing only with regard to the (ordering of) the candidates at the top of the lists. Sometimes parties have also found it tactically advantageous to present special candidate lists with, for example, young candidates or "Christian" candidates. When this method is used, a party's candidate lists are merged into a joint rank ordering of candidates (depending of the number of votes for the list varieties) in the course of the allocation of seats. What happened in 1985 was something different, however. The Center Party and the Christian Democrats agreed to use the label "The Center" as a common label. Under that label, there was a Center Party candidate list and a Christian Democrat candidate list, identifiable by the candidate names on the list types. By this strategy the Christian Democratic Leader, Mr. Alf Svensson, was elected in the constituency which was his special stronghold. The Christian Democrats won no other seats, but the Center party, of course, gained somewhat because the Center's share of the national vote was increased a little. This was a strategy that caused no little anger amongst the other parties, but it seems generally agreed by constitutional experts that it was perfectly legal. Yet it has, so far, not been used in any subsequent election.

The 1991 election was a disaster for the Social Democrats. The Greens dropped out of the *Riksdag*, but this time two other small parties gained representation. One was the Christian Democrats, who at last managed to pass the threshold in their own right. The other was a party on the extreme right, the New Democrats. None of the other non-socialist parties really wished to have anything to do with this populist and xenophobic movement that had appealed to anti-immigration feelings in the electorate, yet there was no non-socialist majority in the parliament unless the New Democrats were counted in. The result was that a four-party bourgeois government, which included the Christian Democrats but not the New Democrats, was formed. Although the coalition did not command an overall majority, it had more seats than the Social Democrats and the Left taken together. The non-socialist coalition government had to cope with a deepening economic crisis and was fraught by internal tensions. Towards the end of the election period, the Center Party leader even resigned from the government over an issue disagreement, although the party as such remained in the coalition government. The Social Democratic government survived the 1988 election, although its share of the vote declined. But, for the first time in decades a new party entered the *Riksdag* when the Greens (*Miljöpartiet de gröna*) succeeded in passing the threshold. The Social Democrats continued in office as a minority government, again relying primarily on the Left as part of its parliamentary base, although in practice it often sought collaboration with one of the parties in the Center.

The 1994 election changed the scene again. The New Democrats — discredited by internal splits — dropped out, but the Greens came back. The Social Democrats returned as a minority government. Together with the Left they held a clear majority and if supported also by the Greens they could count on a very substantial majority. In the course of the following years — and especially in the first autumn after the election — the Social Democrats actually established quite close collaboration with the Left and from time to time also with the Greens. After a while the balance has shifted, however. The Social Democrats chose to establish a parliamentary base that is politically firmer by entering agreements and collaboration with the Center Party on a broad range of issues. The Social Democrats seem happy in this constellation, especially since it has enabled them to split the bourgeois front — a perennial strategic target for the party. The Center Party leadership has also been satisfied by an arrangement that has enabled them to exercise a considerable measure of influence on government policy. But there are signs that sections of the Center Party's rank-and-file membership and electoral base feel rather uneasy. The dividing line between "socialist parties" and "the bourgeois parties" is certainly still a very important political reality. The price to be paid for the Social Democrats is a measure of discontent among its own voters because of concessions to the Center Party and the — almost certain — prospect of losses of support to the Left because of the policy of financial austerity that it has had to pursue. The Social Democrats seem — at the time of writing — likely to suffer a setback in the 1998 election. It remains to be seen if the Social Democratic and Center Party collaboration can survive if the next election outcome creates a bourgeois majority in the *Riksdag*, or if it even can last all the way to the election.[4]

Much of the recent volatility in the working of Swedish parliamentary system is undoubtedly the result of the weakening of the Social Democrats. Yet the new election system and the unicameral *Riksdag* seem to have contributed to weakening rather than strengthening the country's parliamentary system of government. Although the emergence of small parties has not been the result of any change in the threshold of representation, it seems plausible that general uncertainty in the parliamentary situation has created room for small parties outside the framework of the traditional five-party system and helped them to surmount the threshold. Sweden now has (at least) a seven-party system. If we are to believe Sartori's typology, this may signify a significant change in the mode of operation of the party system (Sartori, 1976).

In a quite remarkable move, the parties agreed on at least one constitutional change that was intended to increase stability in the political system,

4.In the election of 1998, the Social Democrats suffered a historic setback receiving only 36.4 percent of the vote; the worst result for the party since general suffrage was introduced to all adults in the election of 1921. After the 1998 election, the collaboration between the Social Democrats and the Center Party ceased although the Social Democrats continued on as a minority government but now supported by the Left Party and the Greens instead.

namely to lengthen the election period — for parliamentary as well as local government elections — from three to four years. Constitutional changes require that the decision be taken by two parliaments with a general election occurring between the decisions. The second step was taken by the *Riksdag* elected in 1994, which thus lengthened it own election period.

Electoral System Change: Candidate Preference Voting Within the Party List System

A recent change in the Swedish constitution has reshaped the electoral system in a way that has significantly changed the character of the choice offered to the voter. The voter will be offered not only a choice between candidate lists but also an opportunity to express a personal preference for one of the candidates in the list on the ballot he chooses to cast.

In *Riksdag* elections the new system was used for the first time in the election of 1998. It works as follows: On the parties' candidate list ballots, there will be a space for the marking of the voter's preference at each candidate name. If the voter so wishes, he/she can put a mark in *one* of these spaces and thereby indicate that he wants to give a *personal preference vote* to that candidate in addition to his voting for the list as a whole. Use of the preference voting option is thus voluntary. Independently of whether the voter has indicated a candidate preference, the vote will count towards the total number of votes cast for the party. (Regeringens proposition 1996/97:70. Statens offentliga utredningar, 1993:21, *Ökat personval.* Statens offentliga utredningar, 1996:66, *Utvärderat personval.*)

At a first step in the ballot counting procedure, the number of preference votes each candidate has received is counted. If a candidate's personal votes amount to at least 8% of the party's vote, the name of the candidate will be moved to the top of the rank-ordering of the candidates. (Otherwise his/her preference votes are ignored.) If more than one candidate passes this requirement, their names will be ordered according to the number of preference votes each of them has received. Thereafter, other candidates on the list follow in the rank ordering, ordered in the same way as on the ballot. Preference voting can thus create a rank-ordering of candidates that differs from the one that the party has indicated through its ordering of the names on the party list. This new rank ordering provides the basis for the allocation of the seats that a party is entitled to. (As before, the modified Sainte-Laguë formula is used.) Otherwise the procedure is unchanged with regard to both fixed constituency seats and additional seats. The same preference vote method will be used in local elections, except that the required percentage of personal votes is somewhat smaller: 5% rather than 8%.

The personal vote system was tried in local government elections in a few communes in 1994 and it was also used nationally in the elections to the European Parliament in 1995. The personal vote option attracted only limited public interest in the communes where it was used in 1994. Moreover, a large proportion of the personal votes went to candidates at the top of the lists who would have won seats even without personal voting. Yet, a few of those elected succeeded because their preference votes had indeed placed them higher in the rank ordering of candidates than they otherwise had been. In the European Parliament election, 46% of the voters cast a vote with a candidate preference. In this election, the entire country formed one constituency with 22 seats. Of those elected, 11 won their seats on personal preference votes. However, most of the personal votes had been cast for candidates who were already at the top of the party lists. Had there been no personal preference voting, every one of these 11 would have been elected owing to their place on the party list.

A price has been paid in connection with the introduction of personal preference voting. In the past, it has been possible for a voter to delete one or more names on the party list, thereby denying the deleted candidate(s) his support. It has also been possible to "write in" a candidate name. Both of these options have been abolished in order to avoid making the vote-counting procedure unmanageable. In practice, none of these ways of expressing feelings has had any significant political effect, so the loss is negligible. More important is that the parties henceforth will need to register all their candidates when they protect their party labels by registering them officially (as all major parties will do). If a ballot contains names that are not registered, those names will be considered non-existent in the vote counting. This means that it will no longer be possible for a grouping within a party to put forward its own candidate list, provided only that the two top names on such a list are officially registered candidates. At least theoretically the new requirement that all candidates must be registered by the party could limit the scope for within-party competition. Yet even in the future it will be possible to put forward more than one candidate list under the same party label, although all the names on the different list types will need to be registered candidates.

Looking to the Future

One may guess that a quite large proportion of these preference votes will be used to secure the election of candidates at the top of the parties' candidate lists. If so, the effect of personal voting may be minimal.[5] [*Editor's Note*: All in all, a bare 30% of the voters exercised their right to mark a preferred candidate in the parliamentary election of 1998. As a consequence, only 12 candidates who otherwise would not have been elected were elected as members of the *Riksdag*. Roughly the same number of voters took the opportunity to use the candidate preference vote in the local and regional election, 35% in the local elections and 28% in the regional elections.] One may also speculate about how much more we will see of intra-party campaign competition among candidates. In the past, there has been very little of candidate competition. Campaigns have been organized and financed by parties. Individual candidates have rarely attempted to pursue any personal campaign and no fundraising by individual candidates has been required. Even when there has been within-party competition between different lists, this has usually been a low-key affair. In the future, candidates may find it necessary to pursue their own personal campaigns, organize staff and campaign supporters, and engage in their own fundraising. One could perhaps endeavor to divine the future by looking at Finland and Denmark, which have candidate preference voting — albeit in quite different forms — but at this stage it is hardly worthwhile to make any too specific predictions on that basis. Suffice it to wager that in the Swedish context the parties will likely be able to keep within-party competition within limits that entail no real threat to party cohesiveness. Most of the national campaign will, as in the past, happen on television, within the framework provided by public service television, and will be entirely dominated by the national party leaderships. In that context, there is not likely to be much room for highly visible candidate constituency campaigns. Such complacency may, on the other hand, be unwarranted. If so, we may see entirely new campaign scenarios enfold.

5.However, some voters will undoubtedly cast personal votes for candidates lower down on the party list. One reason may be that the voter indeed hopes the he and like-minded voters may get the candidate elected, despite his low place on the party list. Another reason may be that the voter fears that a candidate who is placed on an 'electable' place on the party list may actually be defeated because other candidates take precedence on the strength of their personal votes. In that case it may be prudent to use one preference vote to support a candidate who may be under threat. Regrettably such tactical consideration will have to be based on assumptions so uncertain that the voter's decision can hardly be supported by any well-grounded rational calculation.

Appendix

Table A1. Share of votes in percent, the number of seats for each party and share of seats in percent in the Second Chamber elections between 1911 and 1998.

SWE III

Year	Share	Party							
		Left party	Social Democr.	Center party	Peoples party	Conser-vatives	Chris-tian Democr.	Green party	Other parties
1911	Votes in%		28.5		40.2	31.2			
	# of seats	-	64		102	64	-	-	0.1
	Seats in%		27.8		44.3	27.8			
1914(I)	Votes in%		30.1		32.2	37.7			
	# of seats	-	74	-	70	86	-	-	0.0
	Seats in %		32.1		30.4	37.3			
1914(II)	Votes in%		36.4		26.9	36.5			
	# of seats	-	87	0.2	57	86	-	-	0.0
	Seats in %		37.8		24.7	37.4			
1917	Votes in%	8.1	31.1	8.5	27.6	24.7			
	# of seats	11	86	14	62	57	-	-	0.0
	Seats in %	4.8	37.4	6.1	27.0	24.8			
1920	Votes in%	6.4	29.7	14.2	21.8	27.9			
	# of seats	7	75	30	47	71	-	-	0.0
	Seats in%	3.0	32.6	13.0	20.4	30.9			

Table A1. (Continuation)

SWE IV

Year	**Share**	**Party**							
		Left party	Social Democr.	Center party	Peoples party	Conser- vatives	Christian Democr.	Green party	Other parties
	Votes in%	7.8	36.4	11.1	18.8	25.9			
1921	# of seats	13	93	21	41	62	-	-	0.0
	Seats in%	5.6	40.4	9.1	17.8	27.0			
	Votes in%	5.1	41.1	10.8	16.9	26.1			
1924	# of seats	5	104	23	33	65	-	-	0.0
	Seats in%	2.2	45.2	10.0	14.3	28.3			
	Votes in%	6.4	37.0	11.2	15.9	29.4			
1928	# of seats	8	90	27	32	73	-	-	0.1
	Seats in%	3.5	39.1	11.7	13.9	31.7			
	Votes in%	8.3	41.7	14.1	11.7	23.5			
1932	# of seats	8	104	36	24	58	-	-	0.7
	Seats in%	3.5	45.2	15.7	10.4	25.2			
	Votes in%	7.7	45,9	14.3	12.9	17.6			
1936	# of seats	11	112	36	27	44	-	-	1.6
	Seats in%	4.5	48.7	15.7	11.7	19.1			
	Votes in%	4.2	53.8	12.0	12.0	18.0			
1940	# of seats	3	134	28	23	42	-	-	0.0
	Seats in%	1.3	58.3	12.2	10.0	18.3			
	Votes in%	10.3	46.7	13.6	12.9	15.9			
1944	# of seats	15	115	35	26	39	-	-	0.6
	Seats in%	65	50.0	15.2	11.3	17.0			
	Votes in%	6.3	46.2	12.4	22.7	12.3			
1948	# of seats	8	112	30	57	23	-	-	0.1
	Seats in%	3.5	48.7	13.0	24.8	10.0			

SWE V

Year	Share	Party							
		Left party	Social Democr	Center party	Peoples party	Conser- vatives	Christian Democr	Green party	Other parties
	Votes in%	4.3	46.1	10.7	24.4	14.4			
1952	# of seats	5	110	26	58	31	-	-	0.1
	Seats in%	2.2	47.8	11.3	25.2	13.5			
	Votes in%	5.0	44.6	9.4	23.8	17.1			
1956	# of seats	6	106	19	58	42	-	-	0.1
	Seats in%	2.6	45.9	8.3	25.1	18.3			
	Votes in%	3.4	46,2	12.7	18.2	19.5			
1958	# of seats	5	111	32	38	45	-	-	0.0
	Seats in%	2.2	48.1	13.9	16.5	19.5			
	Votes in%	4.5	47.8	13.6	17.5	16.5			
1960	# of seats	5	114	34	40	39	-	-	0.1
	Seats in%	2.2	49.1	14.7	17.2	16.8			
	Votes in%	5.2	47.3	13.4	17.1	13.7			
1964	# of seats	8	113	36	43	33	1.8	-	1.5
	Seats in%	3.4	48.5	15.5	18.5	14.2			
	Votes in%	3.0	50.1	15.7	14.3	12.9			
1968	# of seats	3	125	39	34	32	1.5	-	2.6
	Seats in%	1.3	53.6	16.7	14.6	13.7			

Table A1. (Continuation)

SWE VI

Year	Share	Party							
		Left party	Social Democr	Center party	Peoples party	Conservatives	Christian Democr	Green party	Other parties
	Votes in%	4.8	45.3	19.9	16.2	11.5			
1970	# of seats	17	163	71	58	41	1.8	-	0.4
	Seats in%	4.9	46.6	20.3	16.6	11.7			
	Votes in%	5.3	43.6	25.1	9.4	14.3			
1973	# of seats	19	156	90	34	51	1.8	-	0.5
	Seats in%	5.4	44.6	25.7	9.7	14.6			
	Votes in%	4.8	42.7	24.1	11.1	15.6			
1976	# of seats	17	152	86	39	55	1.4	-	0.3
	Seats in%	4.9	43.6	24.6	11.2	15.8			
	Votes in%	5.6	43.2	18.1	10.6	20.3			
1979	# of seats	20	154	64	38	73	1.4	-	0.8
	Seats in%	5.7	44.1	18.3	10.9	20.9			
	Votes in%	5.6	45.6	15.5	5.9	23.6			
1982	# of seats	20	166	56	21	86	1.9	1.6	0.3
	Seats in%	5.7	47.6	16.0	6.0	24.6			
	Votes in%	5.4	44.7	10.1	14.2	21.3	2.3[a]		
1985	# of seats	19	159	43	51	76	1	1.5	0.5
	Seats in%	5.4	45.6	12.3	14.6	21.8	0.3		
	Votes in%	5.9	43.2	11.3	12.2	18.3		5.5	
1988	3 of seats	21	156	42	44	65	2.9	20	0.7
	Seats in%	6.0	44.7	12.0	12.6	18.6		5.7	
	Votes in%	4.5	37.7	8.5	9.1	21.9	7.2		7.7[b]
1991	# of seats	16	138	31	33	80	26	3.4	25 (ND)
	Seats in%	4.6	39.5	8.9	9.5	22.9	7.4		7.2
	Votes in%	6.2	45.4	7.7	7.2	22.3	4.1	5.0	
1994	# of seats	22	161	27	26	80	15	18	2.2
	Seats in%	6.3	46.1	7.7	7.4	22.9	4.3	5.2	
	Votes in%	12.0	36.4	5.1	4.7	22.9	11.8	4.5	
1998	# of seats	43	131	18	17	82	42	16	2.6
	Seats in%	12.3	37.5	5.2	4.9	23.5	12.0	4.6	

a. 1985 had the Centre Party and the Christian Democrats formed an electoral alliance. The percentages given in the table are those for each party list. One Christian Democratic Member of parliament was elected.

b. 6.7% of these votes were for New Democracy.

Table A2. Percent constituencies with direct elected members to the Second Chamber 1866 - 1908

Electoral system	Election year	Percent constituencies with direct elections	Total number of constituencies
SWE I			
	1866	23%	173
	1869	Not available	
	1872	55%	176
	1875	59%	176
	1878	62%	183
	1881	65%	184
	1884	68%	185
	1887 (I)	66%	187
	1887 (II)	77%	187
SWE II			
	1890	79%	188
	1893	87%	186
	1896	90%	196
	1899	92%	196
	1902	95%	196
	1905	97%	196
	1908	99%	197

Table A3. Under-representation of the rural population in the Second Chamber 1866 - 1908

Electoral system	Election year	Per cent of those eligible to vote living in rural districts	Per cent of seats elected by the rural population	Per cent under-representation of the rural population
SWE I				
	1866	Not available		
	1869	Not available		
	1872	87.7	71.1	16.6
	1875	86.1	69.7	16.4
	1878	84.3	68.6	15.7
	1881	83.8	68.9	14.9
	1884	83.2	67.8	15.4
	1887 (I)	79.8	66.1	13.7
	1887 (II)	81.6	65.8	15.8
SWE II				
	1890	80.2	64.5	15.7
	1893	79.7	63.6	16.1
	1896	78.7	65.2	13.5
	1899	77.6	65.2	12.4
	1902	74.8	65.2	9.6
	1905	72.5	65.2	7.3
	1908	69.0	65.2	3.8

Table A4. Percent share of employers in four different branches of business in Sweden between 1870 and 1994

Electoral system	Year	Agriculture and forestry	Industry	Trade and communications	Public adminis-tration and other services	Total
SWE I						
	1870	72.4	14.6	5.2	7.8	100
	1880	67.9	17.4	7.3	7.4	100
SWE II						
	1890	62.1	21.7	8.7	7.5	100
	1900	55.1	27.8	10.4	6.7	100
SWE III						
	1910	50.3	26.5	12.0	11.2	100
	1920	43.5	31.1	14.6	11.0	100
SWE IV						
	1930	38.0	32.4	17.6	12.0	100
	1940	30.7	36.1	20.1	13.1	100
SWE V						
	1950	21.5	41.2	23.9	13.4	100
	1960	13.5	44.0	22.3	20.2	100
SWE VI						
	1970	8,1	40.2	26.5	25.1	100
	1980	5.5	33.7	27.6	33.2	100
	1990	3.4	29.0	29.8	37.6	100
	1994	3.4	25.0	31.0	40.5	100

Source: National Central Bureau of Statistics, *Historical Statistics of Sweden — Part 1. Population*, Allmänna förlaget, Stockholm, 1969 and Hadenius, S., *Svensk politik under 1900-talet*, Tidens förlag, Jyväskylä, 1995.

*Table A5. Percent share of the Swedish population living in densely populated areas / sparsely populated areas between 1860 and 1990**

Electoral system	Year	Per cent share of the Swedish population living in densely populated areas	Per cent share of the Swedish population living in sparsely populated areas	Total
SWE I				
	1860	12.7	87.3	100
	1870	14.8	85.2	100
	1880	17.2	82.8	100
SWE II				
	1890	21.4	78.6	100
	1900	28.2	71.8	100
SWE III				
	1910	34.0	66.0	100
	1920	45.2	54.8	100
SWE IV				
	1930	48.5	51.5	100
	1940	56.2	43.8	100
SWE V				
	1950	66.2	33.8	100
	1960	72.7	27.3	100
SWE VI				
	1970	81.4	18.6	100
	1980	83.1	16.9	100
	1990	86.3	13.7	100

Source: National Central Bureau of Statistics, *Historical Statistics of Sweden — Part 1. Population*, Allmänna förlaget, Stockholm, 1969 and Hadenius, S., *Svensk politik under 1900-talet*, Tidens förlag, Jyväskylä, 1995

*Table A5 illustrates the increasing share of the Swedish population living in densely populated areas from 1860 to 1990. The criterion defining densely populated area is has unfortunately not been constant in the actual time period. Up to 1920 areas which were diffusely defined as administratively governed villages and towns were categorized as densely populated. From 1920 even areas within administrative rural districts with more than 200 inhabitants and less than 40% agriculture population was counted as densely populated. In 1950 the criterion was changed once again. From 1950 villages with more than 200 inhabitants and less than 200 meters between the houses were categorized as densely populated.

REFERENCES

Aardal, Bernt and Henry Valen. 1995. *Konflikt og Opinion* (Conflict and Opinion), Oslo: NKS-Forlaget.

Aardal, Bernt and Henry Valen. 1997. The Storting Elections of 1989 and 1993: Norwegian Politics in Perspective. In Kaare Strøm and Lars Svåsand (eds.) *Challenges to Political Parties. The Case of Norway*, Ann Arbor, MI: Michigan University Press, 61-76.

Aardal, Bernt. 1990a. "Green Politics: A Norwegian Experience." *Scandinavian Political Studies*, 13(2): 1-18.

Aardal, Bernt. 1990b. "Ny valgordning – nye koalisjonsmuligheter?" (A new electoral system – new coalition opportunities?). *Norsk Statsvitenskapelig Tidsskrift*, 3:213-223.

Aardal, Bernt. 1993. *Energi og miljø. Nye stridsspørsmål i møte med gamle strukturer* (Energy and Environment. New Issues Facing Old Structures), Report 93:15, Oslo: Institute for Social Research.

Aardal, Bernt. 1994. "Hva er en politisk skillelinje? En begrepsmessig grenseoppgang" (What is a Political Cleavage? A Conceptual Demarcation). *Tidsskrift for samfunnsforskning*, 35: 217-248.

Aardal, Bernt. 2003?. "Electoral Systems in Norway 1814-1997." Paper for the UCI Conference on Evolution of Electoral Systems and Party Systems in the Nordic Countries, Laguna Beach, California; December. Oslo: Institute for Social Research.

Aardal, Bernt. 1997. "Electoral Systems in Norway 1814-1997." Paper originally prepared for the UCI Conference on Evolution of Electoral Systems and Party Systems in the Nordic Countries, Laguna Beach, California; December, 1997. Oslo: Institute for Social Research. Updated and revised as Chapter 4 in the current volume.

Aars, Jacob. 1998. *Rekruttering og personskifte i lokalpolitikken. En sammenligning av Finland og Norge* (Recruitment and Turnover in Local Politics. A Comparison of Finland and Norway), Rapport 58, Bergen: Department of Administration and Organizational Science, University of Bergen.

Aasland, Tertit. 1965. "Valgordningen 1906-1918" (The Electoral System 1906-1918), *Historisk Tidsskrift*, Bd. 44: 267-297.

Althingismannatal 1845-1995. 1996. Reykjavík: Skrifstofa Althingis.

Ames, Barry. 1995. "Electoral Strategy under Open-List Proportional Representation." *American Journal of Political Science* 39(2):406-434.

Andersen, Johannes, Ole Borre, Jørgen Goul Andersen, & Hans Jørgen Nielsen. 1999. *Vælgere med omtanke. En analyse af folketingsvalget 1998*, Aarhus: Systime.

Andersen, Jørgen Goul and Tor Bjørklund. 1990. "Structural Changes and New Cleavages: The Progress Parties in Denmark and Norway", *Acta Sociologica*, 33(3): 195-217.

Andræ, Poul. 1905. *Andræ og hans Opfindelse Forholdstalsvalgmaaden. Et Mindeskrift i Anledning af 50-Aars-Dagen for Forholdstals-Valgmaadens Indførelse.* Copenhagen: Gyldendalske Boghandel.

Andrén, G. 1937. *Tvåkammarsystemets tillkomst och utveckling*. Stockholm: Sveriges riksdag band IX.

AR (Althingi Records) – Althingistídindi. Proceedings from the Althingi since 1845.

Aranson, Peter, and Peter C. Ordeshook. 1972. Spatial Strategy for Sequential Elections. In R. Niemi and H. Weisberg (eds.) *Probability Models of Collective Decision Making*, Columbus, OH: Merrill.

Arnórsson, Einar. 1945. *Réttarsaga Althingis*. Reykjavík: Althingissögunefnd.

Barnes, Samuel H., Max Kaase et al. 1979. *Political Action. Mass Participation in Five Western Democracies.* Beverly Hills and London: Sage Publications.

Bawn, K. 1993. "The Logic of Institutional Preferences—German Electoral Law as a Social choice Outcome." *American Journal of Political Science*, 37(4): 965-989.

Berglund, Sten and Lindström, Ulf. 1978. *The Scandinavian party System(s)*. Lund: Studentlitteratur

Bergsgård, Arne. 1964. *Norsk historie 1814-1880* (Norwegian History 1814-1880), Oslo: Det Norske Samlaget.

Betænkning (1922). *Betænkning afgivet af den i Henhold til Lov af 29. April 1921 nedsatte Valglovskommission*, Copenhagen: Schultz.

Bjørn, Claus. 1998. *1848. Borgerkrig og Revolution*. Copenhagen: Gyldendal.

Blais, Andre, and R. K. Carty. 1990. "Does Proportional Representation Foster Voter Turnout?" *European Journal of Political Research*, 18(2):167-181.

Blais, Andre, and R. K. Carty. 1991. "The Psychological Impact of Electoral Laws: Measuring Duverger's Elusive Factor." *British Journal of Political Science*, 21:79 93.

Blom, Ida. 1974. "Partier og pressgrupper i norsk politikk 1905-1914" (Parties and Pressure groups in Norwegian Politics 1905-1914), *Historisk Tidsskrift*, 1:37-55.

Boix, C. 1999. "Setting the Rules of the Game: The Choice of Electoral Systems in Advanced Democracies." *American Political Science Review*, 93(3): 609-624.

Borre, Ole & Jørgen Goul Andersen. 1997. *Voting and Political Attitudes in Denmark. A Study of the 1994 Election*. Aarhus: Aarhus University Press.

Bowler, Shaun and Bernard Grofman (eds.) 2000. *Elections in Australia, Ireland and Malta under the Single Transferable Vote*. Ann Arbor: University of Michigan Press.

Brams, Steven J. 1975. *Game Theory and Politics*. New York: Free Press.

Cain, Bruce, John A. Ferejohn, and Morris Fiorina. 1987. *The Personal Vote: Constituency Service and Electoral Independence*. Cambridge, MA: Harvard University Press.

Carey, John M., and Matthew Shugart. 1995. "Incentives to Cultivate a Personal Vote: A Rank Ordering of Electoral Formulas." *Electoral Studies* 14(4):417-440.

Carstairs, A. M. 1980. *A Short History of Electoral Systems in Western Europe*. London: George Allen & Unwin.

Christensen, Raymond, and Paul Johnson. 1995. "Toward a Context-Rich Analysis of Electoral Systems: The Japanese Example." *American Journal of Political Science*, 39:575-598.

Coleman, James S. 1972. "The Positions of Political Parties in Elections." In *Probability Models of Collective Decision Making*, ed. R.G. Niemi and F. Weisberg. Columbus, OH: Charles E. Merrill, 332-57.

Cox, Gary W. 1987. "Electoral Equilibrium under Alternative Voting Institutions." *American Journal of Political Science*, 31(1):82-108.

Cox, Gary W. 1990. "Centripetal and Centrifugal Incentives in Electoral Systems." *American Journal of Political Science*, 31:82-108.

Cox, Gary W. 1996. "Is the 1994 Non-Transferable Vote Superproportional? Evidence from Japan and Taiwan." *American Journal of Political Science*, 40(3):740-755.

Cox, Gary W. 1997. *Making Votes Count: Strategic Coordination in the World's Electoral Systems*. New York and London: Cambridge University Press.

Cox, Gary W., and Frances Rosenbluth. 1994. "Reducing Nomination Errors: Factional Competition and Party Strategy in Japan." *Electoral Studies*, 13:4-16.

Dahlerup, Drude. 1978. "Women's Entry into Politics: The Experience of Danish Local and General Elections 1908-20." *Scandinavian Political Studies*, 1(2-3): 139-162.

Damgaard, Erik. 1974. "Stability and Change in the Danish Party System over Half a Century." *Scandinavian Political Studies*, 9: 103-125.

Damgaard, Erik. 1992. "Denmark: Experiments in Parliamentary Government." In Erik Damgaard (ed.), *Parliamentary Change in the Nordic Countries*, Oslo: Uniersitetsforlaget, 19-49.

Damgaard, Erik. 1997. "Dänemark: Das Leben und Sterben von Koalitionsregierungen." In Wolfgang C. Müller & Kaare Strøm (eds.), *Koalitionsregierungen in Westeuropa. Bildung, Arbeitsweise und Beendigung*, Vienna: Signum-Verlag, 2889-326.

Danielsen, Rolf. 1964. *Det Norske Storting gjennom 150 år. Bind II. Tidsrommet 1870-1908* (The Norwegian Storting through 150 years. Volume I. The Period 1879-1908), Oslo: Gyldendal Norsk Forlag.

Danielsen, Rolf. 1984. *Borgerlig oppdemningspolitikk, Høyres historie* Bd. 2 (Nonsocialist containment politics. The History of the Right Party Vol. 2), Oslo: Gyldendal.

Davidson, Chandler and Bernard Grofman, (Eds.). 1994. *Quiet Revolution in the South: The Effects of the Voting Rights Act, 1965-1990*. Princeton, NJ: Princeton University Press.

Dodd, Lawrence C. 1976. *Coalitions in Parliamentary Governments*. Princeton, NJ: Princeton University Press.

Dokument nr. 1. 1896. *Forslag til forandring i Formanskabslovene af 1837* (Proposals Suggesting Changes in the Local Laws of 1837), Oslo: Det norske Storting.

Downs, Anthony. 1957. *An Economic Theory of Democracy*. New York: Harper.

Dunleavy, Patrick and Helen Margetts. 1995. "Understanding the Dynamics of Electoral Reform." *International Political Science Review*, 16(1): 9-29.

Duverger, Maurice. 1984. "Which Is the Best Electoral System?" In Lijphart, Arend and Bernard Grofman (eds.), *Choosing An Electoral System*. New York: Praeger Publishers, 31-39.

Eckstein, Harry. 1975. "Case Study and Theory in Political Science." In Greenstein, Fred and Nelson W. Polsby (eds.) *Political Science: Scope and Theory* (Handbook of Political Science, Volume I). Reading, MA: Addison-Wesley, 79-137 (reprinted in Eckstein. 1992, 117-178).

Eckstein, Harry. 1992. *Regarding Politics: Essays on Political Theory, Stability and Change*. Berkeley, CA: University of California Press.

Eide, Tor Myrland. 1998. "Her er det godt å sitte, la oss i tillegg gjøre det tryggere. Norske valgsystemreformer i perioden 1952-1988." (Here it is good to sit, let us in addition make it better. Norwegian Electoral Reforms 1952-1988), Master Thesis, Department of Comparative Politics, The University of Bergen.

Eigaard, Søren. 1993. *Idealer og politik. Historien om Grundloven af 1953*. Odense: Odense University Press.

Einarsson, Indridi. 1884. "Um kosningar og kjósendr til alþingis" in *Tímarit hins íslenska bókmenntafélags*. 5:1-35.

Elklit, Jørgen & Nigel S. Roberts. 1996. "A category of its own? Four PR two-tier compensatory member electoral systems in 1994." *European Journal of Political Research*, 30(2): 217-240.

Elklit, Jørgen & Ole Tonsgaard. 1978. "Folkeafstemningen i september 1978 om 18 års valgret." *Politica*, 10(3): 33-62.

Elklit, Jørgen and Anne Birte Pade. 1996. *Parliamentary Elections and Election Administration in Denmark*, Copenhagen: Ministry of the Interior.

Elklit, Jørgen. 1980. "Election Laws and Electoral Behaviour in Denmark until 1920." In Otto Büsch, (ed.), *Wählerbewegungen in der europäischen Geschichte*, Berlin: Colloquium Verlag, 366-397.

Elklit, Jørgen. 1981. *Det tyske mindretals parlamentariske repræsentation.* Aabenraa: Det tyske mindretals sekretariat.

Elklit, Jørgen. 1983. "Mobilization and Partisan Division. Open Voting in Fredericia, Denmark." *Social Science History*, 7(3): 235-266.

Elklit, Jørgen. 1984. "Det klassiske danske partisystem bliver til." In Jørgen Elklit, and Ole Tonsgaard (eds.), *Valg og vælgeradfærd. Studier i dansk politik*, Aarhus: Politica. 21-38.

Elklit, Jørgen. 1985. "Open Voting in Prussia and Denmark, or: The Complexity of Comparison. Some Post-Rokkanian Reflections." *Historical Social Research/Historische Sozialforschung*, 35: 2-16.

Elklit, Jørgen. 1988a. *Fra åben til hemmelig afstemning. Aspekter af et partisystems udvikling*, Aarhus: Politica.

Elklit, Jørgen. 1988b. "'Den laveste partiegoismes allerbrutaleste fjæs?' Eller: Noget om valglovene 1915 og 1920." In Hans Chr Johansen, Mogens N. Pedersen and Jørgen Thomsen (eds.) *Om Danmarks historie 1900-1920. Festskrift til Tage Kaarsted*, Odense: Odense University Press. 61-96

Elklit, Jørgen. 1992. "The Best of Both Worlds? The Danish Electoral System 1915-20 in a Comparative Perspective." *Electoral Studies*, 11(3): 189-205. Also in Peter Gundelach, and Karen Siune (eds.), *From Voters to Participants. Essays in Honour of Ole Borre*, Aarhus: Politica, 1992, pp. 236-254.

Elklit, Jørgen. 1993. "Simpler than Its Reputation: The Electoral System in Denmark since 1920." *Electoral Studies*, 23(1): 41-57.

Elklit, Jørgen. 1999a. "The Danish March 1998 parliamentary election." *Electoral Studies*, 18(1): 137-142.

Elklit, Jørgen. 1999b. "What Was the Problem If a First Divisor of 1.4 Was the Solution?" In Erik Beukel, Kurt Klaudi Klausen and Poul Erik Mouritzen (eds.), *Elites, Parties and Democracy. Festschrift for Professor Mogens N. Pedersen*, Odense: Odense University Press. 75-101

Esaiasson, Peter. 1990. *Svenska valkampanjer 1866-1988*. Stockholm: Allmänna förlaget.

Espeli, Harald. 1983. *Høyre og landbrukspolitikken 1945-1965* (The Conservative Party and the Agricultural Policy), Master Thesis, Department of History, The University of Oslo.

Fink, Jørgen. 2000. *Storindustri eller middelstand. Det ideologiske opgør i Det konservative folkeparti 1918-1920*, Aarhus: Aarhus Universitetsforlag.

Fjölnir. 1844. A periodical published by Icelandic intellectuals in Copenhagen. 7:110-136.

Furre, Berge. 1972. *Norsk historie 1905-1940* (Norwegian History 1905-1940), Oslo: Det norske Samlaget.

Gallagher, Michael. 1992. "Proportionality, Disproportionality and Electoral Systems." *Electoral Studies*, 10(1): 33-51.

Geddes, Barbara. 1995. "A Comparative Perspective on the Leninist Legacy in Eastern Europe." *Comparative Political Studies*, 28:230-274.

Ginsberg, Georg. 1981. "Slaget om valglovens spærreregler." *Weekendavisen Berlingske Aften*, 26 June - 2 July.

Glans, Ingemar. 1984. "Fremskridtspartiet - småborgerlig revolt, högerreaktion eller generell protest?" In Jørgen Elklit and Ole Tonsgaard (eds.), *Valg og vælgeradfærd. Studier i dansk politik*, Aarhus: Politica, 195-228.

Greenberg, Joseph and Shlomo Weber. 1985. "Multiparty Equilibria under Proportional Representation." Presented at Weingart Conference on Models of Voting. California Institute of Technology, March 22-23.

Greve, Tim. 1964. *Det Norske Storting gjennom 150 år. Bind III* (The Norwegian *Storting* through 150 Years. Vol. III), Oslo: Gyldendal Norsk Forlag.

Grímsson, Ólafur Ragnar. 1970. "Political Power in Iceland: Prior to the Period of Class Politics 1845-1918". Unpublished Ph.D. thesis, University of Manchester.

Grímsson, Ólafur Ragnar. 1976. "The Icelandic Power Structure 1800-2000." *Scandinavian Political Studies*, 11:9-33.

Grímsson, Ólafur Ragnar. 1977. Thróun íslenskrar kjördæmaskipunar. Reykjavík: Félags-vísindadeild. Mimeo.

Grofman, Bernard, William Koetzle, and Thomas Brunell. 1997. "An Integrated Perspective on the Three Potential Sources of Partison Bias: Malapportionment,

Turnout Differences, and the Geographic Distribution of Party Vote Shares." *Electoral Studies*, 16(4): 457-470.

Grofman, Bernard and Chandler Davidson. 1994. "The Effect of Municipal Election Structure on Black Representation in Eight Southern States." Davidson, Chandler and Bernard Grofman, *Quiet Revolution in the South: The Effects of the Voting Rights Act, 1965-1990*. Princeton, NJ: Princeton University Press, 301-334.

Grofman, Bernard N. (ed.). 1993. *Information, Participation and Choice: An `Economic Theory of Democracy' in Perspective*. Ann Arbor, Michigan: University of Michigan Press.

Grofman, Bernard, Evald Mikkel, and Rein Taagepera. 1999. Electoral Systems Change in Estonia, 1989-1993. *The Journal of Baltic Studies*, 30(3): 227-249.

Grofman, Bernard, Michael Migalski and Nicholas Noviello. 1986. "Effects of Multimember Districts on Black Representation in State Legislatures." *Review of Black Political Economy* 14(4): 65-78.

Grofman, Bernard, Sung-Chull Lee, Edwin Winckler, and Brian Woodall (eds.) 1999a. *Elections in Japan, Korea and Taiwan under the Single Non-Transferable Vote: The Comparative Study of an Embedded Institution*. Ann Arbor, MI: University of Michigan Press.

Grofman, Bernard, Sung-Chull Lee, Edwin Winckler, and Brian Woodall. 1999b. "Introduction." In Bernard Grofman, Sung-Chull Lee, Edwin Winckler, and Brian Woodall (eds.), *Elections in Japan, Korea and Taiwan under the Single Non-Transferable Vote: The Comparative Study of an Embedded Institution*. Ann Arbor, MI: University of Michigan Press.

Grofman, Bernard. 1989. "The Comparative Analysis of Coalition Formation and Duration: Distinguishing Between-Country and Within-Country Effects." *British Journal of Political Science* (19):291-302.

Grofman, Bernard. 1996. Political Economy: Downsian Perspectives. In Robert Goodin and Hans-Dieter Klingemann (eds.) *New Handbook of Political Science*. New York and London: Oxford University Press, 691-701.

Grofman, Bernard. 1999a. "Preface: Methodological Steps toward the Study of Embedded Institutions." In Bernard Grofman, Sung-Chull Lee, Edwin Winckler, and Brian Woodall (eds.) *Elections in Japan, Korea and Taiwan under the Single Non-Transferable Vote: The Comparative Study of an Embedded Institution*. Ann Arbor, MI: University of Michigan Press, i-xvii.

Grofman, Bernard. 1999b. "SNTV: An inventory of theoretically derived propositions and a brief review of the evidence from Japan, Korea, Taiwan and Alabama." In Bernard Grofman, Sung-Chull Lee, Edwin Winckler, and Brian Woodall (eds.) *Elections in Japan, Korea and Taiwan under the Single Non-Transferable Vote: The Comparative Study of an Embedded Institution*. Ann Arbor, MI: University of Michigan Press, 375-416.

Grofman, Bernard (ed.). 2001. *Political Science as Puzzle Solving*. Ann Arbor: University of Michigan Press.

Grofman, Bernard (ed.) 2001a. "Introduction." In Bernard Grofman (ed.) *Political Science as Puzzle Solving*. Ann Arbor: University of Michigan Press, 1-11.

Gudgin, Graham and Peter J. Taylor. 1979. *Seats, Votes and the Spatial Organization of Elections*. London: Pion.

Hadenius, S. 1995. *Svensk politik under 1900-talet – konflikt och samförstånd*. Stockholm: Tidens förlag.

Hardarson, Ólafur Th. 1995. *Parties and Voters in Iceland*. Reykjavík: Social Science Research Institute – University Press.

Hardarson, Ólafur Th. 2001. "Vedfé frambjódenda – stjórnarskrárbrot Althingis 1902?" in Gardar Gíslason, Davíd Thór Björgvinsson, Gudrún Kvaran, Páll Hreinsson, Skúli Magnússon, Sverrir Kristinsson (eds.) *Líndaela*. Reykjavík: Hid íslenska bókmenntafélag.

Hardarson, Ólafur Th. and Gunnar Helgi Kristinsson. 2000. "Iceland." *European Journal of Political Research*, 38:3-4, 408-419.

Hardarson, Ólafur Th. and Gunnar Helgi Kristinsson. 2001. "The 1999 Parliamentary Election in Iceland." *Electoral Studies*, 20: 325-331.

Hart, Jenifer. 1992. *Proportional Representation. Critics of the British Electoral System 1820-1945*, Oxford: Clarendon Press.

Helland, Leif and Jo Saglie. 1997. "Strategisk koordinering i fire stortingsvalg 1909-1918" (Strategic Coordination in four *Storting* Elections 1909-1918), Unpublished paper, Department of Political Science, University of Oslo.

Hibbing, John R. & Samuel C. Patterson. 1992. "A Democratic Legislature in the Making. The Historic Hungarian Elections of 1990." *Comparative Political Studies*, 24(4): 430-454.

Historical Statistics 1994, NOS C188, Oslo: Statistics Norway, 1995.

Hoff, Kristin Taraldsrud. 1995. "Stortingets endring av valgordningen i 1988: symbolpolitikk eller instrumentell konstruksjon?" (The Storting's amendment of the electoral law in 1988: symbolic politics or instrumental construction?). Term paper, Graduate course on Electoral Systems (STV-817), Institute for Political Science, University of Oslo, Spring 1995.

Holm, Axel. 1969. "Rigsrådsvalget efter Fællesforfatningen af 1855 i Sjællands Stift." *Historiske Meddelelser om København*, 165-198.

Iceland in figures 2001-2002. 2002. Reykjavík: Hagstofa Íslands (Statistics Iceland).

Inglehart, Ron. 1997. *Modernization and Postmodernization: Cultural, Economic and Political Change in 43 Societies*. Princeton: Princeton University Press.

Inglehart, Ronald. 1977. *The Silent Revolution: Changing Values and Political Styles among Western Publics*. Princeton: Princeton University Press.

Inglehart, Ronald. 1990. *Cultural Change*. Princeton: Princeton University Press.

Innst. O. Nr. 36-1984-85:13 (Proposals presented to the "lower" chamber, 1984-85).

Ishiyama, T. John. 1993. "Founding Elections and Development of Transitional Parties: The Cases of Estonia and Latvia, 1990-1992." *Communist and Post-Communist Studies* 26(3): 277-99.Ishiyama, T. John. 1996. "Electoral Systems Experimentation in the New Eastern Europe: The Single Transferable Vote and the Additional Member System in Estonia and Hungary." *East European Quarterly* 29(4): 487-507.

Jansson, Jan-Magnus. 1992. *Från splittring till samverkan*. Helsingfors: Söderström & Co Förlag.

Johansen, Hans Chr. 1985. *Dansk økonomisk statistik 1814-1980*. Danmarks historie Bind 9, Copemhagen: Gyldendal.

Jónsson, Gudmundur and Magnús S. Magnússon. 1997. *Hagskinna (Icelandic Historical Statistics)*. Reykjavík: Hagstofa Íslands (Statistics Iceland).

Kaartvedt, Alf . 1964. *Det Norske Storting gjennom 150 år. Bind I. Fra Riksforsamlingen til 1869* (The Norwegian Storting through 150 years. Volume I. From the Constitutional Assembly to 1869), Oslo: Gyldendal Norsk Forlag.

Karnig, Albert and Susan Welch. 1982. "Electoral Structure and Black Representation on City Councils." *Social Science Quarterly*, 63:99-114.

Katz, Richard S. 1980. *A Theory of Parties and Electoral Systems*. Baltimore MD: Johns Hopkins University Press.

Kerr, Henry 1990. "Social Class and Party Choice." In Sänkiaho, Risto (ed.), *People and their Polities*. Helsinki: The Finnish Political Science Association.

Kivinen, Markku. 1989. *The New Middle Classes and the Labour Process Class Criteria Revisited*. University of Helsinki, Department of Sociology, Research Reports No. 223.

Kjartansson, Helgi Skúli. 1996. "Flokkar og flokkaskipting á Althingi frá upphafi til 1930" in Vigdís Jónsdóttir, Björgvin Kemp, Helgi Bernódusson, Jóhannes Halldórsson, Solveig K. Jónsdóttir (eds.) *Althingismannatal 1845-1995*. Reykjavík: Skrifstofa Althingis.

Komiteanmietintö (1999: 6), *Vaalirahoituskomitean mietintö*. Helsinki: Edita.

Kosningaskýrslur 1874-1946. 1988. Reykjavík: Hagstofa Íslands.

Kristensen, Søren Svane. 1996. *De skandinaviske landes partisystemer - en analyse med udgangspunkt i Giovanni Sartoris teori*, unpublished Master's Thesis, Department of Political Science, University of Aarhus.

Kristinsson, Gunnar Helgi (1996). "Parties, States and Patronage." *West European Politics*, 19(3): 433-457.

Kristinsson, Gunnar Helgi, Halldór Jónsson and Hulda Thóra Sveinsdóttir. 1992. *Atvinnustefna á Íslandi 1959-1991*. Reykjavík: Félagsvísindastofnun Háskóla Íslands.

Kristinsson, Gunnar Helgi. 1991. *Farmers' Parties. A Study in Electoral Adoption*. Reykjavík: Félagsvísindastofnun Háskóla Íslands.

Kristinsson, Gunnar Helgi. 1999. *Úr digrum sjóði. Fjárlagagerd á Íslandi*. Reykjavík: Félagsvísindastofnun Háskóla Íslands – Háskólaútgáfan.

Kristvik, Bjørn & Stein Rokkan. 1966. "Valgordningen" (The Electoral System), *Politiske valg i Norge* (Political Elections in Norway). Oslo: Universitetsforlaget.

Kristvik, Bjørn Inge. 1953. Partiene og valgordningen. Tidsrommet 1885-1906 (The parties and the electoral system. The period 1885-1906), Master Thesis in Political Science, The University of Oslo.

Kuhnle, Stein. 1972. "Stemmeretten i 1814" (The Franchise in 1814). *Historisk Tidsskrift*, 51 (4): 373-390.

Kuhnle, Stein. 1987. "Duvergers lov om to-partisystemet" (Duverger's Law on the Two-Party System). In Stein Ugelvik Larsen, (ed.) *Lov og struktur* (Law and Structure), Bergen: Universitetsforlaget, 78-86

Kuusela, Kimmo. 1995. "The Finnish Electoral System: Basic Features and Developmental Tendencies." In Borg, S. and R. Sänkiaho (eds): *The Finnish Voter*. Helsinki: The Finnish Political Science Association, 23-44.

Laakso, Markku and Rein Taagepera. 1979. "'Effective' Number of Parties: A Measurement with Application to West Europe." *Comparative Political Studies*. 12:3-27.

Laakso, Markku. 1979. "The Maximum Distortion and the Problem of the First Divisor in Different P.R. Systems." *Scandinavian Political Studies*, 2(2): 161-169.

Laakso, Markku. 1980. "Electoral Justice as a Criterion for Different Systems of Proportional Representation." *Scandinavian Political Studies*, 3::249-264.

Lane, Jan-Erik and Ersson, Svante 1997. 'Parties and Voters: What Creates the Ties?', *Scandinavian Political Studies*, 20: 179-196.

Lanslet, Lars Roar (1989): *John Lyng. Samarbeidets arkitekt* (John Lyng. The Architect of Cooperation), Oslo: J. W. Cappelens Forlag.

Lewin, L. 1984. *Ideologi och strategi. Svensk politik under 100 år*. Stockholm: Norstedts.

Lewin, Leif. 1984/88. *Ideologi och strategi. Svensk politik under 100 år*. Stockholm: Norstedts. English translation 1988: *Ideology and Strategy: A Century of Swedish Politics*, Cambridge: Cambridge University Press.

Li, Jin-shan. 1995. "Analyse critique des indices de disproportionnalité electorale et de stabilité. Application aux cas de l'Allemagne et du Japon." *Revue internationale de politique comparée*, 2(2): 369-388.

Lijphart, Arend and Robert W. Gibberd. 1977. "Thresholds and Payoffs in List Systems of Proportional Representation." *European Journal of Political Research*. 5: 219-244.

Lijphart, Arend. 1971. "Comparative Politics and the Comparative Method." *American Political Science Review*. 65(3): 682-693.

Lijphart, Arend. 1984. *Democracies: Patterns of Majoritarian and Consensus Government in Twenty-One Countries*. New Haven: Yale University Press.

Lijphart, Arend. 1986. "Degrees of Proportionality of Proportional Representation Formulas." In Bernard Grofman and Arend Lijphart (eds.). *Electoral Laws and Their Political Consequences*, New York: Agathon, 170-179

Lijphart, Arend. 1994. *Electoral Systems and Party Systems. A Study of Twenty-Seven Democracies 1945-1990*. Oxford: Oxford University Press.

Lijphart, Arend. 1999. *Patterns of Democracy: Government Forms and Performance in Thirty-Six Countries*. New Haven, CT: Yale University Press.

Líndal, Sigurdur. 1963. "Thróun kosningaréttar á Íslandi 1874-1963". *Tímarit lögfraedinga*, 13 (1): 35-47.

Lindman, Sven. 1969. *Fråm storfurstendöme till republik - tillkomsten av 1919 års regeringsform*. Ekenäs Tryckeri Aktiebolags Förlag: Ekenäs

Lipset, Seymor Martin and Rokkan, Stein. 1967. "Cleavage Structures, Party Systems, and Voter Alignments: An Introduction." In Lipset, S.M. and S. Rokkan (Eds). *Party Systems and Voter Alignments: Cross National Perspectives*. New York: The Free Press

Mackie, Thomas T. & Richard Rose. 1982. *The International Almanac of Electoral History*, 2nd Edition. London and Basingstoke: Macmillan.

Mackie, Tom & Richard Rose. 1997. *A Decade of Election Results: Updating the International Almanac, Studies in Public Policy*. Glasgow: Centre for the Study of Public Policy, University of Strathclyde.

Magnússon, Thorsteinn. 1987. "The Icelandic Althingi and Its Standing Committees". Unpublished Ph.D. thesis, University of Exeter.

Mair, Peter 1997. *Party System Change*. Oxford: Clarendon Press

Massicotte, Louis & André Blais. 1999. "Mixed Electoral Systems: A Conceptual and Empirical Survey." *Electoral Studies*, 18(3): 341-366.

McCubbins, Matthew D. and Frances M. Rosenbluth. 1995. "Party Provision for Personal Politics: Dividing the Votes in Japan." In Cowhey, Peter and Matthew D. McCubbins (Eds). *Structure And Policy In Japan and the United States.* New York: Cambridge University Press, 35-55.

Metcalf, M. F. 1987. *The Riksdag: a history of the Swedish Parliament.* New York: St Martins Press.

Mjeldheim, Leiv. 1955. *Ministeriet Konow, 1910-1912: ein studie i parliamentarisme og partipolitikk* (The Konow Cabinet, 1910-12: A Study of Parliamentarism and Party Politics), Oslo: Samlaget.

Mjeldheim, Leiv. 1978. *Parti og rørsle. Ein studie av Venstre i landskrinsane 1906-1918* (Party and Movement. A Study of the Left in Rural Districts 1906-1918). Bergen: Universitets-forlaget.

Mjeldheim, Leiv. 1984. *Folkerørsla som vart parti. Venstre frå 1880åra til 1905* (The Popular Movement That Became a Party. The Left Party from the 1880s to 1905). Bergen: Universitetsforlaget.

Myerson, R. B. and R. J. Weber. 1993. "A Theory of Voting Equilibria." *American Political Science Review*, 87(1):102-114.

Myerson, Roger B. 1993a. "Incentives to Cultivate Favored Minorities under Alternative Electoral Systems." *American Political Science Review* 87(4):856-869.

Myerson, Roger B. 1993b. "Effectiveness of Electoral Systems for Reducing Government Corruption: A Game Theoretic Analysis." *Games and Economic Behavior* 5:118-132.

Myerson, Roger B. and R. J. Weber. 1993. "A Theory of Voting Equilibria." *American Political Science Review* 87(1):102-114.

Nannestad, Peter. 1989. *Reactive Voting in Danish General Elections 1971-1979.* Aarhus: Aarhus University Press.

NAR (National Assembly Records) – Thjódfundartídindi 1851. Proceedings from the National Assembly.

National Central Bureau of Statistics. 1969. *Historical Statistics of Sweden – Part 1. Population.* Stockholm: Allmänna förlaget.

Neergaard, Niels. 1892-1916. *Under Junigrundloven. En Fremstilling af det danske Folks Historie fra 1848 til 1866*, Copenhagen: P.G. Philipsens Forlag. Reprint 1973.

Nerbøvik, Jostein. 1973. *Norsk historie 1870-1905* (Norwegian History 1870-1905). Oslo: Det norske Samlaget.

Nissen, Bernt A. 1945. *Gammel eller ny valgordning* (Old or New Electoral System). Sak og samfunn nr. 8, Bergen: Christian Michelsens Institutt for Vitenskap og Åndsfrihet.

Nohlen, Dieter & Mirjana Kasapovic. 1996. *Wahlsysteme und Systemwechsel in Osteuropa*, Opladen: Leske + Budrich.

Nordby, Trond. 1983. *Venstre og samlingspolitikken 1906-1908. En studie i partioppløsning og gjenreisning* (The Left and the Unification Policy. A Study of Party Disintegration and Consolidation), Oslo: Novus Forlag.

Nousiainen, Jaakko. 1998. *Suomen Poliittien Järjestelmä*. Helsinki: Werner Söderström Osakeyhtiö

Nyman, O. (1966): "Tvåkammarsystemets omvandling". In *Samhälle och riksdag. Band IV*. Stockholm: Almqvist & Wiksell.

Opheim, Ingunn. 1997. "Om kommunevalgordningen i Norge. Hvorfor har vi en annen valgordning ved kommunestyrevalg enn ved *Stortings*- og fylkestingsvalg?" (On the local electoral system of Norway. Why do we have a different system for local election than for national and regional elections?). Paper presented at the Institute for Political Science, University of Oslo.

Overå. Oddvar and Steinar Dalbakk. 1987. *Den norske valgordningen* (The Norwegian Electoral System). Oslo: Sem & Stenersen.

Owen, Guilllermo and Bernard Grofman. 1995. "Two Stage Electoral Competition in Two-Party Contests: Persistent Divergence of Party Positions with and without Expressive Voting." Unpublished manuscript, University of California, Irvine.

Pedersen, Mogens N. 1987. "The Danish 'Working Multiparty System': Breakdown or Adaption?" In Hans Daalder (ed.), *Party Systems in Denmark, Austria, Switzerland, the Netherlands and Belgium*. London: Fr. Pinter, 1-60

Pesonen, Pertti. 1995. "The Evolution of Finland's Party Divisions and Social Structure." In Borg, S. and R. Sänkiaho (eds): *The Finnish Voter*. Helsinki: The Finnish Political Science Association, 9-22.

Rae, Douglas. 1967, 1971 (2nd edition) *The Political Consequences of Electoral Laws*. New Haven, CT: Yale University Press.

Rasmussen, Erik. 1972. *Komparativ Politik 2*, 2nd ed., Copenhagen: Gyldendal.

Reed, Stephen R. 1990. "Structure and Behavior: Extending Duverger's Law to the Japanese Case." *British Journal of Political Science* 20:335-356.

Regeringens proposition (1996/97:70): Ny vallag. Stockholm: Statens offentliga utredningar, p. 70.

Reynolds, Andrew. 2001. *The Architecture of Democracy: Constitutional Design,*

Conflict Management, and Democracy. Oxford: Oxford University Press.

Reynolds, Andrew and Ben Reilly. 1997. *The International IDEA Handbook of Electoral System Design*. Stockholm: International IDEA

Reynolds, Andrew and Bernard Grofman. 1992. "The Main Proposals for Electoral Reform in South Africa." Presented at the UCI Focused Research Program in Democratization Conference on Constitutional Design, University of California Irvine.

Riker, William R. 1982. *Liberalism against Populism: A Confrontation between the Theory of Democracy and the Theory of Social Choice*. San Francisco, CA: Freeman.

Robertson, David. 1975. *A Theory of Party Competition*. New York: Wiley.

Rokkan, Stein and Henry Valen. 1962. "The Mobilization of the Periphery: Data on Turnout, Party Membership and Candidate Recruitment in Norway." *Acta Sociologica*, 6:111-158.

Rokkan, Stein and Henry Valen. 1964. "Regional Contrasts in Norwegian Politics: A Review of Data from Official Statistics and from Sample Surveys", in Allardt, E. and Y. Littunen: *Clevages, and Party Systems. Contributions to Comparative Political Sociology*. Helsinki: Transactions of Westermarck Society, 162-238.

Rokkan, Stein. 1966. "Norway: Numerical Democracy and Corporate Pluralism." In Robert A. Dahl, (ed.), *Political Oppositions in Western Democracies*. New Haven and London: Yale University Press, 70-115

Rokkan, Stein. 1967. "Geography, Religion, and Social Class: Crosscutting Cleavages in Norwegian Politics." In Lipset, Seymour M. and S. Rokkan, *Party Systems and Voter Alignments: Cross-National Perspectives*, New York: The Free Press. 367-444.

Rokkan, Stein. 1968. "Elections: Electoral Systems." In David Sills, (ed.), *International Encyclopedia of the Social Sciences*, London: Crowell Collier & Macmillan, Inc., 6-21.

Rokkan, Stein. 1970. *Citizens, Elections, Parties. Approaches to the Comparative Study of the Processes of Development*. Oslo: Universitetsforlaget.

Rokkan, Stein. 1987. *Stat, Nasjon, Klasse*. Universitetsforlaget: Oslo

Rommetvedt, Hilmar. 1994. "Politisk representasjon – fra nominasjon til iverksetting" (Political Representation – From Nomination to Implementation), in B. E. Rasch and K. Midgaard (eds.): *Representativt demokrati. Spilleregler under debatt* (Representative Democracy. Debating the Rules of the Game), Oslo: Universitetsforlaget.

Rosensweig, Jeffrey A. 1981. "Highest Average Methods of Allocating Seats Under Proportional Representation: A Clarification." *Political Studies*, 29(2):Vol. 29(2): 279-281.

RP 48/1998. Regeringens proposition till Riksdagen med förslag till vallag och till vissa lagar som har samband med den.

Rueschemeyer, Dietrich, Evelyne Huber Stephens & John D. Stephens. 1992. *Capitalist Development and Democracy*. Cambridge: Polity Press.

Ruin, O. 1968. *Mellan samlingsregering och tvåpartisystem*. Stockholm: Bonniers.

Rusk, Jerrold M. and Ole Borre. 1974. "The Changing Party Space in Danish Voter Perceptions." *European Journal of Political Research*, 2(4): 329-361.

Saarela, Tauno. *Suomalaisen Kommunismin Synty 1918-1923*. Kansan Sivistystyön Liitto: Helsinki

Sänkiaho, Risto. 1995. "The Social Basis for Party Support." In Borg, S. and R. Sänkiaho (eds): *The Finnish Voter*. Helsinki: The Finnish Political Science Association, 9-22.

Särlvik, Bo 1983. "Scandinavia". In Bogdanor, V. and D. Butler (eds): *Democracy and Elections*. Cambridge: Cambridge University Press.

Särlvik, Bo. 1983. "Scandinavia." In Vernon Bogdanor and David Butler (eds.), *Democracy and Elections. Electoral Systems and Their Political Consequences*. Cambridge: Cambridge University Press, 122-148.

Sartori, Giovanni. 1968. "Political Development and Political Engineering." In Montgomery, J. D. and A.O. Hirschman, (Eds), *Public Policy*, 261-298,

Sartori, Giovanni. 1976 . *Parties and party systems. A framework for analysis*. Cambridge: Cambridge University Press

Sartori, Giovanni. 1997. *Comparative Constitutional Engineering*. London: Macmillan

Sawyer, Jack and Duncan MacRae, Jr. 1962. "Game Theory and Cumulative Voting in Illinois 1902-1954." *American Political Science Review* 56:936-946.

Seip, Jens Arup. 1974. *Utsikt over Norges historie. Første del* (Overview of Norwegian History. Part One). Oslo: Gyldendal Norsk Forlag.

Seip, Jens Arup. 1981. *Utsikt over Norges historie. Annen del* (Overview of Norwegian History. Part Two). Oslo: Gyldendal Norsk Forlag.

Shugart Matthew Sobert and Martin P. Wattenberg (eds). 2000. *Mixed-Member Electoral Systems: The Best of Both Worlds?* Oxford: Oxford University Press

Shugart, Matthew. 1992. "Electoral Reform in Systems of Proportional Representation." *European Journal of Political Research*. 21:207-224.

Skjeie, Hege. 1992. *Den politiske betydningen av kjønn. En studie av norsk topp-politikk* (The political importance of gender. A study of Norwegian top politics). Ph.D. thesis, published in *Rapport* 92:11, Oslo: Institute for Social Research.

Skjeie, Hege. 1997. "A Tale of Two decades: The End of a Male Political hegemony." in Kaare Strøm and Lars Svåsand (eds.). *Challenges to Political Parties. The Case of Norway*. Ann Arbor: Michigan University Press, 289-319.

Skýrsla um breytingar á kjördaemaskipan og tilhögun kosninga til Althingis. 1998. Reykjavík, Forsaetisráduneytid.

Solberg, Per. 1964. "Valgordningen av 1919/20 og dens partipolitiske forutsetninger" (The Electoral System of 1919/20 and its party political preconditions). Master Thesis in History, University of Bergen.

SOU. 1972. Grundlagberedningen, *Ny regeringsform. Ny riksdagsordning*. Stockholm: Statens offentliga utredningar, p. 15.

SOU. 1993. *Ökat personval*. Stockholm: Statens offentliga utredningar, p. 21.

SOU. 1996. *Utvärderat personval*. Stockholm: Statens offentliga utredningar, p. 66.

Statistical Yearbook 1997, Oslo: Statistics Norway.

Steen, Sverre. 1964. "Hvordan Norges Storting ble til" (How the Norwegian Storting came into being), in Kaartvedt, Alf. *Det Norske Storting gjennom 150 år. Fra Riksforsamlingen til 1869* (The Norwegian Storting through 150 years. From the Constitutional Assembly to 1869), Oslo: Gyldendal Norsk Forlag. 1-47.

Stephensen, Oddgeir and Jón Sigurdsson. 1864. *Lovsamling for Island* Vol. 12. Copenhagen: Copenhagen Press.

Stjernquist, N. 1966. "Sweden: Stability or Deadlock". In Robert A. Dahl, (ed.) *Political Opposition in Western Democracies*. New Haven: Yale University Press.

Stortingsforhandlinger 1987-88, nr. 31 (The Storting Debates 1987-88, No. 31, Oslo: Stortinget.

Stortingsproposisjon nr. 76 (1903-1904) Om grundlovsbestemmelse angaaende forandring i grundlovens regler om valg af Stortingsrepresentanter (Storting proposal no. 76 1903-1904. About Changes in the Constitution's Regulations Concerning Election of Members to the Parliament), Kristiania: Stortinget.

Stortingsproposisjon nr. 76 (1903-1904). Bilag 2. Historisk Oversigt over represæntasjonsordningen siden 1814 og de angaaende samme foreslaaede Forandringer, (Storting proposal no. 76 1903-1904. Historical Overview over the Representation rules since 1814), Kristiania: Stortinget.

Strøm, Kaare and Lars Svåsand (eds). 1997. *Challenges to Political Parties. The Case of Norway*, Ann Arbor: Michigan University Press.

Strøm, Kaare. 1985. "Party Goals and Government Performance in Parliamentary Democracies." *The American Political Science Review*, 79(3): 738:754.

Strøm, Kaare. 1990. *Minority Government and Majority Rule.* Cambridge: Cambridge University Press.

Sugden, Robert. 1984. "Free Association and the Theory of Proportional Representation." *American Political Science Review,* 78(1):311-343.

Sundberg, Jan. 1985. *Svenskhetens Dilemma i Finland.* Finska Vetenskaps-Societeten: Helsingfors.

Sundberg, Jan. 1997. "Compulsory Party Democracy. Finland as a Deviant Case in Scandinavia." *Party Politics,* 3:9-22.

Svensson, Palle and Lise Togeby. 1992. "Post-Industrialism and New Social and Political Classes." In Gundelach, Peter & Karen Siune (eds.), *From Voters to Participants. Essays in Honour of Ole Borre.* Aarhus: Politica, 108-131.

Svensson, Palle. 1993. "The Development of Danish Polyarchy or How Liberalization also Preceded Inclusiveness in Denmark." In Tom Bryder, (ed.), *Party Systems, Party Behaviour and Democracy. Scripta in honorem professoris Gunnar Sjöblom sexagesimum annum complentis.* Copenhagen: Political Studies Press. 169-189

Svensson, Palle. 1996a. "Denmark: the referendum as minority protection." In Gallagher, Michael and Pier Vincenzo Uleri (eds.), *The Referendum Experience in Europe,* Houndmills, Basingstoke: Macmillan/New York: St. Martin's Press, 33-51.

Svensson, Palle. 1996b. *Demokratiets krise? En debat- og systemanalyse af dansk politik i 1970'erne,* Aarhus: Politica.

Taagepera, Rein and Matthew Shugart. 1993. "Predicting the Number of Parties-A Quantitative Model of Duverger Mechanical Effect." *American Political Science Review,* 87(2): 455-464.Taagepera, Rein and Bernard Grofman. 1985. "Rethinking Duverger's Law: Predicting the Effective Number of Parties in Plurality and PR systems--Parties Minus Issues Equals One." *European Journal of Political Research* 13:341-352.

Taagepera, Rein, and Matthew Soberg Shugart. 1989. *Seats and Votes: The Effects and Determinants of Electoral Systems.* New Haven, CT: Yale University Press.

Taagepera, Rein. 1986. "Reformulating the Cube Law for Proportional Representation Elections." *American Political Science Review,* 80(2): 489-504.

Tarasti, Lauri. 1998. *Suomen vaalilainsäädäntö.* Edita: Helsinki.

Taylor, Peter J., Graham Gudgin, and R.J. Johnston. 1986. "The Geography of Representation: A Review of Recent Findings." In Grofman, Bernard and Arend Lijphart, (Eds), *Electoral Laws and Their Political Consequences.* New York: Agathon Press.

Thermaenius, E. 1935. *Riksdagspartierna.* Stockholm: Sveriges Riksdag Vol XVII.

Thorsteinsson, Thorsteinn. 1938. "Althingiskosningar 1937." *Almanak hins íslenska thjóðvinafélags* 64: 76-85.

Timelin, E. 1928. *Ministärerna Lindman och representationsreformen 1907-1909.* Karlskrona: J. A. Krooks Bokhandel.

Törnudd, Klaus. 1968. *The Electoral System of Finland.* Hugh Evelyn: London.

Urwin, Derek W. 1997. "The Norwegian Party System from the 1880s to the 1990s." In Strøm, Kaare and Lars Svåsand (eds.) *Challenges to Political Parties. The Case of Norway*, Ann Arbor: Michigan University Press, 33-59.

Utheim, J. 1895. *Statistik vedkommende Valgmandsvalgene og Storthingsvalgene 1815-1885.* (Statistics Concerning the Elections to Electoral Colleges and to the Storting 1815-1885), Kristiania: Det statistiske Centralbureau.

Valen, Henry & Stein Rokkan. 1974. "Norway: Conflict Structure and Mass Politics in a European Periphery." In Richard Rose, (ed.), *Electoral Behavior: A Comparative Handbook*, New York: The Free Press, 315-370.

Valen, Henry and Rokkan, Stein. 1974. "Conflict Structure and Mass Politics in a European Periphery." In Richard Rose (ed.), *Electoral Behavior: A Comparative Handbook*. New York: The Free Press

Valen, Henry, Hanne Marthe Narud and Ólafur Th. Hardarson. 2000. "Geography and Representation" in Esaiasson, Peter and Knut Heidar (eds.) *Beyond Westminster and Congress. The Nordic Experience.* Columbus: Ohio State University Press, 107-131.

Valen, Henry. 1980. *Valg og politikk* (Elections and Politics). Oslo: NKS-Forlaget.

Valen, Henry. 1988. "Norway: decentralization and group representation." In Gallagher, Michael, and Michael Marsh (eds.): *Candidate Selection in Comparative Politics. The Secret Garden of Politics.* London: Sage Publications, 210-235.

Valen, Henry. 1994. "List Alliances: An Experiment in Political Representation." In Jennings, M. Kent and Thomas E. Mann (eds.): *Elections at Home and Abroad. Essays in Honor of Warren E. Miller.* Ann Arbor: The University of Michigan Press, 289-321.

Vallag 714/1998 Finlands Författningssamling.

von Sydow, B. 1989. *Vägen till enkammarriksdagen. Demokratisk författningspolitik i Sverige 1944-1968.* Stockholm: Tiden.

von Sydow, Björn. 1989. *Vägen til enkammarriksdagen. Demokratisk författningspolitik i Sverige 1944-1968.* Stockholm: Tidens förlag.

Wallin, G. 1961. *Valrörelser och valresultat. Andrakammarvalen i Sverige 1866-1884.* Stockholm: Ronzo boktryckeri.

Wildavsky, Aaron B. 1959. "A Methodological Critique of Duverger's *Political Parties.*" *The Journal of Politics*, 21: 303-318.

Yamakawa, Katsumi. 1984. "A Lorenz Curve Analysis of the Allocation of the Seats in the House of the Representatives by the General Elections." *Kansai University Review of Law and Politics* 5:1-26.

Yearbook of Nordic Statistics 1996, Copenhagen: Nordic Council of Ministers

INDEX TERMS

O

P

Printed in the United States
1165100003B/7-36

9 780875 861388